DIVERSITY IN FAMILY COMMUNICATION

FIRST EDITION

Edited by James Honeycutt and Laura Hatcher

Louisiana State University

cognella®
academic publishing

Bassim Hamadeh, CEO and Publisher
Michael Simpson, Vice President of Acquisitions
Jamie Giganti, Managing Editor
Jess Busch, Senior Graphic Designer
Zina Craft, Acquisitions Editor
Monika Dziamka, Project Editor
Natalie Lakosil, Licensing Manager
Mandy Licata, Interior Designer

First published in the United States of America in 2015 by University Readers, an imprint of Cognella, Inc.

Trademark Notice: Product or corporate names may be trademarks or registered trademarks, and are used only for identification and explanation without intent to infringe.

Printed in the United States of America

ISBN: 978-1-62661-786-5 (pbk) / 978-1-62661-787-2 (br)

www.cognella.com   800-200-3908

CONTENTS

PART III: FAMILY PHEROMONES AND PHYSIOLOGY

PART IV: DIVORCE AND FAMILY RECONFIGURATION

PART V: EFFECTS OF INFIDELITY AND ABUSE

Acknowledgments

I would like to thank my wife Elizabeth for her continued support in our ongoing research. I also thank Abby who provides a constant source of support for us. We would like to thank our colleagues who contributed to the volume as well as our valued mentors over the years, including Mark L. Knapp and John M. Gottman who helped inspire the continuing research of communication and psychology, respectively. Our work would not have been possible without the Matchbox Interaction Lab, which was modeled after John's "love lab" in Seattle. Finally, we thank our students who have had us for numerous courses over the years and function as task and social families. In some cases, they apply and pass course concepts on to their families and friends. I also thank Laura and her family. It has been productive and a pleasure working with Laura over the past few years. The influence of Zoey is apparent on Abby. May the legacy continue onward and upward.

—JMH

I would like to thank my husband Matt for his ability to remind me of what is really important in life. Without his constant love and support (and his occasional insistence that I put the laptop away), I know my life would be much less fulfilling and much less wonderful than it is now. I also thank Zoey, who is a source of constant joy and laughter. No one knows how to put a smile on my face quite like her. I thank my parents for teaching me how to live life well and for somehow managing to be encouraging without being pushy. I have no idea how they pulled it off, but they have always supported me without controlling me. I also thank them for allowing me to fail at times. It is a truly loving parent who conquers the urge to save their children and instead allows them to falter occasionally. It is only through the stumbles that we learn to walk. I thank my siblings for being the same brand of crazy as I am. And I thank them for every single bickering match we've ever engaged in. That near-constant sparring helped me develop the ability to present a scientific argument today. Of course, the student has by far surpassed the masters now. No one can ever understand you like a brother or a sister and I am truly grateful to have one of each in my life. Finally I thank Jim, Elizabeth, and Abby. I thank Jim for believing in me and taking chances on me. I thank him for each lesson he has taught me. Without those who came before us pointing out the way, we would all be doomed to stumble in the darkness searching for the path ourselves. I thank Elizabeth for her support and understanding. If ever there was a saint in this world, it is she. And I thank Abby for her friendship and the joy she brings into the world. With so many wonderful people in my life, I can only pray that I am a worthy steward of whatever torches I am asked to carry.

—LCH

Introduction

By James Honeycutt & Laura Hatcher

This book deals with the diversity of family types and communication, including chapters dealing with the "dark side" of family abuse and breakup. The antiquated definition of a nuclear family is changing. A classic definition of the nuclear family was a family group consisting of a pair of adults and their children. This is in contrast to the smaller single-parent family, and to the larger extended family. Nuclear families typically center on a married couple, but not always; the nuclear family may have any number of children. There are differences in definition among observers; some definitions allow only biological children that are full-blood siblings, while others allow for a stepparent and any mix of dependent children, including stepchildren and adopted children. As revealed in Table I-1, additional definitions reflect psychological bonding in which there is a feeling of interdependence and connection, including common-law marriage.

This type of marriage, also known as sui juris marriage, informal marriage, or marriage by habit and repute, is an irregular form of marriage that can be legally contracted in an extremely limited number of jurisdictions and is universally recognized as a valid marriage. There is no marriage license issued by a government, no marriage certificate filed with a government, and no formal ceremony to solemnize the marriage before witnesses. The parties must hold themselves out to the world as husband and wife (which, ironically, is not a requirement of statutory marriage).

Basis of the Volume

Diversity is inherent in this book through a variety of facets. Not only are the culturally diverse functions and activities of families examined, but a variety of family forms, which exist and have existed in our United States society over its history, are investigated as well. In combination with and as an outcome of these two perspectives, diversity in family formation, relationship dynamics, communication style, resource utilization, decision-making approaches, and reconfiguration choices following personal and national disasters are examined. The goal is to encourage students to hold less-parochial perspectives and to apply their findings to other areas of study in which they might engage.

Studying family communication provides an excellent context in which students can be encouraged to critically examine a situation familiar to them and, at the same time, expand their knowledge

Table I-1 Diverse Family Definitions

1. A group consisting of married female and male parents and dependent children, living away from other relatives.

2. A fundamental social group in society typically consisting of one or two parents and their children.

3. Two or more people who share goals and values, have long-term commitments to one another, and reside usually in the same dwelling place.

4. All the members of a household are under one roof.

5. A group of people who may or may not live together (long distance) who regularly interact through mediated communication, including telephones, social media, texts, Skype, etc., and feel a close psychological bond and are committed to the maintenance of the group.

6. A locally independent organized crime unit, as of the Cosa Nostra.

7. A group of like things; a class.

Read more: http://www.answers.com/topic/family#ixzz1z86EmS11

about human relationships. The family, as a basic institution of our society, is ubiquitous and disparate. Family historians and literary writers have documented various family forms within the United States. Contemporary family scholars have described numerous family structures and mores throughout the world.

Through these bodies of scholarly literature, the students' popular beliefs and definitions of the family are challenged and altered as they engage in reflective human action. Students acquire a common core of knowledge drawn from humanities, sciences, and social sciences. Students come to recognize key events, ideas, individuals, and institutions that have influenced family life, and understand the way in which the major academic disciplines work together to provide this understanding. Since individual students are members of families, focusing on family relations in a historical and comparative setting broadens the perspectives students hold about the nature and function of the family. Within this book, students are required to read the family-focused work of psychologists, communicologists, historians, sociologists, and family scientists.

Because students readily identify with the concept of "family," and their definitions of family are challenged by this book, it is likely that their intellectual curiosity is aroused. Application of the historical and comparative framework prompts students to examine family structures from a less-parochial perspective and to use the same framework to enrich their understanding of other areas of study. Although some enrollees may find ways to continue their study of family relations beyond the completion of the course, it is hoped that all students, regardless of their major, will recognize family relations as an important field of study. Additionally, all these combinations of experiences for both faculty and students create an atmosphere in which reflective human action is the mode of operation.

WHAT IS A FAMILY?

According to the U.S. Census Bureau, a family is "a group of two or more people who reside together and who are related by birth, marriage, or adoption." Though this definition seems straightforward, where do married couples or parents and children who live in different places fit in this definition of family? What about aunts and uncles who regularly care for their nieces or nephews while the parents work? According to the census bureau's definition, these relatively common family arrangements are not officially recognized as families. While the bureau's definition of families is clear and is easily tracked over time, it is important to recognize that not all of our families fit this definition.

In fact, across time and cultures, using the census bureau's definition of family is an inappropriate way to measure and examine families. In ancient Greece and in feudal Europe, a family was all of the people who contributed to the household financial system, including servants (Coltrane and Collins, 2001). In many cultures today, non-parental adults are also considered part of the family if they play a large role in raising or looking after the children of others. These examples highlight the fact that, though the census definition is clear and helpful, there is no single understanding of what a family is; its definition varies across many groups of people.

How Families Have Changed over Time

The structures, or forms, of the family vary as much as the definition itself. There is no single "true" family form. In Western Europe the nuclear family (a single set of biological parents residing together with their children) was prevalent in the Middle Ages, but at that same time in Eastern Europe multiple generations of the same family lived in the same household (Coltrane and Collins, 2001). Indeed, the United States has seen many types of family forms throughout its short history. Stephanie Coontz's (2005) research on the history of marriage reveals that the family forms we see today in the U.S. are actually the result of an evolution of the family that began with an important shift in the culture of marriage in the mid-18th century.

Coontz (2005) found that only in the mid- to late-18th century in Western Europe and North America "did the notion of free choice and marriage for love triumph as a cultural ideal... [opening] the way for it to become an optional and fragile [institution]," thus influencing the structure of the family at that time and into the future (p. 7). Earlier in history, during the Stone and Middle Ages, marriage was not based on love, and men and women had very little choice about whom they married. In the Stone

Figure I-1. Three-person family walking on the beach. Image courtesy of FreeDigitalPhotos.net.

Age men and women married in order to improve the economic situation of their respective clans, then in the Middle Ages and into the 18th century marriage served the economic and political needs of a particular extended family group (Coontz, 2005).

As marriage evolved in the mid- to late-18th century into a union based on love, other economic, cultural, and political shifts in the U.S. and in other nations were happening that would further influence the structure of the family. In the 19th century an ideal of the husband as breadwinner and the wife as homemaker became popular, but the majority of families could not achieve this ideal, as few jobs paid wages high enough to support a single-earner family. This changed as World War II ended and the U.S. experienced a time of dramatic economic growth. The economic prosperity of the time combined with the popular cultural ideal gave rise to family trends in the 1950s and early 1960s that had never been seen before. "Ozzie and Harriet" families that married young, remained married, and had many children were the major family form at this time (McLanahan and Casper, 2001). The realization of the Ozzie and Harriet ideal did not last long, however. In the late 1960s and 1970s divorce rates rose, births to unmarried women increased, and the average age of first marriage also rose. The reasons for these changes in the '60s and '70s were many: real wages for women rose while those for men fell, the economy weakened, wives joined the workforce due to the downturn in the economy, and women gained access to legal rights, education, birth control, and more meaningful careers (McLanahan and Casper, 2001; Coltrane and Collins, 2001). This historical examination of the evolution of the family and marriage shows that the family has constantly been under pressure to evolve and shift with changes in the economy, our values, and even politics. The evolution of marriage into an institution of love along with changes in the economy, our culture, and the political scene since the 1950s has meant that American men and women have been able to realize their ideals of the male breadwinner and marriage for the sake of love and personal freedom as time changes.

These influences and trends in marriage, divorce, and non-marital fertility did not escape rural America. Comparing urban and rural parts of the country between 1950 and 1970 reveals, however, that rural divorce rates were lower, fewer women age 20–24 were unmarried, and the number of children per 1,000 ever married women age 35–44 was slightly higher in rural America (Brown, 1981). The changes in marriage, divorce, and fertility we observe during the 20th century in all parts of the U.S. demonstrate that the structure of families is changing and becoming more diverse. While there are now many forms available to people, the family itself is not disappearing.

WHY DO FAMILIES MATTER?

The increasing diversity of the family in the U.S. has led scholars to examine if and how different family forms are associated with different groups of people who then may experience different outcomes. Research has found that not all racial groups participate in each family type equally, thus not all family forms are equally available to all people (McLanahan and Casper, 2001). Scholars have also found that each type of family (married with kids, married with no kids, single-parent with young children, etc.) is associated with different economic, child, and health outcomes. Demographers Sara McLanahan and Gary Sandefur (1994) explain that past research has found that, "Children who grow up with only one of their parents … are more likely to drop out of high school, to become teenage and single mothers, and to have trouble finding and keeping a steady job in young adulthood, even after adjusting for differences in parents' socioeconomic background" (p. 6).

They clarify, however, that "about half of the disadvantages associated with single parenthood are due to lower incomes [of single parents]. Most of the rest are due to too little parental involvement and supervision and too much residential mobility" (p. 6). Stephanie Coontz (2005) also clarifies that the psychological, health, and economic benefits of marriage for families are due to a number of factors like the effect of selection (people who are already healthier, more psychologically stable, and better able to manage finances tend to marry more than those who are not), the "expectations about responsibility, fidelity, and intimacy" in marriage, and the freedom to exit psychologically, physically, and economically stressful unhappy marriages (pp. 309–310). While we see increasing diversity in family types in the U.S. across time, it is clear that not all types lead to equal outcomes or are equally available to all.

More than one in three American adults is currently unmarried. Policies that benefit only married relationships routinely exclude this considerable percentage of ordinary people, whose lives and families do not fit the married ideal upheld by the marriage movement.

The family diversity that exists in America today includes people who have chosen not to marry and those who are prevented from marrying, such as same-sex couples. It includes people who have chosen to live together before marriage (the majority of marriages today are preceded by cohabitation) and those who are single. It includes older people and disabled people, who may risk losing needed benefits if they get married. And it includes children, half of whom live in a family structure other than their two married parents.

DEBATE OVER FAMILY DIVERSITY

People with a traditional perspective on defining families reflecting the first definition in Table I-1 may feel anxiety at alternative family forms that have evolved. Stigmatizing people who are divorced, punishing single parents, casting step or blended families as less than perfect, shaming unmarried couples, and ignoring the needs of gay, lesbian, bisexual, and transgender people are not positive approaches for supporting families. Many opponents of diverse families misrepresent and oversimplify both the history and research on which they base their claims. The picture that is painted by these opponents is bleak. In reality, however, there are millions of happy, healthy unmarried families. The challenge is to find effective approaches to supporting these successful families, as well as the ones who are having difficult times.

The debate over same-sex unions and their children draws from and informs a more general literature concerning family structure's effect on children. The literature on family structure has generally focused on structural variations within heterosexual-parented families, contrasting heterosexual married couples, heterosexual remarried couples, and heterosexual single mothers (Cherlin 1992; McLanahan and Sandefur 1994). Even though same-sex couples are a small minority of all couples (1% of all couples in the 2000 census were same-sex couples), the inclusion of same-sex couples provides researchers with more leverage over the key question of how family structure matters in general.

Studies of family structure and children's outcomes nearly universally find at least a modest advantage for children raised by their married biological parents. The question that has bedeviled researchers, and that remains essentially unresolved, is why (Cherlin, 1999). Some results have indicated that socioeconomic status explains most or all of the advantage of children being raised by married couples (Biblarz and Raftery 1999; Gennetian 2005; Ginther and Pollak 2004), while other scholars have found that family structure has an enduring effect on children, net of all other factors (McLanahan and Sandefur

1994; Zill 1996). Married couples tend to be the most prosperous type of family unit, and this economic prosperity undoubtedly has certain advantages for children (Shin, 2005).

Overview of the Volume

Having highlighted the diversity of families, a preview of the volume follows. The volume is divided into five parts based on themes associated with the constituent chapters.

Part I: Family Communication Theories and Cultural Diversity

The first section includes three chapters dealing with theories of family communication and changing family diversity. The first chapter, by Chris Segrin and Jeanne Flora, focuses on classic theories and research findings that have influenced and revolutionized the way social science scholars conceptualize family interaction.

The second chapter, by Rhunette Diggs and Thomas Socha, discusses family vows in terms of famous clichés, including "for richer or for poorer, in sickness and in health." Included is a brief discussion about studies in various cultures, including some in Asia, Africa, India, and Mexico. Family cultural diversity is discussed in terms of dilemmas, fears, and opportunity.

The third chapter, by the first co-editor, discusses the difference between intercultural and interracial marriage. As globalization continues to dominate the international landscape and technology continues to make the world metaphorically flatter, intercultural relations, and very likely intercultural marriages, will increase. This chapter examines key elements of intercultural marriage, including assimilation and acculturation of extended family involvement, gender roles, religious practices, child rearing, moods of emotional expression, and divorce. While achieving a successful balance between cultures may be difficult and is not always achieved, it is not impossible and can result in a rewarding and lasting marriage.

Part II: Emotion, Spirituality, Introspection, and Sexual Orientation

The second section of the volume presents four chapters dealing with intrapersonal processes in terms of the expression of emotions in families as well as the role of spirituality, ethics, religious beliefs, and sexual orientation. How is morality taught in families, if at all? What are the consequences of a culture in which values are in the eye of the beholder? Imagined interactions are discussed in Chapter 6 in which family members daydream about sensitive topics that they may fear discussing because of perceived retribution.

Chapter 4, by Julie Fitness and Jill Duffield, discusses how the expression of emotions serves numerous functions within the family, including expression of needs (e.g., the infant cries to signal the need for milk). Families teach how emotions are to be expressed. Some families are stoic in that the public display of emotions is frowned on, while others have no restraint in communicating selfish needs in public. Sibling emotions are discussed in terms of cooperation as well as competition for parental attention resources (who gets the new electronic game), time, love, and attention. While siblings typically share a deep bond, there is also a lot of sibling jealousy and envy, particularly during childhood.

Chapter 5, by Timothy Muehlhoff, Jonathan Denham, and James Honeycutt, discusses religious values as the core of life for many families in terms of symbolic interactionism. Symbolic maps are discussed, including family themes, rituals, and rules. Challenges to symbolic maps include the internet (religion surfers), doubts and challenges to values, negative religious stereotypes, and the fast pace of technological life compromising family members' patience to simply sit at a dinner table without texting.

Chapter 6, by the two co-editors, discusses the role of a type of mental imagery and cognition within families: imagined interactions. Everyday people daydream and use mental imagery as they have flashbacks of prior conversations while anticipating what might be said next. For example, a daughter has an argument with her mother about using the car. The mother replies she has more important plans. Yet, the daughter anticipates asking the father for the use of the car and strategizes about what to say. Imagined interactions serve six functions in daily life: compensation, relational maintenance, resolving arguments, rehearsal, catharsis, and self-understanding. Graphs of the use of various attributes of imagined interactions are shown. A brief section discusses two types of abusers, pit bulls and cobras.

Chapter 7, by Letitia Peplau and Kristin Beals, discusses the family lives of lesbians and gay men. The chapter focuses on four main elements of societal attitudes about gay men and lesbians, the relations of lesbians and gays to their family of origin, the nature of gay and lesbian couples, and the experiences of homosexual parents and their children.

Part III: Family Pheromones and Physiology

The third section deals with family physiology in terms of smell and physiological arousal during family discussions. The third section deals with family physiology in terms of smell and physiological arousal during family discussions. Chapter 8, by Laura Hatcher, examines family communication through the lens of smell. The chapter reveals that humans are able to subconsciously recognize and interpret the meanings of certain human-generated odors. Genetic diversity, for example, is often demonstrated through a person's unique scent, thus allowing the sense of smell to act as a sort of screening tool for potential mating partners. The same mechanisms that allow us to recognize genetic diversity also allow us to smell genetic similarity—a phenomenon that results in the ability to smell kinship among related individuals.

Chapter 9 discusses physiological arousal in families. Physiological linkage is described in which stress affects heart rate, blood pressure, and adrenalin. Physiological linkage between marital partners has been shown to be higher during conflict conversations than during neutral ones. Physiological arousal is negatively associated with marital satisfaction, with less-satisfied couples showing higher levels of linkage. The chapter summarizes how marital interaction research, using cardiovascular, endocrine, and immune measures, has yielded important insights into the physiological consequences of marital conflict, including negative long-term health consequences.

Part IV: Divorce and Family Reconfiguration

The fourth section discusses the four behaviors that result in divorce based on the legacy of John Gottman's work on observing marital couples over forty years, communication in divorced and single-parent families, and a discussion of remarriage in blended families. Chapter 10 discusses John Gottman's notion of the "four horsemen of the apocalypse," which correctly predicts divorce over 94% of the time based on longitudinal and follow-up studies. These behaviors are criticism, contempt, defensiveness, and stonewalling.

Chapter 11, by Julia Lewis, Linda Johnson-Reitz, and Judith S. Wallerstein, discusses communication styles in divorced and single-parent families, including conflict and meta-communication in which parents directly or indirectly communicate their themes, attitudes, and values or lack of values including history, relational roles, and optimism or pessimism about the future.

Chapter 12, by Chris Segrin and Jeanne Flora, discusses the negotiation of redefined family roles in blended families. "Blended families" is another phrase for step-families. Families are combined in which offspring were born from parents who are no longer together, whether through divorce or death.

Part V: Effects of Infidelity and Abuse

The final section discusses the effects of divorce on children as well as abuse in families. Chapter 13, by Jean Duncombe and Dennis Marsden, discusses when parents fail to consider children in relation to their affairs and presents evidence that children may become involved in parental affairs to a greater extent than adults realize. They discuss how children's symptoms of distress from an affair may persist or emerge after they reach adulthood.

Chapter 14, by Kristin Anderson, Debra Umberson, and Simikka Elliott, explores violence and abuse in the family. For many people around the world, the greatest risk of being a victim of violence occurs within the family. Over 25% of women and 8% of men report that they were physically or sexually assaulted by a partner or spouse in their lives. Over 10% of children report severe violence at the hands of their parents in a given year. An even larger number of children suffer from neglect. Family violence is a global problem, as over forty countries find that 10% to half of women report being a victim of an assault by an intimate male partner at some point in their lives. The global presence of family violence is no excuse for any instance of it.

Discussion Questions /Activities

1. Examine the diverse set of family definitions in Table I-1. Which definition do you most agree with? Why do you prefer this definition?
2. Write your own definition of a family. Where did it come from: your experiences, social media, movies, books, teachers, church, friends?
3. Discuss how various cable shows and Netflix portray families. Can you think of shows where the family is portrayed in a positive way and displays resilience and confidence? Conversely, can you think of shows where it is a satire of the family and people laugh at the characters in a comedy?

References

Biblarz, T.J. and Raftery, A.E. (1999). "Family Structure, Educational Attainment, and Socioeconomic Success: Rethinking the 'Pathology of Matriarchy.'" *American Journal of Sociology, 105,* 321–65.

Brown, D.L. (1981). "A Quarter Century of Trends and Changes in the Demographic Structure of American Families." In R.T. Coward and W.M. Smith Jr. (Eds.), *The Family in Rural Society* (pp. 9–26). Boulder, CO: Westview Press.

Coltrane, S. and Collins, R. (2001). *Sociology of Marriage and the Family: Gender, Love, and Property (5th ed.).* Belmont, CA: Wadsworth/Thomson Learning.

Coontz, S. (2005). *Marriage, a History: From Obedience to Intimacy or How Love Conquered Marriage.* New York: Viking Penguin.

Gennetian, L.A. 2005. "One or Two Parents? Half or Step Siblings? The Effect of Family Structure on Young Children's Achievement." *Journal of Population Economics* 18:415–436.

Ginther, D.K. and Pollak, R.A. (2004). "Family Structure and Children's Educational Outcomes: Blended Families, Stylized Facts, and Descriptive Regressions." *Demography* 41:671–96.

McLanahan, S. and Sandefur, G. (1994). *Growing Up with a Single Parent: What Hurts, What Helps.* Cambridge, MA: Harvard University Press.

Shin, H.B. (2005). School Enrollment—Social and Economic Characteristics of Students: October 2003. *Current Population Report,* 20-554. U.S. Census Bureau, Washington, DC.

U.S. Census Bureau. American FactFinder Glossary. http://factfinder.census.gov/home/en/epss/glossary_f.html. Downloaded June 28, 2012. Technical Documentation: Census 2000 Summary File 1.

Zill, N. (1996). "Family Change and Student Achievement: What We Have Learned, What It Means for Schools." In A. Booth and J.F. Dunn (Eds.), *Family-School Links: How Do They Affect Educational Outcomes?* (pp. 139–184) Mahwah, NJ: Lawrence Erlbaum Associates.

Part I

FAMILY COMMUNICATION THEORIES AND CULTURAL DIVERSITY

1. Theoretical Perspectives on Family Communication

By Chris Segrin & Jeanne Flora

In this selection we review a number of influential theories of family communication and relationships. Although not all of the theories discussed in this selection were explicitly developed as theories of family interaction per se, each has been widely and fruitfully applied in the scientific study of families.

What is a theory, and why do social scientists develop theories? Simply put, a theory is an explanation of a fact pattern. Social scientists generally do not develop theories to explain individual cases or incidents. Rather, theories are developed to explain how and why certain things happen, particularly when those things happen repeatedly. For example, scientists and therapists realized that a lot of couples who get divorced exhibit certain patterns of destructive conflict. For that reason, they attempted to develop a theory that explains how and why conflict can harm a marriage. If only a handful of divorced couples had problems with conflict, scientists probably would not have been motivated to develop an explanation for why conflict harms marriage. Scientific theories serve a number of useful functions. Perhaps the most basic function of a theory is to *explain* how and why a phenomenon occurs or operates. A related function of theories is to *predict* when a phenomenon might or might not happen. For example, in recent years there has been great interest in developing theories of divorce that allow for prediction of who will divorce and who will stay married. In addition, theories sometimes allow scientists and therapists to *control* a phenomenon. If a valid theory of divorce explains the phenomenon as caused by dysfunctional communication patterns, instituting training seminars or therapy techniques that address those communication problems might be a useful way to lower the divorce rate.

In this selection, we present an analysis of family systems theory, symbolic interaction theory, social learning theory, attachment theory, and the dialectic perspective. Notice how each theory offers different explanations of how and why family interactions function as they do. It is important to keep in mind that no theory offers the one and only explanation for a fact pattern. There are often multiple explanations for why family interactions function as they do. The utility of a theory is therefore determined, at least in part, by how well it holds up under empirical scrutiny. In other words, are the available data consistent with the propositions of the theory? All of the theories discussed in this selection have been associated with numerous studies that support the essential components and elements of the theory.

Family Systems Theory

Historical Background

As social scientific theories go, family systems theory has unique beginnings. In fact, family systems theory emerged from a line of work that was more closely related to engineering and biology than to families or human relationships. Family systems theory was derived from general systems theory (GST), which is a theoretical perspective developed for explaining how elements of a system work together to produce outputs from the various inputs they are given. A "*system*" is nothing more than a "set of elements standing in interrelation among themselves and with the environment" (Bertalanffy, 1975, p. 159). Two key figures in the development of GST were biologist Ludwig von Bertalanffy and mathematician and engineer Norbert Wiener (e.g., Bertalanffy, 1968; Wiener, 1948). Wiener is most noted for his work on *cybernetics*, which is the science of self-correcting systems. An early application of GST came from work on antiaircraft gunnery during World War II. An essential realization of this work was the necessity to constantly compare the aim of the weapon, and the resultant course of its munitions delivery, to the position of the target. When the ammunition was being delivered too far ahead of the plane or too far behind, the operator of the weapon had to take this into consideration and adjust the aim of the antiaircraft gun. In the abstract, this concept is known as *cybernetic feedback* and would be an essential component of GST.

Whitchurch and Constantine (1993) identified three basic assumptions of GST. First, systems theories can unify science. The principles of GST are thought by many to cut across traditional academic boundaries. That is to say, they apply to systems in the natural as well as in the social sciences. For this reason, concepts and processes that describe the functioning of an automobile engine (mechanical engineering) could be equally applicable to a description of the functioning of a family (family science), or the functioning of a particular ecosystem (biology). A second assumption of GST is that a system must be understood as a whole. This concept, known as *holism*, is fundamental to all systems approaches. A system cannot be understood by merely studying each of its components in isolation from each other. There is little to be learned about the functions and outputs of an automobile engine by carefully examining the alternator and oil filter. That would not be much more useful than trying to learn about a family by carefully studying their cat and their daughter. The concept of holism implies that "the whole is greater than the sum of its parts." To understand the system, one must look at it holistically, considering all elements and how they relate to each other. A third assumption of GST is that human systems are self-reflexive. *Self-reflexivity* means that we can develop our own goals and monitor our own behavior. This is inherent in the fact that human systems are cybernetic systems that can process feedback, which is what allows for adjustments in behaviors in order to reach a goal.

The Family as a System

At first glance, the connection between "family" and such concepts as engines, anti-aircraft artillery, and ecosystems may not be obvious. However, the family is a system that operates in accord with many of the same principles as these other systems. At the same time, the family is a special type of system with some characteristics that set it apart from some other types of systems. The family is often characterized as an open and ongoing system (Broderick, 1993). Systems that are *open* take input from the environment and produce output back to the environment. The input that families take from the environment includes things as simple as food bought at the grocery store to more complex matters such as information on the best colleges to send their children to. Output also includes a vast range of things from garbage to professional work to children who become members of society. Although no family is truly a closed system, families vary in the extent to which they are open. Families that are extremely open are said to have permeable *boundaries*. Boundaries are simply dividing lines that determine who is in and who is out of the system (Yerby, Buerkel-Rothfuss, & Bochner, 1995). The permeable boundaries of the very open family suggest that people can come and go with ease, into and out of the family system, Such a family, for example, may allow a distant cousin to move in for an extended period of time. At the same time, a teenage child might move out of the home to study in Europe as an exchange student. Families that are less open are more inclined to keep to themselves and send clear messages about the limited extent to which they will tolerate "outsiders" entering into the system.

Any system that is *ongoing* has a past, present, and future. If one considers the extended family, most families could be viewed as perpetual. Obviously, we all have ancestors, and barring some catastrophe, our families will all continue long after we are gone. In the grand scheme of things, when people think about their families (e.g., parents, siblings, grandparents, aunts, and uncles) they are really considering a mere snapshot in time. The greater ongoing system has a very long history and is sure to have a very long future.

The fact that families are open and ongoing systems means that they have a number of qualities that distinguish them from other types of systems (Broderick, 1993). For instance, all open and ongoing systems are *dynamic*. The relationships among their elements and the environment are not static; rather, they change over time. The way that a mother relates to her child at age 1 is very different from the way she relates to her child at age 15. The qualities of open and ongoing systems are *emergent*. The elements of the family interact to produce something that is more than just a collection of individuals. Systems theorists often make an analogy to baking a cake. Combining eggs, flour, sugar, and milk and baking it results in something very different from a mere collection of the individual ingredients. Families have a similar quality of emergent properties. Families also exhibit regular patterns from which we can deduce *rules*. For example, observing a family over a long period of time might reveal that whenever a member has a birthday, he or she is excused from any household chores. To the extent that this pattern is evident, one could say that this is a "rule" in the family It is also the case that these patterns of interaction, or rules, are *hierarchically structured*. This means that rules exist at different levels of abstraction, and some take precedence over others (see chap. 4). Open and ongoing systems also *regulate relationships among their components*. In order to maintain the integrity of the system, it is essential to have some rules or patterns that hold the elements together and allow for the smooth functioning of the overall system. Parents who scold their children for fighting with each other are, in the abstract, attempting to regulate their relationships. Constant and intense fighting among family members could otherwise threaten the family's well-being and ability to realize their goals. Finally, open and ongoing systems *regulate relationships between the system and the environment*. All families exist in a greater society ecosystem or suprasystem. Because they are open, interaction with elements outside of the immediate family system is essential. For this reason, families develop rules and patterns of conduct for these interactions, with the goal of protecting the integrity of the family system. A family rule that children cannot go out on dates until they are 15 is an example of a rule designed to regulate relationships between the family and the external environment.

The family's distinction as an open and ongoing system helps to delineate it from a variety of other systems. However, the family is not the only open and ongoing system. Many animal societies and environmental ecosystems could also be characterized as open and ongoing systems. To more fully appreciate the concept of family systems it is necessary to look closer at some of the family processes that are inherent in family systems theory.

Major Processes in Family Systems Theory

System processes are the characteristics that describe how the family system functions as a whole unit (Bochner & Eisenberg, 1987). One way to understand family systems theory is to examine the family processes that are assumed to play an important role in the family's day to day functioning.

Mutual Influence

According to family systems theory, all family components are interdependent. That is to say, what happens to one member affects all other members of the family. The actions of every family member will influence the actions of other family members. Family systems theorists feel that families are constantly in the processes of influencing each other, and that this process never ends. So, for example, a child graduating from college is not just an individual achievement; it is a family event. For parents, it may represent the culmination of years of child rearing, a reduced financial burden, and the possibility of a more distant relationship with the child as he or she moves away to start a new job. To a sibling, this event may represent more freedom to use the family car, no longer having to share a bedroom, and the absence of a reliable tennis partner. Either way, the graduation of one member of the family impacts all other members of the family. Keep in mind, however, that there is no linear cause (child graduates) and effect (more distant relationship with the child) relationship in this hypothetical family. The act of going to college, graduating, and moving away to take a job is also influenced by the family. For example, a child without a close relationship to his or her parents might be more likely to move out of state after graduation. The concept of mutual influence suggests that all family members influence each other.

Stability

All families seek some level of regularity in their lives. Regularity brings predictability, and at least some degree of predictability allows for smooth functioning of the family. The tendency to seek stability is called *morphostasis*. Patterns, routines, and rules all allow families to function with some level of stability. A total lack of stability, or chaos, could easily destroy a family system. In a state a chaos, family roles are unclear, the behavior of family members is unpredictable, and important tasks may go undone because everyone thought that someone else would do them. Alternatively, family members may waste energy duplicating one another's efforts. It is easy to see how such a scenario would make the family such an inhospitable place as to motivate most of its members to leave the system. Although some degree of flexibility and change is healthy for the family (see section on family functioning in chap. 1) all families need and seek some stability.

Change

Just as families need some stability, healthy families must experience some change. In fact, families are also driven to seek change. This tendency is known as *morphogenesis*. Morphogenesis is the tendency to reorganize and evolve over time. As family members marry, have children, age, and die, the family evolves. This is a natural and unavoidable evolution. Families also exist is a larger society, and as society itself changes, so do most families. Fifty years ago family members may have looked down on a mother who took a full-time job while her children were still young. Given the changing economic and social conditions of society, families today may be more inclined to not only accept but also honor someone who takes on so many tasks.

Feedback and Calibration

Families are information processors. They perform the cybernetic function of examining their own behavior and trying to correct it so as to achieve goals. In a feedback loop, the family examines its output, and if that output is not meeting the goal or reaching some standard, they send a message (which becomes new input) to correct the behavior that led to the deviant outcome. An obvious example of this would be rearing children. Families will often correct or punish deviant behavior of their children in hopes that the children will ultimately grow up in accord with some standard defined by the family. The goal of feedback and control is to reach some level of *homeostosis*, or equilibrium. A married couple with full-time jobs that often keep them apart from each other may plan a vacation together to allow them to re-establish some balance between separateness and connection in their relationship. *Negative feedback*, also know as error-actuated feedback, occurs when the family initiates corrective action upon awareness of a deviation from some standard. This is the way that most thermostats operate. Once the temperature deviates from a set point, the thermostat sends a signal to the furnace or air conditioner to produce more heating or cooling. Parents who punish their children for bad behavior operate on negative feedback. *Positive feedback*, or deviation-amplifying feedback, works to enhance changes from a set point. For example, if a young adult child who lives with his parents and works a part-time job suddenly starts looking into colleges to attend, the parents might respond by verbally encouraging him, offering financial assistance with tuition, and relieving him of household chores so that he can pursue his studies. In this way, the parents use feedback to actually encourage change in their son's behavior, once they realize that he is contemplating a change from the norm of his part-time job.

Equifinality

The concept of equifinality refers to the fact that the same end state may be reached in many different ways. Different families can achieve the same goals by traveling down very different paths. Consider, for example, the goal of providing for the family. Some may do this through the father's employment. In other families, both the mother and the father work. In still other families, teenage children may work and contribute some of their wages to the family. In all cases, the family system generates income to provide for their needs, but in very different ways. The family systems concept of equifinality is useful and important because it is a reminder that there is no single version of family well-being and functionality. Instead, there are many different ways that families can pursue the same goal. A related systems concept, *multifinality*, indicates that the same set of inputs may lead to different outputs. Two middle-class, suburban families with similar incomes and resources may end up raising very different children. This is because different families will process the same inputs differently.

Table 1-1. Key Concepts in Family Systems Theory

FAMILY SYSTEMS CONCEPT	DEFINITION
• Boundaries	The border between the system and its external environment
• Enmeshment	A lack of differentiation between family members so as to minimize the development of individual identities
• Equifinality	The idea that the same end state can be reached by many different paths
• Feedback	The family's response to a behavior or process that is observed
• Goals	The family's desired outcomes or end states
• Holism	The family can only be understood by examining it in its entirety; the whole is more than the sum of its parts; also known as nonsummativity
• Homeostasis	Maintaining a state of equilibrium through feedback and calibration
• Interdependence	The idea that all components of the system are interrelated; what happens to one happens to all; the actions of one element affect the actions of the others
• Morphogenesis	The family's tendency to evolve and change with time
• Morphostasis	The tendency to seek stability or equilibrium
• Multifinality	The idea that the same set of inputs can lead to different outputs in different families
• Mutual Influence	Family members influence each other
• Negative Feedback	Error-actuated feedback that is engaged when actions deviate from a family standard; this feedback attempts to suppress the deviation
• Positive Feedback	Deviation-amplifying feedback that is designed to stimulate and enhance deviation for a norm
• Requisite Variety	Having the necessary range of resources and responses to adequately address the demands encountered in the environment
• Rules	Prescribed patterns of behavior in the family; they contribute to the family's stability
• Subsystem	A smaller system within the family system such as husband–wife or parent–child
• Suprasystem	The larger system in which the family is embedded such as the extended family or society more generally

These, and additional concepts and processes in family systems theory, are assembled in Table 1-1.

Evaluation of Family Systems Theory

Family systems theory is the dominant paradigm in family science. It has been noted that "Many, if not most, family communication specialists have a systems theory worldview" (Whitchurch & Dickson, 1999). Nevertheless, family systems theory has been criticized on several grounds (see Klein & White, 1996, and Whitchurch & Constantine, 1993, for reviews). One position is that family systems theory is not really a true theory, but rather a philosophical perspective. There is some ambiguity and generality in family systems theory that makes it hard to generate concrete, testable hypotheses. Also, some people feel that family systems theory goes too far in emphasizing the role of all family members in influencing the phenomena that the family experiences. If a father loses his job, more often than not he is more responsible for that outcome than the family's 1-year old child is. On a related point, family systems theory has also been criticized by feminist scholars who argue that systems conceptualizations do not recognize the fact that women and children often have less power and resources than do men. For that reason, it may be unwise to view the contribution of women and children to family matters as equal to that of men. This criticism has become particularly heated when topics such as family violence and sexual abuse are discussed. Although systems theorists would not "blame" the victim, they would try to understand family problems as a function of the relationships among family members, instead of the behavior of an individual perpetrator. Whitchurch and Constantine argue that this later critique is based on a misunderstanding of GST, and that recent developments in family systems theory actually recognize different levels of power in the family through the concept of hierarchy.

Symbolic Interaction Theory

Historical Background

Even before the development of symbolic interaction theory, 20th-century pragmatists, such as John Dewey and William James, began to argue that reality is not objectively "set in stone"; rather, it is constantly changing. This way of thinking about reality was somewhat novel for the early 20th century. Furthermore, this new notion of reality advocated that participants constantly co-create a subjective social reality as they interact. Inspired by the ideas of these earlier thinkers, George Herbert Mead is credited with articulating the foundations of the theory later named symbolic interaction (SI) theory. Along with Mead, Manford Kuhn is recognized for contributing to and affirming the unique ideas of SI. Mead was a very popular and respected teacher at the University of Chicago, and, after his death, his students compiled lecture notes from his classes to produce a book they titled *Mind, Self, and Society* (1934). One of Mead's students, Herbert Blumer (1969), termed Mead's theoretical tenets "symbolic interaction theory."

Mead and others were interested in the way humans create, react to, and redefine the shared, symbolic meanings in their social environment. Mead began with the premise that words and nonverbal behaviors are the primary symbols to which humans assign meaning. He stressed the idea that meaning only occurs when people share common symbols and interpretations in a state of intersubjectivity. He also elaborated on the idea that symbolic meanings are heavily influenced by perceptions, including people's own perceptions and other people's perceptions of them and the social structure around them, For example, imagine a college student who comes home over a break from school with baskets full of dirty laundry. Her mother washes and folds the clothes for her. What does this behavior symbolize? Because SI sees meaning as occurring between people, we cannot know the meaning until we study the mother and daughter's interaction and perceptions. Perhaps (a) the daughter perceives herself as mature and self-sufficient; (b) based on prior interaction, the mother views and accepts the daughter as self-sufficient; and (c) the two come to a common interpretation that the mother is not obligated to do the laundry, but chooses to do so as a symbol of care for her busy daughter. In another mother–daughter relationship, this very same behavior could symbolize an obligatory caretaking duty full of resent, guilt, and the perception of a lazy daughter.

Mead (1934) and Blumer (1969) felt that the study of human beings required methods different from those of the study of physical objects or laws of nature. This is because human behavior can only be understood by knowing what it means to the person who is actually performing the behavior. Because SI emphasizes individuals' perceptions and the intersubjectivity shared by participants, it is difficult to observe and understand communication from the outside. Not until researchers know the perspective of the individual, can they understand him or her. Mead and Blumer advocated the use of case studies and examination of stories and personal histories in order to understand people's behaviors from the perspective of the people themselves.

Today, SI can be thought of as a diverse collection of theories rather than as a particular theory (Klein & White, 1996). Over time, many branches of the theory developed (e.g., social construction theory, role theory, and self-theory), emphasizing slightly different aspects of symbolic, human interaction. For instance, social construction theory spun off SI to explain co-constructed meaning rather than shared meaning. That is, social construction theory builds on the ideas of SI to further emphasize that "meaning does not reside inside one person's head, waiting to be shared with another. Rather, meaning exists in the practice of communication between people" (Turner & West, 2002, p. 61; see also Chen & Pearce, 1995). To illustrate the social construction of meaning, consider what happens when people become grandparents for the first time. They are often assigned a new title (i.e., grandma, nana, grammy, etc.), which is already loaded with basic cultural meaning. However, the title takes on further meaning as the grandparent–grandchild relationship develops. Through family interaction, the family co-constructs what they mean by the term *grandma*. In some families, grandma is a distant relative who sends gifts on holidays. For others, Grandma is a primary caretaker, acting more like some "moms." In sum, society's expectations for grandparents influence the meaning assigned to the role, but an additional layer of meaning is generated through the family's own interaction.

Central Themes, Assumptions, and Concepts in SI

There are at least three central themes of SI and several underlying assumptions associated with these themes (Klein & White, 1996; LaRossa & Reitzes, 1993; West & Turner, 2000). Each theme relates to one of the three concepts that title Mead's (1934) book, *Mind, Self, and Society*. The first theme involves the importance of meanings for human behavior and relates to Mead's concept of *mind*. Three assumptions reveal this theme (Blumer, 1969; West & Turner, 2000, p. 76):

1. Humans act toward others on the basis of the meaning those others have for them.
2. Meaning is created in interaction between people.
3. Meaning is modified through an interpretive process.

This collection of assumptions acknowledges that human minds have the capacity to use symbols to represent thought. In particular, people rely on common, significant symbols that have shared, social meaning. As a symbol system, language works because people act in accordance with shared meanings. Even though people have many shared symbols, symbolic meaning is always being modified in interaction. Through perspective taking and other interpretive processes, people come to understand others' views. For instance, in symbolic role-taking, people try to take another person's perspective, or step inside his or her mind, in order to see how another person sorts out meaning. Very young children have a difficult time perspective taking. In a game of hide and seek, young children may think that if their own eyes are closed, then no one else can see them. They soon learn that what they see is not what other people see.

The second theme addresses how humans develop self-concepts and relates to Mead's (1934) concept of *self*. Two assumptions reveal this theme (LaRossa & Reitzes, 1993; West & Turner, 2000, p. 78):

1. Individuals develop self-concepts through interaction with others.
2. Self-concepts provide an important motive for behavior.

Mead (1934) describes the *self* as an *I* and a *Me*. During interaction, the *I* simply acts, impulsively and spontaneously. The *Me* is more reflective, concerned with how people come across to their social world. The Me employs social comparisons and considers the way other people view the self. More specifically, the Me attends to reflected self-appraisals. *Reflected self-appraisals* refer to the appraisals or evaluations other people make of the self. The extent to which another person's view affects one's self-concept depends on how much one values the other person's opinion. Young children often take the comments of their primary caretakers very seriously, because they have few other referents in their lives. Some college students, on the other hand, only take their parents' opinions with a "grain of salt" because they are receiving a great deal of reflected self-appraisal from other important sources including friends, romantic partners, professors, and so forth. As SI indicates, the way people view their *self* motivates their future behavior. For example, people who have been told they are bad at math and who view themselves as bad at math have little reason to be motivated to major in math. Their self-concept may even set forth a self-fulfilling prophecy, whereby they see little reason to try hard at math because they already perceive they are bad. Putting forth little effort at math helps them meet their already low expectations.

Finally, the third theme describes the relationship between individuals and society and relates to Mead's (1934) concept of *society* (West & Turner, 2000, p. 79):

1. People and groups are influenced by cultural and social processes.
2. Social structure is worked out through social interaction.

Mead (1934) states that *society* is comprised of particular others and generalized others. *Particular others* refer to close significant others, such as family and friends, and *generalized others* refer to the larger community or society. According to SI, people act in the context of societal norms and values, whether they be the norms and values of their particular others or generalized others. For example, family members know what is normal behavior for their family culture (i.e., their particularized others), and they act with those norms in mind. Some families have a ritual of eating dinner together around a table every night. Other families do not expect members to eat at the same time or in the same place. Just as the interaction in one's family creates a set of norms and values, society (i.e., generalized others) influences what is viewed as normal family interaction. The media, for instance, is one societal force that shapes standards for family interaction.

Evaluation and Application to Family Communication

Sociologist and symbolic interaction theorist Ernest W. Burgess was "the first to define family in terms of its interaction: 'a unity of interacting personalities,' by which he meant a family as a living, changing, growing thing, 'a unity of interacting persons,' rather than 'a mere collection of individuals'" (as cited in Whitchurch & Dickson, 1999, p. 691). Burgess' pioneering approach viewed interaction as the defining feature of families. His work became a theoretical cornerstone of family research. SI inspired a new way of studying families, by examining family interaction and the creation and maintenance of family symbols and themes.

In particular, SI has guided research on topics such as the socialization of family members, symbolic interpretations of family events, and family identities and narratives. As Steinmetz (1999) states: "We are not born with a sense of who we are, but must develop a sense of 'self' through symbolization with other people" (p. 375). Symbolic interaction draws attention to the critical role that parents, siblings, and other outside forces play as socializing agents for children (Bohannon & White, 1999; Cheng & Kuo, 2000). Children observe appropriate behavior for certain roles, and they receive reflected self-appraisal from the significant others in their family. Second, SI explains how families symbolize both routine and extraordinary events, though a great deal of attention has been given to extraordinary events, such as marriage, death, or major family illnesses (Book, 1996; Rehm & Franck, 2000; see also chap. 3). Informed by the society around them, families develop rituals for family events, such as weddings or funerals, or rituals for routine events, such as bedtime rituals to put a child to sleep. Finally, families generate stories to symbolize one family member's identity or the whole family identity (Hequembourg & Farrell, 1999; Stone, 1988).

There are a number of obvious strengths and weaknesses of SI. As a strength, SI highlights that meaning is dynamic and subjective, and understandings are worked out as family members interact with one another and with society. The problem is that researchers sometimes have a difficult time studying family meanings and symbols because they are often so subjective. Apart from actually living with a family, the only way researchers can learn about these subjective understandings is by asking family members to report their perceptions and tell their own story. Some family members may not even be aware of their own subjective meanings, and, if they are, they may be unwilling to report or may adjust their story for someone outside the family. Nonetheless, SI and its theoretical offshoots continue to inspire a great deal of research in family studies.

SOCIAL LEARNING THEORY

Background

Social learning theory was developed by Stanford University psychologist Albert Bandura (Bandura, 1977). Bandura developed social learning theory, not as a theory of family communication per se, rather as a more general theory of behavioral acquisition. More recently, Bandura has expanded social learning theory into the more general social cognitive theory (e.g., Bandura, 1986, 1994). However, for purposes of the present discussion we will contain our presentation largely to explanation of the basic principles of social learning theory.

In the premier study of what was later to become social learning theory, Bandura, Ross, and Ross (1963) documented that children will imitate a model who is reinforced for performing certain behaviors. To explore this issue, they randomly assigned nursery school students to watch a filmed portrayal of a child model. Under one condition, the model behaved aggressively and was rewarded for doing so. Under the second condition the model behaved aggressively and was punished for doing so. In the control group the model did not behave aggressively at all. Shortly thereafter, the children were allowed to play, and researchers measured their aggressive behavior during the play session. They found that children who observed the aggressive model get rewarded exhibited significantly more aggressive behavior themselves than either those under the aggression-punished condition or those in the control group. Also, those who saw the model get punished for aggressive behavior behaved much less aggressively than those under the other conditions. Bandura and his colleagues theorized that the children learned the consequences of behaving aggressively by observing what happened when the model behaved aggressively. When the model was rewarded, the nursery school children imitated or enacted the same behavior that produced the reward for the model. When the model was punished, the children seemed to avoid performing the behavior that resulted in punishment for the model. This idea of observational learning through modeling would become a central element of Bandura's social learning theory.

One can think of the process of social learning as a search for "if-then" relationships (Smith, 1982). Consistent with the more general principles of behavioral theory, according to social learning theory, people seek rewards and try to avoid punishments. Bandura notes that, fortunately, people are able to learn what brings rewards and what brings punishments at least some of the time through observing what happens to other people. Imagine what life would be like if the only way we could learn about the consequences of driving without a seatbelt, playing with a loaded gun, picking up rattlesnakes, and drinking household chemicals was through direct experience. Most people would not live to see their 20th birthday. Fortunately, we are able to learn about the consequences of these behaviors by observing other people's misfortunes. Similarly, we are able to learn about behaviors that bring more positive consequences by also observing others. Once the "if-then" rule (e.g., "If I touch a hot stove, then I will burn my hand" or "If I scream and cry, then my mother will give me candy") is learned, most people act accordingly to secure the reward or avoid the punishment.

Learning About the Consequences of Behavior

In social learning theory, people are assumed to gain most of their knowledge about the consequences of performing various behaviors through two possible sources. The first, and the most obvious, is through *direct experience*. In this rudimentary mode of learning, people acquire knowledge of behavioral consequences by actually experiencing them. For example, if a child eats a chili pepper and it burns his or her mouth, that experience teaches the child to avoid eating chili peppers in the future. If the child eats a chocolate candy bar, and it tastes good, the child would learn the reinforcing value of eating chocolate and would presumably perform the behavior frequently in the future. The idea of learning through direct experience and the rewards and punishments that are associated with our behaviors is a basic element of behavior theory, and is a mode by which even the simplest of animals can and will learn. However, because of their ability to form mental representations and their ability to abstract rules from observations of actions and their consequences, humans (and some other animals) are also able to learn through observation and the vicarious experience that it presents. Learning by vicarious experience happens when we take note of the effects of other people's behaviors. For example, if John observed his parents reward his sister with $20 for bringing home a report card with straight As, he is likely to abstract the following if-then rule: "If you get straight As in school, then mom and dad will give you money" So long as receiving money is seen by John as a positive outcome, he is likely to try to enact that behavior (i.e., working hard in school to get good grades) himself. Note that John did not learn the if-then rule by directly experiencing the effects of getting good grades. Rather, he learned the rule vicariously, through observing what happened when his sister got good grades.

The Process of Social Learning

Let us dissect the process of observational learning, or learning by modeling, a bit further. Learning through vicarious experience is dependent on several interrelated processes. To start, there must be some *attention* paid to the model. Each day people are exposed to dozens, hundreds, and in some cases, thousands of other people. Each of these people is a potential model from whom others can learn about the consequences of enacting various behaviors. However, social learning can only happen if we pay attention to both the model's behavior and its associated consequences. Without attention to the model, there can be no observational learning. Second, there must be *retention* of the if-then rule that is learned by observing the model. That is to say, we have to form a mental representation of what was learned, and store that in memory, perhaps as a more abstract rule. Bandura (1986) notes that retention can be enhanced by rehearsal. The more people rehearse the socially learned rule (e.g., if I apologize for doing something wrong, people will forgive me) the more likely they are to have access to it at critical times, and therefore to perform the appropriate behavior for either securing rewards or avoiding punishing responses from the social environment. Next, there are a number of *behavioral production processes* that are vital to performing the observed behavior. People must have the ability to produce or enact the behavior that they observed. This often requires organization of constituent subskills into a new response pattern. Sometimes people are able to enhance their ability to perform observed behaviors by receiving informative feedback from others on troublesome aspects of their behavior. For example, a father might teach his daughter how to kick a soccer ball by modeling the behavior. If the daughter does not perform the behavior with the same competence as the father's, he might give her feedback on what she has done incorrectly in order to help her perform the behavior in the best way possible. Finally, there has to be *motivation* to perform the modeled behavior. In the previous example, the father might model the proper way to kick a soccer ball 100 times in the presence of his daughter. However, even if she pays attention to him, remembers how to do it, and has the competence to perform the modeled behavior, she will not do so unless she has sufficient motivation.

Where does the motivation to perform behavior come from? Social learning theory recognizes that incentives can be inherent in the behavior, vicariously produced, or self-produced (Bandura, 1986). Some behaviors are inherently satisfying to most people. For example, people generally like to eat ice cream. The motivation to eat ice cream comes from consequences that are inherent in the behavior itself, not from some abstract or complex rule that is learned (e.g., "eating ice cream will keep the dairy farmers in business and will therefore be good for the state economy."). Bandura refers to the effects of such behaviors as eating ice cream or drinking water when thirsty as "direct incentive." Sometimes the incentive for performing a behavior is *self-produced*. With self-produced incentives, people essentially reward themselves for a job well done. There is nothing inherently satisfying about bowling a strike. However, bowling enthusiasts will mentally congratulate themselves upon bowling a strike because they have come to value this sort of performance. To people who do not care about or understand bowling, knocking down 10 pins with a heavy ball may seem like a meaningless behavior. Most important to social learning theory, people are sometimes motivated to perform behaviors because of vicarious incentives. People often acquire and perform behaviors because they see other people do so and get rewarded. The fashion and clothing industry—an industry that relies heavily on modeling—is constantly trying to impart vicarious knowledge of the consequences of performing various behaviors (e.g., wear this brand of shoes and you will be a good athlete; wear this style of pants and you will look great and gain the admiration of your peers, etc.).

Application to Family Communication

Even though social learning processes operate throughout the life span, and through observation of virtually any person, their applicability to child learning in the family context is undeniable. Smith (1982) noted that "we acquire most of our basic values and personal habits by initially observing our parents' behavior and later the behavior of admired friends and reference groups" (p. 201). Children often grow up to hold political and religious values similar to those of their parents, pursue many of the same hobbies and occupations that their parents do, and sometimes even drive the same brand of car that their parents drive. Social learning theory provides a compelling account for how and why this happens. The theory is a reminder that anything that parents do in the presence of their children can and often will communicate abstract if-then rules to the children. If the surrounding circumstances are right, these rules may then become prompts for behavior, or inhibitors of behavior, depending on the content of the mental representation.

Smith (1982) described a number of conditions that affect the success of modeling, several of which have obvious applicability in the family setting. One such factor is the similarity between the model and the observer. The more similar the model is to the observer, the more likely the observer is to enact the modeled behavior. Similarity between the model and the self contributes to self-efficacy in the observer. When people experience self-efficacy, they feel that they are able to adequately perform the behavior. Supposedly the thinking with models similar to the self is that "if they can do it, then I can do it." It is obvious that there is considerable perceived similarity within family groups. For this reason, family members can be ideal models of behavior. Smith also notes that modeling is more successful when models have high status. Certainly parents and older siblings have very high status in the eyes of young children. Because most children start out in life looking up to their parents, they naturally use their parents as a benchmark for appropriate behavior. Also, modeling is most successful when there are multiple models. In the family context, it is often the case that more than one person performs a particular behavior. So, for example, if two or three members of the family are avid golfers, children raised in that family will have multiple models to observe, and are consequently very likely to adopt the same behaviors (i.e., take up golfing) themselves.

Family science researchers have continued to apply social learning theory to the explanation of many functional and dysfunctional aspects of family interaction. For example, there are many who feel that people learn how to be spouses and how to be parents by observing their own parents in these roles. In the area of family dysfunction, there is compelling evidence for social learning processes in family or partner violence, substance abuse, and even divorce (e.g., Andrews, Hops, & Duncan, 1997; Mihalic & Elliot, 1997; Swinford, DeMaris, Cernkovich, & Giordano, 2000; see chaps. 11, 13, and 15 for more in-depth analysis of these family issues). When parents engage in physical violence or substance use in the presence of their children, they inadvertently communicate that this is an acceptable form of behavior. This is because young children lack the reasoning skills to independently determine what is right and what is wrong. Therefore, they use their parents as a benchmark for appropriate conduct. The idea is that, if the parents do it, it must be the correct thing to do. So if the mother and father resort to physical violence when engaged in conflict or consume large amounts of alcohol when stressed, children who observe that behavior are likely to enact it themselves later in life. Similarly, when children observe their parents' divorce, they are likely to learn the if-then rule that goes "if you have problems in your marriage, then you get divorced." This is one of several hypotheses for the intergenerational transmission of divorce. It is apparent that social learning processes are so powerful that the if-then rules learned in family contexts and the behaviors that they prompt will often hold up in the face of intense challenges. For example, most people know that divorce and domestic violence are not positive experiences. Yet, the template for behavior that is learned in the family of origin through social learning can be nearly impossible for some people to modify or escape. Despite "knowing" that family violence is wrong, when confronted with intense conflict, that becomes the default response. As disturbing as these family patterns are, they are a testimony to the power of social learning.

Attachment Theory

Background

Attachment theory was originally developed by John Bowlby and was based on his observational studies of children who experienced separation from their parents during World War II (Bowlby, 1969, 1973, 1980). Bowlby was also influenced by ethological theories that explore similarities and differences in behavior across species. Ultimately he argued that attachment processes outlined in the theory are evident in nonhuman as well as human primates and serve an adaptive function for the survival of the species. Although Bowlby developed his theory as something of an alternative to the orthodox psychodynamic view of child development that was articulated by Sigmund Freud, Bowlby's thinking still preserves many of the trappings of psychodynamic ideology.

Bowlby (1973) observed that human infants are innately driven to seek out and remain in close proximity to their primary caregivers. Indeed, this pattern of behavior is typical of most primates. Bowlby characterized attachment behavior as "any form of behavior that results in a person attaining or retaining proximity to some other differentiated and preferred individual" (p. 292). This type of behavior is viewed as "hardwired" into the brain. That is to say, people do not need to learn proximity seeking to the caregiver, Rather, this tendency is already present at birth. Bowlby felt that this pattern of behavior was the result of natural selection. Because it is adaptive to the survival of the species, those who did not seek the proximity of a caregiver as an infant were less likely to survive and pass on their genes.

Functions of Attachment

As noted earlier, attachment processes between the infant and primary caregiver are assumed to be functional. Bowlby argued that attachment is adaptive to the survival of the species. His writings highlight four distinct functions that are served by attachment, all of which appear to be beneficial to the infant's survival and development. Perhaps the most basic function of attachment is *proximity seeking*. Infants have an innate tendency to seek out their primary caregiver. Given that this person is the source of protection and nourishment, it is obvious how this tendency serves the infant's best interests. *Separation protest* is a second function of attachment. This simply implies that the infant will resist separation from his or her primary caregiver. Behaviorally, it is evident in crying and screaming when the infant is separated from the caregiver. The *safe haven* function refers to the tendency to seek out the caregiver in times of stress or danger. Eventually children will explore their environment apart from their parents. However, attachment will readily send the child back to the presence of the parent for protection during times of stress. Finally, the *secure base* function indicates that an attachment that is felt as secure will motivate or allow the child to explore his or her environment, beyond immediate contact with the caregiver. The idea is that the secure attachment with the caregiver provides a sort of psychological foundation on which the child can mount an exploration into the unknown elements of his or her environment. If the child knows in the back of his or her mind that the caregiver is available for protection, exploration of the environment is not felt to be as risky. All of these functions of attachment should keep the infant out of harm's way and in the presence of the individual who can shelter, protect, and nourish. There can be little doubt about the adaptive nature of such processes. Infants (or animals) who enact attachment behaviors are most likely to survive the perils of early development and grow into functional adults.

Working Models and Attachment Styles

In attachment theory, interactions between the infant and his or her primary caregiver (usually the mother) become the basis for internal *working models*. These are mental representations that summarize and organize interactions between the self and the caregiver. Early attachment experiences contribute to both internal working models of the self and internal working models of others. In the self model, the child views him-or herself as either worthy or unworthy of love and support. Experiences with a parent who is warm and responsive would obviously lead to an internal working model of the self as worthy of love. However, if early childhood experiences with the caregiver are marked by coldness and unavailability, the child will come to view the self as unworthy of love and support. As Reis and Patrick (1996) wisely observed, "just how this internalization occurs remains one of the most important and unresolved issues in attachment research" (p. 526). Internal working models of others are a mental representation of the benevolence of other people. Other models are something of a prototype of other human beings and how they can be expected to treat the child. These representations are summarized along themes of availability, responsiveness, and trustworthiness. Essentially, the child will generalize from experiences with the primary caregiver and assume that this is how most people will treat him or her. According to attachment theory, once these internal working models are established, which may happen as early as age 1 or 2, they are relatively stable throughout the remainder of the life span.

Obviously, different children have different internal working models of the self and others. These various internal working models become the foundation for attachment styles. Bowlby (1973) felt that the nature of the caregiver's response to the child was the dominant factor that determined the infant's attachment style. Originally, attachment theorists suggested that there were three distinct attachment styles. People with a secure attachment style had caregivers who were responsive to their needs, available, and affectionate. Those with an *anxious—avoidant* attachment style had early interactions with caregivers who were cold, not nurturing, and unavailable. If the primary caregiver was inconsistent or unpredictable in his or her responsiveness to the child, the child was thought to develop an *anxious—ambivalent* attachment style. Research on attachment theory has shown that infants with different attachment styles will behave differently around their mothers (Ainsworth, Blehar, Waters, & Wall, 1978). For example, infants with a secure attachment will gladly explore their environment when in the presence of their mothers. Upon separation they become distressed but then readily settle back down when reunited with their mothers. Infants with an anxious—avoidant attachment style tend to avoid close contact with their mothers and keep to themselves. Finally, the anxious-ambivalent infants will exhibit extreme distress upon separation from their mothers. However, when reunited, these children show signs of anger and ambivalence.

More recently, a four-category scheme of attachment styles has been proposed, based on positive and negative models of the self and others (Bartholomew & Horowitz, 1991). In this model, early experiences with caregivers are thought to produce internal working models of the self that are generally positive (worthy of love and acceptable to others) or negative (unworthy of love, unacceptable to others). At the same time, children are assumed to develop internal working models of others that are either positive (others are trustworthy and available) or negative (others are unreliable and rejecting), When the internal working models of the self and others are crossed, there are four possible attachment styles: *secure, preoccupied, dismissing,* and *fearful.* These are depicted in Figure 1-1.

As evident in Figure 2-1, the four-category scheme preserves the secure attachment style of the original three-category scheme. However, it divides the avoidant styles into two substyles: the dismissing and the fearful. In each case, the internal working model of others is negative, but in the dismissing style the internal working model of the self is positive, whereas it is negative in the fearful style. It should be

MODEL OF SELF		

	Positive	Negative
Positive	**SECURE** Comfortable with intimacy and autonomy	**PREOCCUPIED** Preoccupied with Relationships
Negative	**DISMISSING** Dismissing of intimacy Counter-dependency	**FEARFUL** Fearful of intimacy Socially avoidant

MODEL OF OTHERS

Figure 1-1. The Bartholomew and Horowitz (1991) Model of Attachment Styles

Note. From "Attachment Styles Among Young Adults: A Test of a Four Category Model," by K. Bartholomew & L.M. Horowitz, 1991 *Journal of Personality and Social Psychology*, 61, pp. 226–244. Copyright 1991 by the American Psychological Association. Adapted with permission.

noted that this scheme was developed and validated largely on young adults. One might wonder how, for example, a person develops a positive internal working model of the self but a negative model of others. Infants appear much more readily willing to internalize the negative behavior of others as a negative reflection on the self. However, people who start out in life with a positive view of the self, but then have a string of bad experiences with others, could plausibly maintain their positive view of the self while holding a more negative view of other people. Note that this explanation hinges on the person's ability to *not* always internalize the negative actions of others as a poor reflection on the self. This undoubtedly entails a more adult way of thinking about the social world and its relation to the self.

Evaluation and Application to Family Communication

Embedded within attachment theory are some very powerful ideas and statements about family communication early in life. According to Bowlby (1969, 1973, 1980) the nature of the parent–infant interaction sets a template for social relationships that the child will carry with him or her for life. Notably, much of this early parent–child communication is nonverbal. As children grow older, their attachment figures shift from parents to romantic partners and spouses (Hazan & Shaver, 1987; Reis & Patrick, 1996). This implies that communication patterns in the family of origin may be revisited in some way in the family of orientation. For example, people with secure attachment styles have a tendency to end up in traditional or independent marriages, whereas those with dismissing or preoccupied styles are more likely to be in separate style marriages (Fitzpatrick, Fey, Segrin, & Schiff, 1993) (see chap. 6 for a discussion of the different martial types). Those with a secure attachment style are also more likely to report high marital satisfaction compared to those with other styles of attachment (Feeney, 2002; Feeney, Noller, & Callan, 1994; Meyers & Landsberger, 2002). A positive view of the self (i.e., secure or dismissive attachment style) is positively associated with family outcomes such as perceived rewards from marriage and parenting (Vasquez, Durik, & Hyde, 2002). Finally, secure attachment has been linked with less destructive marital conflict patterns and more positive attitudes toward parenting (Cohn, Silver, Cowan, Cowan, & Pearson, 1992; Feeney, Noller, & Roberts, 2000). Findings such as these are useful for employing attachment theory as an explanation for the effects of family of origin experiences on later family of orientation experiences. They also draw attention to the critical role of parent–child communication in the early years of life. Even preverbal children appear very attuned and attentive to their parents' style of relating to them. This early parental communication evidently leads to self-concept development and views of the trustworthiness of others that impacts later communication patterns and relationships.

Attachment theory has been very useful for explaining why people with a history of childhood abuse often find themselves in abusive relationships as adults. This noxious form of parent-child communication has been linked with a host of negative social and psychological outcomes later in life (see chaps. 13 and 15 for a more in-depth analysis). An abused child would be expected to develop a negative internal working model of the self and therefore not feel worthy of love from others. Perhaps the child even feels that abusive conduct from others is somehow deserved or warranted. This sets up a mental representation of close relationships as normatively including abusive behavior. When such a child grows older and begins seeking romantic partners, attachment theorists speculate that this mental model of close relationships causes the person to, perhaps unknowingly, seek out others who will be abusive. In so doing, they recreate their childhood experiences and settle into a social life that is at once painful but familiar.

It would not be an exaggeration to state that attachment theory has been subject to hundreds of studies in the past 25 years. Researchers have used attachment styles to explain so many different phenomena that it begins to strain the imagination of the reader and credibility of the theory. The eagerness with which researchers have studied attachment styles in the past 15 years appears to be fueled by a variable—analytic mentality in which the search is on for any phenomenon, concept, or experience that varies as a function of attachment styles. Regardless of the utility of this approach, it obviously indicates the current mass appeal of attachment theory in the social and behavioral sciences.

One assumption of attachment theory that has been hotly debated is the stability of attachment styles. Bowlby (1969, 1973, 1980) argued that the attachment styles formed in childhood are enduring throughout the life span. However, some scientists disagree with this assumption. For example, Coyne (1999) has been critical of theories that characterize early childhood experiences as frozen in time, like the Wooly Mammoth, unable to be changed. Rather, Coyne argues that we have experiences throughout the life span that are influential in developing and changing our interpersonal perspectives. Further, he argues that early childhood experiences have only modest associations with later adult experiences such as depression. In the research literature there is at least suggestive support for the stability of internal working models and attachment styles over time (e.g., Bram, Gallant, & Segrin, 1999; Feeney et al., 2000). However, when attachment style is measured categorically (e.g., secure and dismissive), about 25% of respondents appear to change their attachment style over periods of 1 to 4 years (Feeney &

Noller, 1996). Further, people may experience a different attachment style depending on the relationship. When considering their 10 "most important" relationships, 88% of respondents reported that these relationships corresponded with at least two attachment styles, and 47% reported correspondence with three attachment styles (Baldwin, Keelan, Fehr, Enns, & Koh-Rangarajoo, 1996). If attachment styles change over time and by relationship, the fundamental importance of parent–child interaction that is postulated by attachment theory could be seriously questioned.

THE DIALECTICAL PERSPECTIVE

Every year, millions of Americans travel home to their family of origin during the holiday season. In most cases people seem eager to reunite with family members and spend time with them. Often, after a week or so, people return back to their homes, jobs, and school, and seem as eager to get back to their life away from the family of origin as they were to see the family members in the first place. Why does it happen that at one moment people want to be united with their family members, and at the next they want to leave family members behind and get back to school or work? The dialectical perspective (Baxter & Montgomery, 1996, 1997) explains that these seeming contradictions are an inherent part of our relationships with other people. Even though the dialectical approach describes forces that operate in virtually all relationships, family theorists have found its principles and ideas to be very useful for explaining the form and function of family relationships.

Contradiction in Family Relationships

In the dialectical perspective, contradictions are seen as an inherent aspect of any relationship. Contradictions cause change in our relationships and they keep relationships growing instead of static. They are relational forces that are unified opposites. By "unified" Baxter and Montgomery (1997) suggest that the opposing relational forces are interdependent. In other words, the meaning or experience of one force is dependent on the other. For example, if one lived in a tropical climate where the outdoor temperature was consistently between 70 and 90° F is there any such thing as it being "hot" or "cold" outside? For people who live in the Midwestern United States where the weather can range from 0 to 100°F "hot" and "cold" have obvious and clear meanings. The point is that the experience of "hot" takes on meaning relative to its alternative: "cold." If there were no such thing as "cold," "hot" would not be very meaningful.

What are some contradictions, or unified opposites, that play a part in family life? One example cited by Baxter and Montgomery (1996) is *autonomy versus connectedness*. Reconsider the previous example about the family reunion over the holidays. In all close relationships, there is an obvious desire for a sense of "connectedness" among the members of the relationship. This might be established and maintained though sharing time and space, engaging in conversation, and engaging in joint activities. Without any of these, it would be hard to say that there is much of a relationship at all. However, there are very few people who want to spend 24 hours a day together. Even the closest married couples and the most attached parent–child dyads seem to desire some time on their own. Consequently, family members must strike a balance in their relationships, over time, between connectedness and separateness. These opposing forces that impinge on the relationship are known as dialectic tensions. Other dialectic tensions that must be managed in family relationships include novelty versus predictability, disclosure versus privacy, stability versus change, and conventionality versus uniqueness (Baxter & Montgomery; Bochner & Eisenberg, 1987). According to the dialectical approach, these oppositional forces are balanced by different families in different ways. Rarely are they handled with an "either-or" approach.

Before leaving the topic of contradictions, it is important to note that the opposing forces described in the dialectical approach are not located in the struggle between one person and another. Rather, Baxter and Montgomery (1996, 1997) note that these oppositional forces are part of the *relationship*. In other words, they are relational, not individual, forces. In a mother–daughter relationship, the disclosure–privacy dialectic is not an issue of the mother expecting and offering full disclosure while the daughter expects and maintains full privacy. That would be an antagonism between two individuals. Rather, this is a relational force that each must manage. There are surely some things that the mother wants to disclose to the daughter and some things that she would like to keep private. Similarly, the daughter would also want to disclose some things to her mother and keep some matters to herself. This dialectical tension calls on the mother and daughter to balance their desires for disclosure and privacy in a way that is comfortable for their relationship. Most people who have been in such a family relationship can attest to the difficulty of negotiating this dialectic tension.

Praxis and Praxis Patterns

According to the dialectical perspective, "people are at once both actors and objects of their own action" (Baxter & Montgomery, 1997, p. 329). This concept is called praxis. People consciously and often freely make choices about how they choose to treat their family members. This is abundantly evident in messages that are sent from one family member to another. At the same time, sent messages and communication patterns have a way of influencing the relationship in such as a way as to impact the original message sender. Consider, for example, a parent with an anger-management problem. If the parent expresses anger with his child through enacting physical violence, he could be seen as a sender of dysfunctional verbal and nonverbal communication, but at the same time, he will be *acted on* by his own communication. Assume, for example, that the Child Protective Services were made aware of the abuse, took the child from the family home, and had the father arrested. Suddenly, his act of communication has massive consequences that come back and act on him and his relationship with the child.

Different relationships use different mechanisms for managing the dialectical tensions that they experience. These mechanisms or tactics are called *praxis patterns*. Baxter and Montgomery (1996, 1997) divide these tactics into those that are dysfunctional and those that are functional. One of the common but dysfunctional praxis patterns is *denial*. Here, members of the relationship simply deny the presence of the contradiction by only honoring one of the poles while excluding the other. In a family that felt the opposing forces of conventionality and uniqueness, family members would be using denial if they simply ignored the pull for uniqueness and honored only the drive for conventionality Another dysfunctional praxis pattern is *disorientation*. This happens when there is no real "management" of the oppositional forces in the relationship. Rather, members of the relationship resign themselves to the fact that these contradictory motives are inevitable and negative. Consequently, they are likely to find themselves in double-bind situations where any behavior or communication will feel like it clashes with one of the opposing relational forces.

Baxter and Montgomery (1996, 1997) have also identified a series of more functional praxis patterns. These are more effective means for managing the dialectical tensions in such a way as to minimize negative relational outcomes. One functional praxis pattern called *spiraling alternation* involves alternating between the opposite poles of a dialectic at different points in time. For example, every Sunday family members may get together for dinner, honoring connectedness, but it may be understood that every Saturday night everyone is free to do their own thing or go out with their friends, honoring the desire for autonomy. In *segmentation*, members of the relationship honor opposing poles of the dialectic, not over time, but over topic or activity domain. For example, a family might be very open when it comes to discussing spiritual beliefs and finances, but very private when it comes to discussing sexuality By having open communication on some topics and treating others with a "hands-off" attitude the family alternates between the two poles of the disclosure-privacy dialectic. *Balance* is a praxis pattern in which members of the relationship try to respond to both ends of the opposition by seeking a compromise. One problem with balance is that neither polarity is fully satisfied at any point in time. *Integration* is something of an ideal in conflict resolution and management of dialectical tensions. When members of a relationship integrate, they find a way of simultaneously satisfying both polarities of a dialectical tension. Baxter and Montgomery (1996) suggest that in some cases family dinnertime can be seen as an integration praxis pattern in which the family bond is established and maintained, and yet individual actions and accomplishments are recognized and embraced though the input of individual members into the interaction. With *recalibration* members of the relationship create "a transformation in the expressed form of the contradiction such that the opposing forces are no longer regarded as oppositional to one another" (Baxter & Montgomery, p. 65). With this praxis pattern, members of the relationship find a way to reframe the contradiction "such that the polarities are encompassed in one another" (p. 65). The phrase "if you love something, set it free" may be a reflection of this mentality. By freeing one's partner to behave as he or she will, members of a relationship can experience security through that freedom. Finally, the praxis pattern of *reaffirmation* "celebrates the richness afforded by each polarity and tolerates the tension posed by their unity" (Baxter & Montgomery p. 66). In some ways, the "for better or worse" part of a marriage vow may represent reaffirmation for some married couples. If the couple accepts both the good times and the bad, and realizes that they will have a better and stronger relationship as a result of working through each, they may be enacting a reaffirmation praxis pattern.

Evaluation and Application to Family Communication

The dialectical approach has proven to be very useful to family theorists and researchers who are interested in explaining various family processes and tasks. For example, the work of Bochner and Eisenberg (1987), which predated the formal development of the dialectical approach, argued that there are two dialectical tensions that are central to family functioning. They characterize the first as *integration versus differentiation*. All families are made up of individuals with their own unique identities. At the same time, families as a collective unit have an identity. One task that faces all families is honoring the desire for a collective identity as a family unit versus allowing individuals within the family to develop their own unique identities as individuals, or their own unique relationships with other family member (e.g., mother–daughter and between two siblings). Another dialectic that has a substantial impact on family functioning according to Bochner and Eisenberg is *stability versus change*. Most families have predictable patterns of interaction. These might be reflected in activities such as the family dinner, picking up children from school, or watching television together in the evening. Some degree of predictability is desirable for most families. On the other hand, too much stability in the family can lead to stagnation. As families evolve through time, they experience changes that are internal to the system (e.g., birth of a child) and changes that are external to the system (e.g., societal changes). There is some need to adapt to these changes, but without entirely abandoning the family's traditions and destroying any sense of predictability in family interaction. According to Bochner and Eisenberg, managing these two important dialects is a significant task that families must address in order to maintain their integrity.

The work of Bochner and Eisenberg (1987) shows how the assumptions and ideas of the dialectical approach can be fruitfully employed for describing certain family processes. At the same time, the dialectical approach does not have all of the elements of a formal theory such as social learning theory. For this reason it more difficult to use the dialectical approach for prediction or intervention to change or improve family functioning. Its major utility is in *explaining* the nature of family relationships. Also, some of the concepts in the dialectical perspective can be difficult to grasp, much less identify, in a practical setting. For example, the praxis patterns of integration, recalibration, and reaffirmation are somewhat vaguely conceptualized and therefore difficult to observe or identify in an actual family setting. Further, these praxis patterns may not be as common as other praxis patterns such as denial, segmentation, or balance.

Conclusion

In this selection we explore several theories that are and have been very influential in the field of family science. These general theories have inspired hundreds of research studies and numerous more specific theories that draw on many of the postulates of the theories presented here. We start by examining family systems theory. According to this perspective, family processes can only be understood by examining the family in its totality. All family processes and events are thought to be connected to the larger family system and social suprasystem in which the family itself resides. Families are assumed to have emergent qualities that make them more than just the sum of their individual parts. Symbolic interaction theory highlights the vital role of the family in creating self-concepts and understandings of the world. Symbolic interaction theorists feel that meaning is at least to some extent negotiated through our interactions with other people. Because the family is the primary source of social interactions and relationships, it has a monumental role in shaping people's self-concepts and what it means to be a father, sister, grandmother, and so forth. Although meanings are negotiated through social interactions over the entire life span, the process starts in the family. Social learning theory explains how people acquire behaviors through observing other people perform behaviors, along with the consequences that they experience subsequent to the behavior. Learning by modeling is a fundamental process in social leaning theory. When people observe a model perform a behavior and get rewarded for doing so, they are likely to start performing the behavior themselves. Like symbolic interaction theory, social learning theory has obvious applications to family interaction because the family provides a multitude of compelling models for children to observe. Attachment theory focuses on early infant–caregiver interactions as the basis for forming enduring internal working models of interpersonal relationships. An internal working model is a mental representation of the self as worthy or unworthy of love and attention and others as reliable and trustworthy or rejecting and uncaring. Attachment theorists feel that the nature of early interactions with a caregiver will inform young children's internal working models which then influence the nature of their interpersonal relationships well into adulthood. Finally, we examine the *dialectical perspective*. This approach to understanding family processes is built around dialectical tensions or functional contradictions that are an inherent part of any family relationship. In the dialectical perspective, family members are seen as having to balance or manage tensions such as connectedness—separateness, stability—change, and novelty—predictability. The dialectical perspective also explains how families manage dialectical tensions through a variety of techniques known as praxis patterns.

Of all the theories that we discuss in this selection, only *family systems theory* was explicitly developed as an explanation of family dynamics (although it was derived from the more general version of systems theory). All of the other theories were developed as explanations of more general interpersonal processes. However, the family either plays a prominent role in the reasoning of the theory (as in attachment theory) or the theory has obvious and immediate applicability to the family. In either case, scholars have seized on these theories as some of their primary tools for explaining and understanding family interactions and relationships. Their continued application to the understanding of issues such as child abuse, alcoholism in the family, marital satisfaction, divorce, and parent–child interaction is a testimony to the utility of these family interaction theories.

2. Communication, Families, and Exploring the Boundaries of Cultural Diversity

By Rhunette Diggs & Thomas Socha

Socha and Diggs (1999), Gudykunst and Lee (2001), and others developed a preliminary rationale for the study of family communication framed by ethnic culture. This selection adds to that work in three ways by: (a) increasing understanding of the role of culture (ethnic and otherwise) in framing how family communication scholars conceptualize and study communication in family units and relationships, (b) reviewing recent family communication studies and communication studies from allied fields with an eye to how this work might illuminate and challenge current understandings of family communication, and (c) utilizing insights gained from these sources to offer future directions for scholarship. Before addressing these aims, we discuss some of the complexities of the terminology to be used, specifically culture and cultural diversity, and the particular ideologies[1] on which this selection is built. We begin by considering the term "cultural diversity" at some (p. 4). The goal of critical and qualitative research is to reveal participants' ideologies; however, as researchers, we often overlook our own invisible ideologies or taken-forgranted assumptions that impact on our work unbeknownst to us. length, because of the recent popular and public debates about this concept, especially in the context of communication and family.

Satellites, television, tourism, computer communications, cheap oil, cheap transport— these have brought images, foods, clothing, entertainment from various corners of the world into one place, collapsing distance, eliding space, compressing time, and glossing over cultural difference.

—Weiner (1997, p. 110)

CULTURE AND DIVERSITY

Prevailing ideas and definitions about communication, family, and diversity are connected explicitly and implicitly to scholars' attitudes, teachings, and the way they position culture in their research. For example, researchers' worldviews and traditions operate, perhaps unconsciously *and* strategically, to perpetuate cultural homogeneity rather than cultural diversity in scholarship and teaching. Scholarly references often are familiar or "known" (here to be interpreted as similar in ideology, theory, and race or ethnicity) as opposed to unfamiliar and "unknown" (here to be interpreted as different ideology, theory, and race or ethnicity) (see Socha & Diggs, 1999). The quote by Weiner (1997) that opens the present selection situates well the current emphasis on globalization in the field of communication studies (e.g., Braman & Sreberny-Mohammadi, 1996; Chen & Starosta, 2000; Collier, 2000; Mowlana, 1996). However, the extent to which current trends of globalization have seeped into family communication studies is not clear. That is, the acknowledgment of cultural differences has been common in the theory and research on family communication, but the depth of their representation is debatable. Mowlana (1996) frames this problem in broad terms:

> … lack of conceptual clarity, epistemological and disciplinary rigidities, insufficient amounts of skill in language and cultural studies, a high level of ethnocentrism and parochialism, and ideological biases. Consequently, our knowledge of communication, cultural and social systems, is provincial rather than universal. (p. 200)

Historically, family communication textbooks and conceptualizations have mentioned family "cultures" (e.g., Fitzpatrick & Ritchie, 1993; Galvin & Brommel, 1996; Whitchurch & Dickson, 1999), and more recently family communication scholars have been challenged to go beyond their "cultural habits" (characterized by ethnocentricism) to include other worldviews and approaches in their theoretical research perspectives (e.g., Gudykunst & Lee, 2001; Socha & Diggs, 1999). However, even one's allegiance to a particular perspective on diversity is potential for adherence to a certain view of families, families' roles in society, and thus the directions that research on family communication should take.

To understand cultural diversity in the contexts of domestic life, we begin with the term "culture." Definitional treatments of this term can range from a stable, unchanging characteristic to something that is unstable and fluid. The definitions correspondingly fit within epistemological[2] frameworks that consider knowledge in a variety of ways ranging from knowledge as given and universal (objective reality) to knowledge as contextual and constructed (social construction). These epistemological and ideological perspectives undergird public and scholarly conversations about cultural diversity as well.

Matthew Arnold's (1971) contribution to early debates about the value of culture (or high culture) in England during the 1860s offers a start to a brief tour of the historical lineage of culture. Arnold notes:

> Culture seeks to do away with classes; to make the best that has been thought and known in the world current everywhere; to make all men [sic] live in an atmosphere of sweetness and light, where they may use ideas, as it uses them itself, freely,—nourished, and not bound by them. This is the *social idea;* and the men [sic] of culture are the true apostles of equality. The great men [sic] of culture are those who have had a passion for diffusing, for making prevail, for carrying from one end of society to the other, the best knowledge, the best ideas of their time; who have laboured to divest knowledge of all that was harsh, uncouth, difficult, abstract, professional, exclusive; to humanise it, to make it efficient outside the clique of the cultivated and learned, yet still remaining the best knowledge and thought of the time, and a true source, therefore of sweetness and light. (p. 56)

This modern sense of culture is still evident in our contemporary society.

In contrast to Arnold's (1971) description of culture, the anthropological understanding of culture as the study of the human species has evolved from primarily examining how different ("remote" or "isolated") groups subsisted and sustained, physically and socially. Eventually, anthropologists and others came to see that "all peoples have unique histories" (Singer, 1987, p. 6). For example, Hecht, Collier, and Ribeau (1993) offered a socially constructed perspective in their definition of culture: "… whether national, ethnic, professional, organizational, or gender based, as a social organization. By this we mean that a culture is the common pattern of interaction and perception shared by a group of people" (p. 15).

Other conceptions of culture include the following characteristics: shared language or code that manifests the perceptions, attitudes, values, beliefs, and disbelief systems of the group; change; a way of life of a people; patterns of behavior (e.g., see Asante, 1988; Gudykunst & Kim, 1997; Kim & Gudykunst, 1996; Myers, 1998; Singer, 1987). It is these latter perspectives that can best serve the study of family communication because they speak to concepts at the foundation of family interaction including communication in service of socializing the young. Common to all of these definitions is that culture is a set of shared meanings or understandings about a group or organization and its problems, goals, and practices.

However, wholesale use of the term "culture" is not unproblematic. As implicated by the study of different groups with different values, beliefs, and language, critical perspectives have argued for particular ways of approaching the study of culture and communication. Critical scholars in a range of disciplines (e.g., anthropology, communication, ethnic studies, sociology, and psychology) have cautioned against cultural imperialism and cultural consumption (Asante, 1988; Bodley, 1976; Braman, 1996; Myers, 1998). These critical perspectives suggest that different family meanings, family values, and family work and leisure are inextricably tied to larger societal and mainstream cultural conceptual systems. Also these perspectives alert us to the terrain facing scholars who explicitly choose to intersect family, communication, and cultural diversity.

In spite of the challenges that face researchers who study cultural diversity and family interactions, it is generally accepted that culture is important to communication because of its impact on language, behavior, perception, and interpretation. Cognizant of our words and endeavors, we have chosen to use the terms race and ethnicity interchangeably. We have chosen to use the term "co-culture" rather than "minority" to refer to groups that are deemed other than the "majority" within their society (see Orbe, 1998, for a complete commentary on this choice).

Scholars' treatments of culture have impacted on present hopes, fears, anxieties, and conversations about cultural "diversity." Based on public debates and existing scholarship on diversity, the current selection organizes the meanings of cultural diversity into four categories, that is, culture as: Aspiration, Dilemma, Fear, and Opportunity. These four categories attempt to convey general themes rather than mutually exclusive categories. In brief, cultural-diversity-as-aspiration suggests an ideal positive rhetoric that implies cultural diversity will improve people's personal, private, and public lives. This perspective views any tensions experienced as potential positive by-products of difference (e.g., Freedman, 2002; Makau, 1997; Orbe, 1998; Socha & Diggs, 1999). Cultural-diversity-as-dilemma reflects the anxiety or discomfort experienced and felt about difference (e.g., Benhabib, 1999; Chen & Starosta, 2000). Cultural-diversity-as-fear emphasizes what is lost or the fear of threat to self and civil society (e.g., Wuthnow, 1999). Finally, cultural-diversity-as-opportunity is offered as an extension of the somewhat polarized perspectives (aspiration and fear) to acknowledge real struggles (optimistic orientation vs. anxiety orientation) within the contexts of cultural differences (e.g., Clark & Diggs, 2002; Diggs & Clark, 2002).

Cultural Diversity as Aspiration

Mowlana's (1996) summary and critique of the efforts of the International Communication Division of the Association for Education in Journalism and Mass Communication (AEJMC) to examine globalization seem instructive in terms of building an understanding of the term culture and how it fits with the study of family communication. He explains:

> The birth of nations from the 1950s through the 1990s, and the upheavals and changes occurring in the old nations, are not simply the result of drastic changes in demographic or economic sectors. They also indicate an important development on the intellectual level. Advances in communication technologies and transportation, for example, have helped to lessen cultural isolationism and to increase the cultural awareness of minorities by making them more conscious of the distinctions between themselves and other groups. (pp. 95–96)

This statement implies that people (including families) take notice of their environments, near and far, to determine their moves. When individuals observe their life experiences, events in the world (i.e., 911 or September 11, 2001, "Attack on America"), and local and transnational events, then they begin to move globally. That is, families are aware of their local communication environments but also are aware that other families in other parts of the world communicate differently. In a recent lecture, Socha (2002) modified the 1960s' environmental movement slogan to capture this idea: Families need to think globally, but communicate locally.

Makau (1997) wants to "celebrate" differences and believes that "problems commonly attributed to diversity are actually problems of communication ethics" (p. 49). She used varied scholarship to recount the history of the "construction" of diversity in the United States. She argued that this construction was influenced by discourses around changing demographics, the myth of changing demographics rather than the reality of economic shift, cultural standpoints and locations, and "context specific conceptions of identity," with essentialization of groups (pp. 49–53). Makau advocates a healthy dose of tension around the topic of diversity. Such a perspective, she believes, allows the individual and group culture to simultaneously manifest in each communicative encounter.

Freedman (2002), believes that "it is persons least like ourselves who teach us the most about ourselves" (p. 32). This ideal is pointed especially at the young college student to promote campus diversity. This promotion of diversity seems to fit the concept of high culture whose aim is to generate leaders and the elite. Freedman points out that it is our obligation to seek diversity, "as it always has been for positions of national leadership" (p. 32). At the same time that this clearly is an aspiration, a focus on cultural diversity as a commodity (something to be bought and sold) creates a dilemma, especially for those who become the "objects" blamed for the cultural diversity "problems."

Cultural Diversity as a Dilemma

Contained within this perspective is a tension between "essential" and "constructed" identities. Benhabib (1999) addressed this tension in her analysis of nationalist groups:

> Whereas identity claims are said to be fundamental, essential, nonnegotiable, and clearly distinguishable from the claims of competitors, in the process of social and political mobilization and cultural articulation, identity claims are "created" that are negotiable, contestable, and open to political redefinition and redescription. … All identity/difference movements struggle

for the distribution of resources as well—be these land, power, representation, cultural space, or linguistic access—although the political grammar ... is dominated by the vocabulary of recognition rather than redistribution. (pp. 295 and 307)

Benhabib seems to present this perspective as a dilemma in that there are real and serious struggles that exist within and between those who identify themselves as part of a collective that provokes some discomfort. Although the existence of struggles over identity issues should be acknowledged, the essential versus constructed identity can be viewed as an acknowledgment of the Afrocentric principle that "all things work together" (not necessarily in opposition). There is not simply one way to think of oneself; potentially developmental or cyclical, essential and constructed identities both are operative in how people think of themselves and their families. Benhabib's concern for citizenship challenges researchers to theoretically account for this (i.e., offer a theory that explains how this fundamental and negotiable/created identity works). How are identity claims communicated in different kinds of families? To what extent do these identity claims create obstacles to dialog between different kinds of families?

Chen and Starosta (2000) also raised the dilemma about what the "dialectic tension between cultural identity and cultural diversity poses for the future global society" (p. 5). How do people maintain a balance between their sense of identity and their understanding and acceptance of *other* as different? The authors are interested in how communication scholars might address (via research) the cultural competence that is needed in a global society that assumes "as the world becomes more interdependent and interconnected, the nation-state becomes more culturally heterogeneous" (p. 1).

Philosopher, Çinar (2002), reviewed Parekh's "pro-multiculturalism" book which addressed strengths and weaknesses in thinking about multiculturalism. In the review, he asserts that a problem or weakness is the conceptualization of culture. For Çinar, the view of culture as stable or unchanging without internal differences reflects passive and not active people, who can be overtaken by the powerful economic and political structures; this is cause for anxiety.

Cultural Diversity as Fear

Underlying many of the popular discussions about diversity is the "fear factor." Wuthnow (1999) asserts that:

> Questions have arisen about the extent to which the nation is being fragmented by tensions separating racial, ethnic, and religious groups, and about Americans' willingness to shoulder the difficult tasks of working together for the common good. ... Many interpreters sense that Americans are neither maintaining their traditional values nor responding well to social diversity. (p. 19)

In this statement, "Americans" are assumed to be "White" Americans who are suddenly sensing "tensions" and "fear." These emotions, however, have been a staple of the Black experience in America. In Withnow's terms, diversity involves questions about how White people overcome their fear that Black people and other persons of ethnic difference are entering space on a somewhat equal footing.

Wuthnow's (1999) sociological analysis questions these fear-based assumptions. For example, "Much of the recent anxiety about the condition of civil society points directly or indirectly to diversity as a major source of America's current problems" (p. 23). The civil rights movement is indirectly blamed as part of the problem when people point to "African Americans, Hispanics, women, and gays and lesbians as sources of a perceived retreat from common values and responsibilities" (p. 23). Wuthnow concludes that diversity "challenges the social order" but is unjustly blamed for the potential demise of civil society and societal discontent. Rather it is the "loosening of social bonds or porousness compared to tightly bounded institutions" and their fragility that prompt Americans' worry (p. 28). In addition, there are examples of what we term as the commodification of diversity: The diversity slogan is used as a means to gain votes or to buy or sell things.

Cultural Diversity as an Opportunity

Critics in varied disciplines (e.g., Asante, 1988, in African and African American Studies and Intercultural Communication; Lather, 1991, in Cultural Education; West, 1989, in Philosophy and Religion) have argued that now that people of color, women, and others of different groups are impacting academia and gaining equality, there is a broadening of ideas and some resistance to those perspectives that they bring. From a family communication perspective, these conversations about culture, whether stable or changing, can be viewed as opportunities. The conversations and debates are a prime opportunity for family communication scholars to ask themselves personal questions about culture and to inspect how they enter into the discussion with co-cultures within the United States and with families beyond the United States (e.g., Diggs & Clark, 2002, autoethnography of interracial talk). For certain, family communication research has embraced a perspective on culture as noted earlier, but scholars need to question the fruitfulness of the perspective in enabling them to see their own ethnic thinking and its impact on who they study, what they study, and how they study various phenomena.

Implications for Researchers

Ethnicity is defined as "givens (objective perspective), such as blood, customs, language, ritual, religion, social values" (Mindel, Habenstein, & Wright, Jr., 1998, p. 6). The problems associated with entering into the discussion of culture as synonymous with ethnicity (as we have) abound, as it obscures the diversity contained within particular ethnicities or races. These problems, however, are unavoidable. To place culture as synonymous with ethnicity places a boundary on the term "culture." In this sense culture is defined as a focus on different races or ethnic peoples. This categorization should not be limiting for prospective researchers as they can pick and choose or argue for the interdependence of many aspects of the ethnic person. Rather than take rigid positions in the debate over pluralism, cultural diversity, or multiculturalism, family communication scholars would do well to continue to openly examine their assumptions and pursue both respect for their research on participant families and sensitivity to the myriad of cultural ways of knowing.

Fitzpatrick's and Ritchie's (1993) assertion that, "our variable field focuses attention across many levels of analysis to study" can be viewed as a strength of the vision to intersect communication, family, and culture. Whitchurch and Dickson (1999) more specifically described a communication approach to the study of family relationships that emphasized the meaning of family as grounded in verbal and nonverbal communication. Certainly this perspective accommodates family diversity, in that the suggestion is that researchers can understand different families by examining their communication. It is important to note, however, that such conceptualizations about family will not necessarily ensure that diversity makes it into our studies. For example, Nicholson (2001) argued that the family communication literature has focused its attention primarily on the parental and marital subsystems. His study on sibling relationships reflects how researchers can attempt to go deeper inside the family to

pursue a particular level of analysis (i.e., subsystems). However, such a pursuit also may keep researchers inside only one kind of family culture rather than encourage them to venture outside into the
cultural world to examine the communication and creation of different racial and ethnic families.
Gudykunst, Ting-Toomey, and Nishida (1996) indicate that interpersonal communication researchers
"ignore the relationships between culture and communication and study communication in a cultural
vacuum" (p. 3).

Conceptualizations of family communication and family relationships have always accommodated
the examination of diverse families, yet, it is researchers' worldviews, theoretical orientations, and habits
that are, perhaps, their greatest challenges (and obstacles) to the study of communication of different
families. What cultural standpoint do researchers begin from? Have they examined their worldviews
and ethnocentrism? What ideological values are implied by their studies? By examining published
studies in the family communication literature and in allied fields, scholars can draw conclusions and
advance an agenda about the current state of communication and the boundaries of diversity in research
and pedagogy.

DIVERSITY IN FAMILY COMMUNICATION STUDIES

Although the goal of this selection, ultimately, is to expand the scope of our understanding of family
communication in diverse families, it is important to first acknowledge the progress researchers have
made in their back yard (see Amason's, 2002, review of family communication textbooks; Socha &
Diggs, 1999). To accomplish this latter goal, a review of recent studies of family communication, culture,
and diversity was conducted. Empirical studies that focused on different culture samples and family
communication as independent or dependent variables and those studies that simply described the
ethnic makeup of the sample were examined.

A number of studies reported "diverse" demographics or identified the sample by race but did not
conceptualize culture as a relevant or substantive variable (see Aune & Comstock, 2002; Koesten, Miller,
& Hummert, 2002; Pecchioni & Nussbaum, 2002; Segrin & Flora, 2001). Studies that addressed family
context (culture), communication characteristics, and ethnicity or race also were examined (see Day &
Remigy, 1999; Diggs, 2001; Duneier, 1992; Durrheim & Dixon, 2001; Fisherkeller, 1997; Georgas et al.,
2001; Jenkins, 1991; Julian, McKenry, & McKelvy, 1994; Kane, 2000; Mosby, Rawls, Meehan, Mays, &
Pettinari, 1999; Schönpflug, 2001; Socha & Diggs, 1999; Socha & Stamp, 1995; Xu & Burleson, 2001).
In these studies culture was conceptualized as a specific, concrete, objective ethnic category (by virtue of
the distinctive labeling) and as socially constructed by virtue of the discourse and social influences that
shape family meanings, values, and family identities. Even though we cannot draw specific conclusions
about who benefits from the culture conceptualizations of the studies, we can say that knowledge of
these ethnic families is enhanced when descriptions of contexts, communication and behavior patterns,
and interpretations of particular family members and families communication are provided.

If scholars remain aware of the varied metatheoretical, epistemological, and methodological assumptions and purposes underlying scholarly work about families, then the literature about families and
domestic life outside the United States has something important to offer. It can provide researchers
with information about families from cultures beyond the borders of the United States and it can be
used to study those cultures.

Table 2-1. A Preliminary Primer of Selected Books About Families and Familial Relationships in Countries Outside the United States

COUNTRY	AUTHOR	SYNOPSIS
Africa South Africa	Mathabane (1994)	An ethnography of three generations of women (the author's grandmother, mother, and sister) spanning the time of apartheid in South Africa, to their flight, and adjusting to life in the United States.
Africa Middle East	Fernea (1985)	An edited volume that includes six chapters pertaining to women and family life in the Middle East (featuring Saudi Arabia and Egypt).
Asia China	Baker (1979)	A study of traditional Chinese family composition, lineage, worship, and kinship patterns. The book includes sections about terms of address for kin and non-kin as kin.
Asia Korea	Lee & Kim (1979)	A sociological study that focuses on values and family practices concerning children in South Korea. A volume in a series of studies about the value of children conducted in China, Japan, Philippines, Thailand, and U.S. (Hawaii).
Asia Vietnam	Van Bich (1999)	A sociological dissertation from Sweden that examined traditional Vietnamese family life, historical changes, husband–wife relationships, and the influence of Confucianism and Marxism on family living patterns.
India	Ramu (1977)	A sociological dissertation from the University of Illinois that reports an in-depth case study of the daily life of a family living in urban south India with particular attention to the role of India's caste system in family life.
India	Khatri (1983)	A sociological study of familial relationships that uses content analysis of Indian fictional novels to examine familial relationships including: courtship, marriage, parent–child, siblings, and in-laws.
North America Mexico	Lewis (1959) Lewis (1961)	A University of Illinois anthropologist writes extensively about families living in poverty in Mexico. These two volumes represent case studies of five families (Lewis, 1959) and one poor family in Mexico city (Lewis, 1961). These are classic works of extensive "thick" description.

Table 2-1 offers a limited preliminary primer of readings that can begin to add to the picture of family communication as a global activity. The table includes books that display countries not often appearing in family communication studies, as well as works that provide a flavor for the different kinds of research that have been conducted. Some of the books are considered "classic" studies. These include the work of anthropologist Oscar Lewis, who examined five families living in poverty in Mexico (Lewis, 1959) and a family living in Mexico City (Lewis, 1961). The methods typically used to study different family cultures include detailed, in-depth chronicles of day-to-day family lives, sociological portraits, and content analysis.

EXPLORING THE BOUNDARIES OF DIVERSITY IN FAMILY COMMUNICATION STUDIES

In addition to providing a summary of the literature on cultural diversity and family communication, this review offers an opportunity to reflect on some of the factors that have yet to be systematically examined by those who study family interaction.

For Richer or Poorer

In communication studies, some scholars have examined "the poor" or those in poverty (e.g., Daniel, 1970), but those experiencing economic prosperity have not received attention, nor have these studies examined domestic poverty–prosperity and communication in domestic contexts. Studies in allied fields, in particular those of sociologist Lillian Rubin (1976, 1994), stand out in providing insight into blue-collar family life (e.g., especially see Rubin, 1994, chapter 4—"Mother Goes to Work"). This work focuses on the development and interconnections of macroeconomic policies and their effects on the microlevel of everyday family life. It seems that economic poverty–prosperity can exert a tremendous force on how families communicate (e.g., research in mass communication about Internet use shows differences so large between rich and poor as to create a "digital divide"), and conversely how families communicate can affect their relative levels of poverty–prosperity. But, research on family communication to date has not systematically considered the role of economic diversity in explaining family communication processes and outcomes. This would seem to be an important and fruitful area for future study. For example, does the relative importance of communication in family and family relationships change with a family's socioeconomic status? How do qualities of communication in families and family relationships change with high or low, rising or falling income levels? Also, what commitments and conceptions of culture exist in rich, workingclass, and poor families (e.g., Duneier, 1992)?

In Sickness and in Health

Family members and their systems confront a wide array of physical and mental illnesses over the life span, and, at any given point families can vary widely in wellness–illness. That is, some families have members who struggle with chronic illness and debilitation, whereas others experience years of wellness. The family communication literature and textbooks have attempted to consider issues associated with "wellness–illness." For example, many textbooks cite the therapeutic literature extensively (individual psychological as well as family systems) and seek to develop models of family communication that incorporate concepts of wellness (e.g., satisfaction, optimal family functioning). Communication scholars have also examined "illness" as a communication act (Chesebro, 1982). However, to date there have not been systematic research efforts to examine the array of communication that occurs in families along the wellness–illness continuum. It would seem that wellness–illness would have great potential to affect family communication processes and outcomes and that family communication in turn can affect managing illness (e.g., Henry, 1973).

Religion

A search for studies that examine participation in organized religion (i.e., Baptist, Buddhist, Catholic, Hindu, Jewish) and family communication revealed that this, too, is uncharted territory on the landscape of diversity. In contrast, a search of nonacademic literature yielded a variety of publications from a wide array of religions that seek to have a say in everyday family life. For example, texts of homilies given in the early 1700s show that early colonial pastors were preaching about ways to achieve "the well-ordered family" (Wadsworth, 1712). Families vary not only in terms of religious participation but also in terms of the extent to which a chosen faith tradition is lived or practiced. Similar to ethnic culture, there is much diversity of adherence to and identification with religious beliefs and prescriptions that also needs to be considered. Theological approaches and families of various religious traditions, rather than being ignored, potentially, could be sources for culturally diverse interrogation of family communication (e.g., Barton, 1996; Furrow, 1998; Hughes & Dickson, 2001).

Urban-Rural

Sociologist Richard Sennett (1970), among others, has examined the effects of urban environments (as well as rural ones) on family life in the United States. Studies in family communication, however, have been less concerned with diversity of family space. This might be due in part not only to the overuse of convenience samples and the difficulties in recruiting and gathering diverse samples (e.g., due to lack of funding) but also to the relative homogenization of life in the United States. Stepping outside the United States, one finds the contrast of the lives of those who live in the cities and those who live in rural, often remote environments to be quite stark. For example, during a visit to South Africa, the second author viewed (albeit briefly) the radically different worlds of living in beehive huts in rural Kwazulu-Natal near the Shlu-Shluwe game reserve (home to white rhino and others of the "big seven") to living in modern condos in Cape Town; from living in tin-roofed shanty houses of Soweto Township to living in a mansion in a suburb of Johannesburg. Diversity of place seems to matter a great deal in setting the context for communication in families and familial relationships and seems worthy of future study (also see Al-Oofy & McDaniel, 1992; Durrheim & Dixon, 2001).

CONCLUSION: FUTURE DIRECTIONS

At this stage in the history of family communication studies, there is a need to keep at the forefront the goal of creating a portrait of family communication that is diverse, complex, and inclusive. As family communication textbooks suggest, efforts to show openness toward diversity by including pictures of diverse families (see Amason, 2002) have sketched an orientation toward embracing diverse families, but the image is inadequate nationally and does not go far enough globally. As research moves forward, scholars need to look for ethnically and racially diverse samples (substantive to research questions, of course), to ask questions that reveal similarities as well as differences in our diversity, and to understand differences in family communication.

Mowlana (1996) stated, "the decline of nationalism and secular national ideologies patterned on European and Western schools of thought and the concurrent discourse and revival of notions of community along sociocultural lines open an entirely new area of inquiry and research that needs to be studied by those interested in societal change and evolution" (p. 92). Collier (2002) stated that "scholars, teachers, and practitioners construct and produce what nation and culture are known to be in historically situated sites and moments of time" (p. xi). How do these statements affect scholars interested in family communication? First, these statements suggest that researchers need to include families in their studies that substantively (as cultural variables) bring the diversity of interest to the research situation. Next, these statements suggest that scholars and professionals need to critique themselves in their apolitical and noncommittal stance toward diversity in their scholarship. Perhaps our most evident expressions of studying family communication and diversity suggest that scholars are bound to all of the ideologies about cultures, particularly culture as fear and culture as dilemma. Personal narratives and empirical data on researchers' culture-based fears and dilemmas could reveal how these ideologies influence theorizing, research decisions, and outcomes. Cultures as opportunity and aspiration are more apparent when we see special calls for diversity in research and convention programs that generate works in progress toward publication. The question now is, "What direction should we take to promote diversity in future family communication research and pedagogy?"

Who Do We Study?

Studies of varied family subsystems and communication contexts (i.e., parent–child communication, sibling communication, gay and lesbian families) offer the opportunity to describe the family culture that members create and the kind of communication that constructs and impacts personal, social, and cultural or ethnic identities within a changing social context. The challenges of a global society (e.g., not meeting face to face; children communicating via email) urge family communication scholars to study varied national and international families. For example, a model for studying families globally is reflected in collaborative studies that take advantage of technology and the international contacts that such technology affords. Georgas and 17 other researchers (2001) situated in various countries studied a 16-country sample. Although multiple researcher studies offer a model for collaboration, researchers still are tied to the single, two-, or three-co-author model that is most likely attached to existing Western tenure and promotion practices.

A commitment to diversity in sampling with substantive questions of culture will require openness to creativity and ways of knowing, inclusive of objective, qualitative, rhetorical, and critical paradigms. For example, Diggs' (2001) qualitative study asked diverse Black and White participants to talk about their experiences with racial profiling in a public library setting. In reflection, Diggs speculated that the discussion of racial profiling was viewed as a "threatening and fearful" topic to most non-Black library patrons, due to mediated information rather than to personal experiences with racial profiling and the very real current events surrounding the topic. Therefore, the study generated more Black participants than White ones. In this context, age, sex, and location differences within the predominantly same-race sample were deemed important.

What Do We Study?

A conceptualization of family communication and culture that recognizes the larger social influence on family communication as evidenced in media and other institutional messages prompts us to move beyond the private-home site to the public as well. For example, Diggs' (2001) study that examined family and community racial profiling discourse used a family member's spontaneous response to a media message about racial profiling to frame family and community experiences with racial profiling. Media (TV/film, visual, and print) continue to be a prime source of subject matter for family communication research as traditional family meanings and family values are being contested in the public arena (e.g., MTV reality TV shows such as *Real World* and more recently, *The Osbourne's*).

Gudykunst and Lee (2001), Collier (2000, 2001), and McAdoo (2001) are among communication and family researchers who emphasize caution in treating ethnic or racial groups monolithically. For example, theoretical models from cross-cultural and intercultural communication research grounded in sensitivity to intragroup difference are offered by the first two sets of authors. Gudykunst and Lee offer concepts of strength and content, and Collier (2000) offers co-construction, salience, and overlapping identities as concepts to help researchers attend to differences within ethnic or racial groups. These conceptualizations direct researchers to consider how family communication varies by virtue of cultural valuing of ethnic and cultural identity, how members are affected by family discourse, and how the family discourse creates family cultures (or patterns) and distinctiveness.

Comparisons of family meanings within ethnic families and cross-culturally will be able to reveal those differences that seem to make a difference. For example, Day and Remigy's (1999) study of Mexican and French preschool to school-age children revealed that those children who were from two-parent, traditional families typically viewed "family" to mean the presence of both parents in the physical setting, whereas those children from single-parent homes were less likely to reference the presence of both parents to mean "family."

How Do We Study?

Closely related to what we study is how we conduct our studies. Scholars (e.g., Stephen, 2001; Turner & West, 2002) have called for greater diversity in the methods used by researchers. Some researchers have begun to respond to this call. For example, Alexander (2001) examined the concept of a self-defined family. This study is undergirded by a constructivist view of culture (or culture as constituted through communication); that is, one can create a family through language and interaction. In this ethnographic study, Alexander examined a self-defined family at a local bar (no characterization of race or ethnicity). The importance of future studies of this kind is explicated in this statement concerning the study's findings: "as our society becomes increasingly global and fast-paced and hectic, individuals are likely to become progressively more stressed … and more inclined to look towards a self-defined family for kinship" (p. 25).

What Is Our Responsibility?

We are preparing ourselves, our community, and society for a world that is postcolonial (e.g., Collier, 2000; Cooks, 2001) and open to all. Even though this openness is acknowledged in our civil rights laws and national commitment, many people of co-cultures are still navigating spaces where this is fiction. As scholars who study family communication and family relationships, we are in a unique position to teach, to learn, and to study cultural diversity from a variety of vantage points. As we engage in all of these tasks, we need to continually seek "an earnestness and good faith that in the end will create a far better climate for the achievement of true equality" (Freedman, 2002, p. 33).

NOTES

1. The term ideology is taken to mean that which we accept unconsciously, without reflection. It is defined by Palermo (1997) as "not recognized; the world naturally as the normal state of affairs of the taken for granted"

2. The term epistemology is defined as the basis of knowledge. For example, in Western philosophy and science, the realm of ideas was separated from that of matter which created a dualism between theory and practice (Mowlana, 1996, p. 208); "knowledge is validated through a combination of objectivity and scientific method" (Harris, 1998, p. 19). Mowlana believes that we currently have an ethnocentric epistemological approach operating, which is a barrier to cultural understanding. Harris (1998) indicated that "Afrocentric epistemology validates knowledge through a combination of historical understanding and intuition; what is known is a harmonization of the individual consciousness with the best traditions of the African past" (p. 18).

REFERENCES

Al-Oofy, A., & McDaniel, D. (1992). Home VCR viewing among adolescents in rural Saudi Arabia. *Journal of Broadcasting and Electronic Media, 36*, 217–223.

Alexander, A. L. (2001). *Regulars at the Hole in the Wall: An ethnographic study of a self-defined family at a local bar.* Paper presented at the National Communication Association Conference, Atlanta, GA.

Amason, P. (2002). Choosing an undergraduate text from a limited range of options: A review essay of family communication textbooks. *Journal of Family Communication, 2*, 41–56.

Arnold, M. (1971). *Culture and anarchy: An essay in political and social criticism.* New York: The Bobbs-Merrill Company.

Asante, M. K. (1988). *Afrocentricity* (Rev. ed.). Trenton, NJ: Africa World Press.

Aune, K. S., & Comstock, J. (2002). An exploratory investigation of jealousy in the family. *Journal of Family Communication, 2*, 28–39.

Baker, H. D. R. (1979). *Chinese family and kinship.* London: Macmillan.

Barton, S. C. (1996). Biblical hermeneutics and the family. In S. C. Barton (Ed.), *The family in theological perspective* (pp. 3–23). Edinburg: T&T Clark.

Benhabib, S. (1999). Civil society and the politics of identity and difference in a global context. In N. J. Smelser & J. C. Alexander (Eds.), *Diversity and its discontents: Cultural conflict and common ground in contemporary American society* (pp. 293–312). Princeton, NJ: Princeton University Press.

Bodley, J. H. (1976). *Anthropology and contemporary human problems.* Menlo, CA: Cummings. Braman, S. (1996). Interpenetrated globalization: Scaling, power, and the public sphere. In S. Braman & A. Sreberny-Mohammadi (Eds.), *Globalization, communication and transnational civil society* (pp. 21–36). Cresskill, NJ: Hampton Press.

Braman, S., & Sreberny-Mohammadi, A. (Eds.). (1996). *Globalization, communication and transnational civil society.* Cresskill, NJ: Hampton Press.

Chen, G. M., & Starosta, W. J. (2000). Communication and global society: An introduction. In G. M. Chen & W. J. Starosta (Eds.), *Communication and global society* (pp. 1–6). New York: Peter Lang.

Chesebro, J. W. (1982). Illness as a rhetorical act: A cross-cultural perspective. *Communication Quarterly, 30*, 321–331.

Çignar, D. (2002). Cultural diversity and dialogue: On Bhikhu Parekh: Rethinking multiculturalism. Cultural diversity and political talk. Review section of polylog. *Forum for Intercultural Philosophizing* 2, 1–11. Retrieved March 12, 2002, from http://www.polylog.org.org/lit/2/rvw1-en.htm

Clark, K., & Diggs, R. C. (2002). Connected or separated?: Towards a dialectical view of interethnic relationships. In T. A. McDonald, M. Orbe, & T. Ford-Ahmed (Eds.), *Building diverse communities: Applications of communication research* (pp. 3–25). Creskill, NJ: Hampton Press.

Collier, M. J. (2000). Reconstructing cultural diversity in global relationships: Negotiating the borderlands. In G. M. Chen & W. J. Starosta (Eds.), *Communication and global society* (pp. 215–236). New York: Peter Lang.

Collier, M. J. (2001). Constituting cultural difference through discourse: Current research themes of politics, perspectives. In M. J. Collier (Ed.), *Constituting cultural difference through discourse* (pp. 1–25). Thousand Oaks, CA: Sage.

Collier, M. J. (Ed.). (2002). Introduction. *Transforming communication about culture: Critical new directions* (pp. ix–xix). Thousand Oaks, CA: Sage.

Collier, M. J., Hedge, R. S., Lee, W., Nakayama, T. K., & Yep., G. A. (2002). Dialogue on the edges: Ferment in communication and culture. In M. J. Collier (Ed.), *Transforming communication about culture: Critical new directions* (pp. 219–277). Thousand Oaks, CA: Sage.

Cooks, L. (2001). From distance and uncertainty to research and pedagogy in the borderlands: Implications for the future of intercultural communication *Communication Theory 11*, 339–351.

Daniel, J. (1970). The poor: Aliens in an affluent society. *Today's Speech, 18*, 5–21.

Day, E. D., & Remigy, M. J. (1999). Mexican and French children's conceptions about family: A developmental approach. *Journal of Comparative Family Studies, 30*(3), 95–112.

Diggs, R. C. (2001). Optimizing family/community places and spaces for racial profiling discourse [Special Issue]. *The Journal of Intergroup Relations, 28*(3), 42–58.

Diggs, R. C., & Clark, K. D. (2002). It's a struggle but worth it: Identifying and managing identities in an inter-racial friendship [Special issue]. *Communication Quarterly, 50*, 368–390.

Duneier, M. (1992). *Slim's table: Race, respectability, and masculinity.* Chicago: The University of Chicago Press.

Durrheim, K., & Dixon, J. (2001). The role of place and metaphor in racial exclusion: South Africa's beaches as sites of shifting racialization. *Ethnic and Racial Studies, 24*, 433–450.

Fernea, E. W. (Ed.). (1985). *Women and the family in the Middle East.* Austin, TX: University of Texas Press.

Fisherkeller, J. (1997). Everyday learning about identities among young adolescents in television culture. *Anthropology and Education Quarterly, 28*, 467–492.

Fitzpatrick, M. A., & Ritchie, L. D. (1993). Communication theory and the family. In P. G. Boss, W. J. Doherty, R. LaRossa, W. R. Schumm, & S. K. Steinmetz (Eds.), *Sourcebook of family theories and methods: A contextual approach* (pp. 565–589). New York: Plenum Press.

Freedman, J. O. (2002). Dealing with difference: Why it's important to attend a college that's racially, culturally, and ethnically diverse. *Private Colleges and Universities*, 32–33.

Furrow, J. L. (1998). The ideal father: Religious narratives and the role of fatherhood. *The Journal of Men's Studies, 7*, 17–32.

Galvin, K. M., & Brommel, B. (1996). *Family communication cohesion and change* (4th ed.). New York: HarperCollins.

Georgas, J., Mylonas, K., Bafiti, T., Poortinga, Y. H., Christakopoulou, S., Kagitcibasi, C., et al. (2001). Functional relationships in the nuclear and extended family: A 16-culture study. *International Journal of Psychology, 36*, 289–300.

Gudykunst, W. B., & Kim, Y. Y. (1997). *Communicating with strangers* (3rd ed.). New York: McGraw-Hill.

Gudykunst, W. B., & Lee, C. M. (2001). An agenda for studying ethnicity and family communication. *Journal of Family Communication, 1*, 75–85.

Gudykunst W. B., Ting-Toomey, S., & Nishida, T. (Eds.). (1996). *Communication in personal relationships across cultures.* Thousand Oaks: CA: Sage.

Harris, N. (1998). The philosophical basis for an Afrocentric orientation. In J. D. Hamlet (Ed.), *Afrocentric visions: Studies in culture and communication* (pp. 15–25). Thousand Oaks, CA: Sage.

Hecht, M. L., Collier, M. J., & Ribeau, S. A. (1993). *African American communication.* Thousand Oaks, CA: Sage.

Henry, J. (1973). *Pathways to madness.* New York: Random House.

Hughes, P. C., & Dickson, F. C. (2001). *Keeping the faith(s): Religion, communication, and marital satisfaction in interfaith marriages.* Paper presented at the National Communication Association, Atlanta, GA.

Jenkins, K. W. (1991). Inside the family's culture: A communicative-oriented analysis of culture within the family unit. *Dissertation Abstracts International, 51*(12), 4288A. (UMI No. 9112814).

Julian, T. W., McKenry, P. C., & McKelvey, M. W. (1994). Cultural variations in parenting: Perceptions of Caucasian, African-American, Hispanic, and Asian-American parents. *Family Relations, 43*, 30–37.

Kane, C. M. (2000). African American family dynamics as perceived by family members. *Journal of Black Studies, 30*, 691–702.

Khatri, A. A. (1983). *Marriage and family: Relations through literature: A study of Indian fiction*. Bayside, NY: General Hall.

Kim, Y. Y., & Gudykunst, W. B. (Eds.). (1996). *Theories in intercultural communication* (pp. 299–321). Newbury Park, CA: Sage.

Koesten, J., Miller, K. I., & Hummert, M. L. (2002). Family communication, self-efficacy, and White female adolescents. *Journal of Family Communication 2*, 7–27.

Lather, P. (1991). *Feminist research in education: Within/against*. Geelong, Victoria: Deakin University Press.

Lee, S. J., & Kim, J. O. (1979). *The value of children—A cross national study: Korea*. Honolulu, HA: East-West Population Institute.

Lewis, O. (1959). *Five families: Mexican case studies in the culture of poverty*. New York: Basic Books.

Lewis, O. (1961). *The children of Sanchez: Autobiography of a Mexican family*. New York: Random House.

Makau, J. (1997). Embracing diversity in the classroom. In J. M. Makau & R. C. Arnett (Eds.), *Communicating ethics in an age of diversity* (pp. 48–67). Urbana: University of Illinois Press.

Mathabane, M. (1994). *African women: Three generations*. New York: HarperCollins.

McAdoo, H. P. (2001). Point of view: Ethnicity and family dialogue. *Journal of Family Communication, 1*, 87–90.

Mindel, C. H., Habenstein, R. W., & Wright, R., Jr. (Eds.). (1988). *Ethnic families in America: Patterns and variations*. New York: Elsevier.

Mosby, L., Rawls, A. W., Meehan, A. J., Mays, E., & Pettinari, C. J. (1999). Troubles in interracial talk about discipline: An examination of African child rearing narratives. *Journal of Comparative Family Studies, 30*, 89–521.

Mowlana, H. (1996). *Global communication in transition: The end of diversity?* Thousand Oaks, CA: Sage.

Myers, L. J. (1998). The deep structure of culture: Relevance of traditional African culture in contemporary life. In J. D. Hamlet (Ed.), *Afrocentric visions: Studies in culture and communication* (pp. 3–14). Thousand Oaks, CA: Sage

Nicholson, J. H. (2001, November). *Relational effects of sibling alliances*. Paper presented at the National Communication Association, Atlanta, GA.

Orbe, M. P. (1998). *Constructing co-cultural theory: An explication of culture, power, and communication*. Thousand Oaks, CA: Sage.

Palermo, J. (1997). Reading Asante's myth of *Afrocentricity*: An ideological critique. Retrieved April 1, 2002, *http://www.ed.uiuc.edu/EPS/PES-Yearbook/97 docs/ palermo.html*

Pecchioni, L. L., & Nussbaum, J. F. (2002). Mother-adult daughter discussions of care-giving prior to dependency: Exploring conflict styles of European-American women. *Journal of Family communication, 1*, 133–150.

Ramu, G. N. (1977). *Family and caste in urban India: A case study*. New Delhi, India: Vikas Publishing House.

Rubin, L. B. (1976). *World's of pain: Life in the working-class family*. New York: Basic Books.

Rubin, L. B. (1994). *Families on the fault line: America's working class speaks about the family, the economy, race, and ethnicity*. New York: HarperCollins.

Schönpflug, U. (2001). Intergenerational transmission of values: The role of transmission belts. *Journal of Cross-Cultural Psychology, 32*, 174–85.

Segrin, C., & Flora, J. (2001). Perceptions of relational histories, marital quality, and loneliness when communication is limited: An examination of married prison inmates. *Journal of Family Communication, 3*, 151–173.

Sennett, R. (1970). *Families against the city: Middle class homes in industrial Chicago*. Cambridge, MA: Harvard Press.

Singer, M. R. (1987). *Intercultural communication: A perceptual approach*. Englewood Cliffs, NJ: Prentice-Hall.

Socha, T. J. (2002, April). *Diversity and family communication*. A lecture given at the Family Communication and Stress Forum, University of Nebraska-Lincoln, Lincoln, NE.

Socha, T. J., & Diggs, R. C. (1999). *Communication, race, and family: Exploring communication in Black, White, and Biracial families.* Mahwah, NJ: Lawrence Erlbaum Associates.

Socha, T. J., & Stamp, G. H. (Eds.). (1995). *Parents, children and communication: Frontiers of theory and research.* Mahwah, NJ: Lawrence Erlbaum Associates.

Stephen, T. (2001). Concept analysis of the communication literature on marriage and family. *The Journal of Family Communication, 1,* 91–110.

Turner, L. H., & West, R. (2002). Call for papers: Communication with diversity in contemporary families [Special issue]. *Journal of Family Communication, 2,* 57–58.

Van Bich, P. (1999). *The Vietnamese family in change: The case of the Red River delta.* Surry, UK: Curzon.

Wadsworth, B. (1712). *The well-ordered-family: Relative duties—Early American Reprints.* Boston and New York: Readux Microprint [No. 1591].

Weiner, A. B. (1997). The false assumptions of traditional values. In S. Dreman (Ed.), *The family on the threshold of the 21st century: Trends and implications* (pp. 103–112). Mahwah, NJ: Lawrence Erlbaum Associates.

West, C. (1989). *The American evasion of philosophy: A genealogy of pragmatism.* Madison, WI: The University of Wisconsin Press.

Whitchurch, G. G., & Dickson, F. C. (1999). Family communication. In M. B. Sussman, S. K. Steinmetz, & G. W. Peterson (Eds.), *Handbook of marriage and the family* (pp. 687–704). New York: Plenum Press.

Wuthnow, R. (1999). Democratic liberalism and the challenge of diversity in late-twentieth century America. In N. J. Smelser & J. C. Alexander (Eds.), *Diversity and its discontents: Cultural conflict and common ground in contemporary American society* (pp. 19–35). Princeton, NJ: Princeton University Press.

Xu, Y., & Burleson, B. R. (2001). Effects of sex, culture, and support type on perceptions of spousal social support. An assessment of the "support-gap" hypothesis in early marriage. *Human Communication Research, 27,* 535–566.

3. ELEMENTS OF INTERCULTURAL MARRIAGE

By James Honeycutt

The number of intercultural marriages is significantly increasing worldwide. This is due to the expansive amount of globalization occurring between different countries and cultures. Interracial marriages in the U.S. have climbed to 4.8 million—a record 1 in 12—as a steady flow of new Asian and Hispanic immigrants expands the pool of prospective spouses. Blacks are now substantially more likely than before to marry Whites according to the Pew Research Center. As globalization continues to dominate the international landscape and technology continues to make the world metaphorically flatter, intercultural relations, and very likely intercultural marriages, will increase. With a better understanding of the processing and communication that go into what elements effect the success and satisfaction experienced in these relationships, our society will continue on a path of healthy intercultural interactions. This chapter discusses intercultural marriage by looking at some if its key elements, including assimilation and acculturation, extended family involvement, gender roles, religious practices, child rearing, moods of emotional expression, and divorce. While achieving a successful balance between cultures may be difficult and is not always achieved, it is not impossible and can result in a rewarding and lasting marriage.

Two people coming together from different backgrounds bring about many differences that may lead to conflict. Therefore, a better understanding of what these conflicts are, what causes them, and how to deal with them in a positive way is greatly needed to help these marriages last. In this chapter, several controversial topics within intercultural marriage are discussed, including assimilation and acculturation, involvement of the extended family, gender roles, religious practices, child-rearing, mood expression styles, and divorce. Taking these topics into consideration when trying to successfully maneuver intercultural marriage may be what allows the marriage to last and thrive.

Not all interracial marriages are intercultural. First, it is necessary to define the difference between race and ethnicity. Very few people can accurately describe the difference between ethnicity and race because they tend to lump them into the same definition. We can say that a Caucasian is white, but that doesn't describe his or her ethnicity. If we lined up a Caucasian from Ireland, Israel, France, Russia, or Spain in a photograph, it would be difficult to discern from which country each person originates. Yet,

Table 3-1 Interracial Married Couples in the United States in 2010 (thousands)

	WHITE WIFE	BLACK WIFE	ASIAN WIFE	OTHER WIFE
White Husband	50,410	168	529	487
Black Husband	390	4,072	39	66
Asian Husband	219	9	2,855	28
Other Husband	488	18	37	568

Source: U.S. Bureau of the Census "Table 60. Married Couples by Race and Hispanic Origin of Spouses," 15 Dec 2010. (Excel table. Detailed data can be found in the Statistical Abstract of the United States, from 1979 to 2011)

if we gave them appropriate items from their culture, it becomes easier to determine their country of origin. Ethnicity is about tradition, socialization, learned behavior, and customs. It is about celebrating the traditions and ideas that are part of a region. At one time it was easy to tell one's ethnicity, but as the global conglomeration offered more choice and change (as well as borrowing styles and ideas from other cultures), it has become impossible to identify ethnicity based solely on distinctive features.

Race is your biologically engineered features. It can include skin color, skin tone, eye and hair color, as well as a tendency toward developing certain diseases. It is not something that can be changed or disguised. Race does not have customs or globally learned behavior. Ethnicity does not always describe color either. One can claim to be African, which indicates an entire multi-regional, multi-cultural continent. You can enhance the definition by assigning a subculture to the ethnicity, such as South African, or Ethiopian. There can be a wide range of skin colors and tones throughout Africa, ranging from the white skin and fair-haired faces many associate with the Aryan race to the dark skin, black-haired faces that many associate with African regions. As revealed in Table 3-1, marriages can be racial (black–white), ethnic (Taiwanese-born Chinese married to an American-born Chinese), or both ethnic/racial (a Black Nigerian married to a White American).

Based on figures from Table 3-1, White Americans were statistically the least likely to wed interracially, though in absolute terms they were involved in interracial marriages more than any other racial group due to their demographic majority. In terms of percentages, 2.1% of married White women and 2.3% of married White men had a non-White spouse while 1.0% of all married White men were married to an Asian American woman, and 1.0% of married White women were married to a man classified as "other." Additionally, 4.6% of married Black American women and 10.8% of married Black American men had a non-Black spouse. Eight and a half percent of married Black men and 3.9% of married Black women had a White spouse while 0.2% of married Black women were married to Asian American men, representing the least prevalent marital combination.

ASSIMILATION AND ACCULTURATION

There are many theories concerning how a person's culture changes when marrying someone of a different culture. First, Gordon's (1964) pioneering Assimilation Theory states that the member of the minority group loses their distinctiveness and their cultural identity and assimilates into the culture by marrying someone from the dominant group. Critics argue that intercultural marriage is a sign of acculturation by the dominant host culture (Ezra and Roer-Strier 2006). This is inevitable with social tolerance, but it does necessarily lead to assimilation, the loss of ethnic identity. There are then two types of acculturation with one that occurs at the collective level and the other at the individual psychological level. At the psychological level acculturation occurs when there is contact with another culture. Behavior, identity, values, and attitudes are influenced with the culture in contact. In intercultural marriage, mutual assimilation is most often what occurs. Assimilation is a two-way process influencing both partners; the one in the minority culture as well as the one in the dominant culture (Ezra and Roer-Strier 2006). Along with mutual assimilation, selective acculturation may occur. Selective acculturation implies cultural maintenance and strong ties with the co-ethnic community concomitant to cultural transition, which may often thwart assimilation. Marriage to a native furthers acculturation, but the pace and extent to which this occurs is not necessarily voluntary (Remennick 2009).

Romano (2008) suggests that couples embrace one of four styles in how they manage their differences in culture. In one style, one spouse gives up their culture and fully embraces the culture of the other spouse. A second style consists of couples compromising where both spouses give up aspects of their culture in order to minimize conflict and live harmoniously. A third style that is more severe involving both partners denying that there are any differences and finding a common, neutral territory in which to operate by giving up their traditions and values. The fourth styled is a win-win situation involving "mutuality and flexibility" but the partner keeps what is most important to them about their culture.

Similar findings came from a study on Western women marrying Pakistani men and moving to Pakistan. Four categories of cultural adaptation were discovered. They categorize the wife's feelings about their own culture identities and embracing their partner's culture. First is identity loss. The foreign spouses were insecure in their identity definition, therefore, not really feeling a belonging to either their own culture or the culture of their spouse. Some women remained in this category, whereas others moved on to a different stage; the stages being complete assimilation, compromise, and total rejection. The men's attitudes were not documented but according to the wives, the husbands became more traditional with the move as opposed to before when they were liberal and open-minded. Many did this is favor of the extended family's wishes (Ezra and Roer-Strier 2006).

In a study of Russian immigrants married to native Israelis, the identity dilemma occurred more in the immigrant spouses. They were split between their former and current ways of life as well as incorporating the partner and their culture. Many of the Russians did not want to completely shed themselves of their Russian culture, however, they thought of themselves as doubly rich in culture by partaking in languages and traditions. Dealing with the differences in both cultures was expressed as a daily challenge but the Russian and Israeli spouses thought of it as a positive aspect in that they had a mutual interest and curiosity in the other's culture and that for life, they would continue to make new discoveries (Remennick 2009).

Extended Family Involvement

Different cultures expect their extended family's involvement to different degrees. For example, African heritage emphasizes consanguinity, or family ties, whereas European heritage emphasizes conjugality, or marital kinship. Consanguinity, therefore, has a broader meaning of family. Family may include the immediate nuclear family as well as grandparents, aunts, uncles, cousins, etc. When bringing together two people from these separate backgrounds with different ideas of family, it may cause stress on how much they expect their extended families to be involved (Socha and Diggs 1999). A study conducted by Lewis and Yancey (1995) measured the parental support of children who are part of a biracial couple. The three ethnicities interviewed were Black Americans, Mexican Americans, and Whites. Overall,

Lewis and Yancey discovered that all families were generally supportive; however, fathers were less supportive than mothers. Black Americans (77%) and Mexican Americans (57%) were more supportive of the marriages than Whites (44%). Only 1.6% of Black American parents rejected the marriage, no Mexican-American parents did, but 10.4% of Whites completely rejected their child's biracial marriage. The researchers discovered that minorities are more supportive of intercultural marriage. They defined this idea with the term "color grading," lighter skin is more accepted than darker skin. In conclusion, if the family was supportive from the initial decision to marry, it positively influenced family acceptance after the union was established. This study, however, did not discuss how the parents' opinions affected children's relationships.

GENDER ROLES AND CULTURAL DIFFERENCES

Gender roles reflect the cultural expectations of female and male behaviors. Sex is a biological given (XX and XY chromosome, respectively) while gender is learned. Gender roles are thus heavily dependent on the cultural socialization from the family of origin and can vary widely across cultures. When two individuals enter into a relationship with differing understandings and expectations of gender roles, complications and conflict can arise. In recent decades, in the mainstream society of the United States, gender roles have gradually become more blurred with the prevalence of diverse sources of information across social media and the Internet. Sometimes this change in established gender norms will cause a rift for individuals originating from more traditional gender-role ideals.

Neuliep (2012) discusses how Hispanic cultures tend to emphasis a distinct separation between appropriate husband and wife behavior, in the identification of being machismo for male roles and marianismo for female roles. Machismo has men defined as being dominant, virile, and independent, resulting in a focus on the role as provider for the family unit. Marianismo has women defined as being submissive, chaste, and dependent, with an emphasis on the role of mother and martyr. As Hispanic families and individuals become acculturated into the United States, the continuation of these roles and ideals vary ("Gender Norms" 2007). A prime example of religious acculturation is how some Hispanic Catholics lapse from Catholicism to other Protestant beliefs or secularism after living in the U.S. Putnam and Campbell (2010) claim that over two-thirds of people raised as Catholics in America are no longer practicing Catholics. One third of them are still devout practicing Catholics while another third no longer call themselves Catholics.

While the likelihood of a gender disconnect between an individual raised in the U.S. and one raised in a Hispanic culture outside of the U.S. may seem high, similar struggles are often had by individuals assimilating into the U.S. after living in a predominantly Hispanic country. In their native countries, traditionally, Hispanic women do not work outside of the home and act exclusively as primary caregiver, but once a move is made to the U.S., the likelihood of the wife and mother entering the workforce is higher. This means that the family may now have two providers. The wife may take on part of the role that makes the husband masculine and require the husband to take on more daily chores ("Gender Norms" 2007). While this situation may appear to be exclusively experienced by Hispanic marriages after a move to the U.S., it is also possible for individuals in intercultural marriages to find themselves in a similar situation.

Neuliep (2012) cites a survey of 10,000 Chinese urban men and women where, "92% of the men indicated that they wanted a wife who would be aggressive in her career, yet 96% of the men indicated that they wanted a wife who would do most of the house work. Nearly half the Chinese women surveyed, however, wanted men to share chores more" (Neuliep 2012, p. 228). Should a Chinese male living in the United States marry a female of Hispanic heritage, they may experience a clash of gender role preferences when the wife requires additional assistance with household duties.

As can be seen here, the possibility for a variety of gender role combinations is possible in an intercultural marriage. It is important for couples to establish those expectations upfront in order to avoid confusion and complications later on in the marriage.

Religious and Spiritual Practices

The topic of religion and spirituality in intercultural marriages is one that comes with conflict, controversy, and often compromise between the couple as noted in Chapter 6. It is necessary to differentiate between religious beliefs and values. Religious beliefs reflect a belief in a supernatural power or powers that control human destiny. Even scientists have "faith" in the scientific model. Beliefs are the convictions that we generally hold to be true, usually without actual proof or evidence. They are often, but not always, connected to religion. Religious beliefs could include a belief that God created the earth in seven days, or that Jesus was the son of God. Religions other than Christianity have their own set of beliefs. Non-religious beliefs could include that all people are created equal, which would guide us to treat everyone regardless of sex, race, religion, age, education, status, etc. with equal respect. Conversely someone might believe that all people are not created equal, which results in racist and sexist values and attitudes.

Beliefs are assumptions that we make about the world and our values stem from those beliefs. Our values are things that we deem important and can include concepts like "equality, honesty, education, materialism, effort, perseverance, loyalty, faithfulness, and conservation of the environment," to name a few. Values reflect the rules of how you live or want to live your life. This is important to separate because the focus here is religious views and interfaith marriages. Some would argue that the conflict would not be there if everyone married into their own culture but "because someone has the same religion as you does not make a match made in heaven," which proves that it is not just religion that can cause marital problems, so that should not deter people from interfaith marriage.

When it comes to holidays, celebrating someone else's rituals may seem like you're sacrificing your own and even though this may seem true in some intercultural marriages, the individual can still value their own beliefs and rituals from their personal religion, Deciding what religious practices to follow when raising children also becomes an issue of conflict for marriages that are intercultural and the best thing is that parents lead by example by respecting the religious views and either deciding beforehand on one religion or letting the child decide which they prefer as they grow up.

One of the key religious views of conflict is intercultural marriages between someone who is Muslim following the tenets of Islam and another who is not. Muslims in America represent diverse ethnic and racial backgrounds and this has led to an increase in intercultural and interfaith marriages.. Ezzeldine (2006) claims that individuals preparing for marriage are usually not even consciously aware of their unrealistic expectations and any potential conflicts that can occur in the marriage because of their culture or religion, which can cause problems in the intercultural marriage because the issue of religious views has not even been brought up. But there are five ways to manage these religious differences that interfaith couples may have. The first is transcendent, in which the couple adopts their traditions and beliefs from multiple sources, but this is not usually the case for people brought up in strong religious households and not typical in Muslim families. Second is the secular approach, in which the couple has minimal traditions and rituals and they do not encourage religion in their family or children. The third idea is bicultural, with balanced traditions from both sides of the family. This is common in many Muslim households. Fourth, the modified bicultural, is when the intercultural couple adopts a single religion but they mutually honor both beliefs. This is the most common strategy in Muslim families. Usually the children are raised Islamic but learn about the other traditions, too. And the last strategy is assimilation, in which one partner of the marriage converts his or her beliefs to the other and forgets all about their personal beliefs.

When marriage partners come from two different cultural backgrounds, it is up to them to negotiate and decide what to do in regards to religion; "this is because two individuals come from two different families, and as a couple they will develop their own family identity by choosing the traditions, habits and beliefs they value and want to celebrate in their family and with their own children" (Ezzeldine 2006). Religious traditions and beliefs will probably always be a challenge in intercultural marriages, but there are ways in which the couple can go about deciding what to do in a healthy, constructive way that is beneficial to them and to their families.

Arranged Marriages

In Western cultures, the choice of a partner is up to the individual. We have institutions like hooking up, dating, and Internet matching services like eharmony.com that give young people a chance to accumulate relevant experience over a number of years, so that they can make an informed decision. In a way, dating offers the kind of experience with intimate relationships that summer jobs, externships, and volunteer work provide for youth in making career decisions.

In Southeast Asian societies (e.g., India, Pakistan, Bangladesh, Iran, Egypt) parents or other designated individuals choose a person's spouse (and occupation). These are sometimes called arranged marriages, in contrast to love marriages, though there are many varieties of each. Matches are based on religious compatibility, socioeconomic status and wealth, family reputation, vocation, health of the individuals, and astrology.

A common rationale for arranged marriages is that young people are too immature and impulsive to make a wise choice, and experienced elders are likely to do better. In addition, in the West one chooses a partner to fulfill oneself, while in non-Western collectivist cultures, one's primary responsibility is to the group—to one's parents, kin group, ancestors, and others—all of whom have contributed to make one's current life possible and to whom one is obligated. Advantages of arranged marriage are extended family support and that the risk of incompatibility is diminished. Parallel disadvantages include romantic love being minimized and interference from extended family. A study in India over 30 years ago by Gupta and Singh (1982) found that people in love marriages were more in love for the first five years, while those in arranged marriages were more in love for the next 30 years. People do not expect to love their spouse at first—love is seen as something that develops (when it does) over time and through shared experiences.

A follow-up study done by Myers, Madathil, and Tingle (2005) compared 45 individuals living in arranged marriages in India to individuals in choice marriages in the United States. They found "no support for differences in marital satisfaction or love aspects of wellness in relation to arranged marriages." In addition, studies by Schwartz (2007) on Orthodox Jews and Walsh and Taylor (1982) studying Japanese arranged marriages found no differences in love between arranged versus choice marriage.

Further research on the relationships between cultural differences, cultural values, and characteristics of marriages are needed to explain these relationships and provide a knowledge base for cross-cultural couples counseling.

Child Rearing

The term "Latino" refers to Spanish-speaking people from Mexico, South and Central America, and the Caribbean. According to the 2000 census, Latinos are the largest minority group in the United States. Latinos encompass over 12.5% of the American population. They believe in tight-knit families where the father is the dominant figure and the mother is responsible for taking care of the home. Their methods of child rearing derive from the two terms *Respeto* and *Familismo* (Bornstein 2002, p. 21).

The term *Respeto* refers to the concept of "Proper Demeanor." *Respeto* is intrinsically contextual; it involves, by definition, knowing the level of courtesy and decorum required in a given situation in relation to other people of a particular age, sex, and social status (Bornstein 2002, p. 22). Latinos teach their children the value of hard work and the respect for their elders or authority figures. They believe that physical punishment is more effective than taking away privileges like those in Western cultures. Latinos think that this teaches children respect and discipline. Religion also plays a huge role in disciplining their children. Over 90% of Latinos are Roman Catholic. In Latino culture, family is the most important value. The term *Familismo* is defined as "a belief system [that] refers to feelings of loyalty, reciprocity, and solidarity towards members of the family, as well as to the notion of the family as an extension of self" (Bornstein 2002, p. 22). According to the handbook, there are four different types of *Familismo*: demographic, structural, normative, and behavioral. Demographic refers to the size of the family. Structural *Familismo* means multigenerational households or extended family systems. Normative considers the importance of family solidarity and support. Lastly, behavioral *Familismo* refers to the amount of contact among extended family members. Latino families consist of not only the nuclear family, but the outer members as well such as aunts, cousins, in-laws, et al. They believe that having a large family helps provide more emotional, social, and even financial support.

According to Bornstein there are 5 central issues Black-American parents have with raising their children. They often struggle with a lack of adequate financial resources, roles of education, high proportion of single parents, grandparents being primary parent, and lastly, the task of racially socializing with their children. Financially, the Black-American culture has become less essential to the stimulation of American economy. This is due to offshore and overseas cheap labor. The demand for lesser-educated workers is diminishing in the United States and is affecting the quality of Black-American parenting. According to the University of Michigan Panel Survey of Income Dynamics, the net worth of the Black American family has shrunk by 17% in 1984 to 1999. Education has been the window of opportunity in the Black-American culture for a better life. However, because of the "white flight" of European Americans to suburban areas, the quality of education in intercity schools is far more inferior. Two-thirds of Black-American children are born to unmarried mothers. Therefore, resources are not as readily available to them as if they were in a two-parent household. Also, because of parental issues, a lot of times grandparents become the primary child raiser.

The term "Asian" refers to countries in South East Asia, East Asia, South Asia, and the Philippines and Thailand. Asian cultures are greatly influenced by traditions and cultural values. They believe in authoritarian parenting. Parents in Asian cultures have strict demands for and high expectations of their children. Because of this strict style of parenting, Asian children tend to perform exceptionally well in school and have minimal behavior problems. Asians are also interdependent, meaning they rely on support within the family. They have a large respect for elders. Also, Asian children are required to fulfill a range of financial, instrumental, and caregiving obligations to the family.

Parents of biracial children face several challenges in making their children understand their differences from other children. Studies have shown that multiracial children forced to choose a single-race identity tend to suffer from this inauthentic expression of self. Therefore it is essential to embrace the heritage of both parents. Each parent must familiarize their children with customs, religions, and languages from both cultural backgrounds. Also, parents are encouraged to search for schools and neighborhoods that are more accepting of multiracial marriages. Even though it will not completely eliminate the risk of racism, it lessens the amount their children will potentially receive. When raising children of multiple backgrounds, it is important to teach them that racial identity is more complicated than physical appearance. Some parents even prepare their children for questions their peers might ask in school. Child rearing is a major cause of stress in intercultural marriages and knowing how you express your feelings to your partner is a necessary skill.

Emotion and Mood Expression

Mood expression styles are how we show how we are feeling. Research examining emotions and moods has been dated as far back as 1667. Darwin even considered the face to be the predominant mode of expression for emotions in humans. Our reactions can be voluntary or involuntary. Culture can affect how we express these feelings. From childhood we are socialized as to what are appropriate emotions to display, when it is a right time to display these emotions, and how we should appropriately convey them.

Elsewhere I have discussed the difference between moods and emotions (Honeycutt and Bryan 2011). Batson, Shaw, and Oleson (1992) indicated that emotions are concerned with the present, whereas moods concern anticipation of the future. Furthermore, Schwartz and Clore (1988) argued that emotions have a specific focus, whereas moods are nonspecific. Emotions have an object that moods may not have. Moods do not have to be caused by emotion. In essence, a working definition of <u>mood</u> is a feeling state, "which need not be about anything, whereas emotion refers to how one feels in combination with what the feeling is about" (Clore et al. 1994, p. 326). So learn the distinction in everyday usage.

There are six universal signs of emotions. They are happiness, sadness, surprise, fear, disgust, and anger. Certain stimuli will cause the responses to occur. For example, sadness has shown to invoke a response of the lowering of the mouth corners and raising of the inner portion of the brows. Depending on your culture you may be taught not to show such an emotion. Even in the United States, men are taught that they must be strong when displaying the emotion of sadness; they are not to cry, as it is unmasculine. As the previous example states, we may all have universal signs of emotions, but in some cases we are taught to repress showing these emotions.

According to Markus and Kitayama (2010), one of the biggest problems between eastern and western cultures in conflict is that they view the context of the situation differently. While the North American focuses on the sole individual and what they are actually saying, an East Asian reads the entire social context. Particularly in Japan, as a collectivist society, they are taught to focus on their actions being accommodating to others (Markus and Kitayama 2010). For people in the U.S., behaving appropriately in an argument would probably be to make sure that they clearly get their points across and make sure that they are heard. However, if Japanese marriage partners were to behave properly they would have to adjust their expectations and preferences of other people rather than try to advance their own personal goals. While it seems the American way, being assertive and concerned with self-advancement is seen as childish and selfish in the Japanese culture; they are taught to preserve social harmony and fulfill their expected social role. This more often than not, in the context of marriage, will leave the woman to keep her husband happy, as her social role is to preserve harmony in her family, not cause conflict within it.

In American society, parents and peers encourage emotional expression. Suppression of emotions is often seen as insincere. We believe it may be a risk to our health and well being to keep too many of our emotions inside. Carroll and Russell said, "Most Americans believe that they can infer emotion from other people's faces. This is the focal point in our interactions with others. This can lead to confusion as some other cultures are taught to look at the ground as a sign of respect. How are we supposed to know what they are feeling if we cannot see their face?" For example, the Japanese are taught to repress strong emotions and adapt their expression to the rest of the group's. They infer from the context surrounding, rather than the individual's facial expression. In the same study, they even stated that several East Asians, when given a picture of solely someone's face, said they could not infer what they were feeling as they could not see the surroundings (Markus and Kitayama 2010).

There have been many documented articles on the concept of machismo in the Latin community. According to Ingoldsby (1991), machismo has several characteristics. "To be a macho you must be aggressive, masculine, strong, and physically powerful. Differences must be met with fists or other weapons. They should not be afraid of anything and should be capable of drinking great quantities of liquor without necessarily getting drunk" (Ingoldsby 1991). They are to be strong protectors of the females in the house. Showing affection to other men, even their own sons, would be considerate inappropriate. It has been said that the entire practice is based on an inferiority complex; nonetheless this practice has taught men that anger is an appropriate response, sadness is not.

Latin women in these societies can appropriately show many more emotions. Affection is expected from them and for them. However, they are expected to be submissive and dependent. They are passive creatures created to be dominated. Women seem to happily perpetuate these standards, which has been termed "Marianismo" (Ingoldsby 1991). Although women learn to cater to their fathers and that they are less important than their brothers, women are revered, respected, and thought of as morally superior.

In just briefly looking at a couple of cultures, you can see that how we are taught to show emotions could cause a serious amount of conflict in an intercultural marriage. Partners will have to understand how and what the other is conveying even though it may not necessarily be how they are acting or what they are saying. They will need to understand where they are coming from and why they act the way they do.

In terms of dealing with mood expressions in an intercultural marriage, the biggest thing is to understand why both partners act the way they do. It is very culture specific how men and women are taught to engage with one another. Even if you think about women's roles in India, Japan, and the United States, how they are taught to interact with men and their level of importance in the family structure may be very different. Every culture has their own ways of showing respect, dealing with conflict, and how they should come to decisions. When a part of an intercultural marriage, the partners will have to find a way to mold together their styles of how they express themselves and learn why the other shows or fails to show how they are feeling. We are socialized through our culture the appropriate way to express our emotions. In an intercultural marriage, partners are going to have to understand the other's culture in order to interpret how their partner is feeling.

DIVORCE

All of the issues discussed so far are in all relationships, not just intercultural marriages. However, the stressors and decisions may be increased in an intercultural marriage. Opposites may attract, but every couple must come to mutual agreements, which can be difficult when individuals' perspectives vary or are polar opposites. When decisions cannot be mutually arrived at, this can lead to divorce.

Neuliep (2012) states that the divorce rate in many countries is increasing. As women become more educated and gain more independence, they have other options. People's views in many countries are becoming less stigmatized about those who are divorced, and it is becoming more socially acceptable. The divorce rate in Japan is considerably less than in United States but is growing. according to the Japanese Health, Labor, and Welfare Ministry. About one in three Japanese marriages end in divorce, four times the rate in the 1950s and double the rate in the 1970s. The divorce rate has slowed, partly because fewer couples are getting married. In urban areas of China, the rate has increased from two percent in 1981 to almost twenty percent in 1992. The divorce rate in Russia is rising quickly as women are becoming more financially independent and can afford to support themselves; it is now at about forty percent (Neuliep 2012).

With that being said there are certain cultures where divorce still brings much shame. In India only one in a hundred marriages ends in divorce. Divorced women still face poverty, loss of status, and custody of their children. In rural China, divorce is still highly stigmatized. For those who follow traditional beliefs, breaking up one's family would not be for the greater good. It is a selfish act, and the women's primary tasks are still to care for the children, household, and to fulfill her filial piety duties. To divorce would be against their core beliefs and bring shame upon the family.

The role of gender in interracial divorce has been highlighted by Bratter and King (2008) when examining marital instability among Black/White unions. White wife/Black husband marriages show twice the divorce rate of White wife/White husband couples by the 10th year of marriage, whereas Black wife/White husband marriages are 44% less likely to end in divorce than White wife/White husband couples over the same period.

Referring back to Table 3-1, Black men are more than twice as likely as black women to marry someone outside their race. Yet, Bratter and King (2008) report that interracial marriages are less stable than same-race/ethnicity marriages, but marital dissolution was found to be strongly associated with the race or ethnicity of the individuals in the union. The authors found that the results failed to provide evidence that interracial marriage per se is associated with an elevated risk of marital dissolution. Mixed marriages involving blacks and whites were the least stable with higher divorce rates when the wife is white. In contrast, a white husband/black wife combination was 50 percent less likely to divorce than white/white couples (Bratter and King 2008). Unfortunately, it is hard to get accurate statistics of divorce in many of the less-developed countries. As countries continue to industrialize, women gain more independence, and fewer countrymen follow traditional views, the divorce rate in other countries should continue to rise.

Conclusion

As seen throughout this chapter, there are many different aspects to intercultural marriage that need to be addressed to have a successful marriage. Marriage is something that does not necessarily come easily, but it is something that needs to be worked on. By being aware of "hot topics" that may become controversial, it is easier to handle what controversies may come.

Discussion Questions /Activities

1. The difference between ethnicity and race was briefly discussed. How do you explain the finding that interracial marriages are less stable than same-race/ethnicity marriages? Do you personally believe that interracial or inter-ethnic couples are more likely to divorce than same-race or same-ethnic couples?

2. Compare the following pairs: a) White husband/Black Wife; b) Black husband/White Wife c) White husband/Hispanic wife d) Black husband/Hispanic wife. Are any of these couples likely to be stereotyped or ostracized in various regions of the United States? Why or why not?

3. Do you believe that children of intercultural marriages (distinguish between interethnic and interracial couples) are likely to adopt the practices and ritual of the mother's or father's racial or ethnic heritage?

4. Go to YouTube and search for a brief family documentary dealing with parenting across cultures (e.g., http://www.youtube.com/watch?v=BJic9NrYk0Y&feature=related). Watch the video and see if you empathize with the experiences being discussed. Do you believe in the saying, "Birds of a feather flock together" or "Opposites attract"? Why or why not?

References

(2007). "Gender Norms and the Role of the Extended Family." Administration for Children and Families. Retrieved from http://www.acf.hhs.gov/healthymarriage/pdf/Gender_Norms.pdf.

Blee, Kathleen M. and Tickamyer, Ann R. "Racial Differences in Men's Attitudes About Women's Gender Roles." *Journal of Marriage and Family*, Vol. 57, No. 1 (Feb 1995), pp. 21–30. Published by National Council on Family Relations Article Stable. URL: http://www.jstor.org/stable/353813.

Bornstein, Marc H. *Handbook of Parenting: Social Conditions and Applied Parenting*. Vol. 4. New Jersey: Lawrence Erlbaum Associates, 2002. Print..

Bratter, J. L. and King, R. B. (2008). "'But Will It Last?' Marital Instability Among Interracial and Same-Race Couples." *Family Relations, 57*, 160–171. doi:10.1111/j.1741-3729.2008.00491.x/pdf.

Ezra, D. B. and Roer-Strier, D. (2006). "Intermarriages Between Western Women and Palestinian Men: Multidirectional Adaptation Processes." *Journal of Marriage & Family*, 68(1), 41–55.

Ezzeldine, M. L. (2006). Before the wedding: Questions for Muslims to ask before getting married. Irvine, CA: Izza Publishing.

Gupta, U. and Singh, P. (1982). "An Exploratory Study of Love and Liking and Type of Marriages". *Indian Journal of Applied Psychology, 19*, 92–97.

Gordon, M. M. (1964). *Assimilation in American life: The Role of Race, Religion, and National Origins*. New York: Oxford University Press.

Honeycutt, J. M. and Bryan, S. P. (2011). *Scripts and Communication for Relationships*. New York: Peter Lang.

Ingoldsby, Bron B. "The Latin American Family: Familism vs. Machismo." *Journal of Comparative Family Studies*. Vol. 22, Issue 1, (Spring 1991), 57–62.

Lewis, R. and Yancey, G. (1995). "Biracial Marriages in the United States: An Analysis in Variation in Family Member Support." *Sociological Spectrum*, *15*(4), 443–462.

Markus, H. R. and Kitayama, S. "Culture and Selves: A Cycle of Mutual Constitution." *Perspectives on Psychological Science*. Vol. 5, Issue 4, (July 2010), 420–430. Thousand Oaks: Sage Publications, Inc.

Myers, J. E., Madathil, J., and Tingle, L. R. (2005). "Marriage Satisfaction and Wellness in India and the United States: A Preliminary Comparison of Arranged Marriages and Marriages of Choice." *Journal of Counseling & Development, 83*, 183–190.

Neuliep, J. W. (2012). *Intercultural Communication: A Contextual Approach*. (5 ed.). Sage Publications, Inc. 345–346.

Putnam, R. D. and Campbell, D. E. (2010). *American Grace: How Religion Divides and Unites Us*. New York: Simon & Schuster.

"Ohio State University Fact Sheet." *Understanding the Hispanic Culture, HYG-5237-00*. Web. 19 Mar. 2012. http://ohioline.osu.edu/hyg-fact/5000/5237.html.

"Raising Biracial Children to Be Well Adjusted." *About.com Race Relations*. Web. 19 Mar. 2012.

Remennick, L. (2009). "Exploring Intercultural Relationships: A Study of Russian Immigrants Married to Native Israelis." *Journal of Comparative Family Studies, 40*(5), 719–738.

Romano, D. (2008). *Intercultural Marriage: Promises and Pitfalls*. Boston: Nicholas Brealey.

Schwartz, P. (2007). *Prime: Advice and Adventures on Sex, Love and the Sensuous Years*. New York: HarperCollins.

Socha, T. J. and Diggs, R. C. (1999). *Communication, Race, and Family: Exploring Communication in Black, White, and Biracial Families*. (pp. 147–150). Mahwah, NJ: Lawrence Erlbaum.

Walsh, M. and Taylor, J. (1982). "Understanding in Japanese Marriages." *Journal of Social Psychology, 118*, 67–76.

Part II

EMOTION, SPIRITUALITY, INTROSPECTION, AND SEXUAL ORIENTATION

4. Emotions and Communication in Families

By Julie Fitness & Jill Duffield

amily life is a dynamic, intricately patterned kaleidoscope of feelings and emotions, ranging from the most intense hues of anger, hate, and love to the mildest shades of irritation, hurt, and affection. There are times when the family provides an emotional refuge, a "haven in a heartless world." At other times, the family is a crucible of dark emotions that may fracture and destroy family relationships. The emotional life of the family is rich and extraordinarily complex: a complexity that derives, in part, from the sheer number of the relationships it may comprise, from adult partners/spouses to parents and children, siblings, and extended/blended family members, including aunts, uncles, grandparents, stepparents, and beyond. Every family member is a potentially powerful source of emotion for every other family member, and every family member's expression of emotion has a more or less powerful impact on other family members. Emotions, then, can be thought of as the currency of family relationships, imbuing them with meaning and importance.

> ... interpersonal communication is truly "a reciprocation of emotions—a dance of emotions."
>
> —Zajonc (1998, p. 593)

In recent years, research on emotion has flourished. However, theoretical and empirical work on emotional communication in relational contexts such as the family has been relatively sparse and scattered throughout different literatures (e.g., sociology, social, developmental and clinical psychology, and communication studies). Our aim in this [article], then, is to provide an integrative account of what we know, and do not know, about some of the most interesting and important aspects of emotion communication in families. We begin with a discussion of the functions of emotions, followed by a review of emotion in marital and sibling relationships. We then examine emotion socialization practices within the family, followed by a discussion of emotional transmission and the creation of emotion climates in the family. Finally, we discuss the role of emotion communication in adaptive family functioning and propose an agenda for future research.

The Functions Of Emotion Communication

In 1872 Darwin published a wonderfully insightful account of the origins and functions of human emotional expressions. His general thesis was that many human facial and bodily behaviors, such as smiling, snarling, and crying, are innate and universal and serve vital communicative functions. Recently, a number of emotion theorists have adopted and elaborated Darwin's functionalist perspective, arguing that we are born with several "hard-wired" emotion systems that serve crucial functions in relation to our survival and well-being (e.g., see Andersen & Guerrero, 1998a; Oatley & Jenkins, 1996). According to this perspective, the primary function of emotion is informational: Specifically, emotions inform us about the status of our needs and goals. As Tomkins (1979) noted, if we did not suffer pain when we injured ourselves, or hunger when we needed food, we would soon bleed or starve to death. In the same way, emotions ensure that we will care about our own well-being and survival and that we will be motivated to act when the need arises. Thus, anger lets us know that a goal has been thwarted and mobilizes us to deal with the obstacle; fear stops us in our tracks, alerts us to danger, and motivates us to escape; romantic love tells us that our needs are being well met and urges us on to bond with, and commit to, the source of such rewards (Gonzaga, Keltner, Londahl, & Smith, 2001).

Critically, emotions also inform *others* about what matters to us. Babies, for example, are completely dependent on caregivers to meet their needs and must communicate those needs in ways that will motivate their caregivers to respond to them. Emotional expressions serve this vital function. In particular, researchers have found that babies spontaneously produce expressions of happiness, sadness, and anger within the first few days of life, and that caregivers differentially respond to these expressions (Scharfe, 2000). A baby's cry of distress is aversive and motivates the baby's mother to attend to its needs. In turn, the comforted baby's smile rewards its mother and helps to ensure she will continue to respond to its needs. Similarly, throughout life, expressions of anger communicate goal-frustration and a desire for others to put things right; expressions of fear communicate helplessness and a desire for protection; expressions of joy communicate that one is not currently needy but rather has resources (including positive feelings) to share. This, in turn, reinforces and strengthens social bonds.

Evolutionary psychologists have noted that humans are generally much more inclined to meet the needs of close family and friends than those of acquaintances and strangers. Similarly, humans are much more likely to express their needs and vulnerabilities to kin than to strangers (Buss, 1999). This suggests that emotions are more likely to be expressed within close, communal relationships than in more business-like, exchange relationships, where people feel no particular responsibility for each other's welfare. This hypothesis has been confirmed in a program of research conducted by Margaret Clark and her colleagues (see Clark, Fitness, & Brissette, 2001, for a review). Specifically, they have found that the expression of emotion is an integral feature of communal relationships such as the family, where people feel responsible for others' needs and, in turn, expect that others will be responsive to their own needs.

Another important feature of family life that makes it such a potentially emotional context derives from the complex patterns of behavioral interdependencies that develop among family members over time (Berscheid, 1983; Berscheid & Ammazzalorzo, 2001). Many of these interdependencies are explicit (e.g., son relies on mother to drive him to school; wife relies on husband to fix the car). However, many are implicit and involve expectations that family members will follow certain "rules" (e.g., Buck, 1989; Burgoon, 1993). For example, spouses expect one another to be supportive in times of trouble; parents expect children to love and respect them; and children expect parents to treat them fairly. To the extent that family members follow the rules and meet each other's needs and expectations, life runs smoothly.

However, when explicit or implicit expectations are "interrupted" (Mandler, 1975) or violated (e.g., husband ignores wife's upset; child is rude to parent; parent favors one child over another), the scene is set for negative emotion—and often, strong negative emotion, given that we expect so much from those who are close to us. On the other hand, it is also possible for family members to exceed our expectations, as, for example, when a normally forgetful husband remembers his wife's birthday, or a child behaves well when his grandmother visits. These kinds of expectancy violations may also generate emotions; only they may be positive (e.g., joy or relief) rather than negative (e.g., anger or jealousy).

It is possible to predict which kinds of emotions an "interrupted" family member is most likely to experience if we know how he or she is cognitively appraising, or interpreting, a violated expectation with respect to its importance, cause, controllability, and so forth (see Lazarus, 1991, and Roseman, 1991, for detailed cognitive appraisal-emotion models). In their study of marital emotions, for example, Fitness and Fletcher (1993) found that both anger and hate were associated with violated expectations about how spouses should treat one another (i.e., with love and respect). However, whereas spouses' anger in response to a marital transgression was associated primarily with cognitive appraisals of partner-blame, unfairness, and predictability, spouses' hate was associated with appraisals of relative powerlessness and a perceived lack of control over the situation.

Different emotions are also associated with different motivations, or action tendencies (Frijda, 1986), with profound implications for what people actually do in emotional encounters. In Fitness and Fletcher's (1993) study, for example, episodes of marital anger were associated with urges to confront the partner and seek redress for an apparent injustice, whereas marital hate was associated with urges to escape from, or reject, the partner. On the other hand, spouses' self-reported feelings of love were associated with urges to be physically close to their partners and to express their feelings to them.

In summary, emotional expressions communicate our needs and desires to others, and family members are expected to care more than anyone else about meeting those needs and desires. Thus, more emotions are expressed in the context of the family than perhaps any other relational context. Moreover, the complex networks of interdependencies that exist within families mean that family members' expectations of one another are likely to be frequently violated. A variety of positive or negative emotional consequences may follow, depending on how family members cognitively appraise the meaning and significance of the violation. In the next section of the [article], we discuss emotion communication within one of the best studied of all familial relationships: marriage.

Emotion Communication In The Marital Relationship

Given that emotional expressions communicate information about needs and provide close others with the opportunity to meet those needs, it is not surprising that marital interaction researchers have found positive associations between marital happiness and spouses' abilities to both clearly express their own emotions and accurately identify their partners' emotions (e.g., Fletcher & Thomas, 1999; Gottman, 1994; Noller & Ruzzene, 1991). In fact, there are a number of ways in which emotional miscommunication can lead to marital distress, principally because spouses' perceptions of how well they communicate their emotions are not necessarily related to how well they *actually* communicate, especially with respect to accurately encoding, or expressing, emotions (Koerner & Fitzpatrick, 2002; see also Thomas, Fletcher, & Lange, 1997). For example, a spouse may believe she is communicating anxiety and a need for support from her partner, but her facial expression, tone of voice, and gestures may actually be sending an angry, rather than an anxious, message. Moreover, because spouses tend to reciprocate the emotions they perceive, accurately or otherwise, are being expressed to them (see Gaelick, Bodenhausen, & Wyer, 1985), her partner is likely to respond to her apparently angry message with anger, rather than with support. Or a spouse may communicate an objectively clear message of anxiety, but her partner may misinterpret her emotional expression as anger and again respond with anger. In both cases the most likely outcome is an escalating spiral of reciprocated hurt and hostility and increasing marital distress (Gottman, 1994).

Researchers have identified several factors that affect emotional communication processes and outcomes in marriage (Bradbury & Fincham, 1987; Fitness, 1996). For example, researchers have found that people in good moods tend to generously attribute the causes of conflict in their intimate relationships to relatively transient, external factors, whereas people in sad moods tend to see the conflict as a function of stable, global factors, such as the partner's personality flaws (Forgas, 1994). Chronic emotional dispositions such as depression and negative affectivity, or the tendency to experience frequent episodes of anxiety, anger, and sadness, cast a similarly gloomy pall over people's habitual ways of interpreting and responding to their spouses' behaviors (Beach & Fincham, 1994; Segrin, 1998). Ironically, depressed spouses' negative expectations and perceptions may elicit the kinds of defensive partner responses that only serve to confirm their pessimistic outlooks. Marital happiness, too, plays a major role in coloring spouses' expectations and perceptions of each other's behaviors, with distressed spouses tending to interpret their partners' behaviors in much the same way as do sad spouses (Fitness, Fletcher, & Overall, in press; Fletcher & Fincham, 1991).

Another important factor that affects emotional communication in marriage derives from spouses' relationship histories and, in particular, their early attachment relationships with caregivers. According to attachment theorists (e.g., see Bowlby, 1969; Shaver, Collins, & Clark, 1996), individuals develop schemas, or mental "working models" about what to expect from intimate relationships, based on the security of their attachment relationships in childhood. Infants develop a secure attachment style when they feel safe, loved, and accepted. This results from sensitive caregiving in which the infant's emotional signals are accurately decoded and responded to. Avoidant attachment, on the other hand, results from perceptions that the caregiver is habitually unavailable and unresponsive. Infants learn that expressing needs does not bring the comfort they desire and that they must rely on themselves in times of trouble. Finally, anxious/ambivalent attachment develops when caregivers respond inconsistently to their infants' needs. Sometimes expressing distress brings comfort; sometimes it brings punishment or no response at all. Accordingly, infants tend to become preoccupied with the caregiver and to express intense anger and anxiety when they have unmet needs in order to maximize the chances of obtaining attention and care.

Within adult romantic and marital relationships, individuals' attachment schemas influence both their own emotion communication styles and their responses to their partners' needs and expressions of emotion. Individuals with secure attachment styles, for example, are comfortable with the expression of a range of emotions and are appropriately responsive to their partners' emotional expressions (e.g., Feeney, 1999). Avoidant individuals, however, tend to discount their partners' needs or react with anger to them and to distance themselves from their partners when experiencing stress themselves (Simpson, Rholes, & Nelligan, 1992). Anxious–ambivalent individuals respond inconsistently to their partners' needs and are vigilant for signs of rejection. They also express negative emotions such as anger and jealousy more intensely and more often than secure individuals (Shaver et al., 1996).

Finally, several reliable gender differences in marital emotion communication have been identified, with women generally better than men at both accurately encoding and decoding emotions (see Noller & Ruzzene, 1991). Furthermore, women tend to express emotions like sadness and fear more frequently than men, whereas men tend to express emotions like anger and contempt more frequently than women (see Brody, 1999). In her theoretical analysis of gender and emotion, Brody claimed that men are less likely than women to express sadness and fear because such emotions signal vulnerability and a need for support. Men's roles, however, are typically associated with the exercise of power and control; thus, men who display "vulnerable" emotions tend to be evaluated more negatively and are less likely to be comforted by others. Men may react to feelings of vulnerability, then, with expressions of anger, an energizing emotion that intimidates others and may provide a feeling of control, at least in the short term (see also Clark, Pataki, & Carver, 1996; Fitness, 2001b).

Expressing contempt serves a similar function. Contempt signals superiority and serves to humiliate and shame its target (see Tomkins, 1979). The destructive nature of this emotion has been demonstrated by findings that contempt expressions in marital interactions are one of most reliable predictors of eventual marital breakdown (see Gottman, 1994). Frequently in such interactions the problem is not so much what is said but rather how it is said. For example, a spouse's sneer, or sarcastic, mocking remarks, may trigger feelings of shame in the partner, who retaliates with anger or rage (Noller & Roberts, in press; Retzinger, 1991; Scheff, 1995; Tangney, 1995). As noted previously, these kinds of escalating spirals of negative emotional expressions tend to characterize unhappy marriages, even in partnerships that span decades (Carstensen, Gottman, & Levenson, 1995).

In summary, accurate encoding and decoding of emotional expressions is a crucial feature of marital happiness. In addition, mood, relationship satisfaction, attachment style, and gender have all been identified as important influences on spouses' expressions and interpretations of emotions in the marital context. We now briefly discuss emotion and emotion communication in another important familial context: sibling relationships.

Emotion In Sibling Relationships

Sibling relationships have been described as quintessentially emotional (Bedford & Avioli, 1996). Evolutionary theorists have noted that siblings are major social allies by virtue of their relatedness (i.e., they share genes with one another); however, they are also major competitors for crucial parental resources, including time, love, and attention (Daly, Salmon, & Wilson, 1997). Sibling relationships, then, involve both cooperation and competition and may be characterized (especially in childhood) by the relatively frequent experience and expression of highly ambivalent emotions including love, resentment, and hostility (Gold, 1989; Klagsbrun, 1992).

Of all the emotions experienced by siblings, jealousy and envy tend to be regarded as prototypical (Dunn, 1988; Volling, McElwain, & Miller, 2002). Historically, however, this has not always been the case. In the 19th century, for example, jealousy-related emotions were associated with adult sexual relationships rather than with childhood ones (Stearns, 1988). In part, this was because families were typically so much larger in that era, and older children were expected to take responsibility for younger children's welfare. Today, however, families tend to be smaller and parental resources do not have to stretch as far as they once did. Children's expectations of parents, then, may be considerably higher, with constant monitoring among siblings for signs of parental favoritism. Furthermore, research suggests that a sizable majority of siblings perceive such signs of preferential treatment. One study, for example, found that 84% of 272 U.S. respondents perceived there had been parental favoritism in the family (Klagsbrun, 1992).[1]

---

1 Interestingly, just under half of these respondents regarded themselves, rather than their sibling, as the favorite. They also reported feeling considerable guilt over their favored status.

With the birth of a second child, first-borns inevitably experience decreasing amounts of attention and other resources from their parents. In response to their perceptions that the exclusive relationship they have enjoyed with their parents is under threat, first-borns may experience intense jealousy, accompanied by urges to protect their resources, grieve for what they have lost, and/or destroy their rival. These mixed emotions may be expressed in anxious, clingy behavior, depression and withdrawal, and/or outbursts of rage and hostility toward the unfortunate later-born (Dunn, 1988; Sulloway, 1996). Later-borns, on the other hand, may experience feelings of envy and resentment in relation to their older sibling(s) if they perceive they are being unjustly treated with respect to parental love and privileges (Smith, 1991). Such feelings may find their expression in behaviors intended to hurt older siblings, such as destroying their possessions and resources, including their reputations.

Sibling jealousy and envy, then, are partly an inevitable function of birth order and the redistribution of parental resources and partly an outcome of perceived parental favoritism and differential treatment. This latter factor may not be a deliberately divisive strategy by parents. In particular, the emotional disruption experienced by maritally distressed spouses may mean they become less vigilant about treating children equally (Brody, 1998). However, the effects of differential treatment have been shown to impact negatively on the disfavored child's sense of competence and self-worth (Dunn, Stocker, & Plomin, 1990) and on his or her attachment security and psychological adjustment (Sheehan & Noller, 2002).

Even so, the picture is not altogether bleak. As noted previously, siblings are as much allies as competitors, and sibling relationships may be a source of support and emotional warmth throughout life. Researchers have found, for example, that when exposed to marital conflict, some older siblings increase protective, care-giving behaviors toward younger siblings (Cummings & Smith, 1989). Similarly, Wilson and Weiss (1993) found that preschoolers who watched a suspenseful TV program with an older sibling were less frightened and liked the program more than did those who viewed alone. Warm sibling relationships have also been identified as powerful contexts for the development of trust, self-disclosure skills, and socioemotional understanding (Howe, Aquan-Assee, Bukowski, Lehoux, & Rinaldi, 2001). There is still much to learn, however, about how and when different emotions are experienced and expressed within sibling relationships, for example, the conditions in which a younger child might admire, rather than envy, his or her older sibling. We also know little about how emotions and emotional expressions might differ depending on the age, birth order, and gender composition of the sibling (and frequently today, stepsibling) relationship.

In summary, sibling relationships are characterized, in part, by the expression of negative emotions such as jealousy and envy as a function of their intrinsically competitive nature. However, siblings may also form strong attachment bonds and experience highly positive emotions toward one another. In the next section, we consider an important facet of emotional communication between parents and children: the socialization of emotion.

SOCIALIZING EMOTION: LEARNING EMOTION RULES IN THE FAMILY

Babies' abilities to express and recognize certain basic emotion expressions appear to be innate and play an essential role in their survival (Oatley & Jenkins, 1996). Similarly, parents appear to be generally well equipped to understand and respond appropriately to their baby's communications (e.g., Izard, 1991; Scharfe, 2000). However, as infants grow and develop motor and language skills, parents spend an increasing amount of time teaching their children the rules of emotional expression, according to the norms of their own family backgrounds and of the wider culture (Buck, 1989).

As might be expected, given the vagaries of parents' own emotional histories, parents display different orientations toward feeling, managing, and talking about emotions with their children (Planalp, 1999). Two general orientations, in particular, have been identified (though there are sure to be others): emotion coaching and dismissing (Gottman, Katz, & Hooven, 1996). The emotion coaching orientation is associated with a parental "meta-emotion philosophy" that endorses family members' feelings as valid and important. Parents holding this philosophy actively teach children about the causes, features, and consequences of emotions and help them to regulate and deal constructively with difficult emotions such as anger, fear, and sadness. The dismissing orientation, on the other hand, is associated with a meta-emotion philosophy that regards emotions like anger, fear, and sadness as dangerous and/or unimportant, to be changed (or even punished) by parents as quickly as possible.[2]

Of course, emotion socialization is a reciprocal process. Thus, although some children have calm, agreeable temperaments and may be easily coached, others may have more difficult temperaments; they may be shy, anxious, irritable, or emotionally labile (Kagan, 1984; Lytton, 1990). These children may pose difficulties for parents who have different temperaments or emotion orientations and who cannot understand, appreciate, or meet their children's (or indeed, stepchildren's) emotional needs. Furthermore, parents within the same family do not necessarily hold the same meta-emotion philosophy. One parent, for example, may favor an accepting, empathic approach to the expression of emotions, whereas the other disapproves of the expression of any emotion other than resolute cheerfulness. These conflicting orientations may only become apparent (or problematic) after their first child is born. Conflict may also arise when two families with different metaemotion philosophies are blended as a result of parental remarriage, although little is known about the manifestation and/or outcomes of these kinds of conflicts.

There is, however, a wealth of evidence confirming the beneficial effects of parental emotion coaching on children's emotion understanding, regulation, and socioemotional competence. Harris (2000), for example, noted that conversations about emotions help children to make sense of their feelings and understand the implications of emotional events (see also Dunn, Brown, & Maguire, 1995). Parents' meta-emotion philosophies are also important in the development of parent–child attachment relationships (Denham, 1998). In a secure attachment relationship, children learn that expressing their emotions elicits parental attention to their needs. Thus, securely attached children tend to be emotionally expressive and are able to both understand and regulate their own and others' emotions (Feeney & Noller, 1996; Scharfe, 2000). These skills are valued and promoted by parents with an emotion coaching philosophy. Conversely, parents with insecure attachment styles tend to endorse emotion socialization practices in line with their own experiences and expectations of attachment relationships. Thus, for example, Magai (1999) found that parents with fearful attachment styles were more likely than other kinds of parents to physically punish and shame their children for expressing their needs, just as they were themselves shamed as children. Parents with an avoidant style, on the other hand, may discourage or dismiss children's emotional expressions altogether.

Gender, too, has an important impact on emotion socialization practices. The results of one longitudinal study found that mothers talked more about emotions, and about a greater variety of emotions, to their daughters than to their sons. By the age of 5 years, the girls talked more than the boys about a variety of emotions and initiated more emotion-related discussions (Kuebli, Butler, & Fivush, 1995). Similarly, Dunn, Bretherton, and Munn (1987) found that mothers used fewer emotion words when

---

2   See also Tomkins' (1979) insightful discussion of humanistic versus normative parental emotion ideologies.

interacting with their 18–to 24-month-old sons than with their same-aged daughters. No doubt this kind of emotion coaching is at least partly responsible for women's abilities to accurately express and identify emotions in their adult relationships (Noller & Ruzzene, 1991).

Our prior observation that men express more anger and contempt in marital interactions than do women, who express more sadness and fear, may also derive from early socialization practices. Brody (1999) noted that boys are typically socialized to behave more aggressively than girls and to control, rather than do express, their feelings. Anger, however, is the exception, with its expression attended to in boys, but ignored or punished in girls. Boys are also rewarded for behaviors that denote dominance (including expressions of contempt), and more aggressive boys are rated as more likable by teachers and peers. Girls, on the other hand, are encouraged to express more nurturing, sensitive emotions such as empathy and cheerfulness, in preparation, presumably, for their future roles as caregivers.

Even so, there are some interesting differences between the socialization practices of mothers and fathers that warrant closer investigation. For example, Parke and McDowell (1998) argued that whereas emotional understanding may be learned in mother–child conversations, father–child exchanges may teach children how to regulate levels of arousal in the context of physical play. Importantly, Brody (1999) reported that when fathers are more involved in child care, their daughters express relatively less emotional vulnerability and become more competent and aggressive in comparison to other daughters. Conversely, their sons express relatively more vulnerability and become less competitive and aggressive in comparison to other sons. This research underscores the important and largely unexplored role for fathers in developing children's socioemotional competence.

It is also important to consider the wider cultural context when exploring emotion socialization practices. Much of the research discussed in this [article] has been conducted with middle-class American families. However, different subcultures (e.g., separated by neighborhoods, ethnicities, or socioeconomic factors) may have different emotion rules and orientations. Miller and Sperry (1987), for example, found that mothers in a tough, working-class neighborhood valued anger in their daughters and encouraged rather than suppressed it because it supported goals of self-protection and motivated them to defend themselves.

Different cultures, too, have different emotion rules depending on the relative importance they place on the self versus the group (e.g., Planalp & Fitness, 1999; Triandis, 1994). In so-called collectivist cultures (e.g., Japan, China, and Korea) family harmony is prized and individual needs are subordinated to the needs of others. Accordingly, the open expression of anger is discouraged because it disrupts social relationships and puts individual needs ahead of group needs. Conversely, in so-called individualist cultures (e.g., North America), independence and individual achievement are prized and the expression of anger is encouraged in the pursuit of individual needs and goals. These cultural differences were demonstrated in a study that found U.S. children showed much more anger and aggression in symbolic play than did Japanese children (Zahn-Waxler et al., 1996). In addition, U.S. mothers encouraged their children's open expression of emotions, whereas Japanese mothers fostered sensitivity to other children's emotional needs (see also Eisenberg, Liew, & Pidada's, 2001, study of emotional expressiveness in Indonesian families and Yang & Rosenblatt's, 2001, analysis of the role of shame in Korean families).

In summary, some parents actively coach their children about emotions and help them develop sophisticated understandings of their own and others' emotional lives, whereas other parents discourage or even punish the expression of emotions. Clearly, there is still much to learn about other styles and philosophies of emotion within the family and about the content and function of emotion rules according to gender, family history, and cultural differences. In the next section, we discuss the dynamics of emotion communication within the family and the creation of emotional family climates.

The Dynamics Of Emotion Communication Within The Family

Families are dynamic systems comprising complex patterns of interdependencies and expectations. Every family member, then, is affected by what happens to every other member. This has important implications for emotion communication within the family. For example, highly interdependent relationship contexts provide opportunities for participants to experience the same emotions at the same time ("emotional co-incidence"), such as when parents are jointly thrilled over a child's success (Planalp, 1999). In such circumstances, family members' needs and goals are aligned, expectations are exceeded, and shared positive emotions create feelings of group cohesion and closeness. However, emotion sharing is not always a positive experience. For example, when one spouse is depressed, the degree to which the couple is emotionally close is a risk factor for the other spouse also becoming depressed (Tower & Kasl, 1995). In close relationships, people feel responsible for meeting each other's needs; however, the partner of a depressed spouse may well become disheartened by his/her inability to relieve his/her spouse's chronic neediness. The potency and contagiousness of negative emotions were also demonstrated by Thompson and Bolger (1999), who found that depression in one partner reduces happiness in the other, rather than the other way around (see also Baumeister, Bratslavsky, Finkenauer, & Vohs, 2001).

Parental depression also has a variety of negative effects on children (Segrin, 1998; Zahn-Waxler, 2000). Depressed parents tend to be less affectionate toward their children, feel more guilt and resentment toward them, and experience more difficulty in communicating with them (Brody, 1998). Not surprisingly, such children tend to exhibit behavioral problems that may then aggravate their parents' depression. Even transient negative moods may be passed onto children, only to rebound on parents. For example, parents in bad moods may pay selective attention to their children's undesirable behaviors and interpret them in ways that aggravate the situation ("he is doing this deliberately to annoy me"; Jouriles & O'Leary, 1990). Children are thus more likely to be punished, with their angry reactions exacerbating parental negativity.

Parental anger has a particularly negative impact on children, with the results of several studies suggesting that children exposed to overt and intense displays of parental anger are at risk for behavioral problems such as aggression, anxiety, and depression (Grych & Fincham, 1990; Jenkins & Smith, 1991). These and other researchers have suggested that parental anger and children's emotional dysregulation may be linked, in part, because angry parents model dysfunctional ways of behaving and impart a hostile attributional style to their children. Boyum and Parke (1995), for example, observed parental emotional expressions during a family dinner and found that negative emotional exchanges between parents were associated with teacher ratings of children's verbal aggression. In effect, these children appeared to be acquiring anger scripts comprising such beliefs as "if I feel threatened, I should attack"; "if something bad happens, someone else is always to blame" (see also Fehr & Baldwin, 1996; Fitness, 1996).

Emotions, then, may cascade through families and create emotional atmospheres, or climates, that affect the day-to-day feelings and functioning of family members. Belsky, Youngblade, Rovine, and Volling (1991), for example, reported that as men became more unhappy in their marriages, they became more negative in their interactions with their children. Their children, in turn, reciprocated the negative emotions that were being expressed to them, which exacerbated their fathers' dissatisfaction with parenting and the marital relationship. Thus, fathers withdrew further from their wives and children, which exacerbated their wives' and children's distress. Given that in such circumstances siblings may be more likely to fight with one another, which further upsets their parents (Brody, 1998), it is not difficult to imagine how a whole family may become immersed in a climate of hostility and unhappiness.

There are many other kinds of emotional family climates, though few have been well studied. One kind that has been extensively investigated is the so-called high "EE" (expressed emotion) family climate, characterized by high levels of negative emotional expression, including criticism, hostility, and intrusiveness (Blechman, 1990). This kind of volatile, aggressive emotional climate is especially detrimental to mentally ill (particularly schizophrenic) patients, who tend to relapse quickly after returning home (see Kavanagh et al., 1997). In contrast, other families are distinguished by a climate of coldness and emotional disengagement; others again may be dominated by a highly controlling family member who terrorizes the rest of the family, effectively creating a climate of fear (e.g., see Dutton, 1998). On the other hand, Blechman (1990) has documented the existence of very positive emotional family climates characterized by high levels of mutual trust, affection, and warmth. Such nurturing family climates have been found to promote children's empathy for others, including their siblings (Brody, 1998; Zahn-Waxler, 2000).

One interesting aspect of positive family climates concerns the role of women in creating and maintaining them. Some researchers have argued that women still do the bulk of nurturing "emotion work" in the family by supporting and meeting the emotional needs of their spouses and children (DeVault, 1999; Hochschild, 1979). Studies of emotional transmission in the family have demonstrated the existence of an emotional hierarchy, with men's emotions having the most impact on family members overall (Larson & Richards, 1994). This implies that, although the family is a communal context in which family members feel mutually responsible for meeting each other's needs, it is women who feel most responsible for meeting the needs of their spouses and children (see also Brody, 1999). Thus, women's emotional expressions tend to revolve around empathic responding to others' needs, whereas men's emotional expressions tend to be associated with asserting their dominance in the family (Roberts & Krokoff, 1990).

Other research supporting this interpretation comes from studies of women's mediational roles in the family. Seery and Crowley (2000), for example, noted that women are frequently responsible for nurturing the relationship between fathers and children. This involves offering suggestions for father–child activities, praising fathers for engaging with their children, and maintaining positive images of fathers to their children. Women may also initiate peace-keeping strategies when fathers and children are unhappy with one another and encourage reconciliation. However, it is important to note that family structures, norms, and gender/power relations are undergoing accelerated change, with expanding roles for men as family "emotion workers" in their own right. In particular, Rohner and Veneziano (2001) noted that despite the widespread assumption that fathers express less affection toward children than do mothers, there is a growing body of literature showing that father love is as important as mother love in child outcomes, although the expression of such love (e.g., in shared activities) may not fit the traditional feminine model (see Baumeister & Sommer, 1997). Amato (1994) also found that perceived closeness to fathers for both sons and daughters made a unique contribution, over and above perceived closeness to mother, to adults' happiness and psychological well-being.

In summary, family emotion communication patterns are dynamically interwoven. Both positive and negative emotions are transmitted among family members in ways that affect the wellbeing of all. Families also develop distinctive emotional climates, although there is much to be learned about their origins and features. We now move on to discuss the role of emotion communication in adaptive family functioning.

Emotion Communication And Adaptive Family Functioning

According to Blechman (1990), adaptive family functioning is characterized by the open exchange of information about feelings and emotions, the frequent expression of positive emotions, and the ability to monitor and regulate the expression of emotions. There is a growing amount of evidence to support each of these assertions. For example, researchers have found that spouses generally regard emotional expressiveness as both positive and desirable in marriage, and that more emotionally expressive spouses tend to have happier partners (Feeney, 1999; Huston & Houts, 1998). However, it is the ratio of positive to negative emotional expression that counts, with spouses in long-term, happy marriages expressing negative emotions like anger and sadness to one another much less frequently than they express affection and good humor (Carstensen et al., 1995).

Open exchange of information about feelings and emotions between parents and children has also been implicated in children's health and happiness. Berenbaum and James (1994) found that people who reported having grown up in families where the open expression of emotions was discouraged showed higher levels of alexithymia, a term describing an inability to identify and talk about one's emotions. This, in turn, has been associated with health and adjustment problems in adulthood. Again, however, it is the frequent expression of positive emotions that is most crucial factor for adaptive functioning. As Cummings and Davies (1996) noted, it is not just the absence of fear and anger in children's lives that leads to optimal development, but the presence of love, joy, and contentment that allows children to feel emotionally secure (see also Halberstadt, Crisp, & Eaton, 1999).

Finally, there is a growing body of research attesting to the importance of emotion regulation in adaptive family functioning. In particular, happy spouses have been found to be more likely to inhibit their impulses to react destructively when their partners express anger and to try to respond instead in a conciliatory manner (e.g., Carstensen et al., 1995; Rusbult, Bissonnette, Arriaga, & Cox, 1998). Similarly, Fitness and Fletcher (1993) found spouses reported making efforts to control the expression of anger in the interests of marital harmony (see also Fehr & Baldwin, 1996). Children, too, who are taught by their parents how to effectively regulate their emotions display greater socioemotional competence and have more positive relationships with parents, siblings, and peers (Denham, 1998; Planalp, 1999).

This emphasis on the role of open, positive emotion expression and emotion regulation in adaptive family functioning is echoed in the growing literatures on emotional competence (e.g., Eisenberg, Cumberland, & Spinrad, 1998; Saarni, 2001) and emotional intelligence (e.g., Fitness, 2001b). Typical definitions of these closely related constructs include such features as the ability to accurately encode and decode emotions, the ability to understand the meanings of emotions and to be able to respond appropriately to them, and the ability to effectively manage and regulate both one's own and others' emotions. This raises the question of whether there might be such an entity as the emotionally intelligent family and what kinds of behaviors it might exhibit.

The work of marital and family researchers provides some clues. For example, Gottman (1998) reported that marriages become distressed when spouses become too busy to respond fully or appropriately to one another's needs. In the process of turning away from one another, they also neglect to listen to one another, fail to make "cognitive room" for each other, rarely soothe and comfort one another, and are more likely to express anger and contempt rather than spontaneous admiration and affection, in their interactions with one another (see also Huston, Caughlin, Houts, Smith, & George, 2001). This suggests that one distinctive feature of the emotionally intelligent family might be what Gottman and Levenson (2002) referred to as a culture of appreciation, whereby family members regard one another with fondness and respect; accept and respond to the emotional expression of one another's needs; and cultivate interpersonal warmth, compassion, and emotional connectedness with one another (see also Andersen & Guerrero, 1998b).

It is important to note, however, that positive emotions are not generated automatically in the absence of negative emotions. As Berscheid (1983) noted, relationships in which people are well meshed and meeting each other's needs on a day-to-day basis tend to be emotionally tranquil and may even be perceived as boring. It is not until an interruption to the well-meshed routine occurs that individuals pay attention and the scene is set for emotion. Generating positive emotions in the family, then, requires making active efforts to exceed each other's expectations; planning and delivering pleasant surprises, facilitating each other's hopes and plans, and helping each other to deal with life's problems. There is also an important role for positive emotions like interest and excitement to play in enhancing family functioning (e.g., Aron, Normans, Aron, McKenna, & Heyman, 2000; Gonzaga et al., 2001). Sharing novel and exciting activities generates feelings of cohesion and mutual pleasure and strengthens social bonds. In this sense, families that play together may well stay together.

In summary, adaptive family functioning involves the open exchange of emotions, the frequent expression of positive emotions, and the ability to effectively regulate and manage emotions. Emotionally intelligent families may be those in which family members feel validated and embraced within a culture of mutual regard. In the final section, we revisit some earlier themes and suggest further avenues for future research.

AGENDA FOR FUTURE RESEARCH

As noted in the introduction, the study of emotion communication in families has been relatively sparse. There are still large gaps in our understanding of how different kinds of emotions are communicated and miscommunicated in families, for what purposes, and with what outcomes. In addition, much of the research conducted so far has focused on dyads (i.e., spouses, or parents and children, or siblings), rather than on the family system as a whole (Duck, 1992). In researchers' defense, it should be noted that although the "family as a system" metaphor is a powerful one (Reis, Collins, & Berscheid, 2000), the scientific study of such complex patterns of interdependent relationships poses some extraordinary methodological (and ethical) challenges. It is important to acknowledge, though, that the emotional functioning of the family overall is not a simple function of the sum of its parts.

Another distinctive feature of much of the research on this topic to date has been its relatively atheoretical stance, particularly with respect to the dynamic and functional features of emotion within the family context. Certainly, interdependence theory provides a powerful framework for understanding the conditions under which emotions may arise within familial interactions. However, this theory takes us only part of the way. In particular, it does not tell us what family members' expectations of one another are, how different kinds of emotions (e.g., anger versus contempt) are generated, or what is the impact of individual differences and contextual factors on familial emotion rules and orientations.

Social–cognitive researchers have made some progress in mapping the structural features of laypeople's understandings of the causes and consequences of interpersonal emotions such as love, anger, hate, and jealousy (Fitness, 1996). They have found, for example, that individuals hold beliefs about the typical causes of angry marital interactions (e.g., unfair partner behaviors) and the typical motivations (e.g., the urge to yell) and behaviors (e.g., retaliatory insults and/or apologies) that are likely to occur as the drama of what has been described as the "anger script" unfolds over time (Fitness, 2001a; see also Fehr, Baldwin, Collins, Patterson, & Benditt, 1999). Whether accurate or not, these understandings about the whys and wherefores of emotions are important in that they are held to drive people's expectations, perceptions, and memories of emotional interactions. We still know little, however, about people's theories of the causes and consequences of specific emotions in the context of different family relationships, such as those between siblings, and of the ways in which such understandings impact on people's cognitions, motivations, and behaviors over time.

Another fascinating area about which we still know little concerns the ways in which people use their emotion knowledge strategically within the context of the family to achieve their goals. Clark et al. (1996), for example, reviewed a body of evidence showing that individuals may deliberately express sadness in order to obtain sympathy and support, feign anger in order to intimidate others and procure obedience, and suppress anger and/or feign happiness in order to appear more likable or ingratiate themselves to others. Similarly, people may feign or exaggerate hurt feelings in order to make another feel guilty, an emotional state that tends to motivate compliance with the hurt person's wishes (Vangelisti & Sprague, 1998). These kinds of strategic emotion expressions are doubtless an important aspect of emotional interactions in the family, ranging from mild, everyday manipulations to garner sympathy or persuade children to do their homework, to full-scale "emotional blackmail," such as when a parent manipulates a grown child through hurt and guilt to put the parent's interests first, regardless of the cost.

Finally, there is much we do not know about the dynamics of emotional communication with respect to family members' ongoing feelings and motivations. Again, there is a need for strong theory to help us ask the right questions about these complex processes. One sociological approach with the potential to help illuminate such dynamics is Kemper's power/status model of emotions in social interactions (e.g., Kemper, 1984). According to this model, there are two, basic dimensions underlying every human interaction: power (feelings of control, dominance) and status (feelings of worthiness, esteem, holding resources). Every relational exchange takes place along these two dimensions, with emotions signaling shifts in power/status dynamics.

To illustrate, a perceived loss of power (e.g., when a father punishes his son) triggers fear and anxiety; gaining power (e.g., when a daughter wins an argument with her mother) triggers feelings of pleasure and triumph. Gaining status (e.g., when a boy invites his younger brother to the movies) elicits the happiness that comes from feeling that one belongs and is a valued relationship partner. However, losing status (e.g., when a child must present a bad report card to his parents) elicits emotions such as shame (if the child holds himself to blame), depression (if the child feels helpless to change the situation), or even anger (if the child blames the teacher or his squabbling parents). Furthermore, within the family, as in other kinds of relational contexts, individuals' power and status are frequently signaled by others, as when a parent's praise confers status and triggers warm feelings of pride, or when a parent's contemptuous remark depletes a child's status and triggers feelings of shame (Tomkins, 1979).

One of the strengths of this theory is that it accounts for a range of subtle feeling states that often escape attention in the emotion literature, for example, the warm feelings that a child's smile may elicit (signaling a gain in status); the heart-sinking feeling that a parent's cold glance may elicit (signaling loss of status); the tense, stomach-tied-in-knots feeling that an older brother's teasing may elicit (signaling loss of power); the pleasant rush of blood to the head when one's older brother is punished for his behavior (signaling a gain of power). It is within these shifting patterns of give and take, power and status, that feelings and emotions are experienced and exchanged among family members.

It also seems likely that these feeling states are fundamental, in the sense of being hard-wired and having an evolutionary history. It is critical for humans, who are so socially interdependent, to be constantly monitoring their social environments for information about how they are doing, relative to others (i.e., how much power/ control do they have, how much do others appear to care about whether they live or die). Feelings of being (figuratively speaking) "one-up" or "one-down," resource rich or resource poor, provide such information and motivate people to take particular kinds of action (e.g., retaliation, ingratiation, escape, etc). Accordingly, we believe that exploring family members' ongoing feelings about their power and status, relative to each other, may provide some fascinating insights into the complex dynamics of both spontaneous and strategically motivated emotion communication within the family context.

Of course, although it is relatively easy to identify interesting and unexplored research topics in this field, choosing appropriate methodologies is more difficult and requires considerable ingenuity and resourcefulness. No doubt, laboratory-based observational studies will continue to be important, as will more naturalistic observations in different kinds of familial contexts. The use of diaries, interviews, surveys, and experimental work also have valuable contributions to make. The most important point, however, is that the choice of method is theoretically driven so that with each piece of the puzzle we uncover, we obtain a richer, more coherent, and more integrated picture of emotion communication processes and functions within family life.

CONCLUSION

Families are profoundly emotional contexts. When we express our emotions within the family, we expose our deepest needs and vulnerabilities. In turn, the response of family members to the expression of our emotions colors our perceptions and beliefs about ourselves and others and helps form the template from which we, in turn, respond to others' needs. Throughout this [article], we have stressed the potentially adaptive nature of emotions and the functions they serve in informing ourselves and others about our needs. Certainly, emotions can run amok and motivate dysfunctional or destructive behaviors. Nevertheless, emotions always tell us something important about who we are and what we care about, and nowhere is this informational function more important than in the context of the family.

Clearly, there is still much to discover about the processes involved in the communication of family emotion. However, given the rapidly growing scholarly interest in this topic, we are optimistic about the progress that will be achieved, particularly if researchers take a theoretically informed and integrative approach to their empirical work. Above all, it is our belief that understanding, supporting, and encouraging emotionally adaptive family functioning will ultimately be to the benefit of us all.

REFERENCES

Amato, P. R. (1994). Father-child relations, mother-child relations, and offspring psychological wellbeing in adulthood. *Journal of Marriage and the Family, 56*, 1031–1042.

Andersen, P., & Guerrero, L. K. (1998a). Principles of communication and emotion in social interaction. In P. Andersen & L. Guerrero (Eds.), *Handbook of communication and emotion* (pp. 49–96). New York: Academic Press.

Andersen, P., & Guerrero, L. K. (1998b). The bright side of relational communication: Interpersonal warmth as a social emotion. In P. Andersen & L. K. Guerrero (Eds.), *Handbook of communication and emotion* (pp. 303–329). New York: Academic Press.

Aron, A., Norman, C., Aron, E., McKenna, C., & Heyman R. (2000). Couples' shared participation in novel and arousing activities and experienced relationship quality. *Journal of Personality and Social Psychology, 78*, 273–284.

Baumeister, R., Bratslavsky, E., Finkenauer, C., & Vohs, K. (2001). Bad is stronger than good. *Review of General Psychology, 5*, 323–370.

Baumeister, R., & Sommer, K. (1997). What do men want? Gender differences and two spheres of belongingness. *Psychological Bulletin, 122*, 38–44.

Beach, S., & Fincham, F. (1994). Toward an integrated model of negative affectivity in marriage. In S. Johnson & L. Greenberg (Eds.), *The heart of the matter: Perspectives on emotion in marital therapy* (pp. 227–255). New York: Brunner/Mazel.

Bedford, V. H., & Avioli, P. S. (1996). Affect and sibling relationships in adulthood. In C. Magai & S. McFadden (Eds.), *Handbook of emotion, adult development, and aging* (pp. 207–225). New York: Academic Press.

Belsky, J., Youngblade, L., Rovine, M., & Volling, B. (1991). Patterns of marital change and parent-child interaction. *Journal of Marriage and the Family, 53*, 487–498.

Berenbaum, H., & James, T. (1994). Correlates and retrospectively reported antecedents of alexithymia. *Psychosomatic Medicine, 56*, 353–359.

Berscheid, E. (1983). Emotion. In H. H. Kelley, E. Berscheid, A. Christensen, J. H. Harvey, T. L. Huston, G. Levinger, E. McClintock, L. A. Peplau, & D. R. Peterson (Eds.), *Close relationships* (pp. 110–168). New York: Freeman.

Berscheid, E., & Ammazzalorso, H. (2001). Emotional experience in close relationships. In G. J. O. Fletcher & M. S. Clark (Eds.), *Blackwell handbook of social psychology: Interpersonal processes* (pp. 308–330). Malden, MA: Blackwell.

Blechman, E. A. (1990). A new look at emotions and the family: A model of effective family communication. In E. Blechman (Ed.), *Emotions and the family* (pp. 201–224). Hillsdale, NJ: Lawrence Erlbaum Associates.

Bowlby, J. (1969). *Attachment and loss.* New York: Basic Books.

Boyum, L. A., & Parke, R. D. (1995). The role of family emotional expressiveness in the development of children's social competence. *Journal of Marriage and the Family, 57*, 593–608.

Bradbury, T. N., & Fincham, F. D. (1987). Affect and cognition in close relationships: Toward an integrative model. *Cognition and Emotion, 1*, 59–87.

Brody, G. H. (1998). Sibling relationship quality: Its causes and consequences. *Annual Review of Psychology, 49*, 1–24.

Brody, L. (1999). *Gender, emotion, and the family.* MA: Harvard University Press.

Buck, R. (1989). Emotional communication in personal relationships. In C. Hendrick (Ed.), *Review of personality and social psychology, Vol. 10: Close relationships* (pp. 144–163). Newbury Park. CA: Sage.

Burgoon, J. (1993). Interpersonal expectations, expectancy violations, and emotional communication. *Journal of Language and Social Psychology, 12*, 30–48.

Buss, D. (1999). *Evolutionary psychology: The new science of the mind.* Boston, MA: Allyn & Bacon.

Carstensen, L. L., Gottman, J. M., & Levenson, R. W. (1995). Emotional behavior in long-term marriage. *Psychology and Aging, 10*, 140–149.

Clark, M. S., Fitness, J., & Brissette, I. (2001). Understanding people's perceptions of relationships is crucial to understanding their emotional lives. In G. J. O. Fletcher & M. S. Clark (Eds.), *Blackwell handbook of social psychology: Interpersonal processes* (pp. 253–278). Malden, MA: Blackwell.

Clark, M. S., Pataki, S. P., & Carver, V. H. (1996). Some thoughts and findings on self-presentation of emotions in relationships. In G. J. O. Fletcher & J. Fitness (Eds.), *Knowledge structures in close relationships: A social psychological approach* (pp. 247–274). Mahwah, NJ: Lawrence Erlbaum Associates.

Cummings, E. M., & Davies, P. T. (1996). Emotional security as a regulatory process in normal development and the development of psychopathology. *Development and Psychopathology, 8,* 123–139.

Cummings, E. M., & Smith, D. (1989). The impact of anger between adults on siblings' emotions and social behavior. *Journal of Child Psychology and Psychiatry, 25,* 63–74.

Daly, M., Salmon, C., & Wilson, M. (1997). Kinship: The conceptual hole in psychological studies of social cognition and close relationships. In J. Simpson & D. Kenrick (Eds.), *Evolutionary social psychology* (pp. 265–296). Mahwah, NJ: Lawrence Erlbaum Associates.

Darwin, C. (1872/1965). *The expression of the emotions in man and animals.* Chicago: University of Chicago Press.

Denham, S. A. (1998). *Emotional development in young children.* New York: Guilford Press.

DeVault, M. (1999). Comfort and struggle: Emotion work in family life. *Annals of the American Academy of Political and Social Science, 561,* 52–63.

Duck, S. (1992). *Human relationships.* Newbury Park, CA: Sage.

Dunn, J. (1988). *The beginnings of social understanding.* MA: Harvard University Press.

Dunn, J., Bretherton, I., & Munn, P. (1987). Conversations about feeling states between mothers and their young children. *Developmental Psychology, 11,* 107–123.

Dunn, J., Brown, J. R., & Maguire, M. (1995). The development of children's moral sensibility: Individual differences and emotion understanding. *Developmental Psychology, 31,* 649–659.

Dunn, J., Stocker, C., & Plomin, R. (1990). Nonshared experiences within the family: Correlates of behavioral problems in middle childhood. *Development and Psychopathology, 2,* 113–126.

Dutton, D. G. (1998). *The abusive personality.* New York: Guilford Press.

Eisenberg, N., Cumberland, A., & Spinrad, T. (1998). Parental socialization of emotions. *Psychological Inquiry, 9,* 241–273.

Eisenberg, N., Liew, J., & Pidada, S. (2001). The relations of parental emotional expressivity with quality of Indonesian children's social functioning. *Emotion, 1,* 116–136.

Feeney, J. (1999). Adult attachment, emotional control, and marital satisfaction. *Personal Relationships, 6,* 169–185.

Feeney, J., & Noller, P. (1996). *Adult attachment.* Thousand Oaks, CA: Sage.

Fehr, B., & Baldwin, M. (1996). Prototype and script analyses of laypeople's knowledge of anger. In G. J. O. Fletcher & J. Fitness (Eds.), *Knowledge structures in close relationships: A social psychological approach* (pp. 219–245). Mahwah, NJ: Lawrence Erlbaum Associates.

Fehr, B., Baldwin, M., Collins, L., Patterson, S., & Benditt, R. (1999). Anger in close relationships: An interpersonal script analysis. *Personality and Social Psychology Bulletin, 25,* 299–312.

Fitness, J. (1996). Emotion knowledge structures in close relationships. In G. J. O. Fletcher & J. Fitness (Eds.), *Knowledge structures in close relationships: A social psychological approach* (pp. 195–217). Mahwah, NJ: Lawrence Erlbaum Associates.

Fitness, J. (2001a). Betrayal, rejection, revenge, and forgiveness: An interpersonal script approach. In M. Leary (Ed.), *Interpersonal rejection* (pp. 73–103). New York: Oxford University Press.

Fitness, J. (2001b). Emotional intelligence in intimate relationships. In J. Ciarrochi, J. Forgas, & J. Mayer (Eds.), *Emotional intelligence in everyday life: A scientific inquiry* (pp. 98–112). Philadelphia, PA: Psychology Press.

Fitness, J., & Fletcher, G. J. O. (1993). Love, hate, anger and jealousy in close relationships: A prototype and cognitive appraisal analysis. *Journal of Personality and Social Psychology, 65,* 942–958.

Fitness, J., Fletcher, G. J. O., & Overall, N. (in press). Attraction and intimate relationships. In J. Cooper & M. Hogg (Eds.), *Handbook of social psychology*. Thousand Oaks, CA: Sage.

Fletcher, G. J. O., & Fincham, F. D. (1991). Attribution processes in close relationships. In G. J. O. Fletcher & F. D. Fincham (Eds.), *Cognition in close relationships* (pp. 7–35). Hillsdale, NJ: Lawrence Erlbaum Associates.

Fletcher, G. J. O., & Thomas, G. (1999). Behavior and on-line cognition in marital interaction. *Personal Relationships, 7,* 111–130.

Forgas, J. P. (1994). Sad and guilty? Affective influences on the explanation of conflict episodes. *Journal of Personality and Social Psychology, 66,* 56–68.

Frijda, N. (1986). *The emotions.* New York: Cambridge University Press.

Gaelick, L., Bodenhausen, G., & Wyer, R. S. (1985). Emotional communication in close relationships. *Journal of Personality and Social Psychology, 49,* 1246–1265.

Gold, D. T. (1989). Sibling relationships in old age: A typology. *International Journal of Aging and Human Development, 28,* 37–51.

Gonzaga, G. C., Keltner, D., Londahl, E. A., & Smith, M. D. (2001). Love and the commitment problem in romantic relations and friendship. *Journal of Personality and Social Psychology, 81,* 247–262.

Gottman, J. M. (1994). *What predicts divorce? The relationship between marital processes and marital outcomes.* Hillsdale, NJ: Erlbaum.

Gottman, M. (1998). Psychology and the study of marital processes. *Annual Review of Psychology, 49,* 169–197.

Gottman, J. M., Katz, L. F., & Hooven, C. (1996). Parental meta-emotion philosophy and the emotional life of families: Theoretical models and preliminary data. *Journal of Family Psychology, 10,* 243–268.

Gottman, J. M., & Levenson, R. W. (2002). A two-factor model for predicting when a couple will divorce: Exploratory analyses using 14-year longitudinal data. *Family Process, 41,* 83–110.

Grych, J. H., & Fincham, F. D. (1990). Marital conflict and children's adjustment: A cognitive-contextual framework. *Psychological Bulletin, 108,* 267–290.

Halberstadt, A. G., Crisp, V. W., & Eaton, K. L. (1999). Family expressiveness: A retrospective and new directions for research. In P. Philippot, R. S. Feldman, & E. Coats (Eds.), *The social context of nonverbal behavior* (pp. 109–155). New York: Cambridge University Press.

Harris, P. (2000). Understanding emotion. In M. Lewis & J. Haviland-Jones (Eds.), *Handbook of emotions* (2nd ed., pp. 281–292). New York: Guilford Press.

Hochschild, A. (1979). Emotion work, feeling rules, and social structure. *American Journal of Sociology, 85,* 551–575.

Howe, N., Aquan-Assee, J., Bukowski, W., Lehoux, P., & Rinaldi, C. (2001). Siblings as confidants: Emotional understanding, relationship warmth, and sibling self-disclosure. *Social Development, 10,* 439–454.

Huston, T. L., Caughlin, J. P., Houts, R. M., Smith, S. E., & George, L. J. (2001). The connubial crucible: Newlywed years as predictors of marital delight, distress, and divorce. *Journal of Personality and Social Psychology, 80,* 237–252.

Huston, T., & Houts, R. (1998). The psychological infrastructure of courtship and marriage: The role of personality and compatibility in romantic relationships. In T. Bradbury (Ed.), *The developmental course of marital dysfunction* (pp. 114–151). New York: Cambridge University Press.

Izard, C. (1991). *The psychology of emotion.* New York: Plenum Press.

Jenkins, J., & Smith, M. A. (1991). Marital disharmony and children's behavior problems: Aspects of a poor marriage which affect children adversely. *Journal of Child Psychology and Psychiatry, 32,* 793–810.

Jouriles, E. N., & O'Leary, K. D. (1990). Influences of parental mood on parent behavior. In E. Blechman (Ed.), *Emotions and the family* (pp. 181–199). Hillsdale, NJ: Lawrence Erlbaum Associates.

Kagan, J. (1984). *The nature of the child.* New York: Basic Books.

Kavanagh, D., O'Halloran, P., Manicavasagar, V., Clark, D., Piatkowska, O., Tennant, C., & Rosen, A. (1997). The family attitude scale: Reliability and validity of a new scale for measuring the emotional climate of families. *Psychiatry Research, 70,* 185–195.

Kemper, T. D. (1984). Power, status, and emotions: A sociological contribution to a psychophysiological domain. In K. Scherer & P. Ekman (Eds.), *Approaches to emotion* (pp. 369–383). Hillsdale, NJ: Lawrence Erlbaum Associates.

Klagsbrun, F. (1992). *Mixed feelings: Love, hate, rivalry, and reconciliation among brothers and sisters.* New York: Bantam Books.

Koerner, A., & Fitzpatrick, M. (2002). Nonverbal communication and marital adjustment and satisfaction: The role of decoding relationship-relevant and relationship-irrelevant affect. *Communication Monographs, 69,* 33–51.

Kuebli, J., Butler, S., & Fivush, R. (1995). Mother-child talk about past emotions: Relations of maternal language and child gender over time. *Cognition and Emotion, 9,* 265–283.

Larson, R., & Richards, M. (1994). *Divergent realities: The emotional lives of mothers, fathers, and adolescents.* New York: Basic Books.

Lazarus, R. (1991). *Emotion and adaptation.* New York: Oxford University Press.

Lytton, H. (1990). Child and parent effects in boys' conduct disorder: A reinterpretation. *Developmental Psychology, 26,* 683–704.

Magai, C. (1999). Affect, imagery, and attachment: Working models of interpersonal affect and the socialization of emotion. In J. Cassidy & P. R. Shaver (Eds.), *Handbook of attachment* (pp. 787–802). New York: Guilford Press.

Mandler, G. (1975). *Mind and emotion.* New York: Wiley.

Miller, P., & Sperry, L. L. (1987). The socialization of anger and aggression. *Merrill-Palmer Quarterly, 33,* 1–31.

Noller, P., & Roberts, N. (2002). The communication of couples in violent and nonviolent relationships: Temporal associations with own and partners' anxiety/arousal and behavior. In P. Noller & J. Feeney (Eds.), *Understanding marriage: Developments in the study of couple interaction.* New York: Cambridge University Press.

Noller, P., & Ruzzene, M. (1991). The effects of cognition and affect on marital communication. In G. J. O. Fletcher & F. D. Fincham (Eds.), *Cognition in close relationships* (pp. 203–233). Hillsdale, NJ: Lawrence Erlbaum Associates.

Oatley, K., & Jenkins, J. M. (1996). *Understanding emotions.* MA: Blackwell.

Parke, R., & McDowell, D. J. (1998). Toward an expanded model of emotion socialization: New people, new pathways. *Psychological Inquiry, 9,* 303–307.

Planalp, S. (1999). *Communicating emotion: Social, moral, and cultural processes.* New York: Cambridge University Press.

Planalp, S., & Fitness, J. (1999). Thinking/feeling about social and personal relationships. *Journal of Social and Personal Relationships, 16,* 731–750.

Reis, H. T., Collins, W. A., & Berscheid, E. (2000). The relationship context of human behavior and development. *Psychological Bulletin, 126,* 844–872.

Retzinger, S. M. (1991). *Violent emotions: Shame and rage in marital quarrels.* Newbury Park, CA: Sage.

Roberts, L. J., & Krokoff, L. J. (1990). A time-series analysis of withdrawal, hostility, and displeasure in satisfied and dissatisfied marriages. *Journal of Marriage and the Family, 52,* 95–105.

Rohner, R., & Veneziano, R. (2001). The importance of father love: History and contemporary evidence. *Review of General Psychology, 5,* 382–405.

Roseman, I. (1991). Appraisal determinants of discrete emotions. *Cognition and Emotion, 5,* 161–200.

Rusbult, C. E., Bissonnette, V., & Arriaga, X. B., & Cox, C. (1998). Accommodation processes during the early years of marriage. In T. Bradbury (Ed.), *The developmental course of marital dysfunction* (pp. 74–113). New York: Cambridge University Press.

Saarni, C. (2001). Epilogue: Emotion communication and relationship context. *International Journal of Behavioral Development, 25*, 354–356.

Scharfe, E. (2000). Development of emotional expression, understanding, and regulation in infants and young children. In R. Bar-On & D. Parker (Eds.), *Handbook of emotional intelligence* (pp. 244–262). San Francisco: Jossey-Bass.

Scheff, T. (1995). Conflict in family systems: The role of shame. In J. P. Tangney & K. W. Fischer (Eds.), *Self-conscious emotions: The psychology of shame, guilt, embarrassment, and pride* (pp. 393–442). New York: Guilford Press.

Seery, B., & Crowley. M. S. (2000). Women's emotion work in the family. *Journal of Family Issues, 21*, 100–127.

Segrin, C. (1998). Interpersonal communication problems associated with depression and loneliness. In P. Andersen & L. Guerrero (Eds.), *Handbook of communication and emotion* (pp. 215–242). New York: Academic Press.

Shaver, P. R., Collins, N., & Clark, C. (1996). Attachment styles and internal working models of self and relationship partners. In G. J. O. Fletcher & J. Fitness (Eds.), *Knowledge structures in close relationships: A social psychological approach* (pp. 25–61). Mahwah, NJ: Lawrence Erlbaum Associates.

Sheehan, G., & Noller, P. (2002). Adolescents' perception of differential parenting: Links with attachment style and adolescent adjustment. *Personal Relationships, 9,* 173–190.

Simpson, J. A., Rholes, W. S., & Nelligan, J. S. (1992). Support-seeking and support-giving within couples in an anxiety-provoking situation: The role of attachment styles. *Journal of Personality and Social Psychology, 62,* 434–446.

Smith, R. (1991). Envy and the sense of injustice. In P. Salovey (Ed.), *The psychology of jealousy and envy* (pp. 79–102). New York: Guilford Press.

Stearns, P. (1988). The rise of sibling jealousy in the twentieth century. In C. Z. Stearns & P. Stearns (Eds.), *Emotion and social change* (pp. 193–222). New York: Holmes & Meier.

Sulloway, F. J. (1996). *Born to rebel: Birth order, family dynamics, and creative lives.* UK: Little, Brown & Company.

Tangney, J. P. (1995). Shame and guilt in interpersonal relationships. In J. P. Tangney (Ed.), *Self-conscious emotions* (pp. 114–140). New York: Guilford Press.

Thomas, G., Fletcher, G. J. O., & Lange, C. (1997). On-line empathic accuracy in marital interaction. *Journal of Personality and Social Psychology, 76,* 72–89.

Thompson, A., & Bolger, N. (1999). Emotional transmission in couples under stress. *Journal of Marriage and the Family, 61,* 38–48.

Tomkins, S. (1979). Script theory: Differential magnification of affects. In H. E. Howe & R. A. Dienstbier (Eds.), *Nebraska symposium on motivation, 1978* (pp. 201–236). Lincoln, NE: University of Nebraska Press.

Tower, R. B., & Kasl, S. V. (1995). Depressive symptoms across older spouses and the moderating effect of marital closeness. *Psychology and Aging, 10,* 625–638.

Triandis, H. (1994). *Culture and social behavior.* New York: McGraw-Hill.

Vangelisti, A., & Sprague, R. J. (1998). Guilt and hurt: Similarities, distinctions, and conversational strategies. In P. Andersen & L. Guerrero (Eds.), *Handbook of communication and emotion* (pp. 124–154). New York: Academic Press.

Volling, B., McElwain, N. L., & Miller, A. (2002). Emotion regulation in context: The jealousy complex between young siblings and its relations with child and family characteristics. *Child Development, 73,* 581–600.

Wilson, B. J., & Weiss, A. J. (1993). The effects of co-viewing with a sibling on preschoolers' reactions to a suspenseful movie scene. *Communication Research, 20,* 214–248.

Yang, S., & Rosenblatt, P. (2001). Shame in Korean families. *Journal of Comparative Family Studies, 32,* 361–375.

Zahn-Waxler, C. (2000). The development of empathy, guilt, and internalization of distress. In R. J. Davidson (Ed.), *Anxiety, depression, and emotion* (pp. 222–265). New York: Oxford University Press.

Zahn-Waxler, C., Friedman, R. J., Cole, P. M., Mizuta, I., & Hiruma, N. (1996). Japanese and U.S. preschool children's responses to conflict and distress. *Child Development, 67,* 2462–2477.

Zajonc, R. B. (1998). Emotions. In D. Gilbert, S. Fiske, & G. Lindzey (Eds.), *The handbook of social psychology* (4th ed., pp. 591–632). New York: Oxford University Press.

5. Diverse Spirituality in Families

Passing Along Religious Values

By Timothy M. Muehlhoff, Jonathan P. Denham, & James Honeycutt

In studying highly religious families, Marks (2004) notes that many Christian, Muslim, and Jewish families self-report that religious identity is the core of family life and a high priority is to cultivate and pass on religious values (p. 226). As the above quote suggests, it is a challenge to pass along these values in a way that will "stick" with a person into adulthood. Research suggests that 61 percent of today's adults had been churched at one point in their teen years, but now are spiritually disengaged (Barna 2006). A key component of a definition of a family is the expectation that family members will influence each other in significant and lasting ways (Galvin, Bylund, and Brommel 2004). What are the obstacles to cultivating spiritual values that will impact family members? How can families embrace and construct a religious identity in a way that will positively influence and stay with family members? One of the primary ways members wield influence is through the construction of symbolic maps created through dialogue.

Our conclusion is that 40 to 50 percent of kids who are connected to a youth group when they graduate high school will fail to stick with their faith in college .... Only 20 percent of college students who leave the church planned to do so during high school. The remaining 80 percent intended to stick with their faith—but didn't.

—(Powell, Griffin, and Crawford 2011, p. 15)

God's Everywhere

"Faith has always been a central part of the American story, and it has been a driving force of progress and justice throughout our history. We know that our nation, our communities, and our lives are made vastly stronger and richer by faith and the countless acts of justice and mercy it inspires" (2012 Democratic National Platform). Just as faith has played a central role in the American story, faith also plays a key role in the narratives of families.

Turner and West (2006) highlight the importance and centrality of religion's effect on families by explaining how through religion, families are able to survive loss, manage conflict, celebrate fortunes, understand marriage, understand how to raise children, and understand the roles of men and women within a marriage. A family's religion serves as an integral component to how each family member lives their life. People who go to church on a regular basis tend to experience a reduction in depression, which implies an improvement in stress management (Barber 2011). Barber suggests religion can help people to cope with life's uncertainties dealing with economics, uncertainty, disease, or a poor social welfare system. That is, when people experience the variety of challenging things that life can sometimes "throw" at a person, religion helps people to cope with things being thrown. Research shows that faith and religion play an integral role in the lives of millions of Americans (Marks 2004). Whether family members are Muslim, Jewish, Mormon, or Protestant, their religion plays a key role in the daily communication of the family members. More than 85% of Americans report that religion is an important part of their lives while only about 17% of Europeans, Canadians, and Australians take religion seriously (Walsh 2010).

Not all family members share the same values on religious views, which can encourage opportunities for family dialogue (Turner and West 2006). Indeed, some family members will have opposing viewpoints concerning behaviors, life decisions, and values stemming from religious ideals and this can lead to in-depth dialogue. However, families could use a "map" to provide some sort of structure for this kind of communication. For example, when a family goes to Disneyland, everybody wants to do something different and go somewhere different. It would behoove the parents to secure maps for the whole family prior to the start of the Disney journey. The parents would explain the maps to the children and show them how to read the map, where to find restrooms, where to meet if they were ever split up, rides they are not allowed to go on, and other areas they should avoid. Perhaps the parents tell their children they are not allowed to go to California Adventure Park unattended. This is a rule the parents have created and the children know if they break the rule, there are consequences; however, the parents have also explained to their children they can petition to challenge the rules of the map. Similarly, a family may have raised their children in a Catholic church and one day, some of the children want to visit a Protestant church, or Buddhist temple. Families who have maps and rules for behavior similar to the Disney example could thoughtfully engage in communication with children who desire to challenge a religious idea in a family.

A child who was raised in a Christian home by their Christian parents and then goes to college and decides to no longer practice a Christian lifestyle can be difficult for the parents and other family members to accept. Religion is what binds the family together and so when certain family members deviate from how they were raised, it shocks the family system. Nevertheless, this chapter primarily focuses on religion in America, which allows for freedom of religion and so when kids go to college and are presented with hundreds of alternatives to the religion they were brought up in, oftentimes they begin to experiment with other religions through attending religious services, researching on the Internet, or engaging in dialogue about religion with a friend who holds a differing set of beliefs regarding faith and spirituality. Because religion is considered to be a "core of life" to many families, family members struggle in how to select, package, and transmit religious values. Just as a family uses a map to navigate Disneyland, family members create symbolic maps that give shape to religious values.

SIMILARITIES AND DIFFERENCES BETWEEN SPIRITUALITY AND RELIGION

Religion refers to a more organized practice, with some sort of human institution, while spirituality refers to a more personal experience, which may or may not fit within an organized religion. Both religion and spirituality can involve belief in a deity, spiritual or mystical experiences, rituals, as well as value systems and beliefs about morality and ethics, and an understanding of how the world works. These things alone are not necessarily religious or spiritual; they can be both.

Religion is designed to be our spiritual source of comfort and advice, a structure to provide moral guidelines, a caring community, and help for those in need. Yet, religion has been the cause of violence, wars, discrimination, bigotry, pain, and suffering, all of which are a long way from kindness, compassion, comfort, and spiritual reassurance. For example, according to the *Dictionary of Islam,* "jihad" is defined as: "A religious war with those who are unbelievers in the mission of Muhammad ... enjoined especially for the purpose of advancing Islam and repelling evil from Muslims" (Morgan 2010). Religious morality is also used to justify political reasoning and supremacy. In the United States, the First Amendment of the constitution draws a separation between church and state, between religion and politics. Yet every presidential candidate is judged by his or her religious beliefs, as seen in the attempt to prove that President Obama is a Muslim, more so because his name is Barack *Hussein* Obama, which generates hate and fear, even though numerous leaders govern as secularists, agnostics, or atheists.

Prospective Republican candidates sometimes use so-called Christian beliefs in the Southern United States (*Bible Belt* as it has been called) as a form of qualification and go to great lengths to show that a good Christian is a Republican even though the gospel in the New Testament (Love your brother as yourself; turn the other cheek; humble yourselves) is often interpreted as being socialist, thereby implying that Democrats are not good Christians. We recall a documentary upon the declining middle class in America in which a couple was being evicted from their home due to spiraling mortgage costs. As the movers were carrying out their furniture around them, the interviewer looked puzzled and asked why they had voted Republican. They replied: "Because we are Christians!"

At the same time, "spirituality" is a loaded word, often misunderstood, as its practices include meditation, contemplation, and direct communication with universal consciousness. Pope John Paul condemned meditation and yoga as immoral, deluding, and even sinful. Yet spirituality is simply the discovery of our authentic self without any trimmings or labels, which gives us a rich source of values and a deeper meaning to life, whatever our religion.

In the seeking of such meaning, religion and spirituality come together. Spirituality highlights qualities such as caring, kindness, compassion, tolerance, service, and community, and, in its truest sense, so does religion. But where religion is defined by its tradition and teachings, spirituality is defined by what is real in our own experience, arising from an inner search within ourselves, the finding of our own truth. Where religion tends to breed separation—my religion vs. your religion, my God is the only real God, my ethics are better than yours, etc.—spirituality sees all people as equal. We are not an "ism" or a label; we are spiritual beings whose purpose is to awaken to our true nature.

CREATION OF SYMBOLIC MAPS

"Communication is a symbolic process whereby reality is produced, maintained, repaired, and transformed" (Carey 2009, p. 19). There are many diverse definitions of communication. This definition by Carey is quite different from an earlier definition by Weaver (1949), "communication is all of the procedures by which one mind can affect another" (p. 95). Carey's definition focuses on the symbolic nature of producing reality. Carey explains how reality is produced with symbols by illustrating how a blueprint for a house is a representation "for" reality and "of" reality. The blueprint is a representation *for* reality in the sense that it provides directions and guidelines for construction workers and architects to create an actual house that exists in reality. The blueprint is a representation *of* reality in the sense that one can show others the blueprint and say "this represents reality." It is not reality in the sense that the blueprint is a representation of something that does not yet exist. Similarly, families can use religion as a symbolic map for how to facilitate communication and everyday life in their families. For example, the Bible, Quran, or Bhagavad Gita can be used as a representation *for* reality and *of* reality. There are rules, guidelines, values, and ideals that a family can live by. Carey explains how "we first produce the world by symbolic work and then take up residence in the world we have produced" (p. 23). The idea of symbolic maps is theoretically grounded in symbolic interactionism.

Symbolic interactionism involves the process of making sense of ourselves and thus making sense out of our world by looking at the behaviors of others; furthermore, "humans think about and act according to the meanings they attribute to their actions and contexts and humans are motivated to create meaning to help them make sense of the world" (Galvin, Bylund, and Brommel 2007, p. 69). Galvin and her associates assert that symbolic interaction requires humans to pay attention to how people interpret and make sense out of life experiences and then to negotiate meaning through the use of language. Children might observe the way their parents discuss how to make decisions about how to spend money in their household. Some children may want to make sense out of what they were discussing and therefore to understand the meaning of their conversation and how it may impact them. The family accomplishes this through language. Using Carey's (2009) notion of symbolic maps, perhaps the dining room table of a particular family could be an example of symbolic map. That is, the dining room table could be a representation *of* and *for* family decision making. Carey speaks to the dual nature of symbolic forms, "as 'symbols of' they present reality; as 'symbols for' they create the very reality they represent" (p. 23). Indeed, the dining room table represents the reality *of* "this is where our family makes decisions while eating" and the dining room table represents the reality *for* "this is an oak dining table with six chairs and we eat lasagna at this table while talking about where Jenny is going to apply for colleges." Whichever medium serves as the map, it is important to note the diversity of maps.

DIVERSITY OF MAPS

Each family is its own culture and has its own unique structure and is often referred to as "The Stuart Home" or "The Roses" or "The Templeton Residence." Consider the Bundys from *Married … with Children* compared to Lucas and Mark McCain, characters from the classic western series, *The Rifleman*, which aired from 1958 to 1963. The family maps in each family would look very different from one another. The Bundys steal money from their father, tell lies, and lack ambition for doing well in school and in life, while Lucas McCain is a single father who explains to his son why he does the things he does and also explains why other people do the things they do. Lucas McCain lives by a code of honor and integrity. Indeed, the section of McCain's map that deals with values suggests he always acts with integrity; i.e., the integrity part of his map is a representation *of* and *for* his reality. In nearly every episode, Lucas teaches Mark about valuable lessons that are rooted in biblical values; e.g., do good unto others and treat people fairly. Al Bundy typically did not teach biblical values to his children. All families have their own ways of making sense out of their own realities and, as mentioned earlier, most families center their "map construction" on religion. Walsh (2010) points to the diversity of religion in American families: "Increasingly, Americans are combining varied spiritual beliefs and practices as they forge new spiritual paths to fit their lives and relationships" (p. 330). Multi-faith couples are much more common than they used to be; e.g., a Jewish woman marries a Catholic man. This begs the question of how an interfaith couple will raise their children. Should they raise their children with both religions or just one? Should there be multiple symbolic maps for making sense of reality? How does a family negotiate the answers to these questions?

Although several Americans report that religion is an important part of their lives, 44% do not follow the religion of their upbringing and in general, religious affiliation, congregational membership, and worship service attendance has been declining (Walsh 2010). Despite the decline in the trend, Walsh mentions how there are more than 2,000 denominations with nearly 500,000 places of worship in the U.S. Typically, when a person is looking for a map in a gas station or a travel agency, there will be certain features of a map that attract that person to Rome versus Birmingham versus Napa Valley. Some families might have maps that do not offer much variety. For example, the keys and symbols on the map suggest the Stuarts will go to church every Sunday, never question the behaviors of the parents, strictly adhere to the dos and don'ts of their religion, and if something does not make sense, they are instructed to just "pray about it and have faith." Maps like those might be perceived as narrow and not offering much, and perhaps that could be an explanation for why several people do not stick with the religion that was central to their upbringing. How can a family have a map for making sense out of reality that allows for diversity but also provides structure? This is an empirical question. "Rooted in cultural, spiritual, and multigenerational traditions, each family constructs its own spirituality, which is transmitted through ongoing interactions" (Walsh 2010, p. 334). A family is an ongoing, living, breathing organism that is subject to change. Perhaps families need to make revised editions to their map. College students will frequently buy history textbooks that are a 2nd, 3rd, 4th, or 10th edition. History is history; it has not changed. However, new ways to make sense out of the past call for a new way to write about it. Similarly, a family map may need revision because as children age and develop new friends who live according to different religions, revisions might be needed to a family map. For example, Billy Stuart goes to Sunnyside Baptist with his parents and siblings every Sunday … it is part of their map. Billy's best friend is Catholic and he wants Billy to go to Mass with him. What do Billy's parents do? Forbid Billy to go or make a revised edition to the map? That is ultimately up to the family. The point is that a symbolic map can be a very useful tool for families to use to facilitate meaning making; however, families need to be aware of the possible need to change/alter their maps, considering the diversity of religion and faith in the U.S. While the diversity found in symbolic maps often matches the diversity of the families creating them, there are common elements that make up the contours of a family map.

Elements of Symbolic Maps

As family members create symbolic maps defining and prioritizing religious beliefs, the following are some salient components that comprise a map.

Family Narratives

All parents have values, beliefs, convictions, and aspirations they want to pass on to their children. Sometimes these beliefs and convictions are the same ones parents received from their parents and sometimes parents' beliefs depart dramatically from how their parents did things and the values they established. Yet, parents of every generation have struggled with *how* to pass on family values. Many parents do it through stories. Richardson (1990) noted, "narrative is the best way to understand the human experience because it is the way humans understand their own lives" (p. 133). In fact, one key theorist argued that a central characteristic of humans is that we are natural storytellers (Fisher 1987). It's not surprising then that family stories serve as the cornerstones of family culture (Stone 2003).

Family stories are the narratives that "family members construct about life together" (Yerby et al. 1998, p. 74). All stories recall events related in temporal sequence with some element of an ending. While some family stories are told in formal settings—family reunions, anniversaries, birthdays, funerals—many are told "incidentally, because someone says something that sparks someone else's memory in the course of daily living" (Stone 2003, p. 72). Two primary functions of stories are that they create links to the past and teach lessons. Most family stories die off after two generations (Martin, Hagestad, and Diedrick 1988). However, the third author is seven generations removed from the frontiersman Daniel Boone, who is his generational uncle. Family narratives inform members of the history of the family and key moral or spiritual lessons to be learned. Growing up, the senior author remembered his family going through some tough financial times when his father was laid off from General Motors for almost a year. During that time his father never sat the family down to assure them that everything would be fine. However, he would regularly tell stories of how his father migrated to America during the Great Depression. Working two or three odd jobs and saving every penny he could earn, he survived by depending on the kindness of others and his unyielding faith in God. Every morning before beginning an exhausting day of work, often filled with uncertainty, he would first read his Bible and pray. Listening to those stories as a child not only allowed me to learn more about my grandfather, but it also imparted to my brothers and me the importance of faith. Mixed into the lore of the family were rich spiritual lessons that helped us in our present struggles.

Not all stories family members tell about the family are unified or equally recognized. *Stories on the margin* is a phrase coined by Jorgenson and Bouchner (2004) to describe stories that give voice to perspectives often silenced or ignored. For example, while most of the family members may be unified in believing that God is good and faithful even in the midst of financial struggles, one family member may offer a narrative that expresses doubt and questions God's provision. This perspective, if recognized, would exist on the margins of the unified narrative offered by the family. Also, research reveals that most family narratives relate to favorable characters, reflecting a social desirability bias. Common themes extol positive personality descriptions, hard work, motivation, care giving, and overcoming adversity. It is rare when stories are about antagonists such as the family member embezzling from a business or committing other crimes. The family members are clearly seen as protagonists who have worked hard.

Family Theme

Inherent in most family stories is a running theme that gives structure and guidance to the family. The idea of a unifying family theme was first conceptualized by Hess and Handel (1959) who argued that themes provide "a fundamental view of reality and some way of dealing with it" (p. 11). For non-religious or atheistic families, a theme may entail the belief that good things happen through hard work and personal sacrifice, not through divine intervention. For them, expecting a higher power to help them through a difficult time may be seen as a weakness. In contrast, religious families, who may also adhere to a strong work ethic, still believe that the most important asset to a family is prayer. For them, not depending on God is seen as being uncommitted. This theme is reinforced when the first thing a family does when hearing about bad news or an unexpected challenge is to pray. If a family member agrees, he or she is supporting the family theme. If a family member balks at prayer or begins to question its efficacy, then a disturbance within the family may occur.

One of the central challenges to a family theme is the presence of *family myths*. Myths are the "beliefs about the family that are selective or constructed to represent the family in a way that may or may not be objectively true but serves some function for the family" (Turner and West 2006, p. 112). Within the Christian, Muslim, and Buddhist traditions, financial giving to assist the needy is a salient part of being a committed follower. A family may believe that giving is a requirement of their faith tradition, yet in reality they give only sporadically. However, it is important to the family to be seen by themselves and others as a family who sets aside personal wants to in order to give to worthwhile projects. This tension is alleviated, in part, by the telling and retelling of a time where the family gave a substantial amount to a church or synagogue building project. Telling this particular story allows them to perpetuate the myth that they regularly give. Family myths are also maintained by telling edited stories that exclude facts that could challenge the family theme. For example, when telling the story about giving to the church project, the family delights in that salient example as it strengthens the family theme. What are edited out are the arguments about how much to give and that the amount finally given was far less that what was originally pledged. These details are withheld from family members and are never told.

Myths are also perpetuated when private beliefs are contradicted by public actions. Goffman (1959) viewed social interactions as existing on a stage made up of front and back stage performances. The front stage consists of what is visible to an audience, while the back stage is where individuals can act in ways that may undermine or contradict what they presented on the front stage. Myths are perpetuated when a family performs being deeply spiritual at a religious service (front stage), yet at home (back stage) acts in a manner that undermines or belittles the values they espoused in public. Marks (2004) noted in his study of self-identified highly religious families that "practicing what you preach" or behavior–belief congruence was mentioned by every participant as being the most important factor in creating a vibrant religious atmosphere in the home.

Roles

Once a theme has been established through narratives and interaction, family roles are instrumental in preserving the theme. A *role* is a set of norms for a specific situation or part. If a family decides to have private times of worship and prayer within the home, what roles do members assume? Who leads family prayer? What is the role of a child during discussions about faith? Does this role entail merely asking questions, or can a child offer answers? Can these answers ever differ from adults'? What role do family members assume when the family goes out in public? When a family attempts to answer these questions they engage in role negotiation. "Individuals may know what is expected of them in a family, but not all members perform the expected behaviors" (Galvin et al. 2007, p. 185).

Whenever a family adopts and negotiates certain roles, the issue of acting comes into play. Do family members really buy into family rituals, rules, and roles? Or, are their outward expressions mere acting? Acting takes two forms: "Surface acting, which is 'painted on' affective displays, or faking, and deep acting, which is modifying inner feelings to match expressions" (Grandy 2003, p. 86). In *surface acting* the child may act interested when religious topics come up, but he or she may feel bored or resentful toward religion. In *deep acting* a child may also feel resentful toward religious topics but still act interested. The difference is that this particular child feels guilty for his or her feelings and will attempt to bring his or her emotions into line with his or her outward reaction. Rafaeli and Sutton (1987) identified the first scenario as *acting in bad faith* and the later as *acting in good faith*.

Family Rules

Family rules are "relationship agreements, revealed by repetitive patterns of interaction, which prescribe and limit family behavior" (Yerby, Buerkel-Rothfuss, and Bochner 1998, p. 175). While rules are unique to each individual family, rules can generally be broken into two types: constitutive and regulative. Constitutive rules define what is counted as communication. Each family has constitutive rules for what counts as respect (looking adults in the eye when talking), disrespect (checking text messages while talking to parents), solidarity (siblings attending each other's sporting events), affection (giving gifts), and so forth. For families rooted in religious beliefs and practices, constitutive rules are particularly important in answering key questions: What counts as spirituality in our family? What counts as religious devotion? How far can I challenge the faith of parents before it is seen as disrespectful? Does my not wearing a burka count as abandoning my faith? What style of dress counts as modest in my mosque?

Regulative rules "tell us when it is and is not appropriate to speak: when interruptions are acceptable, when responses are called for and what kinds of responses are suitable; when we can interact in various ways; and with whom we can communicate about particular topics" (Wood 1998, p. 49). Baxter and Akkoor (2011) showed that for many families, certain topics are allowed and others are off limits. For religious families regulative rules may mean that it is not appropriate to discuss sexual topics with parents, joke about certain religious or sacred topics, mention religious doubts to siblings, or interrupt a pastor or Imam when he or she is speaking.

Constitutive and regulatory rules fit under two broad categories of rules: conversation and conformity (Koerner and Fitzpatrick 2002). *Conversation orientation* entails the degree of openness and transparency families feel comfortable with in discussing diverse issues. Families with a high level of conversation orientation feel free to discuss varied topics without the fear of exclusion or rebuke. Such families would feel free to discuss the positive attributes of other faith traditions, or possible doubts about aspects of their own tradition. Families with a low conversation orientation limit what topics can be discussed and whether or not private thoughts can be shared. *Conformity orientation* refers to the degree a family stresses uniformity of beliefs, convictions, or values. Families with high conformity value harmony, obedience, and interdependence, while families with low conformity cultivate independence, freethinking, and individuality.

Rituals

Family rituals can occur daily, weekly, or yearly and can be something as simple as saying prayers before eating dinner, or attending religious services on a particular day. Rituals are particularly vital for children to understand the values and priorities of a family and can be defined as a "recurring, patterned communication event whose successful enactment pays homage to some highly valued person, concept, or thing" (Baxter and Clark 1996, p. 254). For Christian families the ritual of observing Communion is vital, while for Muslim families the month of Ramadan is time to focus on fasting and prayer. Researchers, starting in 1950, observe two salient benefits that come through family rituals (Fiese, Tomcho, Douglas, Josephs, Poltrock, and Baker 2002). First, rituals offer families a way to connect with past generations. In order to continue a family tradition, a family may forgo opening presents Christmas morning to first attend a religious service, or volunteer at a homeless shelter once presents have been exchanged. This ritual links past and present generations through a symbolic act. Second, it is through rituals that a family develops a collective identity that communicates to themselves and others what the family values and the collective theme that guides their daily action.

Challenges to the Family

In today's hurried, social media–driven culture, unique challenges are presented to families attempting to live out and pass along religious convictions.

Religion Surfers

Berthrong (1999) notes that traditional boundaries between religions are dissolving and people now feel the freedom to have multiple citizenships in diverse and often conflicting faiths. Vietnamese columnist Anh Do (2006) describes her upbringing in a home that encouraged multiple citizenships:

> My father filled our home with books and music, making sure we had information on the Koran, Hinduism, Confucianism, Quakers and Jehovah's Witness. My mother took us to temple, cooked kosher and navigated us through First Communion all the while garbing us in the right clothes to match secular holidays. Both parents showed us that practicing is believing, yet that there are always more than one belief. (p. 2)

For families who subscribe to a high conformity orientation, the environment that Do describes is most likely unsettling and threatening. High conformity families desire to shield members from being introduced to other faith traditions. For many families, if a child walked into their home with the sacred text of another religion, it would challenge the theme and identity of the family and cause conflict. The attempt to understand another faith tradition is seen as condoning that tradition. Yet, with the increase of social media and the Internet, information is only a click away.

For most Americans, information about other faith traditions comes through the Internet. Nearly 30 million Americans have become what Larsen (2001) identifies as *religion surfers* who skim through the Internet to read the narratives of diverse religious followers. Larsen notes that 62% of religion surfers say that material discovered on the Internet fosters religious tolerance of other views. The fear of having children be introduced to other faith traditions is why many parents create rules regulating access to the Internet (Papadakis 2003). As these fears and rules grow, families will have to negotiate what information or beliefs are off limits. Each family will have to construct constitutive rules that ask: Does the reading of other sacred texts constitute compromise of family values? Does fidelity to our family's faith mean I cannot embrace or practice components found in other religions? Why have we embraced our particular faith tradition? Will I still be a part of this family if I leave our faith tradition?

Changing Religious Affiliation

Children who decide to leave the religious tradition or affiliation of a family present challenges to the family system. The depth of the commitment or loyalty of the parents to a particular denomination or tradition will determine the depth of the difficulty caused by a child leaving. Imagine parents being fourth or fifth generation Baptists and having a child start attending a non-denominational church. This experience is becoming more common.

Religious affiliation is changing in America according to a Pew Forum survey on religion and public life. Indeed, today's children raised in a particular religious denomination are more likely to have left the denomination compared to earlier generations. One in three (32%) who are under age 30 claim no religious affiliation. Today's millennial generation is more unaffiliated than any young generation ever has been when they were younger. Generation Y, also known as the Millennial Generation, is the demographic cohort following Generation X. There are no precise dates for when Generation Y starts and ends. Commentators use beginning birth dates ranging somewhere from the later 1970s or the early 1980s to the early 2000s (decade) (Gardner 2006; Gargiulo 2012). Members of this generation are sometimes called Echo Boomers (narcissists), due to the significant increase in birth rates through the 1980s and into the 1990s. Millennials are mostly the children of baby boomers or Gen Xers. The 20th century trend toward smaller families in developed countries continued, however, so the relative impact of the "baby boom echo" was generally less pronounced than the original boom.

While more than one-quarter of American adults (28%) have left the faith in which they were raised, critics also note that the data reveal that 72% retain their religious beliefs. Interestingly, Atheism had the lowest retention rate (30%). Conversely, other sources reveal that that belief in God rises with age even in Atheist countries (Harms 2012). In the United States, 54% of people younger than 28 said they were certain of God's existence, compared with 66% of the people 68 and older. Looking at differences among age groups, the largest increases in belief in God most often occur among those 58 years of age and older. This suggests that belief in God is especially likely to increase among the oldest groups, perhaps in response to the increasing anticipation of mortality. Table 5-1 presents a summary table of highlights of the Pew survey. Notice how 92% of Americans report belief in some type of spiritual being.

Doubt

Some family members do not merely change religious affiliations, but begin to deeply doubt faith or religion itself. Over time a family member may begin to question the identity, beliefs, and theme of his or her family. How will a family member be treated as he or she begins to question long-held beliefs? Guinness (1976) notes that a person who doubts is in suspension between faith and unbelief, not fully embracing either. "This distinction is absolutely vital because it uncovers and deals with the first major misconception of doubt—the idea that in doubting a believer is betraying faith and surrendering to unbelief" (p. 19). Family members who struggle with doubts in a low conversation, high conformity orientation will find their views ignored, silenced, or chastised and their narratives quickly becoming

Table 5-1 Highlights of Pew Survey on Religious Affiliation in the United States

- Men are significantly more likely than women to claim no religious affiliation. Nearly one in five men say they have no formal religious affiliation, compared with roughly 13% of women.
- Among people who are married, nearly four in ten (37%) are married to a spouse with a different religious affiliation. (This figure includes Protestants who are married to another Protestant from a different denominational family, such as a Baptist who is married to a Methodist.) Hindus and Mormons are the most likely to be married (78% and 71%, respectively) and to be married to someone of the same religion (90% and 83%, respectively).
- Mormons and Muslims are the groups with the largest families; more than one in five Mormon adults and 15% of Muslim adults in the U.S. have three or more children living at home.
- The Midwest most closely resembles the religious makeup of the overall population. The South, by a wide margin, has the heaviest concentration of members of evangelical Protestant churches. The Northeast has the greatest concentration of Catholics, and the West has the largest proportion of unaffiliated people, including the largest proportion of atheists and agnostics.
- While more than nine in ten Americans (92%) believe in the existence of God or a universal spirit, there is considerable variation in the nature and certainty of this belief. Sixty percent believe that God is a person with whom people can have a relationship; but one in four—including about half of Jews and Hindus—see God as an impersonal force. And while roughly seven in ten Americans say they are absolutely certain of God's existence, more than one in five (22%) are less certain in their belief.

Source: Pew Forum on Religion & Public Life. (2010, October 3). U.S. Religious Landscape Survey. Retrieved February 1, 2013 from http://religions.pewforum.org/reports.

stories on the margin. The doubts of a family member will soon test the roles, rules, and identity of the family. Most importantly, the one doubting may begin to question his or her place within the family. Guinness concludes: "Often as people are sharing their problems they are testing us. Do we really accept them? Is there a time-limit to our tolerance? Are we as interested in them as we say we are?" (1976, p. 153)

Negative Religious Stereotypes

"Individuals are influenced not only by their own self-concept, and the values, symbols, and beliefs of the families, but also by the cultural norms and values of the society in which they live" (Ingoldsby, Miller, and Smith 2004, p. 85). The power of the generalized other can have profound effects on children brought up in a religious home. For example, as children brought up in a Christian home gain more exposure to the outside world via television and movies, they may experience a dialectical tension between following the influence of their religious parents and dealing with the identity negotiation of how Christians are portrayed in the media. Children do not want to be perceived as unintelligent, narrow-minded, and judgmental, but they also do not want to abandon the religious mores that have served as an integral component to their self-concept, so what do they do? Many will experiment with other religions and many will cease to be an active member of their religious affiliation by not attending religious services or reading spiritual materials such as the Bible or the Quran. Many of the negative religious stereotypes associated with Christianity and other faith-based religions are perpetuated by TV and movie portrayals of religious figures.

According to Learmonth (2006), "The PTC [Parents Television Council] released the results of its study of the 2005–2006 TV season concluding that religious themes had become more scarce on network TV but that when religion was addressed it was more likely to be portrayed in a negative light." Irrespective of accuracy, people develop perceptions and stereotypes about different genres of persons portrayed through media. For example, the majority of Americans have a negative view of teenagers perceiving them as lazy, disrespectful, and prone to causing trouble (Stern 2005). Clearly, not *all* teenagers can be characterized this way. Stern concludes these stereotypes are largely guided by the way teens are portrayed in movies and television. Similarly, religious characters are often portrayed negatively in movies and television as overzealous, judgmental, and hypocritical.

In Showtime's *Dexter*, Dexter Morgan is a forensics blood spatter analyst by day and a serial murderer by night. He does not believe in God; however, he believes in living and killing by a code. In one episode, Dexter asks a colleague who is Catholic, "How do we even know there is a God?" His colleague does not effectively answer the question and Dexter's response is " ... because it makes no sense." Another one of Showtime's programs, *Shameless*, portrays Eddie Jackson as a Christian who takes his daughter, Karen to a "purity ball." After Karen faces the crowd and admits she has been "unladylike," she is told she needs to be as honest as possible "in order to receive the full gift of purity." Karen recounts her sexually promiscuous past in vivid detail, to which her dad responds in anger, "YOU WHORE!" The ironic ending to this scene reinforces the negative stereotype of the Christian virtue of sexual purity and the negative stereotype of hypocritical Christians. *The Big Bang Theory* follows the antics of a group of quirky, highly educated friends who apply logic to dating, roommate relations, and life. The only two non-intelligent people in the show are a lovable, uneducated blonde waitress and a born-again, meddling mother. The show associates Christians with feeble-minded overzealous religious fanatics. NFL quarterback Tim Tebow, a devout Christian, frequently begins interviews by saying, "First and foremost, I'd like to thank my Lord and Savior Jesus Christ" and frequently mentions how "blessed" he is. Tebow's overly expressive acts of faith have become the subject of Saturday Night Live skits. One skit portrayed

Jesus talking to Tebow in the locker room asking him not to be so enthusiastic and charismatic in the way he prays to him on the field. Indeed, Tebow's public acts of faith have received much criticism. In an online knowledge forum, *Big Think*, Bill Nye the "Science Guy" claimed there is no scientific support of the Biblical account of creation and that parents should not teach it to their children. Nye said, "And I say to grownups … if you want to deny evolution and live in your world that's completely inconsistent with everything we observe in the universe, that's fine. But don't make your kids do it." Nye suggests that it is only a matter of time before the creationist worldview becomes obsolete because there is no evidence for it. Arabs have been associated with the 9/11 attacks and several films have typecast Arabs as terrorists. This reinforces the stereotype that some people have about terrorists being Arab Muslims. However, most Muslims are not terrorists and most Arabs are not Muslim. Indeed, the ways that various religious figures are portrayed in the media through film, television, or sports has a powerful effect on consumers of media. People who possess inherited ethos such as Bill Nye can have a profound impact on their viewers, especially children. As children are introduced to an outside world through media, they encounter a generalized other that may contradict, make light of, or belittle family beliefs.

CONCLUSION

In the prestigious *Princeton Lectures on Youth, Church, and Culture*, Robert Wuthnow (1996) argued that parents feel deeply the "responsibility to pass an understanding of the faith to the next generation" (p. 78). This desire is not new, but was also reflected in the Torah, the sacred writings of Judaism, where parents are encouraged to talk to their children about key truths while "you sit in your house and when you walk by the way and when you lie down and when you rise up" (Deuteronomy 6:7). These ancient writers understood that values are transferred, identities formed, and rituals created through dialogue. They also reflected key elements of symbolic interaction where meaning and the creation of symbolic maps are "negotiated through the use of language" (Galvin et al. 2007, p. 69). While the content of these maps may differ according to different faith traditions, the elements of the map—rituals, themes, rules, narratives—have stayed remarkably similar from the Torah to today and deserve our continued attention.

DISCUSSION QUESTIONS

1. Does your family readily follow family rituals, rules, and roles? Or, are their outward expressions mere acting? Are there any examples of family rituals that your family endorses but you think are unnecessary?
2. Do you think being raised in a secular or nonreligious family results in growing up with a sense of morality or immorality in terms of inherently knowing what is right or wrong (e.g., recall or Google the seven deadly sins of anger, greed, laziness, pride, lust, envy, and gluttony)?
3. Perform a Google search and download from YouTube a video that portrays religious upbringing as instilling moral virtues in children or that makes fun of raising children with a religious upbringing.
4. Has a family member ever questioned or doubted the identity, beliefs, or theme of your family? How was he or she treated when these doubts were expressed? Were these questions or doubts

allowed to be expressed or were their views ignored, silenced, or forced to the margin? When you start your own family, how do you think you'll respond to a child questioning cherished beliefs or convictions?

5. Each family has constitutive rules for what counts as what within the family. In your family, what counts as religious devotion (attending religious services, reading sacred texts, praying before meals, etc.)? What might count as disrespecting family beliefs, rules, or rituals? In your family, what constitutive rules govern how a child can challenge or question the faith of parents before it is seen as disrespectful? What are the most important constitutive rules have you adopted from your family?

6. Consider the section *Negative Religious Stereotypes* under **Challenges to the Family**. Watch one or more episodes of a TV show (or a movie) you feel has portrayed members of a faith-based religious organization in a negative way. How are the persons being portrayed accurately if it all and how are they being portrayed negatively? In light of the power of the *generalized other*, describe the effects this can have for followers and potential followers of the particular religion. For example, how does Fox's *Family Guy* negatively portray Christians and Jews? Considering the *generalized other*, how might a Jew or Christian react to this show?

References

Barber, N. (2011). "A Cross-National Test of the Uncertainty Hypothesis of Religious Belief." *Cross-Cultural Research, 45,* 318–333.

Baxter, L. A. and Akkoor, C. (2011). "Topic Expansiveness and Family Communication Patterns." *Journal of Family Communication, 11,* 1–20.

Baxter, L. A. and Clark, C. (1996). "Perceptions of Family Communication Patterns and the Enactment of Family Rituals." *Western Journal of Communication, 60,* 254–268.

Barna Research Group (2006). "Most Twentysomethings Put Christianity on the Shelf Following Spiritually Active Teen Years." Barna Group Update.

Berthrong, J. (1999). *The Divine Deli: Religious Identity in North American Cultural Mosaic.* Maryknoll, NY: Orbis Books.

Carey, J. W. (2009). *Communication as Culture: Essays on Media and Society.* New York: Routledge.

Do, A. (2006, September 22). "Dalai Lama's Message Universal." *The Orange County Register,* p. A2.

Fiese, B. H., Tomcho, T. J., Douglas, M., Josephs, K., Poltrock, S., and Baker, T. (2002). "A Review of 50 Years of Research on Naturally Occurring Family Routines and Rituals: Cause for Celebration?" *Journal of Family Psychology, 16,* 381–390.

Galvin, K. M., Bylund, C. L., and Brommel, B. J. (2007). *Family Communication: Cohesion and Change.* (7th ed.). Boston: Pearson.

Gardner, S. F. (2006). "Preparing for the Nexters." *American Journal of Pharmaceutical Education, 70,* 87. doi:10.5688/aj70048

Gargiulo, S. (2012, August). "'Generation Y' Set to Transform Office Life." *CNN.* Retrieved from http://edition.cnn.com/2012/08/20/business/generation-y-global-office-culture/index.html.

Goffman, E. (1959). *The Presentation of Self in Everyday Life.* Garden City, NY: Doubleday.

Grandy, A. A. (2003). "When 'The Show Must Go on': Surface Acting and Deep Acting as Determinants of Emotional Exhaustion and Peer-Rated Service Delivery." *Academy of Management Journal, 46,* 86–96.

Guinness, O. (1976). *Doubt.* Downers Grove, IL: InterVarsity Press.

Harms, W. (2012, April 18). "Belief in God Rises with Age, Even in Atheist Nations." Retrieved October 31, 2012 from http://news.uchicago.edu/article/2012/04/18/belief-god-rises-age-even-atheist-nations.

Hess, R. and Handel, G. (1959). *Family Worlds*. Chicago: University of Chicago Press.

Ingoldsby, B. B., Smith, S. R., and Miller, J. E. (2004). *Exploring Family Theories*. Los Angeles: Roxbury Publishing.

Jorgenson, J. and Bochner, A. P. (2004). "Imagining Families Through Stories and Rituals." In A. L. Vangelisti (Ed.), *Handbook of Family Communication* (pp. 513–538). Mahwah, NJ: Erlbaum.

Koerner, A. F. and Fitzpatrick, M. A. (2002). "Toward a Theory of Family Communication." *Communication Theory, 12*, 70–91.

Larsen, E. (2001, December). "CyberFaith: How Americans Pursue Religion Online." *Pew Internet & American Life Project*. Retrieved from http://pewinternet.org/Reports/2001/CyberFaith-How-Americans-Pursue-Religion-Online/Executive-Summary.aspx.

Learmonth, M. (2006, December). "PTC Unhappy with TV's Religious Stereotypes." *Variety*. Retrieved from http://www.variety.com/article/VR1117955772.

Marks, L. (2004). "Sacred Practices in Highly Religious Families: Christian, Jewish, Mormon, and Muslim Perspectives." *Family Process, 43*, 217–231.

Martin, P., Hagestad, G. O., and Diedrick, P. (1988). "Family Stories: Events (Temporarily) Remembered." *Journal of Marriage and the Family, 50*, 533–541.

Morgan, Diane (2010). *Essential Islam: A Comprehensive Guide to Belief and Practice*. ABC-CLIO. p. 87. Retrieved from http://books.google.com/books?id=U94S6N2zECAC&pg=PA87.

Papadakis, M. (2003). "Data on Family and the Internet: What Do We Know and How Do We Know It?" In J. Turow and A. L. Kavanaugh (Eds.), *The Wired Homestead* (pp. 121–140). Cambridge, MA: MIT Press.

Powell, K. E., Griffen, B. M., and Crawford, C. A. (2011). *Sticky Faith: Practical Ideas to Mature Long-Term Faith in Teenagers*. Grand Rapids, MI: Zondervan.

Rafaeli, A. and Sutton, R. I. (1987). "Expression of Emotion as Part of the Work Role. *Academy of Management Review, 12*, 23–37.

Stern, S. R. (2005). "Self-Absorbed, Dangerous, and Disengaged: What Popular Films Tell Us About Teenagers." *Mass Communication & Society, 8*, 23–38.

Stone, E. (2003). "Family Ground Rules." In K. Galvin and P. Cooper (Eds.), *Making Connections: Readings in Relational Communication* (3rd ed., pp. 70–78). Los Angeles: Roxbury Publishing Company.

Turner, L. H. and West, R. (2006). *Perspectives on Family Communication* (3rd ed.). New York: McGraw-Hill.

Walsh, F. (2010). "Spiritual Diversity: Multifaith Perspectives in Family Therapy." *Family Process, 49*, 330–348.

Weaver, W. (1949). "Recent Contributions to the Mathematical Theory of Communication." In C. Shannon and W. Weaver, *The Mathematical Theory of Communication*. Urbana: University of Illinois Press.

Wood, J. T. (1998). *But I Thought You Meant … Misunderstandings in Human Communication*. Mountain View, CA: Mayfield Publishing.

Wuthnow, R. "Religious Upbringing: Does It Matter, If So, What Matters?" *The 1996 Princeton Lectures on Youth, Church, and Culture* (Princeton, NJ: Princeton Theological Seminary, 1996), p. 78.

6. MENTAL IMAGERY AND IMAGINED INTERACTIONS IN FAMILIES

By James Honeycutt & Laura Hatcher

Close your eyes and picture your ideal family. Imagine the perfect home. Visualize your dream mate. What do you see? Some may imagine the ideal family being a mother, father, two kids, and a golden retriever. Others may see six kids and a parrot. Still others might see just a husband and wife with no children. We all have different pictures in our heads, different snapshots of what makes the perfect life. And these mental images influence our life-decisions. Your personal beliefs about the ideal home will undoubtedly influence the type of housing you choose throughout your life. Is home a four-bedroom house in the suburbs with a big yard and a picket fence? Or is it a chic loft in the youthful, up-and-coming part of town? What about a ramshackle old house with lots of history in the countryside? The way you picture the ideal housing situation will influence the types of housing you'll consider. The person who wants to live in a downtown apartment probably wouldn't consider living in an old house in the country. In this chapter, we discuss effects of mental imagery in the family and a type of intrapersonal communication called imagined interactions (IIs), which is a type of mental imagery and daydreaming.

Mental Imagery in the Family

Imagery will even influence how happy you are in your future relationships. Does your significant other completely contradict the picture of your ideal mate? If so, you'll either have to alter your imagery or risk unhappiness in the relationship. Say that in your imagination, a family isn't complete without a dog. In your partner's imagination, however, there are no pets whatsoever. Your partner doesn't really like animals at all. Now what? Your mental images don't match. Without a dog, you feel like something is missing. With a dog, your partner is unhappy. Clashing imagery is a recipe for relational strife. According to Tower (1986), "a great deal of the outcome of a marriage is a direct function of the imagery of the people involved in it, their methods of using that imagery, and their capacities for changing it with experience" (217).

If we all have mental images that shape our life-decisions and influence our happiness, where do these images come from? Since we all have different ideas of perfection, it is obvious they aren't inborn, instinctual traits. They are things we learn over time. Culture and society play a large role in shaping our mental imagery, but of even greater importance is the family, which is the foundation of society and existence.

Tower discusses the ways that the family can influence an individual's imagery. The first and most obvious is through *direct experience*. The direct experiences you have with your father will influence the way you picture what a father should do and how a father should act later in your life. Families also use images to create *concepts* and *scripts* for their members. Through repeated exposure to certain related images, an individual is able to assign meaning to those images. Those meanings are then elaborated on to form concepts and/or scripts for entire encounters. The *ambient stimuli* of the family (i.e., the type of home—messy, clean, noisy, quiet, private, open, etc.) can also influence an individual's imagery. Another important consideration is the family's *interaction with the larger culture*. A family can regulate the availability of information from the outside culture that its members are exposed to. A child who isn't allowed to watch television will have very different mental images from a child for whom the television is a de facto babysitter. The family can also pass judgment on messages received from the outside culture. While one family might characterize *Fern Gully* as a feel-good animated children's film with an important message, another might call it environmentalist propaganda. These judgments, when relayed to other members of the family, influence the way those members picture the world.

The family's influence on an individual's mental imagery is pronounced. And the influence of those images on the individual's life is also striking. As previously discussed, your mental imagery will influence your future family structure—impacting everything from mate selection to number of children to the roles each family member is expected to fill. Imagery will influence how you cope with changing relationships (such as through divorce or death). Imagery will even impact the scripts and expectations you have for your romantic relationship(s).

According to Honeycutt and Bryan (2011), some people have very complex expectations for behaviors in a relationship, while others have very simple expectations. They argue that relationships exist just as much in the minds of the relational partners as in the actual, observable interactions between those individuals. Thus, in addition to examining relationships through the interactions of the partners, one can also study relationships from solely within the minds of the individuals.

The way a relationship is formulated in one partner's mind acts as a guide that partner uses to interpret the behavior of the other. In other words, the way one partner imagines the relationship will color the way that partner sees all the relational encounters. If you see your relationship as one of happiness and equality, you'll interpret a discussion about what to watch on TV as an attempt to accommodate and please both parties. If you see your relationship as a power struggle, you'll interpret the same conversation as a covert struggle to exert dominance.

Imagined Interactions

Imagined interactions (IIs) are a type of social cognition and mental imagery theoretically grounded in symbolic interactionism in which individuals imagine conversations with significant others including family members for a variety of purposes (Honeycutt 2003; 2010). The imagined interaction construct has provided a beneficial mechanism for studying intrapersonal and interpersonal communication within family systems. Imagined interactions are a type of daydreaming that has definitive attributes and serves a number of functions, including rehearsal, self-understanding, relational maintenance, managing conflict, catharsis, and compensation. They often concentrate on ongoing or important events in individuals' daily lives and are associated with a variety of emotions (Klinger 1990).

Imagined interactions are mindful activities (Honeycutt and Ford 2001). Langer et al. (1978) showed how people sometimes process information by not attending carefully to information in their immediate environment. Mindlessness occurs when individuals rely on routine ways of thinking and use scripts such as saying "Hi" as a greeting ritual. Honeycutt and Bryan (2011) have discussed how cognitive scripts are a type of automatic pilot providing guidelines for how to act when encountering new situations. Scripts are activated mindlessly and created through imagined interactions, as people envision contingency plans for actions. In contrast to mindless processing, engaging in imagined interaction requires conscious cognitive processing. For example, you may have an arguing script with a parent in which you know that if a certain topic is brought up (e.g., how much time you spend on social media outlets compared to studying for your courses), the parent is likely to respond with belligerence and anger, and accuse you of social media addiction and not being focused on your studies. His/her intent is to shame you by inducing guilt. This reflects a mindless script in that if you have argued about the issue once, you feel as if you have argued it repetitively with no resolution. When you are doing this, you are having an imagined interaction with your parent.

Functional Theory of Imagined Interactions

A functional theory of imagined interactions explains their purpose in everyday encounters. When assuming a functional approach to analyzing imagined interactions, it is assumed that there may be therapeutic benefits at some level, whether it is increased self-awareness, relief of tension, or having pleasant thoughts about the imagined interaction. Support for this assumption is available in studies reviewed by Honeycutt (2003; 2008), particularly in the use of mental imagery to alleviate depression.

Functions of IIs

There are six functions of imagined interactions. First, they maintain relationships, as intrusive thinking occurs in which the partner is thought about outside of his or her physical presence. It has been found that they occur with friends, family members, intimate partners, roommates, and co-workers (Honeycutt 2003). So while you are at college or away from your distant family, you can think about various siblings, parents, in-laws in your mind, which psychologically maintains the symbolic bond that you may have with them. Our research has found that married couples who live together have frequent IIs among themselves. Additionally, IIs occur among geographically separated family members Hence, the maxim of "absence makes the heart fonder is operating rather than "out of sight, out of mind."

A second function of imagined interactions is rehearsing and planning messages. So, you plan what how you are going to ask your mother for a favor and anticipate her reaction. Individuals report how they prepare for important encounters and even think of various messages depending on their interaction partner's responses. Except for lonely people, rehearsal is often helpful even when there are discrepancies with actual conversations. Rehearsal allows people to develop rapid response contingencies more quickly compared to no rehearsal. It is helpful in preparing for job interviews and in stress situations such as having to tell someone bad news. The rehearsal function acknowledges the vital role communication plays in converting plans to action. Berger (1997) notes that when individuals engage in the planning process by themselves, they likely engage in internal dialogue as a means of testing out several alternatives before enactment. In essence, the individual can rehearse the plan(s) mentally prior to activation. Over 20 years ago, Honeycutt (1989) recounts a famous, pioneering example of rehearsal within the family in which a daughter had to confront her father about moving into a new residence while attending college. Following is an account of an II where rehearsal helped in enhancing confidence, although the real interaction did not fulfill expectations. In a sense, the individual was rehearsing the wrong script. However, she believed that the act of rehearsing was helpful. She was afraid that he would not give his approval due to economic costs. Hence, her imagined interaction reflects the II attribute of discrepancy that occurs whenever what you imagined is different from what actually occurs in the encounter. Research has revealed that discrepancy is associated with lower-quality marital relationships. In fact, we quote Honeycutt (2008–2009) who states that, "the less discrepant that imagined interactions are, the higher the quality of the relationship. Hence, discrepant imagined interactions in close relationships may be filled with ruminating over old arguments and conflicts" (p. 316).

The ensuing table shows the imagined interaction journal account in which rehearsal and discrepancy reflect the intrapersonal communication between the daughter and father:

Table 1 Example of Daughter Rehearsing a Request with Her Father

A couple of weeks ago, you gave to us a survey to do on imagined interactions. After doing the survey, I realized that I never really thought about all of the imagined interactions that I actually have. I guess I just never really paid much attention before our discussions about them in class. Recently, I had to confront my father about moving out of the dorm and into an apartment. I was quite nervous about the whole confrontation, so before I discussed the issue with him, I kind of rehearsed what I was going to say to him and I tried to anticipate his reaction.

Our spring break is when I had to talk to my father, so for about two weeks beforehand, I was rehearsing. I seemed like every time I would think about it, I would change my approach a little bit. But, my father's reaction, in my mind, was always the same. He would tell me that he did not want me to move into an apartment. In my imagination, I would tell him of all the benefits an apartment would have. I would have more privacy, there would not be as much noise so it would be easier to study, and it is less expensive than the dorm and a meal plan and on and on.

The time finally arose when I had to confront him. Again, I imagined what I was going to say to him and then I went ahead and opened the discussion. To my surprise, I did not even use my plan of action. I did not even list the benefits of the apartment vs. the dorm. Nevertheless, we discussed it and my father agreed to my moving out, which also contradicted my imagined interaction. I thought that this was kind of strange because usually my imagined interactions were similar in at least some ways to the actual conversation, but this one was completely opposite. At first I thought that all of that "practicing" was just a waste of time, since I did not use what I had practiced, but I think I was a little more confident about the discussion since I had gone over in my head the points of view that I wanted to get across. Maybe this helped since he agreed to let me move out. In this case, I am glad that they were different from the outcome. If they had gone the way I imagined, I would still be living in the dorm next semester.

A third function of imagined interactions is self-understanding, as imagined interactions allow people to clarify their thoughts and promote understanding of their own views, values, and attitudes. Imagined interactions' role in bettering self-understanding has been revealed in research assessing their use by couples experiencing geographical separation. Geographically separated couples indicate they experience imagined interactions as a means for increasing self-understanding compared to couples who are not geographically separated (Honeycutt 2003). These results suggest that such couples have a greater need to develop better understanding prior to interaction because of the limit on interaction time due to their geographic circumstances. So for example, if you find that your fiancée really believes in disciplining, spanking, or corporal punishment and you do not, you are likely to have a lot of IIs trying to understand why she believes so strongly in paddling.

The fourth function, catharsis, allows people to release emotions and vent feelings of frustration or joy. There is tension relief and anxiety reduction. Individuals and family members use imagined interactions to release anxiety as they are planning for anticipated encounters and relive what has previously taken place. A primary example of this is found in a study discussed by Honeycutt.

This function of imagined interactions in the family often occurs in conjunction with the fifth function, compensation, in which individuals compensate or substitute for the lack of actual conversations. For example, a person may imagine giving his or her supervisor a "piece of their mind," which momentarily relaxes them. Yet, they realize to do this may result in reprisal or sanctions; hence, both compensation and catharsis are used. For example, compensating for the lack of real interaction in long-distance relationships may be used to keep the relationship alive as well as rehearsing what will be said in the next telephone conversation.

The final function is conflict linkage also referred to as conflict management. Family members often relive old disagreements and arguments while simultaneously imagining statements for ensuing encounters. Hence, disagreements may pick up where they left off from prior interactions. The study of imagined interactions explains why there may be long-term, recurrent conflict and particular themes that characterize encounters between relational partners. Imagined interactions link a series of encounters together as individuals replay what was previously said and anticipate what may be said in the future. Conflict is kept alive in the human mind by reliving old arguments and imagining future conversations so that subsequent encounters may become self-fulfilling prophecies as interaction expectancies are enacted (Honeycutt 2003). There has been research on memorable messages in which people report messages given to them by parents, supervisors, teachers, or any person who is important in their life. Often these messages are designed to be motivational and provide guidelines for dealing with conflict. For example, Smith and Ellis (2001) found that the types of *memorable messages* fell into ten general categories: the Ten Commandments; the Golden Rule; be kind, patient, and loyal to others; respect elders; be responsible; live a healthy life; do your best and work hard; enjoy yourself and your life; love your family; and take time for God. Occasionally, a memorable message is negative (e.g., You will never amount to anything), which some people use to motivate themselves in order to "show them" that they were wrong in their prediction.

The conflict linkage function of imagined interactions explains recurring conflict in all personal relationships beyond those of the family. Honeycutt (2003) has presented three axioms and nine theorems for managing conflict, with numerous studies supporting them. Table 1 is a summary of the axioms and theorems from conflict-linkage theory that can be Googled. Some therapists lament how counseling and intervention may not result in longitudinal benefits in getting couples to communicate constructively. Conflict may be maintained through retro- and proactive imagined interactions that link a series of interactions (Honeycutt 1995). People may experience negative emotions as they "replay" such encounters. The conflict management function of imagined interactions helps explain why instruction on rational models for conflict resolution often fail, as people regress to old ways for resolving conflict (e.g., "I win, you lose"). Old interaction scripts that are nonproductive may be mindlessly retrieved from long-term memory. Thus, conflict episodes may pick up where they last left off, despite a period of physical separation. In the meantime, conflict is maintained in the mind using the retro- and proactive (rehearsal) features of imagined interactions. In this regard, imagined conflict linkage theory explains why popular "time-out" strategies advocated by educational interventionists for children may fail regularly.

In a relationship with a recurring, unresolved conflict, partners often feel they "know" how a conversation is going to go beforehand, making having the actual conversation useless. This is due to serial arguing over the same topic. Yet, the communication eventually comes to a halt and IIs are used as a substitute through the compensation function. This type of II may even explain why long-term success of marital counseling is low. Couples therapy often works on overt communicative behaviors, but doesn't address covert, or imagined, communication. Thus, once therapy ends, IIs, particularly IIs dealing with prolonged conflict, can drive the relationship back down the wrong path.

Indeed, poor communication habits are often cited as one of the leading causes of marital strife. Anything from treating the partner with contempt to having a "who cares" attitude toward your partner's complaints can spell trouble for the future of the relationship (Gottman 1994). Communication choices emphasize negative emotions in unhappy relationships and positive emotions in happy relationships. A couple in an unhappy relationship will use more negative behaviors and fewer positive behaviors than a happy couple. This may come as no surprise when considering conflict; however, it also holds true for mundane, everyday talk as well (Krokoff, Gottman, and Hass 1989).

While poor communication habits certainly shoulder some blame for many unhappy relationships, one must also examine the *beliefs about* communication that people hold. Honeycutt and Wiemann (1999) argue that individual differences in beliefs about the functions of talk may lead to marital strife. Should communication be used to assert the equality of the partners? Should it be a tool for controlling the pace and topic of an interaction? Just as your beliefs about the ideal home will influence the houses you'll consider living in, your beliefs about the reasons for communicating will impact the way you communicate, consequently impacting your relational satisfaction. Beliefs about communication will also influence the types and functions of imagined interactions you have.

II Attributes

There are eight characteristics or attributes of IIs (Honeycutt 2003; 2008). The attributes are *frequency* (how often persons experience imagined interactions); *emotional valence* (how enjoyable or uncomfortable they are, i.e., Donald Trump imagines telling an apprentice that they will be fired); *discrepancy* (the degree that IIs are different from actual communication); *dominance* (the amount that the self or other dominates the talk); *proactivity* (whether or not IIs precede anticipated encounters); *retroactivity* (whether or not IIs follow encounters); *specificity* (the amount of detail in IIs); and *variety* (the number of different topics and partners experienced).

Research with married couples finds that the sole predictor of relational happiness and satisfaction is the pleasantness of IIs (Honeycutt 1999; Honeycutt and Weimann 1999) suggesting the relationship maintenance function involves primarily positively valenced IIs. In a similar manner, IIs used for compensation are likely to be positively valenced. Although it is possible that individuals compensate for a lack of negative interaction by having negatively valenced IIs, research to date suggests it is more plausible that substituting for actual interaction is marked by positive emotions. In this regard, Honeycutt (1989) found that elderly residents in a retirement home reporting using the compensation function had more pleasant IIs with children who visited regularly compared with children who rarely visited. More recent research has found that having more specific, frequent, pleasant, self-dominant, proactive, and retroactive IIs predicted higher relationship satisfaction (Honeycutt and Keaton 2012–2013).

Types of Marriage and Imagined Interactions

In order to understand the ways that communication in imagined interactions influences relational satisfaction, we must first understand the different types of marital relationships. There are three broad couple-types. Each couple-type has particular implications for communication patterns within the relationship, particularly in terms of relational conflict (Fitzpatrick 1988). The first couple-type is the *Traditional*. Traditional couples are highly interdependent, believing that autonomy must be sacrificed for the good of the relationship. They typically hold traditional beliefs about gender roles and don't typically argue over small issues; however, Traditionals are perfectly comfortable arguing over salient issues (Fitzpatrick 1988). *Independent* couples emphasize individual autonomy and have less conventional attitudes about gender roles. Self-disclosure is high for Independents, leading to a high level of closeness; however, Independents leave room for personal physical and mental space. Independents actively negotiate many aspects of the relationship, with the result being that they regularly engage in conflict over both small and large issues. *Separate* couples hold traditional beliefs about gender roles, while simultaneously maintaining distance and autonomy in the relationship. Intimacy and interdependence are low and conflict over any issue is generally avoided. In addition to these three couple-types, Fitzpatrick (1988) discusses a fourth: the *Mixed* couple-type is made up of partners with differing views of relationships. An Independent husband with a Separate wife would be an example of a mixed couple-type.

Just as couple-type will influence arguing style in face-to-face interaction, it also impacts imagined interactions. For example, Honeycutt (1999) found Traditionals were less likely to use IIs to rehearse future interactions than Independents. Furthermore, these IIs were more likely to be discrepant from the way the conversation actually went. In the same study, Independents were more likely to think about communication, emotions, and arguing than were Traditionals. It was also discovered that Traditionals and Independents were significantly more likely to engage in pleasant IIs and IIs characterized by listening *as well as* speaking to the partner. Both husbands' and wives' marital happiness were predicted by having pleasant IIs. Separates and Mixed-types were not likely to engage in these types of IIs. In fact, Separates report more unpleasant internal dialogues with their partners than Traditionals or Independents. It is speculated that the conflict-avoidance that characterizes Separate relationships causes these individuals mental anguish by forcing them to live with unresolved, but completely resolvable conflict.

Fitzpatrick (1988) notes that Separates are unlikely to disclose inner feelings and express little emotion while Traditionals represent a type of companionate marriage. Separates may be constrained by external forces such as attempting compliance with traditional roles. Separates have been referred to by Fitzpatrick (1988) as failed Traditionals and emotionally divorced in that they are not as likely to concede individual for group goals.

An interesting profile of the Separates emerges. Their internal dialogues are less pleasant with their partner than Traditional and Independents. Gottman (1994) speculates that Separates (conflict-avoiders) live with the pain of unsolved, solvable problems. He discusses how negative emotions are frightening for Separates and that Separates do not have the communication skills to work out unavoidable conflict. If this is the case, then conflict may be kept alive in the minds of Separates through a series of linked IIs. According to II conflict-linkage theory, recurring conflict is maintained through retro- and proactive IIs (Honeycutt 2010) and conflict is kept alive within your mind by dwelling on it. While Separates are afraid of negative emotions and thus avoid communicating about potentially unpleasant things (Gottman 1994), they also desire a resolution to their problems. They find solace in their imagined interactions, thus causing their IIs to be more unpleasant than others.

While imagined interactions differ among couple-type, they also differ somewhat between married and engaged couples. For example, according to Honeycutt and Wiemann (1999), engaged couples tended to have more positive IIs than married couples, leading to greater degrees of relational satisfaction for engaged couples. Engaged couples are also more likely to use IIs as a means of compensating for the absence of the partner than married couples. Married couples, on the other hand, were more likely to use IIs to rehearse future encounters with their partner.

Table 6-1. Rank order of Spousal Imagined Interaction Topics

Topics	Rank Order Combined	Rank Order Husband	Rank Order Wife
Plans and Goals	1	1 (12)	2 (7)
Sex Life	2*	2 (8)	4 (5)
How we communicate	2*	6 (4)	1 (9)
How we manage our finances	4	3 (6)	4 (5)
Our social life	5*	6 (4)	3 (6)
Our relationship	5*	3 (6)	6 (4)
Children	7*	6 (4)	8 (3)
My job	7*	5 (5)	10 (2)
Feelings and emotions	7*	9 (3)	6 (4)
Fantasies	10	9 (3)	8 (3)

*Denotes tie Numbers in parentheses reflect raw frequencies

Finally, there are sex differences in imagined interactions. While conventional wisdom would indicate women have more IIs than men, research actually shows that men and women in relationships report equal numbers of imagined interactions (Honeycutt and Wiemann 1999). The topics discussed in imagined interactions were slightly, though not significantly, different for men and women. Among husbands, plans and goals was the most imagined topic, followed by the couple's sex life, and then managing finances. For wives, future plans and goals was the second most imagined topic. The first was how the couple communicates, while the third was the couple's social life. When combining the data for husbands and wives, future plans and goals was the most frequent topic, with couple communication and sex life tied for second place. Table 6-1 presents a complete breakdown of topics and sex differences.

Report of Imagined Interactions with Family Members over a Week

We conducted a study in which students kept daily logs of their imagined interactions with family members for a total of seven days. The average of the fathers in the study was 54.56 and ranged from 38 to 73. The average of the mothers was 51.43 and ranged in age from 36 to 71. Over 75% of the parents were still married with the remaining 25% who were divorced, separated, widowed, or never married (one case). The sample was primarily of a Judeo-Christian affiliation (71%) with the remaining being secular or agnostic. The vast majority were of a heterosexual orientation (96%).

They were asked to report how often they had imagined interactions with family members and to identify them. Using a seven-point, Likert-type scale, in which a 1 represents having no IIs with any family member and a 7 represents having IIs many times throughout the week; the average score was 5.54. The vast majority of the topics discussed over the week were imaginary discussions of family and home concerns followed by school and daily activities. Over 50% of these discussions took place with parents followed by younger siblings. Following are the average decreasing percentages of II family interaction partners over the course of seven days: Mother (31.63%), Younger Brother (21.47%), Father (20.9%), Older Sister (5.96%), Someone else (e.g., Aunt, Uncle, Cousin) (4.76%), Older Brother

Estimated Marginal Means of

Frequency

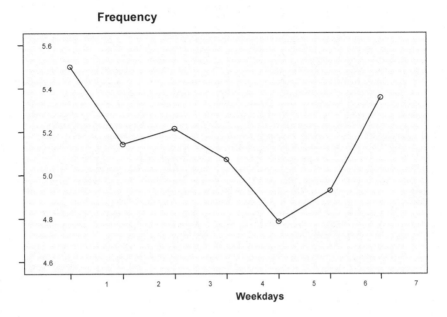

Figure 6-1. Frequency of IIs with a Family Member over a Week*

*Days are numbered in consecutive order from Sunday to Saturday

(4.59%), Grandmother (3.6%), Grandfather (2.56%). Figure 6-1 shows that most family IIs occur on weekends including Sunday (weekday 1) and Saturday (weekday 7).

Figure 6-2 reveals a statistically significant effect for discrepant IIs in which Fridays were the most discrepant IIs with family members while Tuesday, Wednesday, and Thursday were the least discrepant

Estimated Marginal Means of Discrepancy

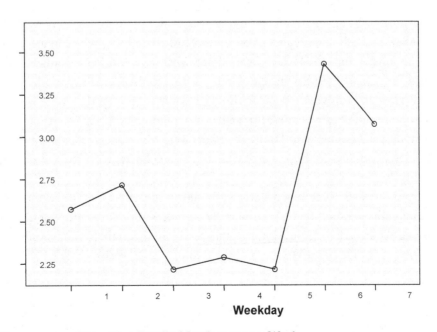

Figure 6-2. Discrepancy of IIs with a Family Member over a Week

Estimated Marginal Means of Valence

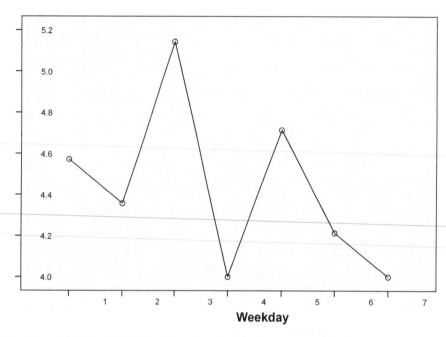

Figure 6-3. Emotional Affect within IIs with a Family Member over a Week

IIs. It could be that IIs on Friday are concerned with anticipating family reactions to weekend events and what was expected is different from the family members' reactions.

Another significant effect was for valence in which Tuesday is the day of the week in which IIs with family members are most positive while Wednesday and Saturday show the most negative emotional affect with family members, as shown in Figure 6-3.

Another statistically significant result we found was how dominant the self was in the IIs with their family member. In a self-dominant II, you do most of the talking while in an "other-dominant" II, you are more in a listening role, such as listening to what your mother or father are telling you to do (McCann and Honeycutt 2006). Figure 6-4 reveals how the students report that they were more dominant in their IIs with family members on Thursday while on Friday, they were in a listening role.

Two functions were statistically significant: self-understanding and dominance. IIs used to understand values, attitudes, and beliefs with family members were more likely to be used on weekends and particularly Monday, as revealed in Figure 6-5, while the Thursday represented the smallest number of self-understanding IIs.

As revealed in Figure 6-6, there was a statistically significant effect for the relational maintenance function in which family members had IIs with family members at the beginning of the week (Sunday–Tuesday even though it drops a little on Monday) that served to maintain bonding and sharing with the family. This function is used least on Wednesday, the middle of the week.

Estimated Marginal Means of Dominance

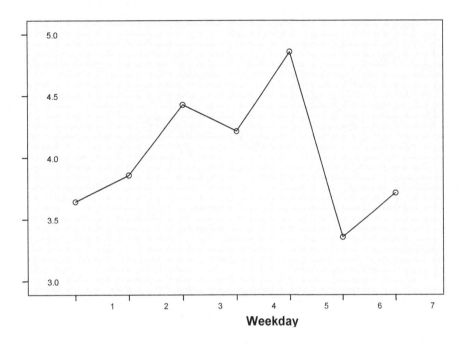

Figure 6-4. Amount of Self-Dominance in IIs with a Family Member over a Week

Estimated Marginal Means of Self-Understanding

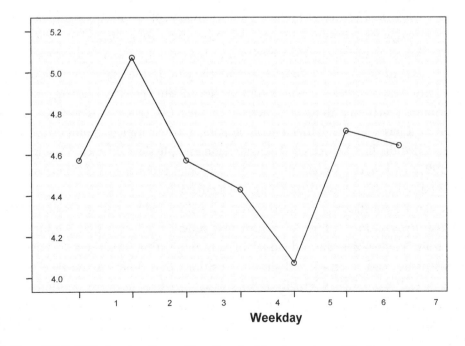

Figure 6-5. Use of II Self-Understanding with a Family Member over a Week

Estimated Marginal Means of Relational Maintenance

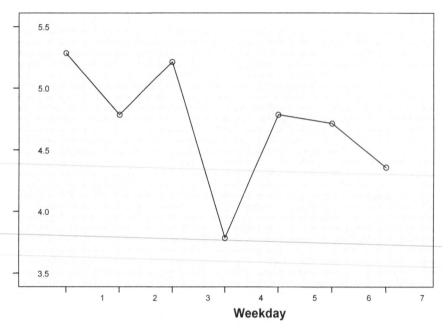

Figure 6-6. Use of Relational Maintenance with a Family Member over a Week

Imagined Interactions Among Different Types of Marriages Abuse: How II can be used to plan aggression with marriage

Intimate partner abuse is a pervasive problem. The estimates of its occurrence range from 960,000 incidents of violence against a current or former spouse, boyfriend, or girlfriend per year to three million women who are abused physically by their husband or boyfriend per year (http://www.endabuse.org/resources/facts/). According to some estimates, around the world, at least one in three women has been beaten, coerced into sex, or otherwise abused during her lifetime (Heise, Ellsberg, and Gottemoeller 1999). Furthermore, nearly one-third of American women (31 percent) report being physically or sexually abused by a husband or boyfriend at some point in their lives (Commonwealth Fund 1998). Research has revealed the link between verbal aggression and physical violence. Vissing, Straus, Gelles, and Harrop (1991) have demonstrated that the psychosocial problems of children are more directly related to parental verbal aggression than to physical aggression.

Aggression can be constructive or destructive. Hostility and verbal aggression are destructive while verbal assertiveness in the form of argumentativeness is constructive. Arguing is defined as a personality trait "predisposes the individual in communication situations to advance positions on controversial issues and to attack verbally the positions that other people take on these issues" (Infante and Rancer 1982; p. 72). A verbally aggressive act produces negative emotional reaction, such as anger, and a covert verbal response, which facilitates recall of the emotional experience at a later date. From this description, it seems likely that imagined interactions (IIs) facilitate the recollection process (Honeycutt 2003).

To the extent that communication skills deficiency is a factor in personal relationships, then there is an important role of intrapersonal communication and cognition in the form of imagined interactions in order to rehearse messages as well as relieving tension. Indeed, prior research has revealed an association between verbal aggression and characteristics of IIs. Honeycutt (2003; 2004) discusses the importance of suppressed rage in abuse. Theorem 4 of II conflict-linkage theory indicates that suppressed rage is the result of an inability to articulate arguments with the target of conflict. As rage mounts, verbal aggression intensifies, possibly culminating in physical violence. If a person experiences heightened arousal but stops short of physical violence, the result can be suppressed rage. Physical aggression is related to verbal aggression. Infante and Wigley (1986) reported a correlation of .32 between physical assault and verbal aggression. Additionally, Infante, Chandler, and Rudd (1989) compared a clinical sample of abused wives from a battered shelter and a sample of abusive husbands undergoing group therapy for wife abuse to a nonclinical sample of men and women. The results revealed that both husbands and wives in violent marriages were lower in self-reported argumentativeness while being higher in verbal aggression than the nonviolent sample.

Honeycutt (2003) tested a model in which the characteristics of frequency, proactivity, and specificity predicted verbal aggression while they were unrelated to persuasive arguments. Honeycutt (2003) speculated that an explanation for this was the slight path from II functions to verbal aggression (.15). That analysis revealed how catharsis and self-understanding reflected II functions that impacted on verbal aggression. Perhaps, individuals who imagine being verbally aggressive as opposed to thinking about rational arguments experience catharsis while also believing that they understand their rage better. Essentially, the abuser does not engage in persuasive arguing.

Later, Honeycutt and Bryan (2011) tested a model in which IIs mediated the relationship between verbal aggression and physical abuse. Essentially, this means the abuser is thinking about his/her actions and verbal taunts. Characteristics of this type of imagined interaction, as revealed in Figure 6-7, are having frequent IIs (activity) that occur before the incidents (Proactivity). Yet, the loading of the specificity factor (.75) on imagined interactions reflects the idea that the abuser is thinking of relatively precise visual and verbal images. For example, he/she anticipates what they are going to say at the anticipated encounter as well as imagining the scene of the interaction. The imagined interaction is characterized by repetitive thoughts about the areas of conflict. For examples, individuals replay arguments in their mind while simultaneously preparing for the next encounter. In addition, the catharsis index is slightly related to imagined interactions in this context as the abuser may report feeling better by using imagined interactions to relieve pent-up emotions, tension, and stress in their mind. Indeed, one of the catharsis items assesses the extent that people report IIs help to get "things off their chest."

To the extent IIs partially mediate the association between verbal aggression and physical coercion, communication intervention may be used for the abuser who plans their violence. Indeed, communication intervention may foster the role of forgiveness, which has been shown to be negatively associated with rumination about seeking revenge (McCullough, Bono, and Root 2007).

Pit-Bull and Cobra Batterers in Marriage

Research has identified two types of batterers in marriage referred to as the pit bulls and cobras (Holtzworth-Munroe, Meehan, Herron, Rehman, and Stuart 2003; Jacobson and Gottman 1998; Waltz, Babcock, Jacobson, and Gottman 2000.) Holtzworth-Munroe and her associates refer to them as "borderline/dysphoric" and "generally violent/antisocial," while Jacobson and Gottman refer to them as "pit bulls" and "cobras." According to Jacobson and Gottman's (1998) study of 60 male batterers, the vast majority (80%) of male batterers were individuals who fit the pit-bull mentality. Pit bulls typically

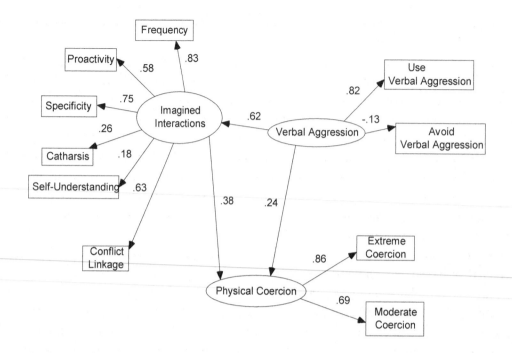

Figure 6-7. Standardized Medional Model of Imagined Interaction, Verbal Aggression, and Physical Coercion

confine their violent behavior to their intimate relationships. They are jealous, and because of a severe fear of abandonment, they seek to deprive their partners of independence (Babcock, Jacobson, Gottman, and Yerington 2000). Their violence is marked by a slow burn that explodes into anger. Hence, they are likely to ruminate about conflict and have imagined interactions in which they may be caught in a self-absorbing state of rage. The more they think about their grievances, the further enraged they are and find it difficult to turn off their internal cognition about grievances.

Cobras, on the other hand, are not emotionally dependent on the relationship, but feel that their every wish should be met. Cobras are prone to aggression toward everyone, and they tend to calm down internally as they become aggressive. Cobras are more likely to threaten with or use deadly weapons. Pit bulls have much more potential for rehabilitation than cobras, who are difficult to treat with therapy (Jacobson and Gottman 1998). Yet, this claim is premised on the assertion that pit bulls ruminate about their aggression. If this is the case, then imagined interactions could mediate the link between verbal aggression and aggression.

These data appear to reflect the pit-bull abuser. The profile of a pit bull suggests that they would have frequent imagined interactions in order to castigate their partners while cobras strike without warning or forethought. Pit bulls metabolize anger in a slow kind of burn as it gradually increases and does not waver (Jacobson and Gottman 1998). While they have unrelenting contempt for women, they are excessively dependent on them and fear abandonment. Ironically, Jacobson and Gottman (1998) discovered that 38% of pit-bull wives left within two years, while none of the cobra wives left during that time period even though 25% of them had left after five years. Control is important to the pit bulls because they feel that they will be abandoned if they do maintain constant vigilance over their partners. Pit bulls usually confine their violence to family members and have had batterers as fathers. Yet, Jacobson and Gottman (1998) believe that there is some potential for rehabilitation.

The potential for rehabilitation may lie in the discovery that imagined interactions partially mediate the direct link between verbal aggression and physical violence. Hence, people are ruminating and thinking about their conflict. Therefore, communication interventionists may attempt to create communication skills for more effective arguing and listening. A number of intervention programs have been tried, including empathy instruction (Warner, Parker, and Calhoun 1984), problem-solving (Markman, Floyd, Stanley, and Storassili 1988), and training in creating persuasive arguments (Rancer, Kosberg, and Baukus 1992).

Intervention is less likely to be effective for cobras who strike without warning. For example, Jacobson and Gottman (1998) believe that young boys are socialized to keep vulnerable emotions submerged and do not develop an emotional vocabulary that allows them to articulate what they are feeling. If you cannot tell sadness from loneliness or the disappointment from rejection from being devalued, bad feelings get overloaded easily. Yet, the strongest emotion is anger, which men have been socialized to vent even through constructive channeling such as athletic competition. Yet, communicating too much anger may also result in anger-management classes or court-mandated intervention. Most programs described in batterer's intervention literature employ some variation of either a cognitive-behavioral or social learning approach. These approaches involve components such as anger-management training, communication skills, modeling, and relaxation. These clinical interventions are used with varying degrees of success, as revealed by recidivism rates in court-referred anger-management therapies (Babcock and Steiner 1999).

Summary and Conclusion

Imagined Interactions within the family are very important in mentally maintaining the family structure. As axiom 1 of imagined interaction conflict-linkage theory states: the relationship exists within the minds of family members. Communication is a conduit and activity that reinforces family bonds. They occur on certain days of the week, including Sunday and Saturday, and most notably on weekends. They are least likely to occur with family members among college students on Thursday. This may be due to the occurrence of other activities including studying, work, and preparation for social activities over the weekend. Popular family topics include discussion of home and family activities followed by sex talk, and how they communicate. The eight attributes are of IIs are frequency, emotional valence, discrepancy, dominance, proactivity, retroactivity, specificity, and variety. The six functions of imagined interactions are relational maintenance, rehearsal, self-understanding, catharsis, compensation, and conflict management. Having happy IIs with a marital partner reflects marital happiness. Couples who are emotionally divorced keep recurring conflict alive in their minds and are called separate, while independent and traditional couples do not do this. Arguing does not predict divorce by itself, but arguing with contempt does. According to II conflict-linkage theory, recurring conflict is maintained through retro- and proactive IIs (Honeycutt 2010) and conflict is kept alive within your mind by dwelling on it. Prior research has revealed how II can mediate the relationship between verbal aggression and physical abuse.

DISCUSSION QUESTIONS AND ACTIVITIES

1. How often do you have imagined interactions with your mother or father? How often do you text them or send them e-mails? Does this serve the relational maintenance and compensation function of imagined interactions?

2. Examine Figure 6-3 in terms of the daily emotional affect. The data reported in this chapter reveal that on Tuesdays, imagined interactions with family members is positively valenced, while the following day, Wednesday, and Saturday show the most negative emotional affect with family members. Do you agree or disagree with this finding? Is this true for you?

3. Recall how Figure 6-4 reveals that college students report that they were more dominant in their IIs with family members on Thursday while on Friday, they were in a listening role. Apply this finding to you. Do you think you listen more to your family members on Friday? Why or why not? How would you explain this finding?

4. As revealed in Figure 6-6, there was a statistically significant effect for the relational maintenance function in which family members had IIs with family members at the beginning of the week (Sunday–Tuesday, even though it drops a little on Monday) that served to maintain bonding and sharing with the family. This function is used least on Wednesday, the middle of the week. Is this true for you? Why or why not? Explain and elaborate.

5. Do you know any pit-bull or cobra abusers?

REFERENCES

Babcock, J. C. and Steiner, R. (1999). "The Relationship Between Treatment, Incarceration, and Recidivism of Battering: A program Evaluation of Seattle's Coordinated Community Response to Domestic Violence." *Journal of Family Psychology, 13,* 46–59. http://dx.doi.org/10.1037/0893-3200.13.1.46.

Berger, C. R. (1997). *Planning Strategic Interaction: Attaining Goals Through Communicative Action.* Mahwah, NJ: Erlbaum.

Commonwealth Fund, Health Concerns Across a Woman's Lifespan: 1998 Survey of Women's Health, May 1999. Retrieved on November 18, 2012 from http://www.endabuse.org/resources/facts/.

Fitzpatrick, M. A. (1988). *Between Husbands and Wives: Communication in Marriage.* Newbury Park, CA: Sage.

Gottman, J. (1994). *What Predicts Divorce.* Hillsdale, NJ: Lawrence Erlbaum Associates.

Heise, L., Ellsberg, M., and Gottemoeller, M. (1999). "Ending Violence Against Women." Johns Hopkins University School of Public Health. Available: http://www.vawnet.org/DomesticViolence/Research/OtherPubs/PopulationReports.pdf. Accessed November 18, 2012.

Holtzworth-Munroe, A., Meehan, J. C., Herron, K., Rehman,U., and Stuart, G. L. (2003). "Do Subtypes of Maritally Violent Men Continue to Differ over Time?" *Journal of Consulting and Clinical Psychology, 71,* 728–740. http://dx.doi.org/10.1037/0022-006X.71.4.728.

Honeycutt, J. M. (1989). "A Functional Analysis of Imagined Interaction Activity in Everyday Life." In J. E. Shorr, P. Robin, J. A. Connelia, and M. Wolpin (Eds.), *Imagery: Current Perspectives* (pp. 13–25). New York: Plenum Press.

Honeycutt, J. M. (1999). "Typological Differences in Predicting Marital Happiness from Oral History Behaviors and Imagined Interactions (IIs)." *Communication Monographs, 66,* 276–291. doi:10.1080/03637759909376478

Honeycutt, J. M. (2003). *Imagined Interactions: Daydreaming About Communication.* Cresskill, NJ: Hampton.

Honeycutt, J. M. (2008). "Imagined Interaction Theory: Mental Representations of Interpersonal Communication." In L. A. Baxter and D. Braithwaite (Eds.). *Engaging Theories in Interpersonal Communication* (pp. 77–87). Thousand Oaks, CA: Sage.

Honeycutt, J. M. (2008–2009). "Symbolic Interdependence, Imagined Interaction, and Relationship Quality." *Imagination, Cognition, and Personality, 28,* 303–320. doi: 10.2190/IC.28.4.b

Honeycutt, J. M. (2010). "Forgive but Don't Forget: Correlates of Rumination About Conflict." In J. M. Honeycutt (Ed.), *Imagine That: Studies in Imagined Interaction* (pp. 17–29). Cresskill, NJ: Hampton.

Honeycutt, J. M. and Bryan, S. P. (2011). *Scripts and Communication for Relationships.* New York: Peter Lang.

Honeycutt, J. M. and Ford, S. G. (2001). "Mental Imagery and Intrapersonal Communication: A Review of Research on Imagined Interactions (IIs) and Current Developments." *Communication Yearbook 25* (pp. 315–345). Mahwah, NJ: Erlbaum. http://dx.doi.org/10.1207/s15567419cy2501_9.

Honeycutt, J. M. and Keaton, S. A. (2012–2013). "Imagined Interactions and Personality Preferences as Predictors of Relationship Quality." *Imagination, Cognition, and Personality, 32,* 3–21. http://dx.doi.org/10.2190/IC.32.1.b.

Honeycutt, J. M. and Wiemann, J. M. (1999). "Analysis of Functions of Talk and Reports of Imagined Interactions (IIs) During Engagement and Marriage." *Human Communication Research, 25,* 399–419. doi: 10.1111/j.1468-2958.1999.tb00451.x

Infante, D. A. and Rancer, A. S. (1996). "Argumentativeness and Verbal Aggressiveness: A Review of Recent Theory and Research." In B. R. Burleson (Ed.), *Communication Yearbook 19* (pp. 319–351). Thousand Oaks, CA: Sage.

Infante, D. A. and Wigley, C. J. (1986). "Verbal Aggressiveness: An Interpersonal Model and Measure." *Communication Monographs, 53,* 61–69. http://dx.doi.org/10.1080/03637758609376126.

Infante, D. A., Chandler, T. A., and Rudd, J. E. (1989). "Test of an Argumentative Skill Deficiency Model of Interspousal Violence." *Communication Monographs, 56,* 163–177. http://dx.doi.org/10.1080/03637758909390257.

Jacobson, N. and Gottman, J. M. (1998). *When Men Batter Women: New Insights into Ending Abusive Relationships.* New York: Simon & Schuster.

Klinger, E. (1990). *Daydreaming.* Los Angeles: Jeremy P. Tarcher, Inc. Langer, E. J., Blank, A., and Chanowitz, B. (1978). "The Mindlessness of Ostensibly Thoughtful Action: The Role of Placebic Information in Interpersonal Interaction." *Journal of Personality and Social Psychology, 36,* 635–642. http://dx.doi.org/10.1037/0022-3514.36.6.635.

Krokoff, L. J., Gottman, J. M., and Hass, S. D. (1989). "Validation of a Global Rapid Couples Interaction Scoring System." *Behavioral Assessment, 11,* 65–79.

Markman, H. J., Floyd, F. J., Stanley, S. M., and Storaasli, R. D. (1988). "Prevention of Marital Distress: A Longitudinal Investigation." *Journal of Consulting and Clinical Psychology, 56,* 210–217. http://dx.doi.org/10.1037/0022-006X.56.2.210.

McCann, R. M. and Honeycutt, J. M. (2006). "A Cross-Cultural Analysis of Imagined Interaction." *Human Communication Research, 32,* 274–301. http://dx.doi.org/10.1111%2Fj.1468-2958.2006.00276.x.

McCullough, M. E., Bono, G., and Root, L. M. (2007). "Rumination, Emotion, and Forgiveness: Three Longitudinal Studies." *Journal of Personality and Social Psychology, 92,* 490–505. http://dx.doi.org/10.1037/0022-3514.92.3.490.

Rancer, A. S., Kosberg, R. L., and Baukus, R. A. (1992). "Beliefs About Arguing as Predictors of Trait Argumentativeness: Implications for Training in Argument and Conflict Management." *Communication Education, 41,* 375–387. http://dx.doi.org/10.1080/03634529209378899.

Smith, S. W. and Ellis, J. B. (2001). "Memorable Messages as Guides to Self-Assessment of Behavior: An Initial Investigation." *Communication Monographs, 68,* 154–168. http://dx.doi.org/10.1080/03637750128058.

Tower, R. B. (1986). "Imagery and Families." In A. A. Sheikh (Ed.), *International Review of Mental Imagery. Vol. 2.* New York: Human Sciences Press.

Vissing, V. M., Strauss, M. A., Gelles, R. J., and Harrop, J. W. (1991). "Verbal Aggression by Parents and Psychosocial Problems of Children." *Child Abuse & Neglect, 15,* 223–239. http://dx.doi.org/10.1016/0145-2134(91)90067-N.

Warner, M. H., Parker, J. B., and Calhoun, J. F. (1984). "Inducing Person-Perception Change in a Spouse-Abuse Situation." *Family Therapy, 11,* 123–138.

7. The Family Lives of Lesbians and Gay Men

By Letitia Peplau & Kristin Beals

Most lesbians and gay men today grew up in a family headed by heterosexual parents. As adults, lesbians and gay men often establish committed partner relationships. Increasing numbers of lesbians and gay men are becoming parents and raising children. Research about these different aspects of the family lives of lesbians and gay men—as children, as romantic partners, and as parents—is relatively new. Of the 1,521 articles published in the *Journal of Marriage and the Family* and the *Journal of Social and Personal Relationships* from 1980 to 1993, only 5 focused on some aspect of sexual orientation (Allen & Demo, 1995). In the past decade, however, there has been a noticeable increase in research on gays and lesbians in families.

This selection reviews empirical research about the family lives of lesbians and gay men. We focus on four main topics: societal attitudes about gay men and lesbians, the relations of lesbians and gay men to their family of origin, the nature of gay and lesbian couples, and the experiences of homosexual parents and their children. Throughout, we highlight areas where additional research is needed.

The Social Climate: Public Attitudes About Lesbians, Gay Men, And Families

The family relationships of lesbians and gay men cannot be understood without recognizing the social climate of sexual prejudice in U.S. society (Herek, 2000). Representative national surveys conducted during the past 30 years show that Americans' attitudes about homosexuality have become more tolerant (see review by Loftus, 2001). Lesbians and gay men are aware of this change. In an important new survey, the Kaiser Foundation (2001) conducted telephone interviews with 405 randomly selected, self-identified gay, lesbian, and bisexual adults from 15 major U.S. cities. In this survey, 76% of respondents said they believed there was more acceptance of homosexuals today than in the past. Nonetheless, 74% also reported that they had experienced some form of prejudice or discrimination because of their sexual orientation, and 32% had been the target of violence against themselves or their property.

Today, a strong majority of Americans (often 75% or more) approves of laws to protect the civil rights of lesbians and gay men in such areas as employment and housing (Loftus, 2001). However, public attitudes about morality and family issues are more strongly divided. In a recent national survey (Kaiser Foundation, 2001), about half of Americans agreed that "homosexual behavior is morally wrong," opposed legally sanctioned gay and lesbian marriages, and indicated that "allowing gays and lesbians to legally marry would undermine the traditional American family." There was somewhat less opposition (42%) to legally sanctioned gay and lesbian unions other than marriage. Approximately half of those surveyed (56%) agreed that "gay and lesbian couples can be as good parents as heterosexual couples," and 46% approved of permitting gay and lesbian couples to legally adopt children. In short, the general public is fairly evenly divided in their views about the morality of homosexuality and the wisdom of same-sex unions and gay adoptions.

RELATIONSHIPS OF GAY MEN AND LESBIANS WITH THEIR PARENTS AND FAMILY OF ORIGIN

Lesbians and gay men are usually raised by heterosexual parents who assume that their children will be heterosexual. The revelation that a child is gay or lesbian often precipitates a family crisis. Perhaps because of the turmoil associated with this event, available research has focused on the individual's initial disclosure of his or her sexual orientation ("coming out") and the parents' reactions to this disclosure.

Disclosing a Minority Sexual Orientation

Many lesbians and gay men anguish about the decision whether or not to disclose their sexual identity to family members. Some individuals who anticipate a negative response and want to preserve family bonds never reveal their sexual orientation. In other cases, family members learn about the person's sexual orientation indirectly, perhaps by overhearing a conversation, or they may suspect a person is gay or lesbian based on the person's choice of friends, hairstyle, or dress. In most cases, however, gays and lesbians intentionally share this important information with at least some family members.

Recent surveys provide information about disclosure to parents and relatives (e.g., Morris, Waldo, & Rothblum, 2001). In a study of nearly 2,300 gay, lesbian, and bisexual adults from northern California (Herek, Gillis, & Cogan, 1996), 79% of respondents said that their mother knew about their sexual orientation, and 65% had talked directly with her about the topic. Siblings were the next most likely to know: 74% of respondents indicated that one or more sisters knew, and 69% reported that one or more brothers knew. Gay men, lesbians, and bisexuals were somewhat less likely to disclose to their father: 62% said that their father knew, but only 39% had talked with him about their sexual orientation. In a national telephone survey (Kaiser Foundation, 2001), 84% of lesbians and gay men said that they were generally open about their sexual orientation with family members. These rates of disclosure are higher than those reported in earlier studies (e.g., Bell & Weinberg, 1978), suggesting that an increasing percentage of gay men and lesbians are coming out to their families.

Studies of adolescents and younger adults show generally similar findings. Based on their review of existing studies, Savin-Williams and Esterberg (2000) estimated that 40 to 75% of young gay men and lesbians have disclosed to their mother and 30 to 55% to their father. These researchers also suggested that "with each passing year, a greater percentage of youths are disclosing to their parents" (p. 201).

In summary, three general findings emerge. First, although most lesbians and gay men are open with their family, a substantial minority conceals this important aspect of their identity from parents or other family members. Second, mothers are more likely than fathers to know about their child's sexual orientation and to have discussed it with the child. Third, the proportion of gays and lesbians who disclose their sexual orientation to parents and relatives appears to be increasing over time.

Research is needed to map systematically the patterns of disclosure in families from diverse backgrounds. First, it appears that a greater proportion of lesbians and gay men are disclosing to their families today than in the past and are doing so at a younger age. Studies systematically examining disclosure among different age cohorts would be valuable. Second, researchers have speculated about the reasons why gay men and lesbians may disclose to some family members before others, but empirical support for these hypotheses is largely lacking. For instance, do individuals tend to come out first to their mother because they have a closer relationship with her and expect a less negative reaction? Do some individuals disclose first to siblings to "test how the family will react" as Crosbie-Burnett, Foster, Murray, and Bowen (1996, p. 400) suggested? Studies examining the transmission of disclosure information among siblings and other family members would also be informative. Third, little is known about the experiences of lesbians and gay men from diverse ethnic, cultural, or religious groups. Some have suggested that lesbians and gay men from traditional ethnic backgrounds may be especially reluctant to disclose their sexual orientation to family members for fear of losing a vital source of social support and connection to their ethnic community (Savin-Williams, 1996). In some cases, ethnic minority lesbians and gay men may also fear that revealing their sexual orientation will bring embarrassment or shame to their family. Finally, prior research has tended to view disclosure as a single, one-time event. In reality, individuals often engage in a continuing process of sharing greater information about their sexual orientation with family members over time. We know little about temporal patterns of disclosure.

Family Reactions To A Gay Or Lesbian Child

Initially, family members' reactions to learning that a son is gay or a daughter is lesbian are often negative (see review by Savin-Williams & Esterberg, 2000). Common reactions include such feelings as shock, disbelief, guilt, and anger (see review by Savin-Williams & Dube, 1998). In a recent survey, 50% of lesbians and 32% of gay men reported that their "family or a family member" had refused to accept them because of their sexual orientation (Kaiser Foundation, 2001).

Many factors contribute to this negativity. Family members may view homosexuality as immoral or a sign of mental illness. They may believe myths about the lives of gays and lesbians, fearing, for example, that their child is doomed to a life of loneliness. Families may also worry about the dangers of sexual prejudice or have concerns about an increased risk of HIV infection. They may fear that they have contributed to their child's being gay or lesbian through their inadequacy as parents. Further, since the lives of parents and children are interdependent in important ways, parents may have concerns about their own future, wondering if they will have grandchildren or if their child's "secret" will affect connections among their extended family and community.

Over time, many families recover from the initial turmoil of disclosure, and relations with the gay or lesbian child improve. We know little about the processes that enable families to restore positive relations, although the quality of predisclosure family relations appears to be important (Patterson, 2000). Popular writers and parent support groups have suggested that parents' reactions follow predictable stages of denial, anger, bargaining, depression, and acceptance. Researchers such as Savin-Williams and Dube (1998) are skeptical of this stage model and note that empirical confirmation of a normative sequence of parental reactions is lacking.

It would be valuable to know more about the ways families cope with having a gay or lesbian child. After the initial disclosure, some parents strive to learn more about their child's personal experiences and about homosexuality in general, perhaps by participating in groups such as Parents and Friends of Lesbians and Gays (PFLAG) that provide support, education, and advocacy opportunities. In contrast, other parents seek to avoid continued discussion and treat the topic of homosexuality as a dark family secret. Research is needed to identify characteristics of the gay or lesbian individual, of the family, and of their social environment that are associated with differing family reactions to disclosure, both immediately and over time. To date, studies of parents' reactions have typically recruited participants from organizations such as PFLAG. As Savin-Williams (2001) has noted, research based on these parents may "distort the reality of how typical parents react to having a sexual-minority child" (p. 249). Investigations of parents who do not join support groups are needed to understand the full range of parental reactions. Another limitation of existing studies is that they describe how families respond to disclosure from only one perspective, either that of a parent or that of the gay/lesbian individual. It is possible, however, that the gay or lesbian person and the family perceive events quite differently. Consequently, studies that include multiple family members would be useful. Finally, the study of disclosure patterns among family members will benefit from the development of more adequate conceptual frameworks and more comprehensive measures (see Beals & Peplau, 2002, for one example).

GAY AND LESBIAN COUPLES

This section provides an overview of research about gay and lesbian couples. We begin with basic information about couples and then consider the initiation of relationships, satisfaction and commitment, the division of labor and power, and needed research on gay and lesbian couples. For more detailed reviews, see Patterson (2000), Patterson, Ciabattari, and Schwartz (1999), Peplau and Beals (2001), and Peplau and Spalding (2000).

Basic Facts About Couples

Many lesbians and gay men want to have a committed love relationship. In a recent national survey (Kaiser Foundation, 2001), 74% of lesbians and gay men said that if they could legally marry someone of the same sex, they would like to do so some day. Most (68%) lesbians and gay men said that legal marriage rights were very important to them. Many studies find that a majority of gays and lesbians are currently in a romantic relationship (see review in Peplau & Spalding, 2000). For example, in a large-scale survey of lesbians, 65% of women reported currently being in a same-sex primary relationship (Morris et al., 2001). Information about the percentage of gay and lesbian adults who live together with a same-sex partner has recently become available from the 2000 U.S. Census and other national surveys (e.g., Black, Gates, Sanders, & Taylor, 2000; Human Rights Campaign, 2001; Kaiser Foundation, 2001). The best estimate is that about 25 to 30% of gay men and lesbians live with a same-sex partner. A recent survey of more than 2600 African American lesbians and gay men found that 41% of women and 20% of men were in a committed relationship (Battle, Cohen, Warren, Fergerson, & Audam, 2002).

The experiences of gay and lesbian couples are colored by the social climate of sexual prejudice. Simply being seen together as a couple can increase the risk of hate crimes and violence against gay men and lesbians. Laws against same-sex marriage deprive gay and lesbian couples of legal benefits in such areas as taxation, health insurance, social welfare, pensions, inheritance, and immigration (Savin-Williams & Esterberg, 2000). In an extreme example of sexual prejudice that took place in 2002, Carla Grayson, her partner Adrianne, and their 22-month old son barely escaped with their lives when an arson fire destroyed their home in Missoula, Montana. A psychology professor at the University of Montana, Carla had been active in efforts to extend the university's insurance benefits to same-sex partners of employees.

Same-sex couples are also vulnerable to daily hassles, inconveniences that are a constant reminder of the stigma of homosexuality. Studies have found that hotels are significantly less likely to make a room reservation for a same-sex couple than for a cross-sex couple (Jones, 1996). In shopping malls, same-sex couples may receive slower service by store clerks and experience more incidents of staring and rude treatment (Walters & Curran, 1996). Taken together, realistic fears about sexual prejudice and chronic daily stressors associated with being gay or lesbian may increase an individual's feelings of psychological distress and adversely affect physical health (Lewis, Derlega, Berndt, Morris, & Rose, 2001). Research is needed to assess how often gay and lesbian couples experience discrimination, the strategies that couples use to cope with these experiences, and the impact of these events on samesex relationships.

Initiating a Relationship

Lesbians and gay men report that they are most likely to meet potential dates through friends, at work, at a bar, or at a social event (Bryant & Demian, 1994). We know very little about how gay men and lesbians identify potential partners or how they communicate romantic and sexual interest verbally or nonverbally. Opportunities to meet potential partners may be more abundant in urban areas with visible gay and lesbian communities. The Internet has rapidly become a new way for gay men and lesbians to meet each other, and research about the use of this technology would be particularly valuable.

Many studies have compared the attributes that lesbians, gay men, and heterosexuals seek in romantic partners (see review by Peplau & Spalding, 2000). Regardless of sexual orientation, most individuals emphasize affection, dependability, and similarity in interests and religious beliefs. Male–female differences have also been found. For example, gay and heterosexual men are more likely to emphasize a partner's physical attractiveness; lesbian and heterosexual women give greater emphasis to desirable personality characteristics.

When gay men and lesbians go on dates, they may rely on fairly conventional scripts that depict a predictable sequence of dating events. One study analyzed gay mens' and lesbians' accounts of typical and actual first dates (Klinkenberg & Rose, 1994). Many common events were listed by both gay men and lesbians, such as discussing plans, getting to know each other, going to an activity like a concert or movie, having a meal, and initiating physical contact. However, gay men were more likely than lesbians to include sexual activity as part of a first date, and lesbians were more likely to evaluate their feelings about the date.

In addition to understanding same-sex dating, it may also be important to understand how same-sex friendships can be transformed into romantic relationships. Rose, Zand, and Cini (1993) found that many lesbian romantic relationships began as friendships, then developed into love relationships, and later became sexual. Some women reported difficulties with this pattern of relationship development, such as problems in knowing if a relationship was shifting from friendship to romance and problems gauging the friend's possible sexual interest.

Relationship Satisfaction and Commitment

Stereotypes depict gay and lesbian relationships as unhappy. In one study, heterosexual college students described gay and lesbian relationships as less satisfying, more prone to discord, and "less in love" than heterosexual relationships (Testa, Kinder, & Ironson, 1987). In reality, comparative research finds striking similarities in the reports of love and satisfaction among contemporary lesbian, gay, and heterosexual couples (see review by Kurdek, 1995a). For example, Kurdek (1998) compared married heterosexual and cohabiting gay and lesbian couples, controlling for age, education, income, and years cohabiting. The three types of couples did not differ in relationship satisfaction at initial testing. Over a 5-year period, all couples tended to decrease in relationship satisfaction, but no differences were found among gay, lesbian, and heterosexual couples in the rate of change in satisfaction.

Like their heterosexual counterparts, gay and lesbian couples benefit from similarity between partners. Further, consistent with social exchange theory, happiness tends to be high when partners perceive many rewards and few costs from their relationship (e.g., Beals, Impett, & Peplau, 2002). Several studies show that satisfaction is higher when same-sex partners believe they share relatively equally in power and decision making (Peplau & Spalding, 2000). For lesbian couples, greater satisfaction has also been linked to perceptions of greater equity or fairness in the relationship.

Research has begun to investigate factors that affect partners' psychological commitment to each other and the longevity of their relationship (see review by Peplau & Spalding, 2000). Of obvious importance are positive attraction forces such as love and satisfaction that make partners want to stay together. The availability of alternative partners is also important: the lack of desirable alternatives is an obstacle to ending a relationship. Finally, barriers that make it difficult for a person to leave a relationship also matter (Kurdek, 2000). Barriers include things that increase the psychological, emotional, or financial costs of ending a relationship. Heterosexual marriage can create many barriers such as the cost of divorce, investments in joint property, concerns about children, and the wife's financial dependence on her husband. These obstacles may encourage married couples to work toward improving a declining relationship, rather than ending it. In contrast, systematic comparisons find that gay men and lesbians experience significantly fewer barriers to ending their relationships than do married heterosexuals, and for all couples, barriers are a significant predictor of relationship stability (Kurdek, 1998). A recent path analysis of data from 301 lesbian couples provided support for the idea that attractions, barriers, and alternatives each significantly predicts psychological commitment that, in turn, predicts relationship stability over time (Beals et al., 2002).

Conflict can also detract from the happiness and stability of same-sex couples, depending on how successfully partners manage their disagreements. Available research documents many common sources of conflict. For example, Kurdek (1994) found that gay male, lesbian, and heterosexual couples had similar ratings of the topics they most often fought about, with intimacy and power issues ranked at the top.

The Division of Labor and Power

A common stereotype is that same-sex couples adopt husband–wife roles as a model for their intimate relationships. Traditional heterosexual marriage has two core characteristics: a division of labor based on gender and a norm of greater male status and power. Most lesbians and gay men today reject both of these ideas.

Several studies have examined the division of labor in same-sex couples (see review by Peplau & Spalding, 2000). Most lesbians and gay men are in dual-earner relationships, so that neither partner is the exclusive breadwinner and each partner has some degree of economic independence. The most common division of labor at home involves flexibility, with partners sharing domestic activities or dividing tasks according to personal preferences or time constraints. In an illustrative study, Kurdek (1993) compared the allocation of household labor (e.g., cooking, shopping, cleaning) in cohabiting gay and lesbian couples and heterosexual married couples. None of the couples had children. Among heterosexual couples, wives typically did most of the housework. In contrast, gay and lesbian couples were likely to split tasks so that each partner performed an equal number of different activities. Gay male partners tended to arrive at equality by each partner specializing in certain tasks; lesbian partners were more likely to share tasks.

Many lesbians and gay men seek power equality in their relationships. In an early study, 92% of gay men and 97% of lesbians defined the ideal balance of power as one in which both partners were "exactly equal" (Peplau & Cochran, 1980). In a more recent study (Kurdek, 1995b), partners in gay and lesbian couples responded to multi-item measures assessing various facets of equality in an ideal relationship. On average, both lesbians and gay men rated equality as quite important, although lesbians scored significantly higher on the value of equality than did gay men. Not all couples who strive for equality achieve this ideal. Social exchange theory predicts that greater power accrues to the partner who has relatively greater personal resources, such as education, money, or social standing. Several studies have provided empirical support for this hypothesis among gay men. In their large-scale couples study, Blumstein and Schwartz (1983) concluded that "in gay male couples, income is an extremely important force in determining which partner will be dominant" (p. 59). In contrast, there is some evidence that lesbians strive to avoid letting financial resources affect power in their relationships.

Needed Research on Gay and Lesbian Couples

One useful approach to studying gay and lesbian couples has been comparative. Studies comparing lesbian, gay, and heterosexual relationships can dispel harmful myths about gay and lesbian couples by documenting the many commonalities across all couples regardless of sexual orientation. Comparative research can also test the generalizability of theories originally developed with heterosexuals. Most comparative research has assessed individual levels of love and satisfaction or such structural characteristics of relationships as the balance of power or the division of labor. Consequently, little is currently known about the patterns of interaction in gay and lesbian couples—the specifics of how gay and lesbian partners talk to each other and seek to resolve the conflicts of interest that inevitably arise in close relationships. These topics of investigation are of interest in their own right but also hold the promise of illuminating ways in which gender influences close relationships. Several interactional topics warrant further examination, including conversational patterns (e.g., Kollock, Blumstein, & Schwartz, 1985), influence tactics (e.g., Falbo & Peplau, 1980), styles of problem solving (e.g., Kurdek, 1998), intimate communication (e.g., Mackey, Diemer, & O'Brien, 2000), and relationship maintenance behaviors (e.g., Gaines & Henderson, 2002). Research might also fruitfully investigate such topics as self-disclosure between partners, the provision and receipt of help and social support, and efforts to resolve conflicts.

Another timely research direction concerns unique issues facing gay and lesbian couples. For example, how do same-sex partners cope with problems created by sexual prejudice both at work and in their social lives? In a recent review, Oswald (2002) outlined some of the strategies that gay men and lesbians use to legitimize and support their relationships, including the creation of "family" networks that combine kin and friends, and the use of rituals such as commitment ceremonies to strengthen relationships. Further, how do partners negotiate issues about concealing versus disclosing their own sexual identity and the nature of their couple relationship to other people (e.g., Beals & Peplau, 2001)? To what extent do couples incorporate elements of gay or lesbian culture into their couple activities, for example, in the social events they attend; the holidays they celebrate; their choice of residence, dress, or friends? How do individuals and couples integrate being gay or lesbian into other important aspects of the lives including religion and ethnicity? How has the AIDS epidemic affected gay and lesbian dating and relationships (e.g., Haas, 2002)?

GAY AND LESBIAN PARENTS AND THEIR CHILDREN

In 2002, gay and lesbian parenting took center stage in the U.S. media when popular television talk show host Rosie O'Donnell revealed on national TV that she is a lesbian mom. O'Donnell and her partner, Kelli Carpenter, went public in part to lend support to a gay couple in Florida who are challenging the state's ban on gay adoption. In the past, most gays and lesbians became parents while in a heterosexual relationship. Today, however, many gay men and lesbians, like Rosie O'Donnell, are deciding to have children either alone or in a same-sex partner relationship. Gay men and lesbians who want to become parents use a variety of approaches including adoption, which is legal in most states, artificial insemination for lesbians, and surrogate mothers for gay men (see review by Buell, 2001). It appears that a growing percentage of gay men and lesbians are considering parenthood. In a recent national poll, 49% of gays and lesbians who were not parents said they would like to have or adopt children of their own (Kaiser Foundation, 2001). Given the obstacles to parenthood faced by self-identified gay men and lesbians, there is a high likelihood that their children are strongly desired and planned.

The best information about the frequency of lesbians and gay men raising children comes from analyses of U.S. census data and other national polls. Black, Gates, Sanders, and Taylor (2000) recently estimated that 22% of partnered lesbians and 5% of partnered gay men currently have children present in the home. A large-scale survey of African American lesbians and gay men found very similar results: 25% of women and 4% of men said they lived with children (Battle et al., 2002). These percentages compare to 59% of married heterosexuals and 36% of partnered heterosexuals who have children at home (Black et al., 2000).

In this section, we review the small body of research about the family lives of gay and lesbian parents, focusing first on the parenting couple, then on their children, and last on special concerns of gay and lesbian parents.

Gay and Lesbian Couples With Children

How does the transition to parenthood affect gay and lesbian couples? For married heterosexuals, parenthood often creates a less balanced division of domestic work, with mothers providing the bulk of child care and household labor. Does parenthood alter the ideology of equality that often characterizes lesbian and gay relationships? Although limited, available research indicates that parenthood does not change this general pattern of shared family responsibilities (see review on lesbian parenthood by Parks, 1998). For example, Chan, Brooks, Raboy, and Patterson (1998) compared

30 lesbian couples and 16 heterosexual couples, all of whom became parents using anonymous donor insemination and had at least 1 child in elementary school. In this highly educated sample, both lesbian and heterosexual couples reported a relatively equal division of paid employment, housework, and decision making. However, lesbian couples reported sharing child-care tasks more equally than did heterosexual parents.

Very little is known about gay male couples with children (see Bigner & Bozett, 1990, for a general review of research on gay fathers). One study found a more even division of child care and housework among gay male parenting couples than among heterosexual couples (McPherson, 1993, cited in Savin-Williams & Esterberg, 2000). Additional studies of gay couples who become parents by choice would provide a unique perspective on fathering. Gay couples who adopt or use surrogate mothers are highly motivated to parent and know that there will not be a woman in the home to provide child care. How do these men perceive the father role and how do they handle their parental responsibilities?

Many questions about the family lives of gay and lesbian parents remain. Available descriptions of gay and lesbian parents tend to be based on relatively older, well-educated, financially secure couples with young children. Lesbian mothers in these studies are likely to have liberal and feminist attitudes. Research is needed with larger, more representative samples. One question concerns the impact of children on the parents' relationship satisfaction. Among heterosexuals, the transition to parenting is often accompanied by a decline in marital satisfaction, sometimes attributed to the uneven division of labor in the couple and the stress of parenting. Does this occur among same-sex couples, or does a pattern of more equal sharing of family work counteract this effect (see, for example, Koepke, Hare & Moran, 1992)? Longitudinal studies of the transition to parenthood among gay and lesbian couples would be particularly valuable.

Another question relevant to some same-sex couples is whether the biological and nonbiological parent are equally involved in child care and paid work. To date, studies on this topic have examined lesbian mothers only, and the results have been inconsistent. Studies of gay male couples with a biological and nonbiological parent would be informative. Finally, it appears that lesbians and gay men who adopt children often parent children from different cultural and racial backgrounds. What impact does this have on their family life?

Children of Gay and Lesbian Parents

A top priority for researchers studying the children of lesbian and gay parents has been to debunk stereotypes that homosexuals are unfit parents whose children are at risk for a variety of psychosocial problems. Several studies have been conducted, most involving children of lesbian mothers (see reviews by Parks, 1998; Patterson, 2000; Stacey & Biblarz, 2001).

There is no evidence that the children of gay and lesbian parents differ systematically from children of heterosexual parents on standard measures of psychological functioning. No significant differences have been found in psychological well-being, self-esteem, behavioral problems, intelligence, cognitive abilities, or peer relations. A recent report by the American Academy of Pediatrics concluded that "no data have pointed to any risk to children as a result of growing up in a family with 1 or more gay parents" (Perrin, 2002, p. 343).

A related research question has been the possible impact of gay and lesbian parents on a child's gender identity and gender-typed behavior (see review by Stacey & Biblarz, 2001). There is no evidence that the children of gay and lesbian parents are confused or uncertain about their gender identity, that is, their self-knowledge that they are male or female (Patterson, 2000). Stacey and Biblarz (2001) suggested that these children may be somewhat more flexible or nontraditional in their views about a range of gendertyped behaviors including clothing, play activities, school activities, and occupational aspiration. Currently, support for this plausible hypothesis is extremely limited. In one study, for example, 53% of the daughters of lesbians aspired to professional careers such as doctor, lawyer, or astronaut compared to 21% of the daughters of heterosexuals (Green, Mandel, Hotvedt, Gray, & Smith, 1986). Additional research on children's gender-typed interests and behaviors would be useful.

A final research question concerns the sexual behavior and sexual orientation of children raised by gay and lesbian parents. For gay rights advocates, this research has the potential to counter the argument that children of lesbian moms and gay dads are at "increased risk" of becoming gay or lesbian themselves. Of course, in a completely accepting society, this would not be a fear, but in our climate of sexual prejudice, this argument has been used in court cases and legislative decisions to limit gay parenting. This research also provides important information about the influence of parents' sexual orientation on child outcomes. Unfortunately, as noted by Patterson (2000), Stacey and Biblarz (2001), and by others, available studies are limited in scope and methodology. Specifically, current research is largely based on small, nonrepresentative samples of White, middle-class, well-educated gay men and lesbians. Most studies rely on self-report questionnaires or interviews collected at one time point. Studies using longitudinal designs or observational methods are not available.

Despite these limitations, two patterns emerge. First, the great majority of children of gay and lesbian parents grow up to identify as heterosexual (Patterson, 2000). Whether the percentage of gay and lesbian offspring differs depending on the parents' sexual orientation is open to debate, and a final conclusion must await more extensive research. Second, children of lesbian parents appear to be more open to same-sex sexual experiences (Stacey & Biblarz, 2001). For example, in the only relevant longitudinal study, Golombok and Tasker (1996) studied 25 lesbian and 21 heterosexual mothers and their children. At the start of the study, the children were on average 10 years old and they were followed into young adulthood. No significant differences were found in the percentage of children identifying as gay or lesbian. However, compared to the children of heterosexual mothers, a greater percentage of children raised by lesbian mothers had had a same-sex sexual relationship or were open to this possibility in the future. Comparable scientific research on the children of gay fathers is not available.

There is a clear need for additional research on the experiences of children of gay and lesbian parents. A promising research direction concerns the resilience of children raised by parents from this socially stigmatized group. Despite teasing and other problems that children of gay and lesbian parents encounter, their psychological adjustment is comparable to that of other children. What processes make this possible? Further, are there compensating benefits of having gay and lesbian parents? For example, are gay and lesbian parents more likely to teach values of tolerance? Stacey and Biblarz (2001) argued that because children of lesbian and gay parents "contend with the burdens of vicarious social stigma" they may "display more empathy for social diversity" (p. 177). As another example, does the lesser concern of gay and lesbian parents about conformity to traditional gender roles provide their children with greater freedom to explore their own individual interests and preferences?

Special Concerns of Gay and Lesbian Parents

The diversity among gay and lesbian parents makes it impossible to characterize a "typical" family. Nonetheless, several issues common to gay and lesbian parenting can be identified (Dundas & Kaufman,

2000; Gartrell et al., 1996). Legal issues are often a major source of worry. Many lesbian and gay parents live in fear that their children can be taken away from them because of their sexual orientation, and some parents engage in lengthy legal battles with a former spouse or family member who disputes their fitness to parent. For gays and lesbians in a couple relationship, there are issues surrounding the legal status of the second parent. Only a few states allow a second same-sex parent to have legal rights and corresponding parental obligations.

Second, gay and lesbian parents have many concerns about the possible impact of sexual prejudice on the experiences of their children at school, in the neighborhood, with friends, with healthcare providers, and so on. Researchers have not yet examined the strategies that gay and lesbian parents use to shelter their children from negative experiences, to help children cope with instances of prejudice, to build resilience in their children, and to create supportive social networks.

Third, gay and lesbian parents, like single heterosexual parents, may have concerns about the availability of other-sex adults to provide role models for their children (e.g., Dundas & Kaufman, 2000). In some cases, siblings, other family members, and friends may fill this role. Gay and lesbian parents may face special problems not experienced by heterosexuals. For example, single heterosexual mothers may encourage their sons to participate in the Boy Scouts as a way to provide models of male leadership, but the anti-gay policies of the Boy Scouts might be discouraging to lesbian mothers.

Fourth, gay and lesbian parents must communicate with their children about potentially sensitive topics, such as the parent's sexual orientation or, in the case of artificial insemination or surrogate motherhood, how the child was conceived (e.g., Barrett, 1997; West & Turner, 1995). Research will need to examine the different aspects of disclosure to children and the consequences of these decisions.

Finally, the experiences of lesbian and gay parents challenge many popular beliefs about "normal" human development. Conceptual analyses of these issues would be beneficial. For example, models of identity development have often emphasized the role that parents play in socializing their children. Yet most gay and lesbian parents avoid socializing their children to conform to the parents' own sexual orientation. In a qualitative interview study, both lesbian and gay parents thought it most likely that their children would be heterosexual (Costello, 1997). All parents emphasized that they would accept their child's sexual orientation, whatever it might be. Parents often taught the value of accepting people in all their diversity. Asked how she thought her sexual orientation would influence her daughter, one lesbian mother replied, "I hope it helps her realize that we need to be true to ourselves, no matter who we are" (cited in Costello, 1997, p. 79).

Author Note

Preparation of this selection was supported in part by a UCLA Academic Senate grant to Anne Peplau and by National Research Service Award 1F31 MH 12836-01A1 from the National Institute of Mental Health to Kristin Beals. Cynthia Carrion provided valuable library assistance. We appreciate the thoughtful comments on an earlier draft by Anita Vangelisti, Adam Fingerhut, and Linda Garnets. Correspondence regarding this selection may be addressed to the first author: Psychology Department, UCLA, Los Angeles, CA 90095-1563. Send email to LAPEPLAU@UCLA.EDU.

REFERENCES

Allen, K. R., & Demo, D. H. (1995). The families of lesbians and gay men: A new frontier in family research. *Journal of Marriage and the Family, 57*, 111–127.

Barrett, S. E. (1997). Children of lesbian parents: The what, when and how of talking about donor identity. *Women and Therapy, 20*, 43–55.

Battle, J., Cohen, C. J., Warren, D., Fergerson, G., & Audam, S. (2002). *Say it loud, I'm Black and I'm proud: Black Pride Survey 2000.* New York: The Policy Institute of the National Gay and Lesbian Task Force. www.ngltf.org

Beals, K. P., Impett, E. A., & Peplau, L. A. (2002). Lesbians in love: Why some relationships endure and others end. *Journal of Lesbian Studies, 6*, 53–64.

Beals, K. P., & Peplau, L. A. (2001). Social involvement, disclosure of sexual orientation, and the quality of lesbian relationships. *Psychology of Women Quarterly, 25*, 10–19.

Beals, K. P., & Peplau, L. A. (2002, July). *Conceptualizing and measuring the disclosure of sexual orientation.* Poster presented at the International Conference on Personal Relationships, Halifax, Nova Scotia.

Bell, A. P., & Weinberg, M. S. (1978). *Homosexualities: A study of diversity among men and women.* New York: Simon and Schuster.

Bigner, J. J., & Bozett, F. W. (1990). Parenting by gay fathers. In F. W. Bozett & M. B. Sussman (Eds.), *Homosexuality and the family* (pp. 155–176). New York: Haworth.

Black, D., Gates, G., Sanders, S., & Taylor, L. (2000). Demographics of the gay and lesbian population in the United States. *Demography, 37*, 139–154.

Blumstein, P., & Schwartz, P. (1983). *American couples.* New York: Morrow.

Bryant, A. S., & Demian (1994). Relationship characteristics of American gay and lesbian couples: Findings from a national survey. In L. A. Kurdek (Ed.), *Social services for gay and lesbian couples* (pp. 101–117). New York: Haworth.

Buell, C. (2001). Legal issues affecting alternative families. *Journal of Gay and Lesbian Psychotherapy, 4*, 75–90.

Chan, R. W., Brooks, R. C., Raboy, B., & Patterson, C. J. (1998). Division of labor among lesbian and heterosexual parents. *Journal of Family Psychology, 12*, 402–419.

Costello, C. Y. (1997). Conceiving identity: Bisexual, lesbian and gay parents consider their children's sexual orientations. *Journal of Sociology and Social Welfare, XXIV*, 63–89.

Crosbie-Burnett, M., Foster, T. L., Murray, C. I., & Bowen, G. L. (1996). Gays' and lesbians' families-of-origin: A social-cognitive-behavioral model of adjustment. *Family Relations, 45*, 397–403.

Dundas, S., & Kaufman, M. (2000). The Toronto lesbian family study. *Journal of Homosexuality, 40*, 65–79.

Falbo, T., & Peplau, L. A. (1980). Power strategies in intimate relationships. *Journal of Personality and Social Psychology, 38*, 618–628.

Gaines, S. O., & Henderson, M. C. (2002). Impact of attachment style on responses to accommodative dilemmas among same-sex couples. *Personal Relationships, 9*, 89–94.

Gartrell, N., Hamilton, J., Banks, A., Mosbacher, D., Reed, N., Sparks, C., & Bishop, H. (1996). The national lesbian family study: Interviews with prospective mothers. *American Journal of Orthopsychiatry, 66*, 272–281.

Golombok, S., & Tasker, F. (1996). Do parents influence the sexual orientation of their children? Findings from a longitudinal study of lesbian families. *Developmental Psychology, 32*, 3–11.

Green, R., Mandel, J. B., Hotvedt, M. E., Gray, J., & Smith, L. (1986). Lesbian mothers and their children: A comparison with solo parent heterosexual mothers and their children. *Archives of Sexual Behavior, 15*, 167–184.

Haas, S. M. (2002). Social support as relationship maintenance in gay male couples coping with HIV or AIDS. *Journal of Social and Personal Relationships, 19*, 87–111.

Herek, G. M. (2000). The psychology of sexual prejudice. *Current Directions in Psychological Science, 9*, 19–22.

Herek, G. M., Gillis, J. R., & Cogan, J. C. (1996, August). *Hate crimes against gay men, lesbians, and bisexuals: Psychological consequences.* American Psychological Association, Toronto.

Human Rights Campaign. (2001, August 22). *Gay and lesbian families in the United States.* Washington, DC: Human Rights Campaign.

Jones, D. A. (1996). Discrimination against same-sex couples in hotel reservation policies. *Journal of Homosexuality, 31*, 153–159.

Kaiser Foundation. (2001, November). *Inside-out: A report on the experiences of lesbians, gays and bisexuals in America and the public's view on issues and policies related to sexual orientation.* Mento Park, CA.

Klinkenberg, D., & Rose, S. (1994). Dating scripts of gay men and lesbians. *Journal of Homosexuality, 26*, 23–35.

Koepke, L., Hare, J., & Moran, P. B. (1992). Relationship quality in a sample of lesbian couples with children and child-free lesbian couples. *Family Relations, 41*, 224–229.

Kollock, P., Blumstein, P., & Schwartz, P. (1985). Sex and power in interaction: Conversational privileges and duties. *American Sociological Review, 50*, 34–46.

Kurdek, L. A. (1993). The allocation of household labor in gay, lesbian, and heterosexual married couples. *Journal of Social Issues, 49* (3), 127–139.

Kurdek, L. A. (1994). Areas of conflict for gay, lesbian, and heterosexual couples. *Journal of Marriage and the Family, 56*, 923–934.

Kurdek, L. A. (1995a). Lesbian and gay couples. In A. R. D'Augelli & C. J. Patterson (Eds.), *Lesbian, gay, and bisexual identities over the lifespan* (pp. 243–261). New York: Oxford.

Kurdek, L. A. (1995b). Developmental changes in relationship quality in gay and lesbian cohabiting couples. *Developmental Psychology, 31*, 86–94.

Kurdek, L. A. (1998). Relationship outcomes and their predictors: Longitudinal evidence from heterosexual married, gay cohabiting, and lesbian cohabiting couples. *Journal of Marriage and the Family, 60*, 553–568.

Kurdek, L. A. (2000). Attractions and constraints as determinants of relationship commitment: Longitudinal evidence from gay, lesbian, and heterosexual couples. *Personal Relationships, 7*, 245–262.

Lewis, R. J., Derlega, V. J., Berndt, A., Morris, L. M., & Rose, S. (2001). An empirical analysis of stressors for gay men and lesbians. *Journal of Homosexuality, 42*, 63–88.

Loftus, J. (2001). America's liberalization in attitudes toward homosexuality, 1973–1998. *American Sociological Review, 66*, 762–782.

Mackey, R. A., Diemer, M. A., & O'Brien, B. A. (2000). Psychological intimacy in the lasting relationships of heterosexual and same-gender couples. *Sex Roles, 43*, 201–227.

McPherson, D. (1993). *Gay parenting couples.* Unpublished doctoral dissertation, Pacific Graduate School of Psychology, Palo Alto, CA.

Morris, J. F., Waldo, C. R., & Rothblum, E. D. (2001). A model of predictors and outcomes of outness among lesbian and bisexual women. *American Journal of Orthopsychiatry, 71*, 61–71.

Oswald, R. F. (2002). Resilience within the family networks of lesbians and gay men: Intentionality and redefinition. *Journal of Marriage and Family, 64*, 374–383.

Parks, C. A. (1998). Lesbian parenthood: A review of the literature. *American Journal of Orthopsychiatry, 68*, 376–389.

Patterson, C. J. (2000). Family relationships of lesbians and gay men. *Journal of Marriage and the Family, 62*, 1052–1069.

Patterson, D. G., Ciabattari, T., & Schwartz, P. (1999). The constraints of innovation: Commitment and stability among same-sex couples. In J. M. Adams & W. H. Jones (Eds.), *Handbook of interpersonal commitment and relationship stability* (pp. 339–359). New York: Kluwer.

Peplau, L. A., & Beals, K. P. (2001). Lesbians, gay men, and bisexuals in relationships. In J. Worell (Ed.), *Encyclopedia of women and gender* (Vol. 2, pp. 657–666). San Diego: Academic Press.

Peplau, L. A., & Cochran, S. D. (1980, September). *Sex differences in values concerning love relationships.* Paper presented at the annual meeting of the American Psychological Association, Montreal, Canada.

Peplau, L. A., & Spalding, L. R. (2000). The close relationships of lesbians, gay men and bisexuals. In C. Hendrick & S. S. Hendrick (Eds.), *Close relationships: A sourcebook* (pp. 111–124). Thousand Oaks, CA: Sage.

Perrin, E. C. (2002). Technical report: Coparent or second-parent adoption by same-sex parents. *Pediatrics, 109*, 341–344.

Rose, S., Zand, D., & Cini, M. (1993). Lesbian courtship scripts. In E. D. Rothblum & K. A. Brehony (Eds.), *Boston marriages: Romantic but asexual relationships among contemporary lesbians* (pp. 70–85). Amherst: University of Massachusetts Press.

Savin-Williams, R. C. (1996). Ethnic-minority and sexual-minority youth. In R. C. Savin-Williams & K. M. Cohen (Eds.), *The lives of lesbians, gays and bisexuals* (pp. 152–165). New York: Harcourt Brace College Publishers.

Savin-Williams, R. C. (1998). Lesbian, gay, and bisexual youths' relationships with their parents. In C. J. Patterson & A. R. D'Augelli (Eds.), *Lesbian, gay, and bisexual identities in families* (pp. 75–98). New York: Oxford University Press.

Savin-Williams, R. C. (2001). *Mom. Dad. I'm gay. How families negotiate coming out.* Washington, DC: American Psychological Association.

Savin-Williams, R. C., & Dube, E. M. (1998). Parental reactions to their child's disclosure of a gay/lesbian identity. *Family Relations, 47*, 7–13.

Savin-Williams, R. C., & Esterberg, K. G. (2000). Lesbian, gay, and bisexual families. In D. H. Demo, K. R. Allen, & M. Fine (Eds.), *Handbook of family diversity* (pp. 197–214). New York: Oxford University Press.

Stacey, J., & Biblarz, T. J. (2001). (How) does the sexual orientation of parents matter? *American Sociological Review, 66*, 159–183.

Testa, R. J., Kinder, B. N., & Ironson, G. (1987). Heterosexual bias in the perception of loving relationships of gay males and lesbians. *Journal of Sex Research, 23*, 163–172.

Walters, A. S., & Curran, M. (1996). "Excuse me, sir? May I help you and your boyfriend?": Salespersons' differential treatment of homosexual and straight customers. *Journal of Homosexuality, 31*(1/2), 135–152.

West, R., & Turner, L. H. (1995). Communication in lesbian and gay families. In T. J. Socha & G. H. Stamp (Eds), *Parents, children and communication* (pp. 147–169). Mahwah, NJ: Lawrence Erlbaum Associates.

Part III

FAMILY PHEROMONES
AND PHYSIOLOGY

8. INFLUENCE OF PHEROMONES IN FAMILIES

By Laura Hatcher

Forgive my bluntness, but ... your house smells. Don't worry though, it's not just your house—it's everyone's. You have probably noticed *other* people's houses having a unique smell, but you are most likely blissfully unaware of your own home's odor. It isn't a bad smell, it's just ... a smell. Partially food, partially people, partially other environmental sources (your pet bird, for instance), the smell of your home is unique to you. In fact, while we are very rarely conscious of it, every individual has a unique olfactory signature (Niolaides, 1975). And this scent goes with you everywhere you go, and is often left behind once you leave. For evidence, consider the search-and-rescue dog. When a person goes missing, the dog is given something they have recently touched in order to track the person. Everywhere that person has recently been will have a trace of their olfactory signature, which acts as a trail for the dog to follow. Human noses are not as gifted. We can't track an individual across long distances the way a dog can. However, I imagine you might be fairly surprised by what our noses *can* do.

HUMAN SCENT

Before we begin to investigate how humans use odors in their daily lives, we must understand where human body odor comes from. Human body odor consists of both a unique olfactory signature (the way you smell under neutral conditions) and a slightly altered scent that arises during times of physiological arousal. Both odors are linked to sweat; however, in times of physiological arousal, the composition of the sweat is altered, which leads to an altered odor.

You are covered in bacteria right now. In fact, there are more cells in and on your body that are *not* you than *are* you. Before you give in to the urge to start bathing in antibacterial hand gel, remember that bacteria are essential for your survival and well-being. In fact, the bacteria that you host are basically an additional organ, as important to you as your lungs or kidneys. We have a symbiotic relationship with the bacteria that live on and in us. We provide them with food, and they protect us from harmful bacteria, help us digest our food, and keep us as healthy as possible. In fact, many people with certain intestinal diseases are lacking some bacteria that other people have. Without these bacteria, those individuals are unable to digest their food properly, which leads to all kinds of nasty symptoms. As gross as it seems, doctors are beginning to experiment with a new treatment for these intestinal diseases—fecal transplants. These transplants allow bacteria from healthy individuals to colonize the intestines of unhealthy individuals.

Why some people lack some bacteria has not been fully investigated and is not fully understood. However, we do know that everyone has a unique set of bacteria, called a *microbiome*. Your microbiome is different from your friends' and coworkers'. It is different from your parents'. It is different from your siblings'. You begin developing your own unique microbiome the moment you are born. Additional colonies are picked up throughout your life—from the air, from the skin of other people, from anything you come in contact with. These bacteria colonies flourish and help prevent more harmful bacteria from setting up shop in your body.

It is these bacteria that are responsible for the way you smell. Most people think sweat is what stinks. This is true, but only to an extent. In reality, it is not the actual liquid secreted by the sweat glands that causes odor, but the bacteria on the skin that consume the sweat. In other words, the smell of sweat is largely derived not from the human producing it, but from the bacteria consuming it. Basically, your skin is almost always secreting a small amount of sweat and oil. The bacterial colonies on your skin use this for food. After eating the sweat, oil, and dead skin on your body, the bacteria create waste that is responsible for your unique olfactory signature. In times of stress, the sweat you secrete in certain places changes, which changes the way you smell.

Interestingly, the type of bacteria found on men and women differs. Women carry more *coccal* bacteria, while men are home to more *coryneform* bacteria (Jackman and Noble, 1983). While most people cannot differentiate a male odor from a female one based on the *way* they smell, they can distinguish male from female based on how *strongly* they smell. Men are largely understood to have a stronger body odor than women (Jacob and McLintock, 2000).

For the most part, the unique olfactory signature is neutral. In fact, most people are barely aware it exists; it runs in the background of our daily lives, making its presence known only when we walk into a loved one's house or are asked to identify who an article of clothing belongs to. However, when someone mentions "body odor," they are not thinking of this subtle smell. Instead, they are thinking of a strong, pungent odor that is associated with humans. We spend billions of dollars every year attempting to cover this smell up. This body odor is not produced by all sweat glands equally. There is a reason deodorant is applied only under the arms rather than over the entire body: the environment under the arms and in a few other key places is much different than the rest of the body—specifically, these areas differ in the types of bacteria present and in the types of food the body provides those bacteria.

The majority of the human body is covered in *eccrine* glands. These glands produce the normal, largely odor-free sweat that is tied to one's olfactory signature. *Apocrine* glands, on the other hand, are concentrated in only a few places (armpits, eyelids, external sex organs, areolas, etc.). Because the apocrine glands host the types of bacteria that produce body odor, they are the glands responsible for the characteristic scent of humans. Those bacteria are not found around the eccrine glands. The largest concentration of apocrine glands is around the axillary glands (i.e., under the arms). Compared to other high-level primates, human axillary glands are both especially large and home to a particularly high concentration of apocrine glands (Monagna, 1964). Just as there are sex differences in terms of type of bacteria consuming human sweat, there are also sex differences in apocrine glands. Women have 75%

more apocrine glands than men; however, though men have fewer apocrine glands, they have much larger ones than do women (Brody, 1975).

In addition to different bacteria in these regions creating a different type of smell (in much the same way one can usually tell the difference between horse waste and dog waste), the sweat the body creates in these areas also contributes to a distinct odor. Sweat produced by the eccrine glands is composed of water and salt and is designed to evaporate quickly, allowing you to stay cool. Sweat produced by the apocrine glands, on the other hand, does little to contribute to cooling the body, but is instead a response to stress. It is oily and milky white, and contains additional chemicals and proteins that are not found in thermoregulatory sweat. This sweat is designed not to evaporate, but to remain behind as long as possible. The apocrine glands are also home to a different type of hair than is found on the rest of the body. This hair is thick, coarse, wiry, and has a larger surface area than most other hairs on the body. In fact, if you want to know where your apocrine glands are, your best bet is to think of all the areas on your body that come with this other type of hair—armpits, genitals, eyes, etc. While we cannot know for sure what purpose this system was meant to serve (since time travel doesn't seem to be panning out), we can make educated guesses about why humans evolved this way. This hair allows the sweat from the apocrine glands more room to spread out, making the smell produced more likely to carry to others in the vicinity. In other words, humans have a form of sweat that is specifically designed to produce body odor. This body odor offers chemical signals about the mood of the individual secreting it, as well as other information about the health and genetics of that individual.

KINSHIP IDENTIFICATION

Have you ever been told you have your father's nose or your mother's eyes or your aunt's ears? Our physical traits are inherited from our family. If you were shown pictures of strangers, you would probably be able to tell which ones made up a family based on their similar appearances. Interestingly, families also appear to have similar olfactory signatures.

There have been a number of studies that seem to confirm this idea. In one study (Russell, Mendelsen, and Peeke, 1983), infants wore a plain t-shirt. Later, the infants' mothers were asked to choose which t-shirt was worn by their child. Ninety-four percent of the mothers participating in the study were able to identify the clothing of their child by smell alone. In another study, infants were exposed to a pad with their mother's lactic scent and a pad with another woman's lactic scent. The infants were able to distinguish between the two pads (Macfarlane, 1975). Porter and Moore (1981) asked both mothers and fathers to identify which clothing belonged to their children. Additionally, the parents were asked to distinguish between the clothing worn by each of their children (could the parents tell which shirt belonged to their youngest daughter and which belonged to their middle son, for example). Eighty-nine percent of the parents were able to successfully identify which clothing belonged to their children *and* which clothing belonged to which child. Siblings are also able to identify each other through smell alone. In the same study design, 79% of the participants were able to correctly identify which t-shirt was worn by their sibling (Porter, Balogh, Cernoch, and Franchi, 1986). On the other hand, identical twin siblings are a trickier case. According to Kalmus (1955), even dogs have a difficult time discriminating between the smells of identical twins. Dogs could be trained to distinguish between fraternal (non-identical) twins who were eating identical diets, as well as identical twins who were eating very different diets (Hepper, 1988). But when identical twins were eating identical diets, the dogs were unable to distinguish between the two individuals. This seems to indicate that the olfactory signature is derived from genetics (and influenced by diet) rather than from purely environmental factors.

When it comes to the human ability to identify kinship based on human odors, the studies outlined so far could easily be attributed to learned associations. After all, when you have lived your life with a person, you tend to be able to recognize many things about them. And if this was as far as the phenomenon extended, it would still be quite intriguing—after all, we typically think of human odor recognition as something only dogs and other species with strong noses can do. However, there is evidence that it goes much further than a simple learned association. In fact, the evidence seems to suggest that we are capable of smelling kinship through shared genetic phenotypes, just as we are capable of seeing kinship through shared physical features. For example, before they had had a chance to meet their newborn grandchildren, grandparents were given a range of t-shirts to smell. These grandparents were able to successfully choose which t-shirt belonged to their grandchild, even though they had never met (Porter et al., 1986). In another study (Porter, Cernoch, and Balogh, 1985), mothers and their children were each asked to wear a plain t-shirt. People who had never met any of the participants engaged in two matching exercises. They were asked to smell a child's shirt and determine which of the offered shirts belonged to the child's mother, and they were asked to smell a mother's shirt and select which of the offered shirts belonged to her child. In both tests, participants were able to successfully match the mother and child at a rate far greater than chance. In order to determine if this ability stemmed from similar environments rather than similar genetics, the researchers ran a similar experiment with husbands and wives. When asked to identify which shirts belonged together, the participants were unable to do so at rates greater than chance.

While we are unable to detect which two individuals have pair-bonded through smell alone, we actually do use our sense of smell in the romance department. Rather than evaluate who of a group of strangers is paired with whom, we use smell to determine who we ourselves should pair with. In short, you may be picking your significant others because you think they don't stink.

MATE SELECTION

Have you ever seen someone who *should* be attractive to you, but isn't? They are physically and mentally appealing, and thus, should make an ideal partner but … you just aren't that into them? Most people have had such an experience, but few can come up with a satisfactory explanation for this lack of chemistry. One theory contends that—quite frankly—they smell. Before we can fully understand how smell is related to sexual attraction, we have to understand a bit of biology.

On a small section of one of your chromosomes (the sixth chromosome, if you're curious), there lies a very important bundle of genetic code. This bit of code is responsible for your Major Histocompatibility Complex (MHC), sometimes known as Human Leukocyte Antigens (HLA). These antigens are found on the surfaces of cells and help tell your immune system what is an invader that should be attacked and what is a harmless part of the body that should be left alone. Your body's immune system analyzes the antigens found on each cell it encounters and determines if it is "self," (and should therefore be left alone) or "non-self," (and therefore should be obliterated). Think of the antigens like a uniform that the cells wear and think of the immune system as security guards. The security guards know what clothing the cells are supposed to be wearing (which antigens should be on the outside of the cells). When the guards encounter a cell that isn't in the right uniform (a cell that has the wrong antigens), they know that that cell doesn't belong and will remove it from the building (your body). In this way, your MHC makes up a very important part of your immune system.

MHCs/HLAs were first studied in organ transplants. Doctors found that many organ recipients would reject the new organ and the immune system would attack it as a foreign body. This reaction was (and is) less likely to happen if the donor and the recipient have similar MHCs. If the two people have matching antigens, the recipient's immune system will see the new organ's cells as self, rather than non-self. If you are ever in need of an organ transplant or a bone marrow donation, you are paired with someone who has an MHC that matches your own. Most people are significantly more likely to find a match from someone who has a similar ethnic background. In essence, the immune system is more likely to see an organ from another person's body as self if that person has a similar ancestral background.

As you know, humans look for genetic diversity in their mates. Without diverse genes, we—as a species—would be much more vulnerable to extinction due to diseases and environmental stressors. It would be detrimental to us as a species if we valued genetic similarity over genetic diversity. In fact, if genetic similarity was advantageous, humans probably would have evolved to be asexual beings—reproducing by making copies of ourselves—rather than sexual beings—reproducing by pairing with other humans. For a real-world example of what happens to a species without enough genetic diversity, consider purebred dogs. These dogs have many more congenital diseases than mixed breeds. In essence, the purebred animals do not have enough genetic diversity in their breeding pools to average out any negative genetic traits. Instead, those negative traits get magnified over time, rather than lessened. This is the precise reason that humans seek out genetically diverse individuals to mate with. In fact, think of the consequences of incest. When enough inbreeding occurs, the offspring produced eventually begin to degrade in quality.

While genetic diversity takes many forms—height, speed, skin color, musculature, etc.—one extremely important variety is immune response. An assortment of immune responses in the population helps to protect the human species from a single infectious disease killing us all off. If we all reacted the same way to every disease, our ancestors would have all died during the Black Plague in the Middle Ages or the Spanish Influenza Epidemic in the 1900s. Fortunately, our genetic diversity meant that, while some succumbed to those diseases, many more survived them and passed their immune systems on to their offspring.

"How is all this related to smell," you may be asking. While the exact mechanism is not understood, there is evidence that humans are able to detect similar and dissimilar MHCs based on smell alone (Wedekind, Seebeck, Bettens, and Paepke, 1995; Chaix, Cao, and Donnelly, 2008; Wedekind and Furi, 1997; Ober, Weitkamp, Cox, Dytch, Kostyu, et al., 1997; Ziegler, Kentenich, Uchanska-Ziegler, 2005). In fact, we generally find the smell of a person with a different MHC from ours to be more sexually appealing than the smell of a person with a similar MHC. While this revelation may be initially surprising, it actually makes a good bit of sense. For example, Wedekind et al. (1995) asked a group of men to wear a plain cotton t-shirt for two days. These t-shirts were then placed in opaque boxes and a group of women were asked to smell and then rate the t-shirts for intensity, pleasantness, and sexiness. Afterwards, the men and women underwent tests to determine their MHC types. After examining the data, the researchers found that the women thought men with different MHC types from their own smelled far sexier than the men with similar MHCs. In short, the women smelled a set of antigens they didn't have, and were very attracted to them.

This attraction comes from a desire to have the healthiest offspring possible. While humanity as a whole has balanced its immune response types to optimize the survival of the species, an *individual* human would want only to optimize the survival of their own offspring. Thus, incorporating two different

MHC types will allow for a stronger, more diverse immune response than pairing the same MHCs together. For instance, let's say you have two people who are very resistant to malaria but not as resistant to influenza and two people who are very resistant to influenza but not very resistant to malaria. If the malaria-resistant people mate with the influenza-resistant people, you have a greater chance of creating children who are resistant to both malaria and influenza, increasing their chances of survival if they are afflicted with either of the two diseases. However, if the two malaria-resistant people mated with each other, their children would remain resistant to malaria, but would still be vulnerable to influenza, decreasing their chances of survival if they are ever infected with the flu. Thus, from an evolutionary perspective, it makes sense that you are more attracted to someone with a different MHC from you. Mating with that person would result in better offspring than mating with someone with a similar MHC.

While this seems very cut and dried on its face (it does elegantly explain the utter lack of chemistry you may have with someone whom you *know* is very attractive), further research begins to complicate matters a bit. Women, as it turns out, are attracted to different things at different points in their menstrual cycles (Thornhill, Gangestad, Miller, Scheyd, McCollough, and Franklin, 2002). Immediately following menstruation until the peak of fertility during ovulation, women far and away prefer men with a different MHC. During menstruation, however, women showed the greatest preference for men with a *similar* MHC. As a woman's fertility fluctuated, her ideal mate also altered. The prevailing explanation for this phenomenon contends that leading up to and during fertility, a woman is subconsciously seeking out a genetically diverse man to mate with. After ovulation and during either menstruation (if the mating was unsuccessful) or pregnancy (if the mating was successful), the same woman seeks out men who are genetically similar to her. Seeking genetic diversity when she is most likely to conceive a child serves to ensure the child will have all the advantages that come with genetic diversity. Conversely, seeking genetic similarity when conception is least likely (or impossible if she is actually pregnant) may be a defense mechanism for the woman. As previously mentioned, genetic similarity is associated with shared ancestry. In other words, seeking genetically similar people is essentially seeking the company of family members. Family members tend to be very protective of each other (one of the perks of being social animals); thus, the theory goes, the pregnant or menstruating woman seeks out kinsmen during the times when she is most vulnerable to attack.

This interesting phenomenon becomes even more interesting when one considers the use of hormonal birth control pills. Hormonal birth control works by preventing a woman from ovulating. If she does not ovulate, she cannot conceive a child. Additionally, if she does not ovulate, she is attracted primarily to similar MHC types, rather than different ones. And studies confirm this. Wedekind and Furi (1997) demonstrated that women on hormonal birth control preferred the smells of men with similar MHCs at any point in the month, while women not using hormonal birth control preferred the smells of different MHCs during ovulation and similar MHCs during menstruation.

Not only are humans able to smell who is a more genetically compatible mate, but we also have the ability to smell when the chances of conception are most probable. Men appear to be able to tell when a woman is ovulating (and thus able to conceive a child). In one study by Singh and Bronstad (2001), women were asked to wear a plain t-shirt during ovulation and another plain t-shirt while not ovulating. After smelling them, men rated the t-shirts worn during ovulation as more pleasant and sexier than the t-shirts worn outside of ovulation. In a similar study (Havlicek, Dvorakova, Bartos, and Flegr, 2006) women were asked to wear a series of cotton pads under their arms during menstruation, ovulation, and the luteal phase (the time between ovulation and menstruation). Men rated the odors of women during ovulation as least intense and most sexually appealing of the categories. Because differences found in a lab don't always translate to differences in behavior outside of the lab, Miller, Tybur, and Jordan (2007) conducted a study to determine how ovulation influences the real-world behavior of men. They chose a strip club to conduct their research. This study asked two groups of strippers—those taking hormonal birth control and those cycling normally—to track their tips and their menstrual cycle for two months. The normally cycling strippers averaged around $185/shift while menstruating, $260/shift during the luteal phase, and $355/shift during ovulation. As you can see from these numbers, there was a distinct spike in the amount of tips the women received during ovulation. For women taking hormonal birth control, there was no such earnings spike. These women averaged around $160/shift during menstruation, $200/shift during the luteal phase, and $210/shift during ovulation. While there were small differences in earnings for the women taking birth control, they were not enough to be considered statistically significant; thus, earnings for women taking hormonal birth control were relatively steady throughout the month.

Obviously, we have a long way to go when it comes to how smells influence human interactions. This area of research has been largely ignored by the scientific community for a number of years. Many believe that the sense of smell is the least influential of our primary senses. However, while most of its influence is subconscious and therefore less obvious, smell is incredibly important to our daily lives. It tells us who we are related to, who is a good genetic match for creating offspring, and when those offspring are most likely to be conceived.

Now that this field is finally getting recognition, many companies are seeking to capitalize on it. There has been a sudden influx in perfumes that are supposed to contain "attraction pheromones." These substances are marketed as a way to subtly and subconsciously attract the opposite sex. While they may seem like a good idea on the surface, remember what we have discussed about MHCs and their influence on attractiveness. Just like your roommate may think your older brother is attractive and you are completely disgusted by thinking about him in that way, which attraction pheromones are appealing to one person will be utterly repulsive to another. This is why these types of perfumes have no hope of universal success. They do not account for the fact that different people will find biological markers sexy; instead, they assume that what is attractive to one person will be attractive to all people. In short they forget the most important element of human mate selection: we seek diversity, not sameness.

Activities

1. Bring an unwashed t-shirt and a clean t-shirt from home. Put all the shirts from the class into a pile. See if you can identify which shirts match each other based on smell alone. Why did you pick the pairs that you did?

2. Have your significant other go for a jog or a very brisk walk. When they return, take a big whiff. What do you think? Now have a friend or a roommate whom you are not sexually attracted to (they should be of the gender you are sexually attracted to, however) do the same thing. Smell them upon their return. Now what do you think? Was there any difference in your reactions?

3. Wear a t-shirt to sleep in for a couple of nights. Now, try to keep yourself from eating onions or garlic for 48 hours. Wear another t-shirt to sleep in. Smell the two shirts. Do you notice a difference in the way you smell when you change your diet?

REFERENCES

Chaix, R., Cao, C., and Donnelly, P. (2008). "Is Mate Choice in Humans MHC-Dependent?" *PLoS: Genetics, 9*, e10000184. DOI:10.1371/journal.pgen.1000184

Havlicek, J., Dvorakova, R., Bartos, L., and Flegr, J. (2006). "Non-Advertized Does Not Mean Concealed: Body Odour Changes Across the Human Menstrual Cycle." *Ethology, 112*, 81–90. DOI: 10.1111/j.1439-0310.2006.01125.x

Hepper, P.G. (1987). "The Amniotic Fluid: An Important Priming Role in Kin Recognition." *Animal Behavior, 35*, 1343–1346.

Jackman, P. and Noble, W. (1983). "Normal Axillary Skin Microflora in Various Populations." *Clinical and Experimental Dermatology, 8*, 259–268. DOI: 10.1111/1365-2230.ep11610201

Jacob, S. and McLintock, M.K. (2000). "Psychological State and Mood Effects of Steroidal Chemosignals in Women and Men." *Hormones and Behavior, 37*, 57–78. DOI: 10.1006/hbeh.1999.1559

Kalmus, H. (1955). "The Discrimination by the Nose of the Dog of Individual Human Odours and in Particular of the Odours of Twins." *Animal Behavior, 5*, 25–31.

Macfarlane, A. (1975). "Olfaction in the Development of Social Preferences in the Human Neonate." *Parent–Infant Interaction, 33*, 103–113. DOI: 10.1002/9780470720158

Miller, G., Tybur, J.M., and Jordan, B.D. (2007). "Ovulatory Cycle Effects on Tip Earnings by Lap Dancers: Economic Evidence of Human Estrus?" *Evolution and Human Behavior, 28*, 375–381. DOI: 10.1016/j.evolhumbehav.2007.06.002

Niolaides, N. (1974). "Skin Lipids: Their Biochemical Uniqueness." *Science, 186*, 19–26.

Ober, C., Weitkamp, L.R., Cox, N., Dytch, H., Kostyu, D., and Elias, S. (1997). "HLA and Mate Choice in Humans." *American Journal of Human Genetics, 61*, 497–504.

Porter, R.H., Balogh, R.D., Cernoch, J.M., and Franchi, C. (1986). "Recognition of Kin Through Characteristic Body Odors." *Chemical Senses, 11*, 389–395.

Porter, R.H., Cernoch, J.M., and Balogh, R.D. (1985). "Odor Signatures and Kin Recognition." *Physiology and Behavior, 34*, 445–448. DOI: 10.1016/0031-9384(85)90210c-0

Porter, R.H. and Moore, J.D. (1981). "Human Kin Recognition by Olfactory Cues." *Physiology and Behavior, 27*, 493–495. DOI: 10.1016/0031-9384(81)90337-1

Singh, D. and Bronstad, P.M. (2001). "Female Body Odour Is a Potential Cue to Ovulation." *Royal Society of Biological Sciences, 268*, 797–801. DOI: 10.1093/beheco/arg043

Russell, M.J., Mendelsen, T., and Reeke, H.V.S. (1983). "Mothers' Identification of Their Infants' Odors." *Ethology and Sociobiology, 4*, 29–31.

Thornhill, R., Gangestad, S.W., Miller, R., Scheyd, G., McCollough, J.K., and Franklin, M. (2003). "Major Histocompatibility Complex Genes, Symmetry and Body Scent Attractiveness in Men and Women." *Behavioral Ecology, 14*, 668–678. DOI: 10.1093/beheco/arg043

Wedekind, C. and Furi, S. (1997) "Body Odour Preferences in Men and Women: Do They Aim for Specific MHC Combinations or Simply Heterozygosity?" *Processes of Biological Science, 264*, 1471–1479.

Wedekind, C., Seebeck, T., Bettens, F., and Paepke, A.J. (1995) "MHC-Dependent Mate Preferences in Humans." *Processes of Biological Science, 260*, 245–249.

Ziegler, A., Kentenich, H., and Uchanska-Ziegler, B. (2005) "Female Choice and the MHC." *Trends in Immunology, 26*: 496–502.

9. Physiological Arousal in Families

By James Honeycutt

Consider a study of positive and negative emotional affect in which siblings are discussing who is favored by their parents. One of the siblings vigorously defends her claims that she is the most deserving, loyal, and obedient child to their ailing father. Yet, she says she is calm, while her sister knows which "buttons to push to elicit a reaction" and hence teases her, hoping for the predictable reaction. We can determine if the so-called calm demeanor is reflected in stable or increased blood pressure. Hence, the appearance of someone being calm may actually be associated with physiological arousal. Physiological measures are more resilient to self-reports in which people may lie about what they are feeling in an attempt to mask emotions.

The goal of this chapter is to introduce you to the marriage, family, and physiology literature in terms of physiological outcomes, including how the autoimmune system is affected when there is recurrent conflict. Physiological arousal involves the autonomic nervous system in a state of adrenalin release and includes pulse (heart rate beats per minute [bpm]), interbeat intervals (IBI), and somatic activity measured on a wrist monitor. Somatic activity tracks wrist and hand movements used while gesturing. It reflects kinetic energy release and tension release through motion. Honeycutt (2010) discusses the importance of physiological variables in order to measure family conflict and affection. Physiological data complement existing methods for measuring family interaction through surveys, interviews, and observation of family members in discussing recent conversations that reflect retroactive imagined interactions (Honeycutt, 2010; Honeycutt, Keaton, Hatcher, and Hample, 2014).

We measure physiological arousal of married couples, engaged couples, and non-romantic pairs (such as siblings) with varying degrees of conflict in their relationships by asking participants to imagine either discussing a topic that they are highly pleased with (e.g., sharing time together) or displeased with (e.g., how they communicate) and then to actually discuss those topics. The former is referred to as an induced imagined interaction. We observe positive and conflictual interaction in the Matchbox Interaction Lab at our university (see link: http://web.archive.org/web/20110927190726/http://www.lsureveille.com/lab-conducts-studies-in-communication-1.903513). The laboratory resembles a living room, containing a comfortable couch, coffee table, end table, round table, computer, magazines, and paintings. Most physiological measures are not under conscious control. Hence, physiological measures offer a means of circumventing the self-presentation bias that is endemic to observational studies of communication.

WHY STUDY PHYSIOLOGY IN MARRIED COUPLES?

Physiological data can be a valuable complement to customary measures of marital interaction. Take for instance a study of positive and negative affect in marital conflict. A typical approach might include self-report (e.g., pre- and post-interaction ratings of affect) and observational data (e.g., behavioral coding of the interaction). Consider an interaction that is mostly positive except for a brief highly negative exchange in the middle. Whereas pre/post ratings of affect would not capture the variability in this case, continuous physiological data would likely reveal a spike in arousal during and after the negative exchange. Though observational coding could capture the behavioral variability in this example, it too could be informed by physiological data. Couples often behave atypically in the laboratory (Foster, Caplan, and Howe, 1997) and a calm demeanor may belie significant internal emotion and arousal. An interaction that appears positive on the surface could be the product of two angry people on their best behavior. Physiological measurement would offer a window into the putative internal turmoil such an interaction might generate. Since most physiological measures are not under conscious control, physiological data offer a means of circumventing the self-presentation bias that is endemic to observational studies of marital interaction (Honeycutt, 2010).

FIGHT OR FLIGHT AND PHYSIOLOGICAL AROUSAL

Early in the 20th century, Walter Cannon's (1929) research in psychobiology led him to describe the fight-or-flight response of the sympathetic nervous system (SNS) to threats. SNS is one of two parts of the autonomic nervous system (autonomic means "out of conscious control"). Cannon found that SNS arousal in response to a perceived threat involves several elements that prepare the body physiologically either to take a stand and fight off an attacker or to flee from the danger.

An evolutionary psychology perspective is that early animals had to react to threatening stimuli quickly and did not have time to psychologically and physically prepare themselves. The fight-or-flight response provided them with the mechanisms to rapidly respond to threats against survival (Goldstein, 2007). Moreover, our ancestors' physiology evolved to deal rapidly with physical threats such as fighting a rival for food or fleeing from predators (Sapolsky, 1998). In contemporary society, the SNS becomes activated when faced with a psychological or social threat. For example, you may be faced with a crucial deadline, you are cut off by a driver in traffic, or you may wonder what a parent will think about your performance in college courses. Once activated, the SNS releases epinephrine, norepinephrine, and cortisol into the bloodstream. Correspondingly, there is increased respiration, blood pressure (BP), heartbeat, and muscle tension. An easy way to remember how the SNS is associated with adrenalin and action is to think how stress begins with an "S" so that the "S" in SNS also reflects stress.

The second part of the autonomic nervous system is the parasympathetic nervous system (PNS). The PNS does essentially the opposite of the SNS: It decreases heart rate, increases digestion, and so on. Hence, the relaxation response turns SNS arousal off by turning on the PNS. So, in essence, we do not control our relaxation response; instead, we do things that result in the PNS taking control. An easy way to remember the PNS is to think how the "P" stands for "peace," which is related to a calm demeanor.

Emotional Coaching In Families

Research by Gottman, Katz, and Hooven (1997) on how parents teach their children to express or withhold emotions reveals that emotional coaching was associated with better ability to regulate stress. As noted above, under conditions of stress, the sympathetic nervous system activates the fight-or-flight response. The parasympathetic nervous system exerts counteracting control, or calming of physical arousal; specifically, the vagus nerve controls parasympathetic response. Children of emotional coaches have high vagal tone. Children can be taught to monitor how they inhale and exhale breaths even though this is not about getting oxygen to the brain. Even saying the word, "calm" while literally counting up the number of breaths in a 15-second time period enables relaxation. This enables them to show quicker recovery to emotional distress and lower levels of overall arousability. Another technique is using the glottis which is at the back of your tongue and it is closed when you are holding your breath. By controlling the glottis you are controlling the air flow, both during inhalation and exhalation. It stimulates your vagus nerve.

Try It Now:

- Inhale diaphragmatically through your nose, with your glottis partially closed, like almost making a "Hhhhh" sound for a count of 7
- Hold your breath for a moment
- Exhale through your nose (or you mouth), with your glottis partially closed, like almost making a "Hhhhh" sound for a count of 11

-Note: See more at: http://antianxietywaves.com/deal-with-anxiety-vagus-nerve/#sthash.7KC9x4mm.dpuf

In summary, parents are involved from the very first days of their child's life in shaping and socializing their child's emotional style. Emotional socialization by family members helps children learn to recognize and label their own and other people's emotions, influences both physiological and behavioral capacities for emotional regulation, and provides children with models and strategies for assisting other people in emotionally charged situations. Although the refinement of these skills is doubtless a lifelong process, individual differences in the basic style of emotional reactivity and emotion-related social behavior are clearly identifiable by the end of the preschool period.

Selected Findings from the Marital Interaction and Physiology Literature

Marriage provides a perfect venue for the study of physiology: happy marriages buffer each spouse from stress and are health promoting (House et al., 1988), while unhappy marriages not only fail to buffer spouses from stress, but also contribute to stress via increased conflict (Kiecolt-Glaser et al., 1993). John

Gottman and his colleagues were the first to study marital interaction and physiology systematically, and in the past twenty years they have gathered a wealth of data on the role of physiological arousal in marital dissolution. The other leader in this field, Janice Kiecolt-Glaser, has accumulated compelling data on the effects of marital conflict on immune and endocrine functioning. The following sections outline the important findings from these pioneers. Table 9-1 presents a summary of how stress induced through conflict and arguing affects physiological variables. Indeed, to the extent that conflict is characterized by negative behavior, it is physiologically arousing. Similarly, distressed couples typically exhibit greater reactivity in laboratory interactions than do non-distressed couples because they engage in more

Table 9-1 Various Findings on Physiological Correlates and Marital Conflict

Effects of Conflictual Discussions on Cardiovascular Variables

1. Marital conflict is reliably associated with heightened blood pressure and heart rate.

2. Other studies involving married couples and cardiovascular physiology have involved impersonal topics instead of relationship issues. In conversations where couples are asked to disagree and to try to influence each other, there is an increase in heart rates and blood pressure among wives, but not husbands.

3. Conversely, evaluative threat and incentive to influence the partner had no effects on women's cardiovascular responses, while men under the same conditions displayed larger heart rate and blood pressure compared to low-threat or no-incentive conditions.

4. When there was an inducement to influence the partner, husbands' elevations in systolic blood pressure were correlated with husbands' hostile and controlling behavior.

5. Lack of desensitization to the same stressor—spouses may not readily adapt physiologically to repetitive or redundant discussions over time. As opposed to becoming desensitized, in which there would be a gradual decline in physiological activation with each conflict discussion, some marriages could be characterized as chronic social stressors composed of repeated hits and a lack of physiological adaptation. Hence, heightened blood pressure due to stress is a good example of the lack of desensitization.

Effects of Conflict on Endocrine System

6. Studies from Kiecolt-Glaser (1996) involving newlywed couples engaged in a thirty-minute conflict resolution task in which they discussed current marital problems revealed that higher levels of hostile and negative behavior during conflict showed elevated levels of epinephrine, norepinephrine, adenocorticotropic hormone (ACTH), and growth hormone, which persisted for fifteen minutes after the discussion had ended, and lower levels of prolactin.

7. Hormone elevations were more pronounced in women compared to men.

8. Wives responded to marital conflict with greater increases in depression, hostility, and systolic blood pressure than husbands; in addition, women's lymphocyte proliferative responses phytohemagglutinin (PHA) decreased following conflict, while those of the men increased. Following conflict, decreases in proliferative responses to PHA were significantly correlated with increases in self-reported hostility.

Immune Function

9. Stress-induced immune changes have consequences for a number of health outcomes, including responses to infectious disease and slower wound healing.

10. The ability to shut off physiological responses after exposure to a stressor is also described as "recovery."

11. Marital interaction studies reveal that hostile and negative conflict behaviors are related to longer recovery following exposure to the conflict.

12. Couples with poorer immunological responses characterized their usual marital disagreements as more negative than individuals who showed better immune responses across areas of disagreement.

negative and less positive behavior. It should be noted, however, that even happily married newlywed couples exhibit elevated stress hormones after conflict (Kiecolt-Glaser et al., 1996).

The importance of measuring cardiovascular variables cannot be stressed enough. Research by Childre and Martin (1999) has revealed how the heart helps us respond to environmental cues through the production of mood-enhancing hormones. The electromagnetic signal that the heart sends to the brain and every other cell is the most powerful signal in the body (Hughes, Patterson, and Terrell, 2005). Furthermore, Damasio (2003) presents evidence that people cannot make decisions without processing emotional information that incorporates beliefs about how positive and negative the situation is. These judgments actually reflect the synthesis of both heart and brain functions weaving together cognition and emotion in a joint, intertwined fabric.

Heart-rate variability is commonly referred to as interbeat interval (IBI). IBI is a measure of the time in milliseconds between adjacent heartbeats (see Honeycutt, 2008, for an extensive discussion). High IBI rates are related to increased levels of adrenalin, anxiety, and arousal (Porges, 1985). The IBI is the time between one R-wave (or heartbeat) and the next and is highly variable within any given time period. Multiple biological rhythms overlay one another to produce the resultant pattern of variability. Interbeat intervals have relevance for physical, emotional, and mental function: The lower the IBI value, the shorter the cardiac beat, which reflects a faster heart rate. Under normal conditions, the heart's rate is under control of the parasympathetic nervous system. Generally, resting heart rates are 70 for men and 80 for women, according to the American Heart Association. Heart rates above 105 are high and above the effects of exercise (Rowell, 1986). A resting heart rate typically decreases with age. It is also affected by environmental factors; for example, it increases with extremes in temperature and altitude. We always take a baseline measure of heart rate before engaging in experimental stimuli. We use the baseline measure and age as a covariate in analyzing subsequent mean differences.

Physiological Arousal

Diffuse physiological arousal (DPA) occurs in terms of adrenalin pumping into the cardiovascular and endocrine systems. It is reflected by elevated heart rate, perspiration, blood pressure, and pulse. DPA can be very high during heated arguments. Gottman and Silver (1999) discuss how marital conflict shows a pattern of *demand change* and *withdraw* from the discussion.

Gottman and Levenson (1988) were pioneering social scientists to study marital interaction and physiology systematically as well as longitudinally, sometimes conducting follow-up data analyses on couples over a fourteen-year period (Gottman and Levenson, 2002). In the past twenty-five years, Gottman and his associates have gathered a wealth of data on the role of physiological arousal in marital dissolution. Another leader in this field, Kiecolt-Glaser, and her associates (2003; 2005) have accumulated compelling data on the effects of marital conflict on immune and endocrine functioning. Sometimes, the groups' conclusions differ. For example, Gottman claims that physiological arousal is more punishing for men, while Kiecolt-Glaser, Bane, Glaser, and Malarkey (2003) argue that it is the women who suffer physiologically from the ill effects of marital duress (also see Kiecolt-Glaser and Newton, 2001). Therefore, Gottman argues that men are more likely to withdraw from discussing sensitive topics in unhappy marriages because subliminally, they are trying to prevent arousal and the release of adrenalin. Once the man is aroused, it takes him longer for heart rates to return to a basal resting state (Gottman, 1994). Furthermore, research by Gottman and his associates (1998) reveals that women are more likely to begin with harsh start-ups, while men are more likely to become flooded and stonewall, and to rehearse stress-inducing thoughts, which reflect imagined interaction conflict linkage as discussed in chapter 6. Additionally, Gottman and Levenson (2002) found that frequent ongoing experience of overdrive in physiological arousal (flooding) in a couple's interactions lead partners to maintain a state of constant hyper-vigilance in the expectation of punishing experiences.

Self-Soothing. Gottman reports that women are better at soothing themselves while arguing. In happy marriages, they are more likely to use what is called the editing function by de-escalating the argument (e.g., calming down a little). Men do this to an extent, but as relational quality declines, men are less likely to soothe themselves. Hence, they use avoidance. Try something that may feel totally foreign in the heights of your distress: breathe. by stimulating the vagal nerve as noted earlier. Practice physiological self-soothing by imagining your favorite place, a place you can get lost in, a place in which you feel untroubled and where you can float peacefully within yourself. Meditate on this place. Do not dwell on your argument or think thoughts that maintain your level of distress. Don't focus on getting even. Avoid thoughts of righteous indignation ("I don't have to take this anymore") and innocent victimhood ("Why is he always picking on me?"). Instead, spend your time doing something relaxing, such as listening to music or exercising.

After spending around twenty minutes in this serene state, you can return to your conversation, centered and calm. Why twenty minutes? According to Dr. Gottman, "the major sympathetic neurotransmitter norepinephrine doesn't have an enzyme to degrade it so it has to be diffused through blood … this takes twenty minutes or more in the cardiovascular system."

General activation of many physiological systems in the body creates the "general alarm response" that spells danger. Physiological arousal may cause increased heart rate, increased myocardial contractility, increased vasoconstriction, increased sympathetic and decreased parasympathetic activation, increased rennin-angiotensin activity, reduced oxygen concentration in the blood, decreased blood supply to non-essential functions like the gut and kidney, catecholamine and cortisol secretion, increased amygdala activation, decreased frontal lobe activation, immunosuppression, and so on. When physiological arousal accompanies relationship conflict, it may lead to:

1. A decrease in one's ability to take in information (reduced hearing, reduced peripheral vision, problems with shifting attention away from a defensive posture)
2. An increase in defensiveness and what we call the "summarizing yourself syndrome"
3. A reduction in the ability to be creative in problem-solving
4. A reduction in the ability to listen and empathize

Physiological Arousal Impacts Health

Low marital quality is associated with greater likelihood of illness and symptom exacerbation. The link between marital quality and health is thought to be physiological arousal during marital conflict. In support of this, Kiecolt-Glaser and colleagues have shown that marital conflict is associated with elevated stress hormones and down-regulation of the immune system (1993). In essence, marital conflict operates as a chronic stressor, weakening the immune system's ability to prevent illness.

It is important that couples avoid the negative (being defensive, sarcastic, withdrawing) while building positive skills. Long-term studies have found that couples who practice effective communication, and anger and conflict management strategies in programs like the Denver-based Prevention and Relationship Enhancement Program see many positive changes. Results include constructive arguing, effective communication, greater relationship satisfaction, fewer sexual problems, fewer instances of physical violence, less dominance, and greater use of problem-solving behaviors.

Gender Differences in Physiological Arousal. The evidence on gender differences in physiological reactivity is decidedly mixed, with studies concluding that husbands are more reactive, wives are more reactive, or that no differences exist (cf., Gottman and Levenson, 1988; 2002; Kiecolt-Glaser et al., 1996). Research conducted over twenty-five years ago revealed that males show increased adrenaline secretion (review, Gottman and Levenson, 1988).

At the risk of oversimplification, Gottman suggests that husbands are more reactive and that this explains husbands' withdrawal behavior (i.e., it is a means of physiological soothing). Kiecolt-Glaser and Newton (2001), on the other hand, suggest that wives are more reactive and that this explains the finding that wives exhibit poorer health than husbands in distressed marriages. Because their studies differ in methods and populations, a direct comparison of Gottman's and Kiecolt-Glaser's gender findings is beyond the scope of this chapter.

Men are more likely than women to have imagined interactions and rehearse distress-maintaining thoughts that may prolong physiological arousal and vigilance (Honeycutt, 2010). Flooding accompanies this arousal, and often leads to what Gottman (1994) called the distance and isolation cascade in terms of the movement toward relationship dissolution (also Google the Gottman Institute). Furthermore, men have a harder time recovering from arousal. Gottman and other social science researchers have demonstrated how men and women are different in their responses to flooding (Bryant and Miron, 2003). Because of biological differences in the way our bodies respond to stress, perhaps stemming from evolutionarily adaptive mechanisms developed in our ancestors in terms of survival, it is more difficult for men's bodies to calm down after an argument. Women calm down more quickly because it takes less time for their cardiovascular system to recover from stress (Gottman, 1994; Gottman and Silver, 1999).

Caught up in the heat of the moment, however, we all experience the physiological signs of stress: sweating, shaking, and being short of breath—a state in which it is completely impossible to think clearly about anything at all, much less to resolve a complicated problem with our loved ones. People shout and sometimes lash out. Gottman and Silver (1999) suggest tips for physiological self-soothing that women are better at. In fact, in happy marriages, it is slightly more likely to be the wife who soothes her husband.

Imagining Conflict Helps Deal with Anxiety and Stress. As noted in Chapter 6, Honeycutt and Hatcher define imagined interactions (IIs) as a type of mental imagery in which we imagine talking with real-life significant others, such as relational partners, family members, roommates, ex-relational partners, individuals in authority, work colleagues, and friends. There are verbal and nonverbal components of IIs to the extent that individuals envision lines of dialogue by self and interaction partners as well as the scenes of the encounters. The catharsis function of IIs helps individuals relieve anxiety, stress, and uncertainty (Honeycutt, 2003; 2010). Individuals can alleviate arousal and symbolically vent and get things off their chest without being encumbered by the reaction of others.

Proactive IIs occur before anticipated encounters in which individuals often rehearse what they are going to do. Conversely, retroactive IIs occur after a real-life encounter in which individuals replay what occurred and how things might be different if alternative actions had been taken. Aside from rehearsal, additional functions of IIs include catharsis, self-understanding, maintaining relationships, compensation for lack of real conversations, and managing conflict.

Honeycutt and his associates examined how in the midst of trauma imagined interactions using the catharsis function to release emotion, deal with anxiety, and for tension relief helped family members in coping with the chaos of Hurricane Katrina. Additionally, theorem six of imagined interaction conflict-linkage theory states that recurring conflict is a function of physiology arousal due to neurotransmitter stimulation in the brain (Honeycutt and Cantrill, 2001; Honeycutt, 2004; 2010). The original theorem is reprinted below and has been modified over the years due to research on cardiovascular reactivity.

- *Old Theorem 6: Recurring conflict is a function of physiology and brain, neurotransmitter activity in which neurons are stimulated.*
- *Corollary: There is a biological and genetic component of conflict engagement that is reflected in neural activity and heart-rate variability.*
- *New Modified Theorem 6: Recurring conflict is reflected in physiological arousal in which anxiety is triggered and persons "fight" or "take flight" in terms of the sympathetic nervous system.*

Indeed, any explanation of conflict must acknowledge the impact of neurology and physiology. In the Matchbox Interaction Lab, we have seen the rise in heart-rate variability as relational partners relive and express ongoing grievances with each other.

Physiological Linkage and Imagined Interactions in a Married Couple

Gottman (1994) defined the notion of physiological linkage in distinguishing happy from unhappy couples in which there would be a reciprocity of negative affect (misery loves company) as well as temporal predictability and "reciprocity in physiology" as well (p. 72). A pioneering study by Kaplan et al. (1964) paired people on the basis of mutual liking or disliking and they found that predictability from one person's electrodermal response to another person existed only for people who disliked each other.

Elsewhere, Honeycutt (2012) reports the results of an intriguing case study involving an engaged couple who had a long-distance relationship for a period of six months. He was 25 and she was 23. He was in graduate school and spent a semester overseas for a cultural exchange internship program studying Dutch pumps. His fiancée studied social work. The couple had an induced II in which he imagined discussing with his fiancée a pleasing topic, which was their shared goals and interests, including their desire to go on a cruise; and a displeasing topic (his separation from her while he would be away). Her pleasing topic was how open she felt he was in communicating with her revealing flexibility and disclosure. The displeasing topic was also the separation due to the cultural exchange program.

These IIs lasted three minutes. Both partners used a talk-aloud procedure to have their II in which they orally stated their views and then responded as they thought their partner would respond. This procedure represents role-playing, except the viewpoint of the partner is orally stated. Then, the couple got together and discussed the displeasing and pleasing topics. This case study presents the results of the analysis of heart-rate variability, also known as interbeat interval (IBI). High-frequency (HF) activity has been found to decrease under conditions of acute time pressure and emotional strain (Nickel and Nachreiner, 2003) and elevated-state anxiety, presumably related to focused attention and motor inhibition (Jönsson, 2007). IBI has been shown to be reduced in individuals reporting a greater frequency and duration of daily worry (Brosschot, Van Dijk, and Thayer, 2007).

In individuals with post-traumatic stress disorder (PTSD), IBI and its HF component are reduced compared to controls, while the low-frequency (LF) component is elevated. Furthermore, unlike controls, PTSD patients demonstrated no LF or HF reactivity to recalling a traumatic event (Hagit, 1998). Higher IBI indicates an optimal cooperation between the sympathetic and parasympathetic nervous systems. Hence, higher IBI results in a balanced equilibrium within the body's autonomic nervous system. Furthermore, larger IBI levels result in a lower heart rate.

The strongest sign of physiological linkage occurred when both partners were discussing their pleasing topic. Additional analysis revealed that before the induced II, the male had larger heart-rate variability than the female during the induced II session. Follow-up tests revealed a statistically significant difference in which he had a higher average or mean IBI ($M = 699.83$, *Standard Deviation (SD)* = 57.80) during the induced II than she did ($M = 642.91$, *SD* = 64.24). Hence this finding denotes that he had a lower heart rate during the induced II.

The same pattern occurred for discussing the pleasing and displeasing topics. Yet, it is worth noting that his highest IB occurred when discussing the displeasing topic ($M = 718.74$, *SD* = 61.72), while her IBI was lower ($M = 617.06$, *SD* = 55.32). Therefore, she had a higher rate while discussing the displeasing topic of separation than he did. It is plausible that since she is staying behind during the separation, she feels lamentation or sadness, while he feels the excitement of traveling abroad. Consequently, her lamentation may be manifested in her elevated heart rate during this discussion. Furthermore, she indicated this to us in a post-experiment debriefing by commenting how she felt left out while he was going to be away and she was disappointed with the situation.

An intriguing study by O'Brien, Balto, Erber, and Gee (1995) examined cognitive and emotional reactions to simulated marital and family conflicts as experienced by college students from homes with physically aggressive (PA) and non-physically aggressive (NPA) marital relationships. The simulations represent Honeycutt and Hatcher's notions of retroactive imagined interactions as discussed in the imagined interaction chapter of this book. Individuals from PA homes reported experiencing more physiological arousal and negative affect in response to simulated marital and family conflict than did individuals from NPA homes. In addition, PA respondents were less likely to provide spontaneous suggestions regarding how marital conflict could proceed more constructively than were NPA respondents. These results suggest that marital conflict witnessed in the home may influence young adults' thoughts and feelings regarding marital conflict in new situations, and present the possibility that marital conflict witnessed between one's parents leads to the development of a marital conflict representation that guides social information processing of newly encountered marital interactions. This reflects social learning theory in which we may model our behaviors from significant others, including parents.

SUGGESTIONS FOR FUTURE INQUIRIES

Life is full of daily stressors such as being cut off in traffic, deadlines at work, and family responsibilities. The way we react to stress can be measured through physiology. With technological apps for iPhones, it is feasible for people to download heart-rate monitors based on the retinas of the eye (see the Cardiio app: https://itunes.apple.com/us/app/cardiio-heart-rate-monitor/id542891434?mt=8). Furthermore, it could be possible to conduct field studies in the home of families where they post their heart rates at various times of the day if they were paid as part of National Institutes of Health grant. The marriage and physiology literature has focused primarily on harmful interactions between spouses and the long-term damage these interactions can cause. While it is important to understand the harm spouses can inflict on one another, it is equally pressing to understand the ways spouses help each other. In fact, one of the most obvious conclusions to be drawn from the marriage and physiology literature is that couples therapy ought to include techniques for soothing the physiological reactivity that accompanies stressful interactions. Social support is a potentially valuable domain for understanding the way marriage buffers spouses from the effects of stress. Physiological arousal during social support interactions found that support (i.e., positive behavior) from a spouse was associated with lower heart rate and blood pressure. This was true only for wives, however. For many husbands, the social support interaction took the form of a confessional, which can be highly physiologically arousing even in the presence of a supportive spouse. Further research is needed to understand the ways that spouses can physiologically soothe one another. Beyond the physiological indicators of stress (e.g., blood pressure, heart rate, cortisol), couples researchers are beginning to study the physiological concomitants of gender (e.g., testosterone), bonding (e.g., oxytocin), and positive affect (e.g., electrical activity in the muscles responsible for smiling), to name but a few.

Neuroscience may hold unique promise in the study of marital interaction. Davidson (1992) has reported that positive emotions are associated with greater activation of the left frontal region, and negative emotions with greater activation of the right frontal region of the brain. What might we learn from EEG or ERPs collected while couples observed a videotape of their interaction? Might satisfied couples exhibit greater left frontal activation? Might this asymmetry be predictive of marital stability or therapeutic outcomes? Because asymmetrical left activation occurs in approach-related emotions and right activation in withdrawal-related emotions (Davidson, 1992), at the behavioral level might we even see neurological concomitants of demand-withdrawal behavior?

CONCLUSION

Robles and Kiecolt-Glaser (2003; 2006) conclude that marital interaction research incorporating cardiovascular, endocrine, and immune measures has yielded important insights into the physiological consequences of marital strain. A chronic stress perspective on physiological processes reveals how ongoing marital conflict can contribute to negative long-term health consequences. Research reviewed by Robles and Kiecolt-Glaser (2003) reveals that there is clear evidence for the importance of incorporating physiological measures in marital interaction research. Though researchers have been studying physiology in marital interaction for over forty years, the field is ripe and many unanswered questions remain.

DISCUSSION QUESTIONS / ACTIVITIES

1. How often are you physically aroused when having discussions with the following people: roommates, boy (girl) friend, siblings, parents? Does arousal occur when you are told good news or having a disagreement?

2. Do you know if you come from a family with a history of high blood pressure? Do you engage in self-soothing in order to deal with feelings of being emotionally flooded? Alternatively, is there a friend who is good at calming you down after an angry argument? Who is this person and why is he/she so helpful in helping your relax or "chill out"?

3. Think about a married couple or two siblings in which one of them appears to be relaxed even in the face of threat (e.g., they are cut off in heavy traffic and late for an appointment), while the corresponding partner is more emotional and would lash out when cut off in traffic. Is the PNS or SNS operating in both partners in this scenario?

4. Interview some members of a family who have recently overcome a stressor event and shown resiliency in the face of the stress (e.g., they were strong in dealing with someone's illness, they got a new job after losing a prior one, they helped someone who needed assistance due a loss). Ask them if they ever thought about feeling tension in their skin (galvanic skin response), their heart raced faster (cardiovascular reactivity), or they had to take some prescription to deal with the stress. Did the resiliency strengthen their faith in family bonding or have no effect?

References

Brosschot, J.F., Van Dijk, E., and Thayer, J.F. (2007). "Daily Worry Is Related to Low Heart Rate Variability During Waking and the Subsequent Nocturnal Sleep Period." *International Journal of Psychophysiology, 63*, 39–47. DOI: 10.1016/j.ijpsycho.2006.07.016

Bryant, J. and Miron, D. (2003). "Excitation-Transfer Theory." In J. Bryant, D. Roskos-Ewoldsen, and J. Cantor (Eds.), *Communication and Emotion: Essays in Honor of Dolf Zillmann* (pp. 31–59). Mahwah, NJ: Erlbaum.

Cannon, W.B. (1929). *Bodily Changes in Pain, Hunger, Fear and Rage: An Account of Recent Research into the Function of Emotional Excitement* (2nd ed.). New York: Appleton-Century-Crofts.

Childre, D.L. and Martin, H. (1999). *The Heartmath Solution.* San Francisco: Harper.

Damasio, A. (2003). *Looking for Spinoza.* Orlando, FL: Harcourt.

Davidson, R.J. (1992). "Emotion and Affective Style: Hemispheric Substrates." *Psychological Science, 3*, 39–43. DOI: 10.1111/j.1467-9280.1992.tb00254.x

Foster, D.A., Caplan, R.D., and Howe, G.W. (1997). "Representativeness of Observed Couple Interaction: Couples Can Tell, and It Does Make a Difference." *Psychological Assessment, 9*, 285–294. DOI: 10.1037//1040-3590.9.3.285

Goldstein, David and Kopin, I (2007). "Evolution of Concepts of Stress." *Stress, 10*, 109–20. DOI: 10.1080/10253890701288935

Gottman, J.M. (1994). *What Predicts Divorce?* Mahwah, NJ: Erlbaum.

Gottman Institute (2014); Retrieved from http://www.gottmancouplesretreats.com/about/relationships-dysfunctional-divorce-predictors.aspx on June 9, 2014.

Gottman, J.M., Katz, L.F., and Hooven, C. (1997). *Meta-Emotion: How Families Communicate Emotionally.* Hillsdale, NJ: Lawrence Erlbaum.

Gottman, J.M. and Levenson, R.W. (1988). "The Social Psychophysiology of Marriage." In P. Noller and M.A. Fitzpatrick (Eds.), *Perspectives on Marital Interaction* (pp. 182–199). Clevedon, England: Multilingual Matters.

Gottman, J.M. and Levenson, R.W. (2002). "A Two-Factor Model for Predicting When a Couple Will Divorce: Exploratory Analyses Using 14-Year Longitudinal Data. *Family Process, 41*, 83–96. DOI: 10.1111/j.1545-5300.2002.40102000083.x

Gottman, J., Coan, J., Carrere, S., and Swanson, C. (1998). "Predicting Marital Happiness and Stability from Newlywed Interactions." *Journal of Marriage and the Family, 60*, 5–22. DOI: 10.2307/353438

Gottman, J.M. and Silver, N. (1999). *The Seven Principles for Making Marriage Work.* New York: Crown.

Hagit, C. et al. (1998). "Analysis of Heart Rate Variability in Posttraumatic Stress Disorder Patients in Response to a Trauma-Related Reminder." *Biological Psychiatry, 44*, 1054–1059.

Honeycutt, J.M. (2003). *Imagined Interactions: Daydreaming About Communication.* Cresskill, NJ: Hampton.

Honeycutt, J.M. (2010). "Physiology and Imagined Interactions." In J.M. Honeycutt (Ed.), *Imagine That: Studies in Imagined Interaction* (pp. 43–64). Cresskill, NJ: Hampton.

Honeycutt, J.M. (2012). "Imagined Interactions: On Knowing What to Say." In K. Lollar, W.M. Monsour, and J. Barwind, (Ed.), *The Talk Within: Its Central Role in Communication* (pp. 181–203). Dubuque, IA: Kendall/Hunt.

Honeycutt, J.M., Keaton, S.A., Hatcher, L.C., and Hample, D. (2014). "Physiological Covariates in Predicting Conflict Escalation in Terms of Advisability and Probability Ratings of Marital Arguing." In J.M. Honeycutt, C.R. Sawyer, and S.A. Keaton (Eds.), *The Influence of Communication on Physiology and Health.* New York: Peter Lang.

House, J.S., Landis, K.R., and Umberson, D. (1988). *Science, 241*, 540–545. DOI: 10.1126/science.3399889

Hughes, M., Patterson, B., and Terrell, J.B. (2005). *Emotional Intelligence in Action.* San Francisco: Pfeiffer.

Jönsson, P. (2007). "Respiratory Sinus Arrhythmia as a Function of State Anxiety in Healthy Individuals." *International Journal of Psychophysiology, 63,* 48–54. DOI: 10.1016/j.ijpsycho.2006.08.002

Kaplan, A. (1964). *The Conduct of Inquiry: Methodology for Behavioral Science.* San Francisco: Chandler.

Kiecolt-Glaser, J.K. and Newton, T.L. (2001). "Marriage and Health: His and Hers." *Psychological Bulletin, 12,* 472–503. DOI: 10.1037//0033-2909.127.4.472

Kiecolt-Glaser, J., Newton, T., Cacioppo, J., MacCallum, R., Glaser, R., and Malarkey, W. (1996).

"Marital Conflict and Endocrine Function: Are Men Really More Affected Than Women?" *Journal of Consulting and Clinical Psychology, 64,* 324–332. DOI: 10.1037//0022-006X.64.2.324

Nickel, P. and Nachreiner, F. (2003). *Human Factors, 45,* 575–590. DOI: 10.1518/hfes.45.4.575.27094

O'Brien, M., Balto, K. Erber, S., and Gee, C.B. (1995). "College Students' Cognitive and Emotional Reactions to Simulated Marital and Family Conflict." *Cognitive Therapy and Research, 19,* 707–724. DOI: 10.1007/BF02227862

Porges, S.W. (1985). "Spontaneous Oscillations in Heart Rate: Potential Index of Stress." In P.G. Moberg (Ed.), *Animal Stress.* Bethesda, MD: The American Physiological Society, 97–111.

Robles, T.F. and Kiecolt-Glaser, J.K. (2003). "The Physiology of Marriage: Pathways to Health." *Physiology and Behavior, 79,* 409–416. DOI: 10.1016/S0031-9384(03)00160-4

Rowell, L. (1986). *Human Circulation: Regulation During Physical Stress.* New York: Oxford.

Sapolsky, R.M. (1998). *The Trouble with Testosterone and Other E*ssays on the Biology of the Human Predicament. New York: Simon & Schuster.

Part IV

DIVORCE AND FAMILY RECONFIGURATION

10. Predicting Divorce and Skills for Effective Communicating

The Legacy of John Gottman's Research

By James Honeycutt

There are four major communication behaviors that predict divorce: criticism, contempt, defensiveness, and withdrawal. These behaviors are corrosive and the couples often feel isolated and distant because their interpersonal needs for respect, inclusion, and affection are not being met. Moreover, these behaviors occur in all interpersonal relationships in varying degrees. Hence, recognition of these signs can potentially help us to improve our interpersonal communication with everyone we encounter.

Gottman (see www.gottman.com) has conducted voluminous research over thousands of couples and states that harsh start-up is a sign that a couple will divorce. Moreover, Gottman states that in marital interaction, he has been able to conclude that 94% of the time the way a discussion starts predicts how it will end. When a partner initiates the discussion using a harsh start-up, such as being negative or accusatory, or using contempt, the discussion is basically doomed to fail. On the other hand, when one partner begins the discussion using a softened start-up, the discussion will most likely end on a similar, positive tone. Honeycutt and Bryan (2011) note, along with Gottman, that it is often women who initiate serious discussion of relational problems with their partners in heterosexual relationships.

John Gottman has spent over thirty-five years studying marriages since the publication of his first paper in *Psychological Bulletin* dealing with marital interaction and parenting (Gottman, Notarius, Bank, Yopi, and Rubin, 1976). Gottman was recognized in 2007 as one of the ten most influential therapists of the past quarter century. His legacy is immense in the area of marital communication. Gottman has been the recipient of four National Institute of Mental Health Research Scientist Awards, the American Association for Marriage and Family Therapy Distinguished Research Scientist Award, the American Family Therapy Academy Award for Most Distinguished Contributor to Family Systems Research, the American Psychological Association Division of Family Psychology, Presidential Citation for Outstanding Lifetime Research Contribution and the National Council of Family Relations, and the 1994 Burgess Award for Outstanding Career in Theory and Research.

Gottman and his associates (1998) claim to be able to predict divorce based on how newlyweds interact. For example, one study with 130 newlywed couples was designed to explore marital communication behaviors that were associated with divorce in a follow-up analysis. They explored seven types of behavioral models: (a) seeing anger as a dangerous emotion, (b) engaging in active listening, (c) reciprocating negative affect, (d) the wife using a negative start-up, (e) attempting to de-escalate conflicts, (f) using positive affect during arguments, and (g) physiological soothing of the male.

The models for seeing anger as a dangerous emotion, engaging in active listening, or reciprocating negative affect, did not indicate a greater incidence of divorce. However, there was a greater incidence of divorce in models where the wife used a negative start-up, the husband did not attempt to de-escalate low-intensity negative affect in the wife, the wife did not attempt to de-escalate high-intensity negative affect in the husband, or there was no physiological soothing for the husband. Additionally, evidence was found for a contingent positive affect model and for balance models (i.e., ratio models) of positive-to-negative affect predicting satisfaction among stable couples. Divorce and stability were predicted with 83% accuracy and satisfaction with 80% accuracy. Additional studies improved the prediction as earlier noted (Gottman and Silver, 1999).

Table 10-1 John Gottman's Four Horsemen of the Apocalypse Leading to Divorce*

---

1. Criticism:
Attacking your partner's personality or character often with the intent of making yourself right and the partner wrong. The use of the second-person singular "you" is indicative of criticisms as opposed to the first-person plural "we."

Examples: "You always …" "You never …" "You're the type of person who …" "Why are you so nasty …"

2. Contempt:
Attacking your partner's self-concept with the desire to insult or verbally abuse him/her:
- Insults and name-calling: "bitch, bastard, wimp, fat, stupid, ugly, slob, lazy …"
- Hostile humor, sarcasm or mockery, ridicule
- Body language and tone of voice: sneering, rolling your eyes, curling your upper lip

3. Defensiveness:
Seeing self as the victim, warding off a perceived attack:
- Making excuses (e.g., external circumstances beyond your control forced you to act in a certain way) "It's not my fault … " "I didn't …"
- Cross-complaining: meeting your partner's complaint or criticism with a complaint of your own, ignoring what your partner said
- Disagreeing and then cross-complaining "That's not true, you're the one who …" "I did this because you did that …"
- Yes-butting: start off agreeing but end up disagreeing
- Repeating yourself without paying attention to what the other person is saying
- Whining "It's not fair."

4. Stonewalling:
Withdrawing from the relationship as a way to avoid conflict. Partners may think they are trying to be "neutral," but stonewalling conveys disapproval, icy distance, separation, disconnection, and/or smugness:
- Stony silence
- Monosyllabic mutterings
- Changing the subject
- Removing yourself physically
- Silent treatment

---

*Based on John Gottman *What Predicts Divorce* (1994). Mahwah, NJ: Erlbaum.

His research has revealed fighting and arguing in and of itself does not predict divorce; it is how people fight that is important. In fact, some couples are conflict engagers and can be called sparring partners. Yet, if they constructively argue, it may be enjoyable for them. He has a website in which people can take marriage quizzes and determine if they are headed for divorce; http://www.gottman.com/. Table 10-1 summarizes the four horsemen followed by a brief explanation of each behavior. It is noted that the four horsemen of the apocalypse is a metaphor depicting the end of times as shown in the New Testament. The Book of Revelations describes conquest, war, hunger, and death, respectively. Dr. Gottman uses this metaphor to describe communication behaviors that can predict the end of a relationship.

CRITICISM

According to Gottman (1994; Gottman and Silver, 1999; 2012), the first of these signs that will predict divorce is the use of criticisms compared to complaints. Criticizing is bad and to be avoided, while complaining is good and should be encouraged. Complaining about one's spouse is normal. Yet the way that we express these complaints is very important. The problem arises when complaints turn into criticisms. A complaint focuses on a specific behavior, while a criticism attacks the character of the person. An example of the difference between a complaint and a criticism is the following:

> Complaint: "You told me earlier that you're too tired to go the concert. I'm disappointed because I thought we could share the quality time."
> Criticism: "Why are you so selfish? It was really nasty of you to lead me on. You should have told me earlier that you were too tired to go to the concert."
> Criticism is very common in relationships, and when used often, can lead to the second horseman.

CONTEMPT

The second horseman, contempt, often follows criticism. This behavior is most predictive of divorce. As noted in Table 10-1, some examples of contempt are when a person uses irony, ridicule, cynicism, name-calling, eye rolling, sneering, mockery, and hostile humor (Gottman and Silver, 1999). Contempt is the worst of the four horsemen because it communicates disgust to the person it is directed toward. Contemptuous nonverbal behaviors such as eye rolling are an implicit way to put a partner down without using verbal statements to do that. Gottman once said on national television that it should be outlawed in marriage. Some research has revealed sex differences, with men more likely to use nonverbal means of communicating contempt through frowning and lip furrowing due to socialization of keeping emotions internalized (Gottman, 1994; 2003; 2012; Gottman and Levenson, 1992; 1998; 2002). The husband's facial expression of contempt are an excellent predictor of his wife's physical illness reported by the wife four years later, while the wife's facial expression at time 1 are correlated at .51 with the number of months the couple will be separated in the next four years (Gottman, 1994). It is difficult to solve a problem when the message being sent is that one partner is disgusted with the other. Often, when a partner uses contempt, the other partner becomes defensive, which is the third horseman.

DEFENSIVENESS

Becoming defensive is a common reaction to being treated with contempt. Many people become defensive when they are being criticized, but the problem is that it never helps solve the problem at hand. Defensiveness is an attempt to ward off or protect one's self from perceived attack. As Gottman (1994) says, "There may be a denial of responsibility for the problems, a counter blame, or a whine" (p. 25). It is really a way of blaming your partner. You're saying, in effect, the problem isn't me, it's you. As a result, the problem is not resolved and the conflict escalates further. Defensiveness often comes across as whining (Gottman, 1994) in which a high nasal tone of voice that is high-pitched. Essentially, the nonverbal message behind defensiveness is "You are not being fair and quit picking on me." The escalating conflict usually leads to one partner tuning out the other, and is the sign that the fourth horseman, withdrawal, has arrived. "You always" or "You never" statements reflect defensiveness.

Whining. Whining is a form of defensiveness that is very common in interpersonal communication. It is signaled by a high-pitched, fluid fluctuation of the voice that can come across as an irritating nasal quality with a syllable being stressed toward the end of the sentence. Gottman (1994) says, "It reflects dissatisfaction in a very childish way … I have noticed that whining almost always has an innocent victim posture behind it. It is as if the whiner is saying that it is not fair. Why are you picking on me? I didn't do anything wrong, I'm good" (p. 27). There is a "poor me" message behind whining.

WITHDRAWAL

Withdrawal is also known as stonewalling because the listener presents a stone wall to the speaker. The usual nonverbal backchannels presented by a listener are missing, including small vocalizations, little gaze at the speaker, and little facial movement; but when there is, it is a negative facial code showing dissatisfaction with the speaker (Gottman, 1994). Silence, leaving the scene of an argument, turning inward, and being introspective while in the middle of an argument reflects withdrawal. In educational psychology, this reflects the "time-out" scenario in which disruptive children are removed from a classroom in order to terminate the temper tantrum in front of the other children. However, time-out seldom works because children are often having retroactive imagined interactions in which they replay what has just occurred while sometimes thinking about revenge in the form of proactive imagined interactions as they mentally envision how they might verbally intimidate someone (Honeycutt, 2014; also see Chapter 6). Additionally, women are more likely to criticize than men and men are more likely to stonewall and withdraw (Gottman and Silver, 1999; Honeycutt and Bryan, 2011). Historically, census data from local municipalities readily reveal that women are more prone to file for divorce than men are.

When couples have a high frequency of these behaviors, isolation and loneliness increase with negative consequences (Gottman, 1994). These cascades of isolation and loneliness increase the likelihood of physiological arousal (see Chapter 9) and marital distress, which often result in divorce. Gottman (1994) notes that withdrawing is perceived as being cold, smug, hostile, and disinterested. Indeed it is physiologically and emotionally punishing (Gottman and Levenson, 2002; Honeycutt and Bryan, 2011; Honeycutt, Keaton, Hatcher and Hample, 2014).

It is intriguing that withdrawal from conflict has been noticed as far back as seventy-five years ago. Terman, Buttwenweiser, Ferguson, Johnson, and Wilson (1938) reported that husbands' complaints about their wives were that the women complained more and criticized more, while the wives' grievances concerned the men's emotional withdrawal. This sequence becomes a closed bidirectional loop of reciprocal causation: he withdraws because she nags, she nags because he withdraws. Neither is right or wrong, they are simply reacting to each other.

Cascade Model of Divorce

Following is a diagram showing correlations between each of the four horsemen. These correlations were originally reported by Gottman (1994) after reviewing a series of studies in which couples were videotaped discussing events of the day, describing the history of their marriage, and arguing while being physiologically monitored as noted in the prior chapter.

.28   .42   .35   94%
CRITICISM → CONTEMPT → DEFENSIVENESS → WITHDRAWAL→ DIVORCE

Figure 10-1 Gottman's Cascade Model of Divorce

While any combination of these behaviors can occur, the diagram reflects a common ordering in a sequence of prototypical precedence. Hence, criticism leads to contempt and so on. The largest correlation is between contempt and defensiveness (.42). Using .30 as the magnitude of a moderate correlation, you can see that all of the correlations are near or beyond a moderate effect size. In terms of nonlinearity, withdrawal can lead to criticism or any combination. The result is divorce. This model also applies to virtually any close, romantic relationship. Recall that Gottman (www.gottman.com) argues that he can predict divorce on the basis of the four horsemen up to 94% of the time. However, the 94% figure was based on analysis of only fifty-two couples and is reported in Buehlman, Gottman, and Katz (1992).

Their study was based on a three-year follow-up in which they conducted an oral history interview and an interaction task to determine what qualities predicted divorce or marital stability. Time 1 variables were able to significantly predict which couples would be separated, divorced, or intact at follow-up. At Time 1, couples who eventually divorced were low in fondness for their partners, high in negativity, low in "we-ness," high in chaos, low in glorifying the struggle, and high in disappointment of the marriage. The behavioral coding of the marital interaction was also consistently related to negativity and the absence of positivity in problem-solving as well as to negative affect.

Similarly, Honeycutt (1999), in a sample of seventy-one couples, found that husbands' marital happiness was predicted by the wives' responsiveness, husbands' and wives' use of we-ness, and fondness for the wife. The wives' marital happiness was predicted by her fondness for the husband and her use of we-ness—the husband's use of we-ness was not related to the wife's marital happiness. Additionally, couples who had a lot of sharing and interdependence (Traditionals) as well as Independents who are prone to argue a lot showed more fondness in their interactions than couples who were labeled as "Separates." Separates are emotionally divorced and share little time together. In addition, having pleasant internal dialogues with a partner predicted marital happiness for Traditionals and Independents compared to Separates.

Anger and the Four Horsemen

Couples get into heated discussions about crucial issues, sometimes giving rise to anger. Anger is often seen as a dangerous and destructive emotion for couples because it is linked to aggression (Honeycutt and Bryan, 2011). Yet, it is normal for couples to express irritability and hurt, to feel pissed off and frustrated. Anger results from frustration with our goals being blocked. Gottman's view is that anger by itself can best be understood as a way of saying "Something is important to me, so please pay attention." Anger itself isn't bad. It doesn't necessarily make the relationship worse, nor is it necessarily good. What is crucial is the way in which the anger is expressed. Research also reveals that in dissatisfied couples, the partners are more likely to interpret their partner's messages being delivered with negative emotions rather than positive affect (Gottman, 2011).

Additionally, in terms of attribution theory, partners in happy marriages are more likely to make both ego- and partner-centric attributions. For example, researchers observed an egocentric attributional bias in married couples in which spouses take greater responsibility for positive behaviors rather than ascribing them to their partners, while others have noted a partner-centric attribution, in which individuals overestimate their contribution to negative events and underestimate their contribution to positive events (Bradbury and Fincham, 1990).

People take credit for success and positive things while discounting failure as being caused by situational or contextual determinants. In social psychology, the fundamental attribution error, also known as the correspondence bias or attribution effect, is people's tendency to place an undue emphasis on internal characteristics to explain someone else's behavior in a given situation, rather than considering external factors. It does not explain interpretations of one's own behavior, where situational factors are more easily recognized and can thus be taken into consideration. The flip side of this error is the actor–observer bias, in which people tend to overemphasize the role of a situation in their behaviors and underemphasize the role of their own personalities (Ross, 1977).

When couples were happy, the strangers and the partners were veridical with one another; that is, their observations matched each other. But when couples were unhappy, the partners observed only 50% of their partner's positive interactions (as measured by the outside observers). Fritz Heider's "fundamental attribution error" is related to these findings. He described a tendency in people to minimize their own errors and attribute them to temporary, fleeting circumstances, but to maximize the errors of others and attribute them to lasting, negative personality traits or character flaws. In our own work, negative attributions made by one partner about the other partner were also related to negatively recasting the history of the relationship. When anger is blended with the four horsemen of the apocalypse, the result is toxic and gives rise to an escalation of negativity: when anger is met with a more intense response, for example:

Sue: "Screw you, Steve. You left your underpants on the bathroom floor again … man, you're a selfish slob."

Steve: "Oh, yeah? Well if you weren't so uptight, like your damn sister … maybe for once you could realize that you're not so perfect yourself."

So meeting anger with defensiveness, contempt, or hostility erodes the trust and is corrosive to intimacy. These interaction patterns are also, not surprisingly, strong predictors of marital meltdown. Additionally, Gottman's website indicates that relationships exist in a state of positive sentiment override (PSO) or negative sentiment override (NSO). PSO occurs with agreements, statements of validation, supportive humor, and smiling. In happy relationships, positive comments and behaviors outweigh negative ones about five to one. It's almost as if there is a positive filter that alters how couples remember past events and view new issues.

For example, Henry and Sylvie have been connecting positively with each other over the past week—a dinner date, lots of sharing, they made love yesterday, and are planning a weekend getaway. Henry sees coffee spilled on the kitchen counter and asks Sylvie to wipe it up when she has a minute because he is busy on the computer. She replies that it's no problem and would he like a cup of coffee.

Yet, consider this different scenario. Unlike Henry and Sylvie, Dickey and Sally have been distant, hardly connecting with each other over the past weeks. They also had a serious argument two days ago and haven't recovered. Dickey sees coffee spilled on the counter and asks Sally in a slightly impatient tone to wipe it up. She replies loudly that she's not his servant and that he should get off his butt and start doing some things around the house for a change. PSO makes a huge difference in relationships for the simple reason that relationships and marriages that thrive also have a strong PSO. Obviously relationships don't automatically have a PSO since the warmth, trust, affection, and caring have to be nurtured and developed over time.

Gottman's Sound Marital House

Gottman's model of the Sound Marital House is based on a symbolic house containing seven stories, which are specific skills that help maintain a solid foundation for thriving relationships. This calls for skills that directly support the likelihood of positive emotions and in turn increase the likelihood of PSO (see http://www.gottmancouplesretreats.com/about/sound-relationship-house-theory.aspx). Gottman and Silver (1999) have a book called *The Seven Principles for Making Marriage Work*. Following is a brief description of the seven skills that can hinder the progression toward divorce.

Skill 1: Build Love Maps

Building love maps is the foundation of a quality marriage. Essentially this symbolizes a road map of each other's inner psychological world and interpersonal needs. It is important to ask *open-ended questions*. It involves the couple knowing one another and periodically updating this knowledge. Trivial, small-talk topics such as updating each other about events that happened in the day as well as news of success and vulnerabilities undergird this skill. Small talk may be like mouthwash: it is necessary for relational hygiene, even if you don't like it!

In terms of Love Maps, ask yourself if you know your partner's best friend. Do you know what your partner is hoping for most, right now, in her life? Do you know what she worries about, is most concerned and troubled about these days? What does she fear the most? These are the kinds of things that people know about their partners when they have well-defined Love Maps.

Skill 2: Share Fondness and Admiration

Here, the partners are affectionate and clear about the things they value and admire in the other. Central to this is letting each other know what it is that they do that the other appreciates. We often take for granted complimenting long-term intimates, assuming that they "know" how we feel. This is called positive mindreading. Yet, many people cherish reminders of fondness, because with them, they do not feel taken for granted.

Skill 3: Turn Toward

State your needs, be aware of emotional bids for connection, and respond to your partner by turning toward them. In this regard, the small moments of everyday life are the building blocks of a strong relationship.

Skill 4: Adopt a Positive Perspective

If the first three levels of the Sound Relationship House are not working, then people are in NSO, as discussed earlier. Yet, partners in conflict-habituated relationships may interpret neutral or positive messages as negative and that their partners are hypervigilant for negativity (Gottman, 1994). Gottman notes that it is not possible to change NSO to PSO, except by changing the quality of the couple's friendship because partners may be in negative sentiment override for good reason: they see their partner as an adversary, not a friend. To change that state, you need to build the couple's friendship, using the first three levels of the Sound Relationship House.

Skill 5: Manage Conflict

The fifth story of the house consists of two styles of conflict management. Couples should identify the core issues that are resolvable (cf., some issues are not resolvable and people agree to disagree) and the pattern of repetitive negative cycles in their relationship (see Honeycutt, 2004, for a discussion of how partners may ruminate about arguing in terms of imagined interactions; also see Chapter 6). In terms of managing conflict, the four horsemen should be avoided, as noted earlier (e.g., criticism, contempt, defensiveness, withdrawal). It is important to note that this skill is about managing conflict, not necessarily resolving it.

Conflicts are one of two types: resolvable and non-resolvable. For couple problems that are resolvable, there are four parts of effective problem-solving. These are softened start-up, accepting influence, repair and de-escalation (including physiological soothing), and compromise. The use of positive affect in the service of de-escalation is a part of this, too, but it is not programmable—it just happens by itself when PSO is in place.

For couple problems that are not perpetual and most likely not resolvable, in order to avoid couple "gridlock," recall the 5:1 positive-to-negative affect ratio. This involves positive affect or even neutral affect—which may be perceived as positive during conflict discussions—and conveying interest, affection, humor, empathy, excitement, and softened vocal tones even when in a disagreement. Again, physiological soothing is a critical part of this process (see Chapter 9).

Skill 6: Make Life Dreams and Aspirations Come True

What is the basis of a continued positive emotional connection during arguments? This level of the Sound Relationship House is about helping one's partner realize important life dreams and making the relationship effective at making dreams and aspirations come true. This aspect of relationship is the basis of unlocking conflict gridlock, in which the couple's values within a position in the gridlocked conflict are explored and understood. Try to create an atmosphere that encourages each person to talk honestly about his or her hopes, attitudes, values, convictions, and aspirations. While this sounds idealistic, think of it as ideal goal. Never give up if you truly value the relationship.

Skill 7: Create Shared Meaning

Finally, we are in the attic of the house, where people either intentionally create or do not create a sense of shared meaning in their life together. Research reveals that the notion of symbolic interdependence characterizes happy relationships as partners negotiate a mutual interpretive framework that filters their observations of the existing culture so that they react to events in similar ways (Honeycutt, 2009). These couples appreciate their unique bond of shared knowledge and may sense that few alternative relationships can provide as much promise for confirmation and understanding. Additionally, shared meaning is created through imagined interactions (again see Chapter 6). While symbolic interdependence stresses how couples negotiate a joint perspective in terms of relationship values, part of this negotiation occurs at an intrapersonal level of communication in terms of mental imagery.

Symbolic interdependence results in non-discrepant, retroactive, proactive, frequent, and positive imagined interactions that in turn predict relational quality. On the one hand, symbolic interdependence directly leads to relationship quality. Yet, symbolic interdependence is positively associated with IIs, while IIs positively affect relationship quality.

The creation of a relationship and a family involve the active creation of a new culture that has never existed before (Gottman and Silver, 1995; 1999). Even if the two people come from the same racial, ethnic, and geographic background, the two families they grew up in will be very different and so their union will always involve the creation of a new world of meaning. Every relationship is a cross-cultural experience.

Discussion Questions /Activities

1. Consider the four horsemen of the apocalypse and the person you are closest to as well as the person you have frequent arguments or disagreements with. Can you identify which of the four behaviors characterize many of your conversations with each individual?
2. Think of the last time you showed either verbal or nonverbal contempt to someone. Who was this person and what was the source of the arguing and contempt? Additionally, is there anyone you know with whom you have frequent arguments and disagreements and feel contempt for during a disagreement (e.g., family member, work associate, roommate, an ex-relational partner, rival, current

partner …)? Is the argument resolvable or non-resolvable? If it is non-resolvable, do you simply withdraw and treat the issue as a taboo topic to be avoided?

3. Numerous research studies indicate that men's biggest complaint in marriage and in close, interpersonal relationships is that the woman nags or complains. Conversely, her biggest complaint is that he withdraws from serious discussion about issues. Do you think this is true in your interpersonal relationships? Is it true of your parents' marriage (if they were married and you knew both biological parents)?

4. Have you ever built a love map with someone? Did you enjoy small talk, discussing trivia, or events of your days with this person? Why or why not? Do you do this with a lot of your friends in your social network?

5. Do you know a couple in your social network whom you think may be headed for divorce? Which if any of the four horsemen of the apocalypse do you see?

REFERENCES

Bradbury, T.N. and Fincham, F.D. (1990). "Attributions in Marriage: Review and Critique." *Psychological Bulletin, 107*, 3–33. DOI: 10.1037//0033-2909.107.1.3

Buehlman, K., Gottman, J.M., and Katz, L., (1992). "How a Couple Views Their Past Predicts Their Future: Predicting Divorce from an Oral History Interview." *Journal of Family Psychology, 5*, 295–318. DOI: 10.1037/0893-3200.5.3-4.295

Gottman, J.M. (1994). *What Predicts Divorce?* Mahwah, NJ: Erlbaum.

Gottman, J.M. (2011). *The Science of Trust: Emotional Attunement for Couples.* New York: W. W. Norton & Company.

Gottman, J.M., Notarius, C., Markman, H., Bank, S., Yoppi, B., and Rubin, M.E. (1976). "Behavior Exchange Theory and Marital Decision Making." *Journal of Personality and Social Psychology, 34*, 14–23. DOI: 10.1037//0022-3514.34.1.14

Gottman, J.M. and Levenson, R.W. (1992). "Marital Processes Predictive of Later Dissolution: Behavior, Physiology and Health." *Journal of Personality and Social Psychology, 63*, 221–233. DOI: 10.1037//0022-3514.63.2.221

Gottman, J.M. and Levenson, R.W. (1988). "The Social Psychophysiology of Marriage." In P. Noller and M.A. Fitzpatrick (Eds.), *Perspectives on Marital Interaction.* Philadelphia: Multilingual Matters.

Gottman, J. and Levenson, R.W. (2002). "A Two-Factor Model for Predicting When a Couple Will Divorce: Exploratory Analyses Using 14-Year Longitudinal Data." *Family Process, 41*, 83–96. DOI: 10.1111/j.1545-5300.2002.401020000

Gottman, J.M., Coan, J., Carrere, S., and Swanson, C. (1998). "Predicting Marital Happiness and Stability from Newlywed Interactions." *Journal of Marriage and Family, 60*, 5–22. DOI: 10.2307/353438

Gottman, J.M. and Silver, N. (1995). *Why Marriages Succeed or Fail: What You Can Learn from the Breakthrough Research to Make Your Marriage Last.* New York: Simon & Schuster.

Gottman, J.M. and Silver, N. (1999). *The Seven Principles for Making Marriage Work.* New York: Three Rivers Press.

Gottman, J. and Silver, N. (2012). *What Makes Love Last.* New York: Simon & Schuster.

Honeycutt, J.M. (2014). "Imagined Interactions." In W. Donsbach (Ed.) *International Encyclopedia of Communication (2nd ed.)* (pp. 249–271). Washington, DC: International Communication Association. DOI: 10.1111/b.9781405131995.2008.x

Honeycutt, J.M. (1999). "Typological Differences in Predicting Marital Happiness from Oral History Behaviors and Imagined Interactions (IIs)." *Communication Monographs, 66,* 276–291. DOI:10.1080/03637759909376478

Honeycutt, J.M. (2009). "Symbolic Interdependence, Imagined Interaction, and Relationship Quality." *Imagination, Cognition, and Personality, 28,* 303–320. DOI: 10.2190/IC.28.4.b

Honeycutt, J.M. (2004). "Imagined Interaction Conflict-Linkage Theory: Explaining the Persistence and Resolution of Interpersonal Conflict in Everyday Life." *Imagination, Cognition, and Personality, 23,* 3–25. DOI: 10.2190/240J-1VPK-K86D-1JL8

Honeycutt, J.M. and Bryan, S.P. (2011). *Scripts and Communication for Relationships.* New York: Peter Lang.

Honeycutt, J.M., Keaton, S.A., Hatcher, L.C., and Hample, D. (2014). "Physiological Covariates in Predicting Conflict Escalation in Terms of Advisability and Probability Ratings of Marital Arguing." In J.M. Honeycutt, C.R. Sawyer, and S.A. Keaton (Eds.), *The Influence of Communication on Physiology and Health* (pp. 73–92). New York: Peter Lang.

Locke, H.J. (1951). *Predicting Adjustments in Marriage: A Comparison of a Divorced and a Happily Married Group.* New York: Henry Holt.

Robinson, E.A. and Price, M.G. (1980). "Pleasurable Behavior in Marital Interaction: An Observational Study." *Journal of Consulting and Clinical Psychology, 48,* 117–118, DOI: 10.1037/0022-006X.48.1.117

Ross, L. (1977). "The Intuitive Psychologist and His Shortcomings: Distortions in the Attribution Process." In L. Berkowitz (Ed.), *Advances in Experimental Social Psychology,* 10 (pp. 173–220). New York: Academic Press.

Terman, L.M., Buttenweiser, P., Ferguson, L.W., Johnson, W.B., and Wilson, D.P. (1938). *Psychological Factors in Marital Happiness.* Stanford, CA: Stanford University Press.

11. Communication in Divorced and Single-Parent Families

By Julia Lewis, Linda Johnson-Reitz, & Judith S. Wallerstein

Communication patterns are a reflection of relationship dynamics, and changes in intra-familial relationships are a central dynamic in the divorce process. Communication per se has not been a primary focus in divorce research, although certain aspects of communication, such as parental conflict, have been intensively studied mostly for their impact on offspring adjustment. In examining the literature with communication as the lens, the yield can be narrow if only those variables that are directly related to expression of communication, such as degree of conflict, quality of affect, and frequency of interaction, are considered. The yield is considerably higher if variables that are more broadly reflective of relationship dynamics are included, as we did for this [article]. Most divorce research has as its aim the elucidation of how parental divorce and its host of related factors affect the adjustment of offspring in the short and, more recently, in the long term. For the purpose of this endeavor, we shift the focus to highlighting changes in communication patterns and relevant relationship dynamics as families go through the divorce process and include the association with outcomes only secondarily.

Defined broadly, communication includes not only verbal, paraverbal, and nonverbal messages exchanged when people are interacting but also the metacommnication over time of themes, attitudes, and values. In families, metacommunication from parents to children involves information imparted from the accumulation of parent–child interactions as they are repeated and evolve over time and information absorbed by children observing and witnessing parental interactions and behavior, again over time. Within the family, metacommunication establishes a shared, internalized sense of family including history, relationships, roles, worldviews, loyalty issues, and orientation to others and to the future (Laing, 1971). In addition to patterns and styles of direct, interpersonal communication that have been observed or reported between members of divorced families, we also discuss the nature of metamessages, particularly those that may be communicated to offspring as a consequence of divorce.

The predominant method of study in divorce research has been through self-report measures in which one or more family members either fill out paper and pencil questionnaires consisting of rating scales and symptom checklists or respond to highly structured scaled items during a short face-to-face or telephone interview. This method is especially useful in large-scale demographic research (Booth, Johnson, White, & Edwards, 1991; Chase-Lansdale, Cherlin, & Kiernan, 1995; Furstenberg, Nord, Peterson, & Zill, 1983). The use of observational methodology in which family members interact together so that the communication between them can be directly observed is rare. Hetherington's early work (Hetherington, Cox, & Cox, 1979, 1982) and more recent research by Gottman and associates (Gottman, 1993; Gottman & Katz, 1989; Gottman & Levenson, 2000; Katz & Gottman, 1993) are exceptional instances. Our own method utilizes individual, facetoface, semistructured clinical interviews with all available family members. Often lasting for hours, these interviews are conducted by highly trained professionals who encourage the participants to explain in detail their feelings, perceptions, attitudes, behaviors, and expectations about targeted areas of their lives (Lewis & Wallerstein, 1987; Wallerstein, Corbin, & Lewis, 1988). These different methodologies result in very different ways of operationalizing and measuring dimensions of human behavior, such as marital conflict. Although being labeled similar names, such as conflict or discord, the actual slices of human behavior each study includes in its designation are often quite dissimilar. Mitigating this apparent confusion is the fact that results from all longitudinal studies of divorce over 10 years show a remarkable convergence in their main findings despite different sample sizes and different approaches to studying the same, critical arenas of divorce-related behavior. In this [article], we focus on the commonalities in the findings across studies and highlight the different methodologies as they inform and illuminate the discussion.

PREDIVORCE COMMUNICATION CHARACTERISTICS

Recent investigation has included a focus on family characteristics that existed prior to divorce, sometimes shown to have predated the divorce by many years. Although it is common sense to assume that there were problems in a marriage prior to the decision to divorce, and that these problems were likely causal in bringing about the divorce, these recent reports have helped elucidate differences in family patterns and the nature of interactions between families who have problems but who continue to stay intact versus families who split up. This line of investigation has also led to intriguing insights regarding the relative influence of family process (communication style) and family structure (divorce) on long-term offspring attitudes and behavior in commitment and marriage.

Frequency of marital conflict has been the most intensively studied process variable in divorce research and has been the main focus of investigations into predivorce family characteristics. Prospective longitudinal studies have found higher levels of marital discord reported in families who later divorced as long as 12 years prior to the decision to separate (Amato, Loomis, & Booth, 1995; Cherlin et al., 1991; Furstenberg & Teitler, 1994). The presence of high amounts of negative affect, including criticism, defensiveness, contempt and "stonewalling," a form of withdrawal, predicted couples who were more likely to divorce within the first 7 years, whereas it was the absence of more positive affect that was the best predictor of later divorces (Gottman & Levenson, 2000).

Poorer and more dysfunctional patterns of parenting have been associated with higher levels of marital discord along with a decrease in quality of parent–child relationships. These factors have been repeatedly shown to affect children's adjustment (Amato & Booth, 1996; Block, Block, & Gjerde, 1986; Cherlin et al., 1991; Emery, 1982). For example, parents in families that later divorced showed more rejection and less involvement with their sons (Shaw, Emery, & Tuer, 1993). In their research on processes linking marital interaction and its impact on child behavior, Gottman and Katz (Gottman

& Katz, 1989; Katz & Gottman, 1993) found maritally distressed couples to show parenting styles which were associated with anger and noncompliance in their children, that were cold, unresponsive, angry, and low in limit setting and structuring. Furthermore, different patterns of marital discord were predictive of different types of child behavior as mutual spousal hostility was predictive of some forms of externalizing behavior, whereas marital strategies containing anger and distancing tended to produce offspring with internalizing problems.

Conflict that directly involves the children is universally regarded as most harmful to children's well-being and is the most detrimental to parent–child relationships (Amato, 1986; Johnston, Kline, & Tschann, 1989; Wallerstein & Kelly, 1980). This includes involving children in physical violence or directly exposing children to parental violence, fighting about the children, and making the child a player, such as enlisting them in loyalty conflicts or bitter alliances or as conduits of negative communication (Buchanan, Maccoby, & Dornbusch, 1992; Davies & Cummings, 1994; Maccoby, Buchanan, Mnookin, Dornbusch, 1993; Maccoby & Mnookin, 1992). A critical distinction may be drawn between those families in which parental conflict is kept within boundaries that protect the children from witnessing, being the focus of, or being involved with the conflict as participants. In some families parents are unhappy and discordant but manage to keep a firm boundary between their marital difficulties and exposing the children in any way to these problems. Both parents have the psychological capability to control and direct their negative feelings to venues away from the children as well as the mutual motivation to keep their parenting functioning well. Their children have a dim sense that conflict happens behind closed doors, but their functioning is not compromised (Wallerstein, Lewis, & Blakeslee, 2000). An intermediate atmosphere exists when children are not directly involved, but marital conflict takes its toll in diminished parenting as parents are more irritable and have less energy and motivation to support and monitor their children's activities (Hetherington, Bridges, & Isabella, 1998).

A critical question currently being discussed is whether children in families where there is toxic conflict that chronically and directly involves the children are better off if their parents divorce. There is little argument that marital conflict and poorer parenting lead to difficulties for children regardless of whether the family later divorces (Hetherington & Stanley-Hagan, 1999). In fact, in a survey of research done throughout the 1980s, children from high-conflict families where the parents did not divorce showed the most adjustment problems followed by children from divorced families (Amato & Keith, 1991a, 1991b). In his meta-analysis of studies done in the 1990s Amato again found relatively better long-term outcomes in offspring from families with chronic, intense, high levels of conflict when the parents did divorce as compared to those who remained in nondivorced chronically high-conflict families (Amato, 2001).

Various explanations and challenges have been raised regarding this issue. Amato, Booth, and colleagues have hypothesized that divorce removes children from highly stressful and destructive family relationships, and the assumed less stressful postdivorce environment mitigates other divorce-related losses such as decline in living standards and less frequent parental contact (Amato et al., 1995). They speculate that having lived through and then escaping a high conflict, difficult family confers a type of resiliency on the offspring, which then helps them in adult relationships (Booth, 1999).

An unaddressed issue that is difficult to research concerns the nature of the high levels of conflict in families who later divorce and in those who remain married. Do families that later divorce have the highest levels and the most destructive types of conflict? Alternatively, do high-conflict families who stay married develop even more toxic destructive cycles of interaction that involve the children? Our own recent research confirms that highly dysfunctional marriages containing violence and involvement of the children in all sorts of unhealthy interactions not only endure over the long term but also can be mutually satisfying to both adults. The only distinguishing feature from these and our group of high-conflict families who divorced was that one of the adults became unhappy and disillusioned and eventually found a way to get out (Wallerstein et al., 2000).

Central to the argument that divorce leads to a decrease in stress for offspring from high-conflict families is the assumption that conflict declines after divorce. In fact, the overwhelming evidence points to the contrary—that conflict is exacerbated by the demands and circumstances of divorce, particularly in the months and years immediately following separation (Hetherington, 1993; Wallerstein & Kelly, 1980). Enduring high levels of acrimony and bitterness was found in over half of our sample of divorced parents 10 years later (Wallerstein & Blakeslee, 1989). A related assumption is that unhealthy, abusive patterns of behavior between spouses and between parents and children will be stopped by divorce. Although less extensively studied, the existing evidence points to a more pessimistic outcome in which patterns of dysfunction and abuse continue despite the divorce, both between former spouses and in new, postdivorce relationships and remarriages (Fitzgerald, 1986; Nelson, 1989; Wallerstein & Blakeslee, 1989). Thus far, we have been considering the impact of high levels of marital conflict on family functioning and its role in the divorce process. But not all families who later divorce can be characterized as high conflict. In our sample, less than 30% reported high, chronic levels of conflict in the predivorce years. Although large-scale survey studies found more predivorce conflict in parents who later divorced, recent statistics indicate that higher levels of enduring conflict do not precede the majority of more recent divorces (Amato, 2001).

There is some evidence that outcomes for offspring in the long term are more compromised when parents divorce following a relatively low-conflict marriage (Amato et al., 1995; Booth, 1999). One of the explanations offered is in low-conflict marriages the children do not anticipate divorce because there have been no overt warning signs, such as open discord. The actuality of the divorce is an unwelcome shock with no preparation. Because the offspring have not been negatively impacted or stressed by ongoing conflict and involvement in dysfunctional interactions, the changes in the postdivorce environment cause a net increase in stress with no positive consequences. The distress of the children in such families may be further exacerbated because of the well-documented rise in conflict around the time of parental separation. This conflict not only may be a new and unwelcome style of parental interaction but also may be the type of conflict regarding custody, child support, visitation, and time sharing—all issues that are likely to involve the children (Booth & Amato, 2001).

Low levels of conflict should not be equated with low levels of marital problems. Conflict is an easily observed, measured, and recordable aspect of communication and certainly is a signal for distress and unhappiness in a relationship. But the presence of conflict is not the only marker of trouble in marriage. Although beyond the scope of this [article], there are forces outside the immediate structure of a marriage that can drastically affect its functioning and course. In our sample, events such as the loss of employment, the death of a parent, the influence of cultural and political movements, and the birth of a child had profound psychological effects on a spouse, which then altered the marital dynamics and precipitated divorce. Other marriages absorbed similar events and remained intact. Some marriages characterized by low levels of overt conflict functioned well enough until an extramarital affair caused disruption.

A commonality between high-conflict marriages that dissolve and apparent low-conflict marriages that end in divorce may be a deficiency in relationship skills and dynamics. One or both spouses has trouble psychologically as well as with communicating, getting their own needs recognized and met, and being able to empathize with and satisfy the needs of the other. This is not a new concept and there are many studies, both recent and over the years, that shed light on the nature of these deficiencies. The underlying assumption is that people who later divorce have psychological attributes that are manifested in communication that are dysfunctional to maintaining interpersonal relationships. Some of these styles of communication result in escalating conflict. These include difficulty in solving problems constructively, in controlling anger and resolving tension along with the tendency to respond to criticism defensively, in being overtly critical, in expressing more negative and less positive emotion, and in experiencing more feelings of moodiness and jealousy. Some interactional styles are dysfunctional in that they culminate in withdrawal and involve suppressing not only conflict but also any constructive exchange of feelings and ideas. People with these characteristics tend to be less articulate and clear in their verbal communication, self-disclose less frequently, avoid or withdraw from conflict and problem solving, maintain stable, negative attributions regarding their spouses' behavior while having difficulty taking in their spouses' communication, and utilize contempt, denial, and withdrawal (Bradbury & Fincham, 1990; Fincham, Bradbury, & Scott, 1990; Gottman, 1993, 1994; Leonard & Roberts, 1998; Matthews, Wickrama, & Conger, 1996; Olsen, 1990). In studies on marital satisfaction over time, levels of disagreement and exchange of anger, commonly viewed as markers of marital discord and dissatisfaction, did not predict long-term deterioration or divorce in families where the marriage had lasted longer than 7 years. Other communication characteristics including defensiveness, stubbornness, and withdrawal as well as the absence of positive valence in affect were better predictors (Gottman, 1993; Gottman & Krokoff, 1989). Communication characteristics highly predictive of marital failure seen even early on in newlyweds as well as in more established couples with young children are indicative of underlying cognitive deficits and learned patterns of perceiving and reacting to others. These deficits and patterns set the stage for nonconstructive communication and in effect predispose the relationship to more negative, less rewarding interaction (Buehlman, Gottman, & Katz, 1992; Carrere, Buehlman, Gottman, Coan, & Ruckstuhl, 2000).

Relationship Between Predivorce And Postdivorce Patterns Of Interaction

Divorce profoundly alters not only the structure of the family but also the essential nature of family interactions and relationships. Early on, divorce researchers found little correlation between pre-and postdivorce behavior in families. Fathers who had previously been distant became more engaged and connected, whereas very involved fathers drifted away following divorce (Wallerstein & Kelly, 1980). Mothers radically altered the nature of their caregiving, and children experienced dramatic and unsettling changes in household routine and management, which could not be predicted by predivorce patterns of parenting (Hetherington, Cox, & Cox, 1979). Adults who were apparently stable and mature in their marriages experienced wildly fluctuating emotions and displayed chaotic and risky behaviors after the marriage ended, and some who had been fragile and insecure showed unexpected strength and fortitude after their divorce (Hetherington & Kelly, 2002; Wallerstein & Blakeslee, 1989).

Although conflict is widely regarded as a harbinger of divorce, recent findings show that predivorce conflict is not a good predictor of postdivorce conflict (Booth & Amato, 2001). Conflict increases after divorce in most families regardless of how much or little conflict was present before. In some families conflict remains high for years, even decades following divorce; in others conflict subsides after the initial period of adjustment.

In contrast, one of the most stable characteristics measured is style of communication between spouses. Partners' communication style has been shown to be consistent over type of interaction (situations involving high vs. low conflict during marriage) and, by inference, across pre-and postdivorce years (Gottman & Levenson, 1999.) The manner in which spouses communicate, including the dysfunctional patterns that promoted dissatisfaction and divorce within the marriage, continues into the postdivorce years. There is no indication that physical separation and the legal event of divorce have power, in themselves, to change deeply ingrained patterns of human behavior. The stress of divorce can exacerbate these modes of interaction so that couples whose marriages were typified by high negativity, much strife, and high involvement would only continue this style as they struggle to confront contentious postdivorce issues. Conversely, couples that tended to avoid conflict and meaningful ongoing engagement in their marriages are forced to engage, with little background or skill, in constructive problem solving after they divorce.

There is general agreement that higher postdivorce parental conflict has negative consequences for children and may be one of the most influential factors affecting children's adjustment, especially in the short term (Amato et al., 1995; Guidabaldi, Cleminshaw, Perry, Nastasi, & Lightel, 1986; Johnston et al., 1989; Linker, Stolberg, & Green, 1999; Shaw et al., 1993). Research delving into nature or type of conflict suggests that postdivorce conflict is more likely to involve the children and to be enacted in the children's presence as much parental contact revolves around child-related issues such as time-sharing and child support. In addition to higher conflict, postdivorce communication styles reflect those reported in families before the divorce. These involve more controlling and demands, more expression of negative affect, less expression of positive emotion, and difficulties in solving problems constructively (Amato & Keith, 1991a; Hetherington et al., 1998; Simons, 1996). Suggesting again that it is the more subtle concomitants related to conflict rather than just conflict in general that make the most difference to offspring, a few studies have shown that factors such as conflict resolution style and degree of cooperation (Camara & Resnick, 1988) and interparent hostility (Linker et al., 1999) are more influential in children's postdivorce adjustment.

COMMUNICATION STYLES BETWEEN FORMER SPOUSES AFTER DIVORCE

Research on what happens to the level of communication between ex-spouses indicates that most couples do not discontinue interacting following finalization of the divorce, but that over time the level of intensity and intimacy in interactions subsides. The most significant decline was present in nonparental couples, where for many contact eventually almost entirely disappears (Metts & Cupach, 1995). In addition to frequency, the content of communication also shifts as time passes after divorce. Topics of communication became less personal and less focused on past and present relationship issues. If communication persists at all it tends to revolve around "safe" areas of mutual concern, such as children (if any) or family or "new experiences" (Metts & Cupach, 1995).

A variety of different patterns of communication have been described between ex-spouses following divorce. "Mutual constructive communication" (Christensen & Shank, 1991) and "cooperative colleagues" (Emery, 1994) is generally designated as the healthiest, most functional postdivorce interactive pattern that is relatively impersonal and involves constructive problem solving and avoidance of conflict. "Demand/withdraw communication" (Christensen & Shank, 1991) and "the pursuer and the pursued" (Emery, 1994) involves a pattern where one partner pursues more closeness and contact, although this may take the form of demands and criticism, while the other partner desires more distance and responds by withdrawing and avoiding. Wives typically have been shown to be the "demanders"; and husbands, the "withdrawers," although recent studies, which include nonconflict interactions that precede these patterns, implicate both spouses (Gottman & Levenson, 1999). A third communication style, referred to as "mutual avoidance" (Christensen & Shank, 1991) and "dissolved duos" (Ahrons & Rodgers, 1987), is typified by both partners avoiding communicating as much as possible or altogether. Another style characterized by positive interactions is "Perfect Pals" (Ahrons & Rodgers, 1987), although the greater level of intimacy it entails may border on enmeshment (Emery, 1994). "Angry Associates" and "Fiery Foes" are different variations of postdivorce relationships that utilize negative communication styles (Ahrons & Rodgers, 1987).

"Distressed" couples seeking counseling for marital problems showed the same types and levels of poorer communicational styles as divorced couples, both being significantly more avoidant and engaging in more demand/withdraw communication (Christensen & Shank, 1991). Communication styles containing more negative affect, hostility, and angry withdrawing characterized marital interactions in couples who were more likely to later divorce (Gottman, 1993).

Communication And Postdivorce Parenting

"Partners who are also parents can never fully divorce" (Emery, 1994). Because parental responsibilities of former spouses do not end, they must instead undergo transformations and adaptations in an attempt to accommodate to their new roles as parents to their mutual children in their respective postdivorce family contexts. It is expected that separated and divorced parents must be willing to interact, communicate, and cooperate with each other regarding child-related issues despite any feelings of rejection, remorse, bitterness, or anger that they may harbor. Optimally, this mode of cooperative communication should be sustained, at least until the children enter adulthood (Metts & Cupach, 1995). Unfortunately, the majority of former spouses never attain the cooperative level of communication needed to maintain effective mutual parenting. Instead, the majority engage in "parallel" parenting where their relationship is disengaged with little or no communication or cooperation between them. A substantial minority maintain highly conflictual relationships in which the children are often actively involved (Ahrons & Wallisch, 1987; Hetherington & Stanley-Hagan, 1999; Maccoby et al., 1993; Maccoby & Mnookin, 1992; Wallerstein et al., 2000).

Parenting is harder after divorce. The often unexpected and overwhelming demands in postdivorce life for single parents temporarily and sometimes permanently derail their energy and ability to parent effectively. Increased external demands, increased stress, the loss of resources, the addition of other adults and responsibilities all take their toll on time, energy, motivation, and emotional availability. For example, at 1 year postdivorce custodial mothers showed less affection, communicated less often, punished more harshly, and showed more inconsistent discipline (Hetherington et al., 1982). Custodial fathers had fewer problems with discipline and control, but they also communicated less, self-disclosed less, and monitored their children's activities less competently (Buchanan, Maccoby, & Dornbusch, 1991). Noncustodial fathers became less parental and authoritative and they interacted in a more peer-related manner with their children (Hetherington & Stanley-Hagan, 1999).

In addition to these increased pressures on single parenting, newly divorced single parents face the enormously complex task of learning to be a co-parent with their ex-spouse. Co-parenting is a qualitatively different form of parenting and one for which few have any experience or skills. Over the years there has been a growing body of knowledge regarding the set of skills and interactive styles that facilitate optimal co-parenting. Co-parents should work together to avoid conflict, share resources, and respect and support each other's parenting. Both parents should maintain authoritative parenting styles in which there is warmth, support, effective monitoring of activities, firm, consistent discipline and control, positive discussion, and responsiveness to children's growing needs and development. Furthermore, co-parents need to communicate often and effectively so that rules, discipline, and parenting styles remain consistent in the two households. The ideal co-parenting arrangement results in the parents maintaining the same level of mutual investment and involvement in parenting their children as they did predivorce and children experiencing the same framework of dual parental focus (Ahrons & Wallisch, 1987; Emery, 1994; Hetherington et al., 1982; Maccoby et al., 1993; Wallerstein & Kelly, 1980).

The ability of divorced parents to co-parent together, to communicate about their children, to cooperate to set limits, to problem solve effectively, and to provide consistent, positive affective messages has been shown to be one of the strongest influences on how well children adjust after divorce (Emery, 1982; Linker et al., 1999; Nelson, 1989). Underlying these skills is the basic task of redefining boundaries and roles in order to separate the former spousal relationship from the new co-parent relationship (Emery, 1994). This renegotiation of relationship dynamics is critical in order for divorced parents to give up or encapsulate old patterns of communication and behavior associated with the marital relationship and move on to create new methods of communication that facilitate co-parenting. Maintaining old roles and patterns of communication in the more ambiguous, acrimonious and stressful post divorce environment serves to exacerbate dysfunctional interactions so that conflict escalates or the likelihood of distancing and withdrawal increases (Serovich, Price, Chapman, & Wright, 1982).

The endurance of conflict and hostility is not only detrimental to the children but its presence in the post divorce family serves to block and break down the communication necessary for co-parenting activities (Linker et al., 1999). For many divorced parents the greater access to children as is present in many time-sharing arrangements promotes more frequent parental contact, which then leads to higher levels of hostile communication including open conflict (Nelson, 1989). The presence of ongoing hostility and conflict can ultimately result in less contact as parents, particularly noncustodial fathers, are driven away (Furstenberg & Nord, 1985; Healy, Malley, & Stewart, 1990; Seltzer, 1991). There is some evidence that custodial mothers control access between fathers and children through the degree of hostility and resentment directed at father, who avoids contact and involvement when negativity is high (Ahrons, 1983; Seltzer & Brandreth, 1994). Frequent and ongoing contact with both parents is promoted as beneficial to children; however, more detailed research indicates contact in the context of high conflict is more detrimental to children's well-being, especially if the conflict occurs in their presence (Amato & Rezac, 1994; Johnston et al., 1989).

Although families who maintain actively high hostility and high conflict are most visible and take up a huge share of professional attention, again, they do not characterize how most divorced parents interact. Over time, the majority settle into patterns of "parallel parenting" where they operate as independent parents, consulting and communicating with the other parent as infrequently as possible, if at all (Furstenberg, 1988). This mode keeps the level of active conflict down but creates two distinct family worlds that may have very different rules, norms, and values for the children to shuttle between (Johnson, 1988). The adjustment to living in parallel worlds that often have little relationship to each other and no access between them compromises psychological development and often imposes economic hardship (Furstenberg, 1990; Wallerstein et al., 2000). This compromised capacity to parent is thrown into bold relief as children grow into adolescence where the natural volatility and need for monitoring and compassionate limit setting tax the resources of even the most competent parents. Communication quality and the level of constructive communication have been repeatedly shown to be poorest in divorced families of adolescents. Although all parents disengage some as children move into adolescence, communication patterns in families of divorce show higher levels of disengagement in both parents and adolescents, less and less effective parental monitoring, less parental involvement, and high negativity and conflict, particularly between mothers and daughters (Hetherington, 1993). More adolescents from divorced families leave home or spend little time at home, avoid communication and interaction with family members, and are more likely to be involved in high-risk behaviors such as early sex, alcohol, and drugs (Hetherington, 1998; Wallerstein et al., 2000).

Postdivorce Parent–Child Relationships

Divorce usually results in less contact between children and their noncustodial parent (Amato et al., 1995; Furstenberg & Nord, 1985), although in some cases contact with the nonresidential parent becomes closer following divorce (Hetherington et al., 1982; Wallerstein & Kelly, 1980). Both the quantity and the quality of noncustodial father–child relationship decrease over time (Amato & Booth, 1996). Noncustodial fathers maintain more contact and more involvement when conflict and hostility are low with their exwives and when they are actively involved in decision making regarding their children (Braver, Wolchik, Sandler, Sheets, Fogas, & Bay, 1993; Cosbie-Burnett & Ahrons, 1985; Seltzer, 1990). Fathers have been more likely to maintain involvement with their sons following divorce (Zill & Rogers, 1988), and father–son involvement has been found to be especially important in the development of sons (Amato & Keith, 1991a).

Divorce results in a lowering of the quality of the child's relationship with the mother as well as with the father (Amato & Keith, 1991a). Although fathers find it hardest to maintain relationships with their daughters in terms of frequency of contact, more overt strain and difficulty have been noted in postdivorce mother–son relationships (Booth & Amato, 1994). In the years immediately following divorce, boys did least well in single-mother households than in other family structures including high-conflict intact families. Girls did as well in mother-headed households when conflict was low as in conflict intact families (Hetherington & Stanley-Hagan, 1999). Girls in mother-headed households often took on the role of helpmate and confidant to their overburdened mothers, which aided in their adjustment in the short-term but, if maintained, negatively affected their adult relationships with men (Wallerstein et al., 2000).

Difficulties persist in parent–child relationships as children from divorced families grow into adulthood. Research suggests that the relationship with the less involved, noncustodial parent was particularly compromised. Earlier feelings of loyalty and yearning for more involvement and contact evolved into counterrejection, lack of respect, and feelings of contempt and pity when children reached adulthood (Wallerstein et al., 2000). Custodial parents who had sacrificed and worked hard to maintain the household during difficult postdivorce years earned respect and admiration, although their adult children felt less closeness and warmth than those for the same parent in nondivorced families. Particularly notable were differences in father–adult son relationships in divorced versus relatively harmonious intact families. We saw a marked increase in closeness and camaraderie as sons grew up and fathers had more time in nondivorced families, whereas sons increased their negative feelings and attributions for their divorced fathers and emotionally disengaged as they grew into adulthood (Wallerstein, Lewis, & Blakeslee, 2000).

Adult children are less likely to spend time with and, importantly as parents become older, less willing to offer financial assistance and feel less responsible for arranging care for their divorced parents, especially for those parents who had been inconsistent, uninvolved, and peripheral in their children's lives (Amato & Booth, 1996). On a more positive note, we found a resurgence in contact and positive communication in some families as the children of divorced parents had their own children. Even parents who had been distant and uninvolved as well as those who had kept in closer contact were drawn in to more rewarding interactions and renewed relationships with their children after they became grandparents (Wallerstein et al., 2000).

Transmission Over Time: Metamessages in Divorced Families

What is the long-term impact of growing up within the communicational and relational context of a divorced family? What dynamics have been shown to be important influences in adult offspring adjustment? What has been transmitted through the years and how does it show up in how adult children conduct their lives and relationships? Both adults from divorced families and adults from conflicted but intact families report more problems in relationships including marriage and show poorer communication skills in dating and in marital interactions (Amato & DeBoer, 2001; Wallerstein et al., 2000).

From their participant–observer perch through countless interactions with and between their parents, it is no surprise that children absorb and then display communicational styles similar to those of their parents. Longitudinal studies demonstrate that adult offspring from both divorced and married but discordant parents showed dysfunctional interactional styles that were negatively affecting the offspring's relationships including their marriages. The content of these interpersonal difficulties sounds very similar to that reported in the marital interactions of the parents: difficulty controlling anger, engagement in more negative, escalating exchanges, more belligerence, criticism and contempt, more denial, and less problem-solving ability (Amato, 1996; Hetherington, 1988; Wallerstein et al., 2000).

Although adults from discordant parental marriages showed similar levels and styles of interactive difficulties as adults from divorced families, these relational difficulties did not lead to higher levels of divorce in their marriages. Although reporting that they had thoughts about divorce, adults from discordant but intact parental marriages were more likely to stay in their marriages, much as their parents had remained in their own troubled marriages (Amato & DeBoer, 2001). Only adults from divorced families showed higher levels of divorce in their own marriages. This higher risk for divorce was present whether or not their parents had high-conflict marriages prior to divorcing (Amato & DeBoer, 2001). Over and above interpersonal interactive problems, what is it that children from divorced families bring to marriage that causes them to leave rather than stay?

Amato and DeBoer (2001) speculate that the additional element is that children of divorce actually experience divorce—they have witnessed and lived through not only their parents' marital difficulties but also one (or both) parents' voluntary decision to end the marriage, the wrenching and highly painful process of separation, and the years of postdivorce readjustment. This actual life experience communicates to children from divorced families a different view of marriage—that difficulties should not be endured and relationship problems are not worked out. Our own intensive interviews with adult children 25 years after their parents' divorce enable us to derive a fuller picture of the metamessages communicated from observing and living through parental divorce.

Experiencing parental separation and the dissolution of the family leaves an indelible impression. Years later adults who were old enough to remember had clear and vivid memories of scenes and images that happened at the time that their parents separated. It is clear that the divorce experience is traumatic for most children and that traumatic events make a profound and lasting psychological and physiological impression. Many children of divorce spend years reacting to this experience—longing for the family to be together, wondering how life would have been different, wishing for more contact and involvement with one or both parents. We found little or no indication that children of divorce have a positive or even a casual attitude toward divorce. Their firsthand experience resulted in a great desire not to repeat what happened to their parents together with an underlying fear that relationships were not to be trusted.

It was striking what was and was not communicated about why parents divorced. At most, the great majority of children received a terse description largely involving who was moving where shortly before the parents separated. In the face of parental pain and reluctance to dredge up traumatic feelings, few children were able to engage in a meaningful dialog with their parents regarding what happened to the parents' marriage and why it failed as the children were growing up. Most were left with explanations largely of their own construction—that their parents had been simply unsuited to one another, that they never should have married in the first place, that one parent had betrayed the other, that their parents had fallen out of love. These children grew into adulthood with no real understanding of what went wrong and certainly with no grasp of the depth and complexity of how two people in a marriage can come to the point of divorce. This lack of a meaningful understanding of marital dynamics that can lead to divorce together with the little they had been told and what they had witnessed left the adult children with a great deal of anxiety regarding relationships. It was hard to trust that love and promises and happiness would really last. Their parents' experience showed otherwise, and they lacked an internal roadmap of how to avoid it happening in their own relationships.

Children of divorce also lacked firsthand experience of how to make a marriage work. They had internalized relational dynamics and methods of communication from their parents that were not facilitative in maintaining a satisfying long-term relationship. They had not developed attitudes, skills, reactions, and expectations that would help them create a successful marriage. Most, having lived through their parents' unsuccessful marriage and divorce as well as subsequent parental relationships and remarriages, had never witnessed two people interacting in a satisfying, lasting relationship.

Tension and conflict were particularly problematic as metamessages that had been absorbed from their families of origin linked relational difficulties with traumatic images of separation and divorce. As adults in their own marriages, they emotionally equated normal stresses inherent in any relationship with the wrenching difficulties, such as betrayal and abandonment, associated with a relationship in trouble and ultimately ending. What had never been communicated was the sense of difficulties being worked through, the expectation that relationships went through high and low periods, and the idea that constructive resolution of conflict and tension could lead to greater intimacy.

What was communicated to children growing up in divorced families were images and skills about how to make it on their own. From watching single parents manage jobs, households, children, and relationships, and from their own experience either living with a single parent who had limited time and availability or living between two parallel parental households, they acquired characteristics that they were proud of as adults. They learned that it was possible to work through difficulty and hardship alone. They learned the value of working hard and what it takes to run a household. They learned self-reliance, independence, and to make their own judgments and decisions. Many learned to be good negotiators and mediators from years of balancing and going between their divorced parents—skills that served them well in the workplace but that were not particularly useful in their own relationships. Although most wished to share their lives with a partner, unlike adults from ever married families, adults from divorced parents had actual life experience being divorced and living in a postdivorce family. All of these metamessages made divorce more painful but more probable for children of divorced families.

Conclusions

The state of the research on communication in divorced and single-parent families presents a complex and provocative picture. Most research has been conducted using self-report measures on a small number of process variables; a smaller number of studies have conducted more in-depth clinical examination across a wider arena of intrafamilial variables, and only a few investigations have directly observed family members interacting together. The same label, such as marital conflict, has been used to describe very different slices of human experience depending on the method of investigation employed. Marital conflict, as rated on a 5-point scale by one of the marriage partners in a short, anonymous telephone interview is probably a different variable from marital conflict assessed by a trained clinician after intensively interviewing both spouses individually, and both of these are different phenomena from the marital conflict observed as marital partners interact together discussing a stressful situation. The time frame of divorce research also spans across an impressive range. A handful of studies have data spanning over 20 years; most examine divorce in the months to 2 or 3 years following parental separation; and a very few prospectively predict divorce from interactions in the first months of a new marriage or even before marriage. Yet, in the past few years, longitudinal studies have reported long-term findings, and there have been meta-analyses integrating decades of individual studies, both of which have contributed to a consolidation and convergence of findings and a clearer perspective on what happens when families divorce.

Nonfacilitative and disruptive communication patterns between spouses have been repeatedly noted both before and after divorce and in marriages that endured but were troubled. These have been linked to less adequate parental behavior, which in turn results in poorer outcomes in offspring. There is evidence to suggest that these maladaptive parental patterns are learned by offspring who then exhibit them in their own adult intimate relationships that are also seen as more troubled. When spouses divorce, additional metamessages about handling stress and conflict, about leaving rather than staying, about surviving after separation, and about forming new relationships after divorce are also communicated to offspring, who then incorporate them into their own tendency to divorce. It seems clear that certain critical points in family life need further, more intensive study and intervention, as they are pivotal in whether communication patterns that are more likely to lead to divorce are maintained and passed on. One point for more study and intervention is in late adolescence and early adulthood as patterns learned from the family of origin begin to emerge in intimate relationships. Related time periods are just before and after marriage when communication systems and patterns begin to be consolidated between the committed couple. Another critical period is at the time of divorce when the stress of divorce exacerbates existing problems and creates new ones. The enormous task of learning new ways to effectively co-parent after divorce, which clearly contributes to better outcomes for the children, is a third arena where more understanding of the processes that derail and facilitate co-parenting would then lead to the development of more informed policies and more focused, effective intervention.

References

Ahrons, C. R. (1983). Predictors of paternal involvement postdivorce: Mothers' and fathers' perceptions. *Journal of Divorce, 6,* 55–69.

Ahrons, C. R., & Rogers, R. H. (1987). *Divorced families: A multidisciplinary, developmental view.* New York: Norton.

Ahrons, C. R., & Wallisch, L. S. (1987). The relationship between former souses. In D. Perlman & S. Duck (Eds.), *Intimate relationships: Development, dynamics, and deterioration* (pp. 269–295). Newbury Park, CA: Sage.

Amato, P. R. (1986). Marital conflict, the parent-child relationship, and child self-esteem. *Family Relations, 35*, 403–410.

Amato, P. R. (1996). Explaining the intergenerational transmission of divorce. *Journal of Marriage and the Family, 58*, 628–640.

Amato, P. R. (2001). Children of divorce in the 1990's: An update of the Amato and Keith (1991) metaanalysis. *Journal of Family Psychology, 15*, 355–370.

Amato, P. R., & Booth, A. (1996). A prospective study of divorce and parent-child relationships. *Journal of Marriage and the Family, 58*, 356–365.

Amato, P. R., & DeBoer, D. D. (2001). The transmission of marital instability across generation: Relationship skills or commitment to marriage? *Journal of Marriage and Family, 63*, 1038–1051.

Amato, P. R., & Keith, B. (1991a). Parental divorce and adult well-being: A meta-analysis. *Journal of Marriage and the Family, 53*, 43–58.

Amato, P. R., & Keith, B. (1991b). Parental divorce and the well-being of children: A meta-analysis. *Psychological Bulletin, 110*, 26–46.

Amato, P. R., Loomis, L. S., & Booth, A. (1995). Parental divorce, marital conflict, and off-spring wellbeing during early adulthood. *Social Forces, 73*, 895–915.

Amato P. R., & Rezac, S. J. (1994). Contact with nonresident parents, interparental conflict, and children's behavior. *Journal of Family Issues, 15*, 191–207.

Block, J. H., Block, J., & Gjerde, P. F. (1986). The personality of children prior to divorce: A prospective study. *Child Development, 57*, 827–840.

Booth, A. (1999). Causes and consequences of divorce: Reflections on recent research. In R. A. Thompson & P. R. Amato (Eds.), *The postdivorce family: Children, parenting and society* (pp. 3–28). Thousand Oaks, CA: Sage.

Booth, A., & Amato, P. R. (2001). Parental predivorce relations and offspring postdivorce well-being. *Journal of Marriage and Family, 63*, 197–212.

Booth, A., & Amato, P. R. (1994). Parental marital quality, divorce, and relations with offspring in young adulthood. *Journal of Marriage and the Family, 56*, 21–34.

Booth, A., Johnson, D. R., White, L., & Edwards, J. N. (1991). *Marital instability over the life course: Methodology report and code book for three wave panel study.* Lincoln, NE: Bureau of Sociological Research.

Bradbury, T. N., & Fincham, F. D. (1990). Attributions in marriage: Review and critique. *Psychological Bulletin, 107*, 3–33.

Braver, S. L., Wolchik, S. A., Sandler, I. N., Sheets, V. L., Fogas, B., & Bay, R. C. (1993). A longitudinal study of noncustodial parents: Parents without children. *Journal of Family Psychology, 7*, 1–16.

Buchanan, C. M., Maccoby, M. M., & Dornbusch, S. M. (1991). Caught between parents: Adolescents' experience in divorced homes. *Child Development, 62*, 1008–1029.

Buehlman, K. T., Gottman, J. M., & Katz, L. F. (1992). How a couple views their past predicts their future: Predicting divorce from an oral history interview. *Journal of Family Psychology, 5*, 295–318.

Camara, K. A., & Resnick, G. (1988). Interparental conflict and cooperation: Factors moderating children's postdivorce adjustment. In E. M. Hetherington & J. D. Arasteh (Eds.), *Impact of divorce, single parenting and stepparenting on children* (pp. 169–195). Hillsdale, NJ: Lawrence Erlbaum Associates.

Carrere, S., Buehlman, K. T., Gottman, J. M., Coan, J. A., & Ruckstuhl, L. R. (2000). Predicting marital stability and divorce in newlywed couples. *Journal of Family Psychology, 14*, 42–58.

Chase-Lansdale, P. L., Cherlin, A. J., & Kiernan, K. E. (1995). The long-term effects of parental divorce on the mental health of young adults: A developmental perspective. *Child Development, 66*, 1614–1634.

Cherlin, A. J., Furstenberg, F. F., Chase-Lansdale, L. P., Kiernan, K. E., Robbins, P. K., Morrison, D. R., & Teitler, J. O. (1991). Longitudinal studies of effects of divorce on children in Great Britain and the United States. *Science, 252*, 1386–1389.

Christensen, A., & Shank, J. (1991). Communication, conflict and psychological distance in nondistressed, clinic and divorcing couples. *Journal of Consulting and Clinical Psychology, 59*, 458–463.

Cosbie-Burnett, M., & Ahrons, C. (1985). From divorce to remarriage: Implications for therapy for families in transition. *Journal of Psychotherapy and the Family, 1*, 121–137.

Davies, P. T., & Cummings, E. M. (1994). Marital conflict and child adjustment: An emotional security hypothesis. *Psychological Bulletin, 116*, 387–411.

Emery, R. E. (1982). Interparental conflict and the children of discord and divorce. *Psychological Bulletin, 92*, 310–330.

Emery, R. E. (1994). *Renegotiating family relationships: Divorce, child custody, and mediation.* New York: Guilford.

Fincham, F. D., Bradbury, T. M., & Scott, C. K. (1990). Cognition in marriage. In F. D. Fincham & T. N. Bradbury (Eds.), *The psychology of marriage* (pp. 118–149). New York: Guilford Press.

Fitzgerald, R. V. (1986). When parents divorce. *Medical Aspects of Human Sexuality, 20*, 86–92.

Furstenberg, F. F. (1988). Child care after divorce and remarriage. In E. M. Hetherington & J. D. Arasteh (Eds.), *Impact of divorce, single parenting and stepparenting on children* (pp. 245–261). Hillsdale, NJ: Lawrence Erlbaum Associates.

Furstenberg, F. F. (1990). Divorce and the American family. *Annual Review of Sociology, 16*, 379–403.

Furstenberg, F. F., & Nord, C. W. (1985). Parenting apart: Patterns of childrearing after marital disruption. *Journal of Marriage and the Family, 47*, 893–904.

Furstenberg, F. F., & Teitler, J. O. (1994). Reconsidering the effects of marital disruption: What happens to children of divorce in early adulthood. *Journal of Family Issues, 15*, 173–190.

Furstenberg, F. F., Nord, C. W., Peterson, J. L., & Zill, N. (1983). The life-course of children of divorce: Marital disruption and parental contact. *American Sociological Review, 48*, 656–667.

Gottman, J. M. (1993). A theory of marital dissolution and stability. *Journal of Family Psychology, 7*, 57–75.

Gottman, J. M. (1994). *What predicts divorce? The relationship between marital processes and marital outcomes.* Hillsdale, NJ: Lawrence Erlbaum Associates.

Gottman, J. M., & Katz, L. F. (1989). Effects of marital discord on young children's peer interaction and health. *Developmental Psychology, 25*, 373–381.

Gottman, J. M., & Krokoff, L. J. (1989). Marital interaction and satisfaction: A longitudinal view. *Journal of Consulting and Clinical Psychology, 57*, 47–52.

Gottman, J. M., & Levenson, R. W. (1999). Dysfunctional marital conflict: Women are being unfairly blamed. *Journal of Divorce and Remarriage, 31*, 1–17.

Gottman, J. M., & Levenson, R. W. (2000). The timing of divorce: Predicting when a couple will divorce over a 14-year period. *Journal of Marriage and the Family, 62*, 737–745.

Guidubaldi, J., Cleminshaw, H. K., Perry, J. D., Nastasi, B. D., & Lightel, J. (1986). The role of selected family environment factors in children's post-divorce adjustment. *Family Relations, 35*, 141–151.

Healy, J. M., Malley, J. E., & Stewart, A. J. (1990). Children and their fathers after separation. *American Journal of Orthopsychiatry, 60*, 531–543.

Hetherington, E. M. (1993). An overview of the Virginia Longitudinal Study of Divorce and Remarriage with a focus on early adolescence. *Journal of Family Psychology, 7*, 39–56.

Hetherington, E. M. (1998) Social capitol and the development of youth from nondivorced, divorced and remarried families. In A. Collins & R. Laursen (Eds.), *Relationships as developmental contexts. Minnesota symposium of child development, 30*, 177–210.

Hetherington, E. M., Bridges, M., & Isabella, G. M. (1998). What matters, what doesn't. Five perspectives on the association between divorce and remarriage and children's adjustment. *American Psychologist, 53*, 167–183.

Hetherington, E. M., Cox, M., & Cox, R. (1979). Family interaction and the social, emotional and cognitive development of children following divorce. In V. Vaughn & T. Brazelton (Eds.), *The family: Setting priorities* (pp. 89–128). New York: Science and Medicine.

Hetherington, E. M., Cox, M., & Cox, R. (1982). Effects of divorce on parents and children. In M. Lamb (Ed.), *Nontraditional families: Parenting and child development* (pp. 233–288). Hillsdale, NJ: Lawrence Erlbaum Associates.

Hetherington, E. M., & Kelly, J. (2002). *For better or for worse: Divorce reconsidered.* New York: Norton.

Hetherington, E. M., & Stanley-Hagan, M. M. (1999). The adjustment of children with divorced parents: A risk and resiliency perspective. *Journal of Child Psychology and Psychiatry, 40*, 129–140.

Johnson, C. L. (1988). *ExFamilia.* New Brunswick, NJ: Rutgers University Press.

Johnston, J. R., Kline, M., & Tschann, J. M. (1989). Ongoing post-divorce conflict: Effects on children of joint custody and frequent access. *American Journal of Orthopsychiatry, 59*, 576–592.

Katz, L. F., & Gottman, J. M. (1993). Patterns of marital conflict predict children's internalizing and externalizing behaviors. *Developmental Psychology, 29*, 940–950.

Laing, R. D. (1971). *The politics of the family and other essays.* New York: Vintage Books.

Leonard, K. E., & Roberts, L. J. (1998). Marital aggression, quality and stability in the first year of marriage: Findings from the Buffalo Newlywed Study. In T. N. Bradbury (Ed.), *The developmental course of marital dysfunction* (pp. 44–73). New York: Cambridge University Press.

Lewis, J. M., & Wallerstein, J. S. (1987). Family profile variables and long-term outcome in divorce research: Issues at a ten-year follow-up. In J. P. Vincent (Ed.), *Advances in family intervention, assessment and theory: A research annual* (pp. 121–142). Greenwich, CT: JAI.

Linker, J., Stolberg, A., & Green, R. (1999). Family communication as a mediator of child adjustment to divorce. *Journal of Divorce and Remarriage, 30*, 83–97.

Maccoby, M. M., Buchanan, C. M., Mnookin, R. H., & Dornbusch, S. M. (1993). Post-divorce roles of mothers and fathers in the lives of their children. *Journal of Family Psychology, 7*, 24–38.

Maccoby, E. E., & Mnookin, R. H. (1992). *Dividing the child: Social and legal dilemmas of custody.* Cambridge, MA: Harvard University Press.

Matthews, L. S., Wickrama, K. A., & Conger, R. D. (1996). Predicting marital instability from spouse and observer reports of marital interaction. *Journal of Marriage and the Family, 58*, 641–655.

Metts, S., & Cupach, W. R. (1995). Postdivorce relations. In M. A. Fitzpatrick & A. L. Vangelisti (Eds.), *Explaining family interactions* (pp. 232–251). Thousand Oaks, CA: Sage.

Nelson, R. (1989). Parental hostility, conflict and communication in joint and sole custody families. *Journal of Divorce, 13*, 145–157.

Olsen, D. H. (1990). Marriage in perspective. In F. D. Fincham & T. N. Bradbury (Eds.), *The psychology of marriage* (pp. 402–419). New York: Guilford Press.

Seltzer, J. A. (1990). Legal and physical custody arrangements in recent divorces. *Social Science Quarterly, 71*, 250–266.

Seltzer, J. A. (1991). Relationships between fathers and children who live apart: The father's role after separation. *Journal of Marriage and the Family, 53*, 79–102.

Seltzer, J. A., & Brandreth, Y. (1994). What fathers say about involvement with children after separation. *Journal of Family Issues, 15*, 49–77.

Serovich, J., Price, S., Chapman, S., & Wright, D. (1982). Attachment between former spouses: Impact on co-parental communication and parental involvement. *Journal of Divorce and Remarriage, 17*, 109–119.

Shaw, D., Emery, R., & Tuer, M. (1993). Parental functioning and children's adjustment in families of divorce: A prospective study. *Journal of Abnormal Child Psychology, 21*, 119–134.

Simons, R. L. (1996). The effect of divorce on adult and child adjustment. In R. L. Simons & Associates (Eds.), *Understanding differences between divorced and intact families: Stress, interaction and child outcome.* Thousand Oaks, CA: Sage.

Wallerstein, J. W., & Blakeslee, S. (1989). *Second chances: Men, women and children a decade after divorce.* New York: Ticknor and Fields.

Wallerstein, J. W., Corbin, S. B., & Lewis, J. M. (1988). Children of divorce: A ten year study. In E. M. Hetherington & J. D. Arasteh (Eds.), *Impact of divorce, single parenting and stepparenting on children* (pp. 114–123). Hillsdale, NJ: Lawrence Erlbaum Associates.

Wallerstein, J. W., & Kelly, J. B. (1980). *Surviving the breakup: How children and parents cope with divorce.* New York: Basic Books.

Wallerstein, J. W., Lewis, J. M., & Blakeslee, S. (2000). *The unexpected legacy of divorce: A 25 Year landmark study.* New York: Hyperion.

Zill, N., & Rogers, C. C. (1988). Recent trends in the well-being of children in the United States and their implications for public policy. In A. J. Cherlin (Ed.), *The changing American family and public policy* (pp. 31–115). Washington, DC: Urban Institute Press.

12. Renegotiating Family Communication

Remarriage and Stepfamilies

By Chris Segrin & Jeanne Flora

When many people think of "family" they imagine two people getting married, having children, and growing old together. This image of the American family is perhaps more stereotypical than it is typical. Because of divorce and widowhood many people will get married more than once in their lifetime. When people with children remarry they create a stepfamily. However, not all Stepfamilies are formed after divorce or widowhood. More people are having children outside marriage, and if these people eventually marry, their first marriage will generate a stepfamily. Remarriages and Stepfamilies face all of the same challenges as first marriages and their associated families. However, remarriages and Stepfamilies appear to have their own unique qualities and burdens that distinguish them from first marriage families. Communication and relationship development issues in Stepfamilies have a different character than what might be observed in first-marriage families. Even though there has been a lot of attention to the negative aspects of remarriage and Stepfamilies, there is reason to believe that they enjoy many of the benefits of first marriage families, and that their relationships are not necessarily more troubled.

We begin this selection by briefly examining the phenomenon of remarriage and answering a common question: "Why is it that marriage does not always work out better the second time around?" Next we present an in-depth analysis of communication and relationships in Stepfamilies. We address questions such as "How are Stepfamilies portrayed in the media?" and "What are societal views of Stepfamilies?" These views and images are mostly negative and are not accurate representations of the complex realities of Stepfamilies. Next, we take on questions such as "How do stepfamily relationships and communication develop in the early years of stepfamily formation?" and "How are roles and relationships defined in different types of Stepfamilies?" Finally, what are the challenges that are particular to Stepfamilies with regard to communication, conflict, and adaptability and cohesion? Addressing this question leads us to consider research findings on child adjustment in Stepfamilies and the importance of stepfamily communication for child well-being. Above all else, the research reviewed in this selection shows that Stepfamilies are exceptionally diverse. There are many different types of Stepfamilies, and these are represented in numerous taxonomies and typologies of Stepfamilies that have been developed by family scientists. Obviously, with all of the various forms and functions in Stepfamilies, sweeping generalizations must be interpreted tentatively.

REMARRIED COUPLES' RELATIONSHIPS

For the majority of people, divorce or widowhood does not mark the end of married life. Most people whose marriages end before they reach the age of 60 eventually remarry. Consequently, about half of all marriages are remarriages for at least one of the partners (Bumpass et al., 1990). About three-fourths of all divorced people eventually remarry (Furstenberg & Cherlin, 1991), Also, remarriage is becoming a more popular trend in society. For example, 10.6% of men in their 40s who were born between 1925 and 1934 were married two or more times. However, 22.3% of men in their 40s who were born between 1945 and 1954 have been married two or more times (Kreider & Fields, 2002). The corresponding figures for women are 12.1% and 22.8%. The median time span between divorce and remarriage is 3 years (Click, 1980). This suggests that people do not move into remarriages with greater caution, as evidenced by longer courtships, than do people embarking on their first marriage. Remarriages also have a higher divorce rate than first marriages. Why is it that people do not "learn from their past mistakes" and experience more success in remarriages than they did in marriage the first time around? Ganong and Coleman (1994) explain that there are multiple reasons for the higher divorce rate of remarried couples that involve a complex mix of individual, interpersonal, and societal factors.

There are several hypotheses for the relative instability of remarriages, especially those that follow a divorce. Ganong and Coleman (1994) suggest that some people have qualities that make them likely candidates for divorce. This is known as the *divorce-prone personality hypothesis*. Imagine a spouse who is very argumentative. That behavior might be perceived as obnoxious and eventually contribute to the deterioration of the marriage. Should this argumentative spouse remarry, the same behaviors and traits are now transported into the new marriage and would be expected to aggravate the new spouse and corrode that relationship as well. According to the *training school hypothesis*, first marriages are training grounds for relationships in subsequent marriages. However, as we noted earlier, people do not seem to learn from past mistakes. Rather, the most likely version of the training school hypothesis is that people learn dysfunctional patterns of interaction and problem solving in their first marriages and bring them into their subsequent marriages (Ganong & Coleman, 1994). In other words, people can develop bad habits in one marriage and continue them in another. The *willingness to leave marriage hypothesis* simply states that people who divorce have an obvious track record for seeing divorce as a solution to marital problems. If divorce was a way of escaping marital problems once, it should operate similarly in subsequent marriages. Because divorced people often marry other divorced people (Wilson & Clarke, 1992), this phenomenon may be compounded by both spouses having more favorable attitudes toward divorce. Another individual-level explanation described by Ganong and Coleman is the *dysfunctional beliefs hypothesis*. According to this explanation, people enter into remarriage with unrealistically high expectations, perhaps fueled by the certainty that they have learned from their past mistakes. When these expectations are not met, the remarried relationship is dissolved. At a more societal level, the *remarriage market hypothesis* predicts that the selection of available mates is often not as good the second or third time around. Divorced people in search of a future spouse may feel that "all of the good ones are taken." Those who are available may not have all of the desired qualities and thus contribute to lower quality marriages. Like so many social phenomena, the higher rate of divorce among remarried relationships is probably influenced by a variety of factors, at least some of which suggest that there are often troubles in these relationships.

Despite the multiple compelling explanations for the higher dissolution rate of second marriages, lower satisfaction does not seem to be a major problem for remarriages. A meta-analysis of 34 studies revealed that people in first marriages were just slightly more satisfied with their marriage than those in remarriages (Vemer, Coleman, Ganong, & Cooper, 1989). The magnitude of the difference was so weak that it could not plausibly account for the higher divorce rate among remarried people. In addition to comparable levels of happiness, Skinner et al. (2002) found that remarried couples reported a similar amount of couple communication and disagreements in their relationships as did first-married or cohabiting couples. Yet other studies show that remarried couples have more open expressions of anger, criticism, and irritation (Bray & Kelly, 1998; Hetherington, 1993). There is some reason to believe that the apparent discrepancies in these results might be explainable by the presence or absence of children in the remarried household (Coleman, Ganong, & Fine, 2000). It seems that opportunities for conflict, anger, and resentment are greater when there are stepchildren in the home.

Adjustment to remarriage is positively related to the extended interpersonal relationships that come with that marriage (Roberts & Price, 1989). These researchers found that the better remarried spouses' relationships were with the couple's families and friends, the better their marital adjustment. Not surprisingly, the quality of these same relationships was also associated with the quality of the remarried couple's own communication. However, there is one interpersonal relationship that predictably interferes with remarried couples' adjustment and that is a relationship with the former spouse. Roberts and Price (1989) found that attachment to the former spouse interfered with marital adjustment among remarried couples.

One obvious difference between remarried and first-marriage relationships is that there is a former spouse in remarried relationships. The act of getting married for a second or third time not only initiates a new marital relationship but also transforms the relationship with the former spouse (Christensen & Rettig, 1995). Christensen and Rettig found that single parents participated in substantial co-parenting (e.g., collectively making decisions about the child and discussing the child's problems), but those who had remarried were far less involved with their former spouse in terms of parenting issues. Additionally, remarried parents reported less parental support from their former spouse and held more negative attitudes toward their former spouse. Despite the seemingly negative tone of these transformations in the relationships with the former spouse, they are probably functional in some ways by creating the psychological space in which people can form a connection with a new spouse. Recall that Roberts and Price (1989) found that attachments to the former spouse could interfere with the adjustment of remarried couples. On the other hand, remarriage almost certainly marks a greater disconnection between biological parents from their children's point of view.

Overall, remarriages have been characterized as both a stressor (Crosbie-Burnett & McClintic, 2000a) and a coping response to the stress of being alone (Gentry & Shulman, 1988). Remarriages that have low levels of marital conflict and high levels of marital satisfaction can bring happiness to spouses and protect against depression (Demo & Acock, 1996). Unfortunately, the high divorce rate in remarriages suggests that the "remarriage as stressor" view is accurate in many cases.

Communication And Stepfamily Relationships

Stepfamilies are quite common in American society. About 30% of all children will live with a stepparent before reaching adulthood (Bumpass, Raley, & Sweet, 1995). It is estimated that one in three Americans is presently a member of a stepfamily and that more than half of all Americans will be a part of a stepfamily at some point in their lives (Larson, 1992). Stepfamilies are also nothing new. American presidents George Washington and Abraham Lincoln each had Stepfamilies. There are a lot of different terms for Stepfamilies including *remarried families, blended families, binuclear families, second families,* and *reconstituted families,* to name but a few (e.g., Bray, 1999; Ganong & Coleman, 1997, 2000). There is something particularly interesting about phenomena that are referenced by multiple terms, such as when two middle-aged people date each other and are described with terms like "partner," "significant other," "boyfriend," "girlfriend," and "lady friend." People often look for different terms when they are somehow uneasy with the concept, or when they feel there is some stigma associated with it. Presumably it is easier to change the label than to change thinking about the concept. Stepfamilies have received a bad reputation in our culture, for reasons that we will get into shortly. However, Stepfamilies are as diverse as families more generally, so broad generalizations about their harm or helpfulness are often difficult to support.

Consider some of the different ways in which Stepfamilies might be formed. People often think of Stepfamilies that are initiated after divorce from a first marriage. That is one of well over a dozen different ways that a stepfamily could be formed. Some people may not find themselves in a stepfamily until they reach their 30s and 40s if an older parent remarries following the death of his or her spouse. Some people may have had children outside marriage and then decide to marry someone other than the biological parent of the children. For both spouses this could be their first marriage, yet one would be a stepparent. The common denominator in all of these cases is that one adult parent has a legal or genetic tie to a child that the other adult does not (Ganong & Coleman, 2000). When these two unite, they form a stepfamily. When only one of the adults has children prior to remarriage, they form what is sometimes referred to as a *simple step-family*. When both have children from previous relationships, they form a *complex stepfamily*. Complex Stepfamilies have a higher likelihood of redivorce (Coleman et al., 2000).

Views of Stepfamilies

In Box 12-1, we examine how Stepfamilies are portrayed in the media. Later in this section, we explore portrayals of Stepfamilies in society more generally.

Box 12-1. Images of Stepfamilies in the Media

Family scientists Lawrence Ganong and Marilyn Coleman remarked that "cultural beliefs about family life exert a strong influence on the ways in which people conduct themselves, evaluate their situations, and expect to be regarded by others" (Ganong & Coleman, 1997, p. 85). Numerous family scholars have argued that Stepfamilies tend to have a bad reputation, due in part to their portrayal in the media (e.g., Bernstein, 1999; Ganong & Coleman, 1997). Although there has been virtually no scientific study of the effects of stepfamily portrayals in the media, it is worthwhile to at least momentarily consider how Stepfamilies are depicted in stories, movies, and television, and how that might influence both society's and individuals' beliefs, attitudes, and expectations for Stepfamilies.

Without doubt, the dominant media image of stepfamily that is referenced in scholarly essays comes from the story *Cinderella* which was made into a popular film in 1950. It was *Cinderella* that popularized the "wicked stepmother" image. Other fairy tales such as *Sleeping Beauty*, *Snow White*, and *Hansel and Gretel* reinforced this often dim view of stepparents. Negative portrayals of stepfamily life, and stepparents in particular, have continued in earnest since *Cinderella*. Films such as *Table for Five* (1983), *See You in the Morning* (1989), *Radio Flyer* (1992), *This Boy's Life* (1993), *Bastard Out of Carolina* (1996), and *Promise to Caroline* (1996) continue to depict stepparents as mean and sometimes abusive and stepfamily life as dysfunctional. The abundance of such storylines illustrates that there is a long history of negative images of Stepfamilies in American media.

With that said, it would be inaccurate to say that media images of Stepfamilies are uniformly negative. A number of dramatic films such as *The Sound of Music* (1965), *Tender Mercies* (1983), *Sarah Plain and Tall* (1990), and *Stepmom* (1998) depict stepparent-stepchild relationships in a much more positive light, sometimes portraying extraordinary caring and kindness on the part of stepparents. Other films such as *Yours Mine and Ours* (1968), *With 6 You Get Eggroll* (1968), *Seems Like Old Times* (1980), *Murphy's Romance* (1985), and *My Stepmother Is an Alien* (1988) present a comedic view of Stepfamilies. Furthermore, television portrayals of Stepfamilies have been almost exclusively positive, as evidenced by shows such as *The Brady Bunch* (1969–1974), *Eight is Enough* (1977–1981), *Major Dad* (1989–1993), and *Hearts Afire* (1992–1995), although more recent programs such as *Once and Again* (1999–2002) have tackled some of the more difficult issues that face contemporary Stepfamilies. For many Americans under the age of 50, it would be difficult to overstate the potential impact of *The Brady Bunch*. This program was first aired 35 years ago and has continued to be broadcast in syndication virtually without interruption. When family scholars discuss the role of unrealistically positive expectations in stepfamily adjustment (e.g., Jones, 1978), images of *The Brady Bunch* and similarly positive portrayals such as *The Sound of Music* immediately come to mind. However, the general belief of media cultivation theorists is that the media does not cause changes in views of the family but rather reflects and reinforces, or cultivates, already established beliefs (Signorelli & Morgan, 2001).

Despite the presence of both negative and positive images of Stepfamilies in the media, on balance, their depiction on television is relatively rare. Robinson and Skill (2001) content analyzed prime time fictional TV shows with a family configuration. In the 1950s, only 1.2% of these shows featured Stepfamilies. By the period 1990 to 1995 this figure had risen to 6.0%—a considerable increase, but still far below their prevalence in the actual American population. The media has been blamed for simultaneously depicting overly negative views of stepfamilies and stepparents in particular, as well as portraying unrealistically positive images of stepfamilies. Overall, depictions of stepfamilies on television and in the movies are still relatively rare; but in some cases, very salient and accessible. The exact role of these media images in shaping cultural as well as individual attitudes toward stepfamilies is still largely unknown to family scientists.

Societal Views of Stepfamilies

Family scientists have argued that most societal views of stepfamilies are negative in tone and based on an idealization of nuclear families (Ganong & Coleman, 2000). For instance, one image of stepfamilies in society is that of *deviant group*. Because stepfamilies and stepparents are sometimes stigmatized through cultural stereotypes, myths, and media images, Ganong and Coleman argue that many people see them as deviant groups. Consequently, stepfamily members sometimes attempt to conceal their status or engage in deliberate impression management strategies to overcome the stigma and prove that they are a worthwhile family. Another prominent view of stepfamilies is evident in the *incomplete institutionalization hypothesis* (Cherlin, 1978). Cherlin's thesis is essentially that stepfamilies lack guiding norms, principles, and methods of problem solving that are enjoyed by members of nuclear families. Further, there is no institutionalized social support for stepfamilies. In some cases, there are not even any appropriate terms for certain step relationships (e.g., the sibling of a stepparent). For these reasons, stepfamilies do not get adequately incorporated into our institutions and have to function under conditions of unclear or ambiguous expectations. Ganong and Coleman are quick to note that some have criticized Cherlin for overstating the case, but that there is at least a kernel of truth in the incomplete institutionalization hypothesis. Another societal view of stepfamilies is that of the *reformed nuclear family*. According to this perspective, stepfamilies are just like nuclear families by virtue of having two heterosexual adults and children. People who endorse this view assume that stepfamilies will function as any nuclear family would and that family membership and household membership are one and the same. This societal view of stepfamilies certainly sounds less negative than the incomplete institutionalization hypothesis or the deviant groups perspective, but it is based on a fundamental misunderstanding of stepfamilies. As we reveal later in this selection, stepfamilies face their own unique set of challenges that often distinguish them from nuclear families. And like nuclear families, stepfamilies have diverse forms and functions. For that reason the reformed nuclear family view appears to stem from a whitewashed vision of what stepfamilies are all about. At the same time, we hasten to point out that the deviant groups and incomplete institutionalization perspectives are perhaps equally off base, just in the opposite direction. In any event, the societal views of stepfamilies described by Ganong and Coleman indicate that myths and stereotypes abound when it comes to understanding stepfamilies.

The Development of Stepfamily Communication and Relationships

Family clinicians such as Papernow (1993) recognize that stepfamilies go through distinct phases in their efforts to form a cohesive "family." At the start of the remarriage, many stepfamilies are in the *fantasy stage*. This stage is represented by hope and perhaps expectation that the new spouse will be a better partner and parent than the previous spouse. The spouse who marries a partner with children will often enter into the relationship with similarly lofty goals and an immediate effort to be a super-parent. The image of stepfamilies portrayed in *The Brady Bunch* is a good illustration of the sort of family communication dynamics that might be hoped for in the fantasy stage. However, as most people are aware, that image of Stepfamily life is just that—a fantasy. Next, stepfamilies enter into the *immersion stage*. In this stage, the stepparent tends to feel like an outsider looking in and their grand expectations are often shattered. Children become more aware of the relationship between their biological parent and stepparent. This can generate feelings of jealousy, resentment, and confusion. The reality of different views toward child rearing, parental roles, and negotiation of new boundaries creates conditions that are ripe for family conflict. The transformation from the fantasy to immersion stages described by Papernow (1993) is clearly evident in research findings on stepfathers and their stepchildren. Stepfathers often enter the Stepfamily with what appear to be the best of intentions, overtly expressing positivity toward the stepchildren in the hope of developing a good relationship with them. However, research shows that they quickly become disengaged from the stepchildren when their positive overtures are rebuffed (Hetherington & Clingempeel, 1992). Despite the fact that sharing information with the children, paying attention to them, and engaging them in shared activities are all positive rapport-building communication behaviors, Stepfamily relationships like all other relationships cannot be forced or rushed. Children have a knack for putting on the brakes when stepparent–stepchild relationships develop too quickly This regulation of relationship development may be interpreted as rejection by the stepfather, resulting in his disengagement from the relationship. This pattern of early Stepfamily relationship development clearly illustrates the sort of changes in behavior that would be expected as stepfamilies progress from the fantasy into the immersion stage.

The development of Stepfamily relationships is often evident in how the family negotiates and develops family rituals. To explore this issue, communication researchers Dawn Braithwaite, Leslie Baxter, and Anneliese Harper (1998) interviewed 20 stepparents and 33 stepchildren and asked them to focus on family rituals during the first 4 years of the stepfamily's history. They found that families had to balance the dialectical opposition between honoring rituals of the "old" family and developing rituals in the "new" family. This management was accomplished in several ways. First, some rituals from the old family were dropped because they could no longer be performed in the new family, they were no longer appropriate, or the new spouse would not participate in the new ritual. It is sometimes the case that family rituals are built around one person (e.g., going to a certain restaurant on the father's birthday) and when that person is no longer a part of the household the ritual is dropped. In other cases, the new spouse may have different religious beliefs and practices that are at odds with the family's adherence to a former ritual. Second, some rituals were successfully imported unchanged into the new family. Braithwaite and her colleagues explain that the perseverance of such rituals functions to honor both the old and the new family. For example, a family that goes on a camping trip every summer might continue to do so after the remarriage of one of the parents. In this way they keep the "old family" tradition alive, while also incorporating the new family member(s) into that tradition ultimately making it the "new family's" ritual as well. Third, some family rituals are imported into the new family but adapted in some way. A family that always gets together for an afternoon barbeque on the 4th of July might have to modify their ritual when their new stepmother, who is a police officer, has to work on that day. Instead, this family may have a dinner and then go to their local park to watch a fireworks display in the evening. The family still celebrates the ritual of getting together for a big meal on the 4th of July, but they adapted it to meet the needs of the new family member. Finally, stepfamilies will often form new rituals of their own. These can help to create a new and unique identity for the stepfamily so long as everyone in the family is a willing participant in the ritual.

In a further analysis of these same interviews Baxter, Braithwaite, and Nicholson (1999) turned their attention to turning points in the development of these stepfamily relationships. When asked to focus on those keys events in the family's early history that brought them to where they are today, respondents most frequently cited "changes in household/family composition" (mentioned by 94% of all respondents), "conflict or disagreement" (72%), "holidays and special events" (67%), "quality time" (64%), and "family crisis" (55%). It appears that these various turning points are characteristic in the development of most stepfamilies. As part of these interviews, Baxter and her associates asked participants to draw a graph where the horizontal axis is time (0–48 months) and the vertical axis is what percent they "feel like a family" (0–100). Analyses of these revealed five distinct stepfamily development trajectories that are summarized in Table 12-1.

Table 12-1. Baxter et al.'s (1999) Taxonomy of Stepfamily Development Trajectories

Trajectory	Prevalence	Description Type
Accelerated	31%	Started out at feeling somewhat like a family and rapidly progressed with an almost 4:1 ratio of positive to negative turning points
Prolonged	27%	Started out not feeling like a family but slowly progressed toward family cohesion with a 3:1 ratio of positive to negative turning points
Stagnating	14%	Started out not feeling like a family and never developed the feeling over the first four years; they experienced a 2:1 ratio of positive to negative turning points but these did not create the feeling of a family
Declining	6%	Started out feeling like a family but that feeling steadily declined over the first four years; they experienced a 2:1 ratio of negative to positive turning points
High-Amplitude Turbulent	22%	Drastic fluctuation in feeling like a family during the first four years; numerous positive and negative turning points that each altered their feeling of being a family

Note. Adapted from Baxter, Braithwaite, & Nicholson (1999).

There are several notable qualities to Baxter et al.'s (1999) findings on stepfamily development trajectories that are evident from Table 12.1. First, it is quite obvious that not all stepfamilies develop in the same way. Some experience a smooth and rapid progression toward feeling like a family, whereas others have a more turbulent development trajectory, or never really develop the sense of being a family. Second, even though the majority of stepfamilies successfully develop a sense of cohesion and unity, it is apparent that some (i.e., "stagnating" and "declining") never successfully achieve that goal. From these data, that appears to be the case for about one in five stepfamilies.

To gain a deeper understanding of what differentiated the stepfamilies, Braithwaite and her associates conducted further analyses of the interviews from these stepfamily members to examine how family processes variables discriminated among the different types (Braithwaite, Olson, Golish, Soukup, & Turman, 2001). They found that *accelerated* stepfamilies rapidly developed traditional family roles, norms, boundaries, and expectations. They seemed to approach stepfamily life expecting traditional nuclear family roles and norms to develop. Their strong solidarity helped them to smoothly work through the conflicts that they experienced early in their development. *Prolonged* families tended to be adaptable, flexible, and generally satisfied with their stepfamily experiences. Even though they started out uncertain, they were willing to negotiate things like family roles and were open to communication about these issues. Unlike the accelerated families, those with a prolonged trajectory did not compare themselves to a nuclear family. Families with the *declining* trajectory seemed to have a lot of trouble from the word go. They started out with great expectations but almost immediately experienced loyalty conflicts, ambiguous and strained family roles, and divisive family boundaries. Their struggles were characterized by eventually developing impermeable and divisive boundaries by bloodline and generation and, ultimately, by avoidance of communication. By the end of their fourth year, these families were around zero on the "feeling like a family" scale. *Stagnating* families experienced awkwardness in their role and felt, as Braithwaite and her associates put it, "thrown together." They wanted a normal or traditional family life, but ironically, the more they tried to create that the more resistance they experienced from within. Obviously, not all members of these families were on the same page when it came to developing a "normal" family life. Loyalty conflicts, resentment, and dissatisfaction were common themes in these families that simply never took off. Finally, the *highamplitude turbulent* families had a diverse and unstable development in their first 4 years. Like many other newly formed stepfamilies they started off with great expectations and quickly collided with realities that were at odds with these expectations. Feelings of betrayal and a lack of trust were common in these family types. Braithwaite et al. noted that a lack of solidarity between the couple was common in these families and prevented them from communicating a unified front to the children. Conflicts typically culminated in a "fork in the road" that was successfully negotiated in some turbulent families. Those who avoided these conflicts were among the least satisfied of the turbulent families. After carefully examining the development trajectories and experiences, Braithwaite et al. concluded that the three key family processes that varied across the different families were boundary management, solidarity, and adaptation. Even though these conclusions were derived from a small sample of stepfamily members, they are generally consistent with the research literature on stepfamilies that highlights the importance of these same critical issues.

Diversity Within Stepfamilies

As we mentioned earlier in this selection, there is no single standard or norm for stepfamilies. Like families, more generally, stepfamilies are quite diverse and can take a variety of forms. In this section we consider the variety of different roles that people might occupy in stepfamilies and some of the many different types of relationships that occur in these different stepfamilies. Finally, this section includes an analysis of different types of stepfamilies based on the members' orientation toward stepfamily life.

Roles in Stepfamilies

Family roles simultaneously shape and are shaped by communication patterns within the family. Although the roles of child and parent are fairly dear in most family contexts, there is considerable ambiguity inherent in being a stepparent. Many stepparents are unsure about assuming the role of parent. After all, in many stepfamilies the children still have two biological parents. What is the ideal role of a stepparent in this family context? Family scientists Mark Fine, Marilyn Coleman, and Lawrence Ganong (1998) investigated this issue by asking parents, stepparents, and children in stepfamilies about what they think the ideal role of a stepparent is. They also asked respondents to describe the actual role of the stepparent in their family. For the ideal role of a stepparent, just over half of the parents and stepparents said "parent." In other words, the stepparent should assume the role of parent just as a biological parent would. In contrast, only 29% of the children offered this response. Evidently, a greater proportion of parents and stepparents, compared to children, think that "parent" is the ideal role for a stepparent. Among these same respondents, 18% of the parents and 18% of the stepparents indicated that "friend" was the ideal role of a stepparent. In contrast, 40% of the children thought that "friend" was the ideal role for a stepparent. So it seems that more children want their stepparent to assume the role of friend, whereas parents and stepparents want the stepparent to assume the role of parent. It is also interesting that 48% of the stepparents said that their actual role in the family was that of parent, whereas only 28% of the children said that their stepparent held the role of parent. Fine et al.'s study illustrates not only how there are different desires within the family for stepparent roles but also how family members do not necessarily agree on what the actual role of the family's stepparent is. For the most part, parents and children have a clearer perception of what the stepparent role is in contrast to stepparents who indicate that their role in the family is not entirely clear (Fine, Coleman, & Ganong, 1999).

The performance of some parental roles in stepfamilies may be specific to the sex of the parent. For example, mothers will often assume a variety of roles to control the development of the relationship between their children and new spouse (Coleman, Ganong, & Weaver, 2001). Mothers will sometimes perform the role of *defender* in which they try to shield their children from unfair discipline, perceived slights, and misunderstanding on the part of the stepfather. In the role of *gatekeeper,* mothers literally control the stepfather's access to their children during both courtship and marriage. For instance, it may take many years before a mother will leave her children alone with their stepfather. Mothers also act as *mediators* between children and their stepfathers. Coleman et al. note that the mediator role is particularly common early in the formation of stepfamilies when disagreements are prevalent. A related role performed by mothers in stepfamilies is that of *interpreter*. Interpreters not only step in and referee conflicts but also explain each family member's perspective to the other. When lines of communication between children and the stepfather may be hindered or nonexistent, the mother's performance of the interpreter role can be vital to salvaging some degree of civility in the family environment.

Remarriage and the formation of a stepfamily often change the interactions between a mother and her children. When mothers remarry, they decrease their use of harsh discipline tactics such as yelling, spanking, and hitting (Thomson, Mosley, Hanson, & McLanahan, 2001). However, remarried mothers supervise their children less than do stable single mothers (Thomson et al.). So remarriage brings not only some obvious improvements to mother–child interactions but also some declines in the form of less supervision.

Stepmothers have a particularly challenging role to fulfill in many remarried families. As mentioned elsewhere in this selection, there is an abundance of negatively toned folklore concerning stepmothers. Stepmothers often feel that they have to go the extra mile to prove that they are not like the wicked stepmother in *Cinderella* (Guisinger, Cowan, & Schuldberg, 1989). In so doing, they often start by forming good relationships with their stepchildren, but their optimistic attitudes toward stepparenting erode noticeably within 3 to 5 years of marriage. Guisinger et al. also found that a quality marriage goes hand in hand with good relationships between stepmothers and their stepchildren. Many stepmothers must also contend with some of the negative emotions that stem from occupying a role that sometimes excludes them or makes them feel less than 100% legitimate. The feminist scholar Elizabeth Church (1999) interviewed 104 stepmothers and found that about half had felt jealous or envious in their role as stepmother. Feelings of jealousy were provoked by three types of circumstances: feeling second best, feeling like an outsider, and feeling like a rival. When stepmothers felt jealous due to a perceived rivalry, it was not the children's biological mother who was the rival. Rather, many felt that they had to compete with their stepchildren for their partner's attention. Church argues that often stepmothers' jealousy is an expression of feeling disconnected from the family and feeling powerless. In many families stepmothers occupy a precarious role. They are expected to form good relationships with the children and get involved in their care—but not too involved. When either biological parent pursues interaction with the children, stepmothers may be expected to step back, never having all of the full rights and privileges of a regular mother.

Stepfamily Relationships and Stepfamily Types

It is customary to describe different types of stepfamilies by their formal structure (e.g., mother with her biological children and stepfather and both spouses with their own biological children). However, Gross (1986) described different stepfamilies from the perspective of their children. To do so, she interviewed 60 children and asked them to describe and explain who was in their family. The children's responses provide insight into the many different ways that some people might define family relationships, and how communication patterns in stepfamilies can sometimes be almost nonexistent, despite the fact that two people may share the same residence. These family structures, defined by children's subjective impressions, appear in Table 12-2. Gross (1986) found that the four different stepfamily structures were

Table 12-2. Gross's (1986) Typology of Children's Perceptions of Family Membership

Stepfamily Structure	Prevalence	Description
Retention	33%	Include both biological parents as family Do not include stepparent as a family member Family identified as prior to divorce Nonresidential parent still very involved in child's life Stepparents play a more negative role in child's life
Substitution	13%	Exclude at least one biological parent from family, usually the nonresidential parent Include at least one stepparent in family Views family as child, one biological parent, and stepparent Household and family are synonymous Children are younger at separation from biological parent and remarriage to stepparent Qualified acceptance of stepparent
Reduction	25%	Fewer than the original two parents viewed as family Stepparent not viewed as family member At least one biological parent (usually nonresidential) not viewed as family member Experience family as "one-parent family" Negative feelings toward stepparent
Augmentation	28%	Both biological parents identified as family, as well as at least one stepparent Stepparent is not a "replacement" but an "addition" Usually involved custodial father and stepmother Many had previously lived with their mother Maintained contact with nonresidential parent Free movement between households, and lack of hostility between biological parents

Note. Adapted from Gross (1986).

about equally common in her sample. In some cases (*retention* and *reduction*) the stepchildren refused to characterize their stepparents as "family." In other cases (*substitution* and *reduction)* the children essentially dropped one of the biological parents from their mental representation of "family." There are also many cases (*substitution* and *augmentation)* where the stepchildren willingly characterized their stepparents as family members. This unique taxonomy developed by Gross is a reminder that children approach stepfamily relationships with vastly differing perspectives. The theory of symbolic interaction would explain these different realities of family life through the children's communication patterns with their parents and stepparents. Where there is little communication at all, as in the case of a noncustodial "deadbeat dad," some children literally revise their mental representation of "family" to exclude that member. On the other hand, where stepparent-stepchild communication patterns reflect issues such as concern, guidance, reasonable discipline, recreation, and so forth, symbolic interactionists would argue that children would more readily incorporate the stepparent into the family's membership.

Much of the research on stepfamily relationships has understandably focused on relationships between children and their stepparents and the marital relationship in stepfamilies. What is sometimes overlooked when people think about stepfamily relationships is the relationship between the two biological parents, only one of whom is currently the custodial parent. Remarriage after a divorce does not represent the end of the relationship between two biological parents. A divorced couple with children often needs to continue some form of relationship to coordinate child care and visitation, even though one or both may have remarried and formed a new family. In such cases, children become part of a *binuclear family*. The communication patterns of formerly married spouses can take on a variety of forms. Ahrons and Rodgers (1987) described these in their taxonomy of postdivorce relationships described in Table 12-3. What is most striking from the descriptions of these relationships is the diverse range of interaction patterns maintained by former spouses. Some (e.g., *dissolving duos*) permanently sever their lines of communication. This is probably a much more common communication pattern in divorced couples without any children. At the other end of the spectrum, the *perfect pals* manage to maintain open communication and continue to participate together in family activities and rituals. It is instructive to compare the types of postdivorce relations in this scheme to the children's subjective impressions of family membership described by Gross (1986). Recall that in some cases (*substitution* and *reduction*) Gross found that children would no longer consider one of their biological parents to be a member of the family. It would not be much of stretch to suppose that the biological parents in such families are *dissolving duos* or perhaps fiery *foes*. Gross also found that children would

Table 12-3. Ahrons and Rogers' (1987) Typology of Postdivorce Relationships

Relationship Type	Description
Dissolving Duos	No contact after divorce
Perfect Pals	Maintain mutual respect for each other after divorce Remain good friends Maintain open communication and family rituals They often remain single
Cooperative Colleagues	No real friendship Cooperate and coordinate efforts at parenting Compromise for the children's benefit Effectively manage conflicts
Angry Associates	Harbor resentment and anger toward each other Both active as parents but in parallel, not collectively Children experience loyalty conflicts
Fiery Foes	Intense anger No acceptance of other parent's rights Attempts to separate ex-spouse from children No cooperation between parents Children become pawns Parents still attached to each other as evidenced by their intense emotional reaction to each other

Note. Adapted from Ahrons & Rodgers (1987).

often still consider a non-custodial parent to be a member of the family, in the cases of *retention* and *augmentation*. One might suppose that the divorced biological parents in these cases would be *perfect pals* or *cooperative colleagues*. One could develop additional hypotheses linking these different stepfamily relationships, but the underlying assumption is that the nature of the postdivorce relationship of the biological parents influences to some extent the child's consideration of these parents as members of the family.

Finally, we present a recent summary of some of the distinct types of stepfamilies that have been identified in past research. Family scientists Coleman, Ganong, and Fine (2004) noted that almost every typology of stepfamilies identifies *Brady Bunch Stepfamilies*. The label that scientists use for these families is a testament to the power of the media in influencing our thinking about families. Needless to say, these are stepfamilies that try to set up a situation that is indistinguishable from a first-marriage family. Members of these families relate to each other as if they were parents and children, not stepparents and stepchildren. Their communication is open and abundant, as is their expression of affection. Coleman et al. observe that such families may be ill-prepared, unrealistic, and in denial. Like the Brady Bunch, these families may be striving not to function like a true first-marriage family but rather as a stereotype of a first-marriage family. As Coleman et al. note, often situational demands for communication and problem solving do not fit the Brady Bunch ideal, and this can be cause for dissatisfaction. For some stepfamilies, however, this mentality may work, particularly when children are very young when the stepfamily is formed.

In contrast to the Brady Bunch Stepfamilies, the *detached stepparent–engaged parent stepfamilies* function with nonequivalent parental roles. Generally the mothers in these families are involved in the upbringing of the children and the stepfathers are detached. Stepfathers in these families show little affection toward the stepchildren; they might not get involved in their supervision and engage in limited communication with them. In contrast mothers in these families are prone to engaging in frequent and intense communication with the children. Before condemning these stepfathers, it is important to realize that their detachment sometimes follows the directives of either the mother or her children (Coleman et al., 2004). Stepfathers are sometimes thrown into relationships with stepchildren merely as a function of their marriage to the mother. The stepparent–stepchild relationship is sometimes an incidental one that families manage by keeping a distance between the two and leaving most of the parenting up to the mother.

A related type of stepfamily can be found in the *couple-focused stepfamilies*. Here the marital union is of paramount importance. In these stepfamilies, the communication is largely between the spouses, and the stepparent is detached from the stepchildren. This pattern is perhaps most likely in cases where the children are older and breaking out on their own or when the children do not reside with the married couple. One might expect to see couple-focused stepfamilies, for example, in marriages that follow the death of a spouse later in life.

Finally, some stepfamilies could be characterized as *progressive stepfamilies*. Communication in these stepfamilies is modified to fit the needs to the family's particular situation and demands. Well-established stepfamilies often develop their own unique and creative style of communication to meet the complexities of their family life. One example cited by Coleman et al. (2004) is when mothers interpret the stepfathers to stepchildren and vice versa. As a way of compensating for the lack of shared history in the stepfamily, the mothers may aid their children's and spouse's understanding of each other by enacting this creative communication behavior. Progressive stepfamilies often exhibit excellent family communication and problem solving. Their relationships are sometimes closer than those of first-marriage families. At this time, family scientists and clinicians do not fully understand how such families are developed. However, it appears that a very flexible approach to family communication coupled with a respect for different family forms, devoid of any preconceived notions, are integral elements of progressive stepfamilies.

Challenges in Stepfamilies

Stepfamilies face a number of challenges in sorting out their relationships that contribute to family stress. Some of the issues that they face, such as conflict, are comparable in kind to those of nuclear families, but perhaps differ in intensity. Other challenges such as negotiating conflicting loyalties to a stepparent and noncustodial parent are unique to stepfamilies. In this section, we examine challenges faced by stepfamilies that include relational communication issues, conflict, adaptability and cohesion, and child adjustment.

Communication Challenges

Although all developing families face a number of communication challenges as they build relationships, trust, roles, and boundaries, stepfamilies have unique dynamics that make these challenges particularly salient. Furthermore, stepfamilies must face a number of unique challenges that differ from nuclear families with both biological parents. To identify these issues Golish (2003) interviewed 90 people (stepparents, biological parents, and children and stepchildren) from 30 different stepfamilies. They were asked how their communication, feelings, and expectations changed over time and to identify their problem areas and strengths. One of the most common challenges cited by participants was *feeling caught*. This typically involved triangulation in the relationship among a child, his or her custodial parents, and his or her noncustodial parent. This challenge caused children to avoid talking to one parent in front of the other or bringing up certain topics of discussion with one of the parents. Interestingly, it was sometimes the parents who felt caught. For example, sometimes the biological parent was used as a go-between by their child and spouse. Instead of the stepchild and stepparent communicating directly, they would air their grievances through the parent. Some families had problems with *ambiguity of parental roles*. Almost all of the stepfamilies studied by Golish (2003) experienced confusion and uncertainty about the stepparent's role in disciplining children. This sometimes causes a clash between the "friend" and "disciplinarian" role performed by the stepparent. Stepfamilies also had to contend with *regulating boundaries with the noncustodial family*. Many children in stepfamilies are still grieving the loss of their family system. This often took the form of having to renegotiate a different kind of relationship with a now noncustodial father. However, sometimes this challenge in regulating relationships was experienced between former spouses. Where there are issues of joint or shared custody, former spouses cannot simply stop communicating, but rather have to work out arrangements for care of the children.

One particularly unique challenge faced by stepfamilies is *traumatic bonding*. It was often the case that mothers and daughters formed a very close bond as the mother made the transition from divorce to single parenthood. The bond formed during these hard times would often persevere during formation of the stepfamily. At this time, the stepparent would be seen as an intruder in the family. At the same time, the stepparent may feel jealous or excluded by this intense mother–daughter bond. Stepfamilies were also challenged by *vying for resources*. Issues like money, space, and privacy are particularly salient in stepfamilies. The desire for one's own territory could be fueled by the feeling of being invaded by outsiders, which could also increase the desire for privacy. Struggling to secure these resources in an environment where they are often scarce sets the stage for abundant conflicts within the stepfamily. A related challenge faced by stepfamilies is *discrepancies in conflict management styles*. The most common scenario for this challenge was a stepparent's desire to openly confront an issue and the biological parent's and children's desire to avoid the issue. Successfully overcoming this challenge often involved all parties adjusting their communication style. The final communication challenge documented by Golish (2003) was *building solidarity as a family unit*. Particularly strong and successful families accomplished this by spending time together, developing their own family rituals, and displaying affection toward each other. In other cases stepfamilies would incorporate humor into their interactions or naturally and gradually introduce the child and stepparent without trying to force the relationship. Even though most families have to deal with at least some of these issues, they are particularly evident in stepfamilies, and their successful negotiation is vital to developing strong stepfamily relationships. Golish observed that the "meta-theme" underlying many of these communication challenges is the negotiation of boundaries within the family and across families.

In a comparable study, Cissna, Cox, and Bochner (1990) interviewed nine stepfamilies that had at least two school-aged children at home and asked them about issues such as managing relationships with the former spouse, problems in reorganizing their family, and strategies for overcoming these problems. All nine of the families mentioned issues related to balancing the marital versus the parental relationships. Cissna et al. found that there were two dominant tasks that families faced in order to manage this dialectic. First, the family needs to *establish the solidarity of the marriage relationship in the minds of the stepchildren*. Marriages are freely chosen by the spouses, but not by their children. As Golish (2003) observed, sometimes children might view the stepparents as an intruder into a close relationship that was established during tough times. For a stepfamily to develop and function effectively, stepchildren need to see the marital relationship as solid and unified. A second major task that stepfamilies face is *establishing parental authority, particularly the credibility of the stepparent*. Once the children appreciate the substantial nature of the parent-stepparent relationship, the next step is to view the stepparent as something of an authority figure. Without that, boundaries can get blurred and conflicts can arise. Cissna et al. observed that one of the difficult chores for the stepparent is building a friendship relationship with the child while at the same time exercising discipline and developing the role of authority figure. This is an unusually challenging dialectic that must be delicately balanced with acute sensitivity and social skills on the part of the stepparent.

Conflict

Because of their unique family structure stepfamilies tend to have their own set of stressors and concerns that contribute substantially to interpersonal conflicts (Burrell, 1995). It is often the case in stepfamilies that an "outsider" comes into a long-established physical environment and relational context. Children sometimes have a close relationship with their custodial parent forged during difficult times. They are often accustomed to their custodial parent's undivided attention when they are home together. In addition children may have their own room and space in the house that does not have to be shared with others. The introduction of a stepparent, particularly one with children in tow, can dramatically upset these norms. Obviously the situation is ripe for conflict and may explain why stepfamilies experience more conflict than do intact families (Barber & Lyons, 1994). A lot of the conflicts in stepfamilies occur between the spouses and often concern the children and stepchildren (Ganong & Coleman, 2000). In stepfamilies, it is sometimes the case that the biological parent has far more history and experience raising children than does the stepparent, who may have no child-rearing experience at all. This immediately sets up a situation where the legitimacy of one person's perspective on child rearing is questioned and almost impossible to substantiate. It is no wonder that conflicts over child-rearing issues are so prevalent among spouses in stepfamilies.

Observations of family clinicians indicate that stepfamily households often have to address multiple sources of potential conflict that include outsiders and insiders, boundary disputes, power issues, conflicting loyalties, triangular relationships, and unity versus fragmentation of the new couple relationship (Visher, Visher, & Pasley, 2003). Scientific researchers have reached similar conclusions, noting that the primary sources of conflict in stepfamilies often revolve around boundary issues (Burrell, 1995; Coleman, Fine, Ganong, Downs, & Pauk, 2001). Subsidiary issues included disagreements over resources, loyalty conflicts, individuals having a "guard and protect" mentality, and conflict with extended family (Coleman et al.). Coleman and her associates documented these family conflicts through interviews of adults and children from 17 stepfamilies. Some of the major resources that they frequently argued about were possessions, space, time and attention, and finances. Loyalty conflicts were often felt by children who seemed to be torn between loyalty to their stepparent and their noncustodial parent. What Coleman et al. characterized as a "guard and protect" ideology involved the mother trying to protect an almost peer-like mother–daughter relationship, attempts to protect the children from an overly strict stepfather, or attempts to protect the children from a nonresidential parent. Instances of these interaction patterns highlighted sharp disagreements and conflicts often ensued. Finally, stepfamilies often experienced conflicts with extended family members who did not view the stepfamily as a legitimate family unit. This type of conflict is a good illustration of a dispute that involves an external boundary issue, whereas most other conflicts in the stepfamilies concerned boundaries within the family.

It is sometimes the case in stepfamilies that role ambiguity and boundary issues collectively contribute to conflicts (Burrell, 1995). For example, role ambiguity occurs when people are uncertain about what actions they are expected to take and exactly what their function is in the family. Of course, boundaries represent the often invisible psychological limits of enacted and accepted behaviors within the family and between its members and outsiders. For a new stepparent, role ambiguity and boundary issues may go hand in hand. The role of disciplinarian is often a very uncertain one for the new stepparent. Stepchildren who are unaccustomed to this new role of the stepparent may reject such forms of communication. At the same time, some stepparents may have a hard time communicating in an authoritarian or authoritative fashion toward their stepchildren. This role ambiguity is entwined in boundary issues. How permeable is the stepparent–stepchild relationship? Does the stepparent have the "right" or authority to command the stepchild to do something or to not do something? Does the stepparent have the right or authority to use corporal punishment (involving nonverbal communication)? Should there be as much physical affection in the stepparent–stepchild relationship as might be expected between biological parents and their children? These are all issues that concern both roles and boundaries. They can be very potent catalysts for conflict in most stepfamilies. These conflicts may occur between stepparent and stepchild, between two spouses who disagree on how the stepparents should interact with the stepchild, or between a child and his or her biological parent who disagree on what is acceptable behavior on the part of the stepparent.

There is an interesting power dynamic in stepfamilies that helps to explain the nature of some common conflicts that occur in these contexts. In stepfather families (perhaps the most common form of remarried families with children), family members agree that the mother has most authority and power for major decision making (Giles-Sims & Crosbie-Burnett, 1989). However, for everyday decisions, adolescents appear to have as much influence as the adults, especially early on in the history of the stepfamily. Further, Giles-Sims and Crosbie-Burnett (1989) found that when it comes to making major decisions, adolescents perceived themselves as having more power than their stepfathers—a view that was not necessarily shared by their stepfathers. This potential power struggle between adolescent and stepparent is undoubtedly manifest in conflict interactions until the family is able to establish some norms, or in systems theory terminology, homeostasis. The struggle for power and the quest to establish new family norms may explain why long-term remarried couples with stepchildren experience more conflict than long-term remarried couples with their own biological children (MacDonald & DeMaris, 1995). When children are born into an intact marriage, power, roles, norms and decisionmaking patterns can be gradually and consistently developed throughout childhood. On the other hand, when a remarried couple has stepchildren, where there is no relational history with one of the parents, these same roles, norms, and decision-making patterns must be negotiated and established from scratch. In long-term marriages, where the stepchildren are likely to be older children and adolescents, the potential for interpersonal conflict is extensive.

What are the communication strategies that stepfamilies use to resolve their conflicts? Coleman et al. (2001) found that stepfamilies would often compromise on rules and discipline, present a unified parental front on rules and discipline, talk directly with the person one is in conflict with, or reframe the problem as less serious, perhaps with a joke. Most communication scholars would agree that these are generally effective ways of handling conflict. This suggests, through their often extensive experience with conflict, that stepfamilies often develop and deploy effective means for managing these conflicts.

Having said that "talking directly" is one way stepfamilies resolve conflict, there are some special exceptions. Sometimes stepchildren handle conflict-laden or other sensitive topics is by avoiding the topic in family interactions. Golish and Caughlin (2002) studied this issue by interviewing 115 adolescents and young adults in stepfamilies, using Petronio's (2000) Communication Privacy Management perspective to develop hypotheses about why and when adolescents would avoid various topics with their parents and stepparents. They found that children reported the greatest topic avoidance with stepparents, followed by fathers, and finally by mothers. The most commonly avoided topic across all types of parental relationships was sex. Other commonly avoided topics included talking about the other parent or family and money (e.g., child support payments). When asked why they avoided these topics, the adolescents' and young adults' most typical replies concerned self-protection, protecting the harmony of the relationship with the parent or stepparent, and conflict. Responses that reflected concerns with conflict included the desire to keep conflicts from happening as well and the desire to keep some conflicts from escalating. Even though people often feel that discussing concerns openly is the best way to develop and manage relationships, in an often fragile context of stepfamily relationships, sometimes the avoidance of certain topics is the more sensible and comfortable strategy—at least from the perspective of a child in the stepfamily.

Before leaving the topic of conflict, it bears mentioning that conflict can be a catalyst for positive change in stepfamilies (Coleman, Fine, et al., 2001). As hard as it is for many stepfamilies to sort out their various issues, establish boundaries, and define new roles, the efforts invested in these conflicts may yield dividends so long as they do not consume the stepfamily. Stepfamilies can achieve harmony and happiness, but that may only come after intense negotiation, or conflict, over issues such as space, roles, expectations, discipline, and privacy.

Adaptability and Cohesion

It is generally the case that stepfamilies have lower family cohesion and adaptability than do first-married families (Pink & Wampler, 1985; Waldren, Bell, Peek, & Sorell, 1990). People in stepfamilies report lower cooperation and greater fragmentation in family relationships than do people in nuclear families (Banker & Gaertner, 1998). Bray and Berger (1993) found not only that newly formed (within

6 months) stepfamilies had lower levels of cohesion than did nuclear families but also that levels of family cohesion dropped even lower in longer established (i.e., 2.5 and 5–7 years) stepfamilies. The fact that stepfamilies have lower cohesion than do first-married families is understandable. After all, the stepparent and any of his or her children often have very little relational history with other family members. Recall that the typical interval between divorce and remarriage is only 3 years. It is therefore plausible to assume that many stepchildren might have only known their stepparent for a year or two prior to sharing a residence with him or her. Therefore, the type of family cohesion that is associated with first marriage families of longer duration may take years to develop, and in a the majority of cases, it may never fully develop. What is perhaps more perplexing is the lower adaptability in stepfamilies. Stepfamilies experience higher levels of stress than do first married families (Waldren et al.). Although extreme adaptability can actually generate stress, some degree of adaptability is necessary to effectively cope with stressors. It is exactly this adaptability that seems to be in short supply in many stepfamilies. It is also worth noting that stepfamilies want levels of cohesion and adaptability similar to those of first-marriage families (Pink & Wampler, 1985), so it is not by design that they have lower adaptability and cohesion.

The lower adaptability and cohesion of stepfamilies is clearly evident in their communication patterns. For example, newly formed stepfamilies rate their family communication more poorly than do newly formed first-marriage families (Bray & Berger, 1993). Also, stepfathers report less positive and more negative communication with family members than do fathers in nuclear families (Pink & Wampler, 1985). Grinwald (1995) asked adolescents aged 12 to 18 to report on various positive (e.g., "my mother or father is always a good listener") and negative (e.g., "my mother or father insults me when he or she is angry with me") aspects of communication with their parent and stepparent. The reports of adolescents from first-marriage families were compared with those of stepfamilies that were formed after divorce and with stepfamilies that were formed after death of a parent. The poorest parent–child communication was reported in the stepfamilies formed after divorce, followed by those formed after death, and the best parent–child communication was reported by adolescents in first marriage families. Grinwald's study points to the fact that at least some of the cohesion and communication problems experienced by stepfamilies may be a continuation of the turmoil experienced in a prior family that ended in divorce. Remarried parents also provide less social support to their children—a level of support that is equivalent to that for divorced parents but less than that for parents in first marriages (White, 1992). White's investigation suggested that the social support deficits from remarried parents can be explained by lower levels of contact with the children and lower quality relationships and solidarity with them.

Elsewhere in this selection we review research findings that show that levels of conflict are often higher in stepfamilies than in first-marriage families. This communication pattern is undoubtedly linked with issues of problematic adaptability and cohesion. One particularly interesting consequent of this higher family conflict and lower cohesion is that children in stepfamilies leave home sooner than do children in nuclear families (White, 1994b). In a very carefully controlled study, 65% of stepchildren were found to leave home before the age of 19, compared to 50% of the children in first-marriage families (Aquilino, 1991). Two compelling explanations for this effect concern weaker relationships or cohesion in stepfamilies, including failure to fully integrate adolescent children into the family system, and children being driven out by or seeking to escape family conflict (Crosbie-Burnett & McClinitic, 2000b; White, 1994b). Obviously, as children depart from stepfamilies, parent–child communication presumably drops as well.

Child Adjustment in Stepfamilies

Given what is known about the special challenges faced by stepfamilies, the nature of their relationships, and their opportunities for conflict, researchers have been understandably concerned with the social and psychological adjustment of children who live in stepfamilies. Although a thorough review of this research is beyond the scope of this selection, there are several highlights that are worth noting. First, children who live in stepfamilies tend to have slightly more externalizing behavior problems and slightly less social competence than do their counterparts in first-marriage families (Bray, 1999). Why is this the case? Obviously many children in stepfamilies undergo difficult life transitions that might include witnessing their biological parents' marriage deteriorate, experiencing the departure of one parent, perhaps living in financial hardship, moving to a new residence, and having a new adult member of the family move in to their residence (Anderson, Greene, Hetherington, & Clingempeel, 1999). These changes can sometimes all occur in a relatively short period of time.

Aside from the obvious structural and residential stressors that children in stepfamilies might have experienced, there is compelling evidence to show that their adjustment problems are also linked to family communication and relationship issues. In remarried families, parental negativity is significantly and positively correlated with child behavior problems (Anderson et al., 1999). This same research team found that adolescents in remarried families displayed more negativity toward their parent and stepparent than did adolescents in nondivorced families. Research also shows that the amount of conflict in stepfamilies is associated with child adjustment problems (Bray, 1999; Dunn, 2002).

Parents in stepfamilies tend to be less involved in the lives of their children than are parents in two-parent biological or adoptive families (Zill, 1994). This effect is especially pronounced for stepfathers (Fine, Voydanoff, & Donnelly, 1993). This is unfortunate because communication with stepfathers appears to be more vital to child adjustment outcomes than does communication with mothers in stepfather families (Collins, Newman, & McKenry, 1995). On the other hand, communication with the father was a stronger predictor of child adjustment than communication with the stepmother in stepmother families (Collins et al). The Fine et al. investigation additionally revealed that positive parental communication behaviors such as praise, hugs, reading to the child, and private talks with the child were positively associated with child adjustment in step-families, whereas negative parental communication behaviors such as spanking and yelling at the child were negatively associated with child adjustment.

Some of the difficulties that children in stepfamilies experience may be more attributable to the legacy of their original family life. A sophisticated longitudinal study that followed over 1,000 school children from age 6 to age 12 indicates that remarriage per se had no appreciable impact on children's aggressive and oppositional behavior, once the effects of parental divorce were taken into account (Pagani, Boulerice, Tremblay, & Vitaro, 1997). This study shows that many of the behavior problems that are evident in children living in stepfamilies may be a legacy of their biological parents' divorce. Contrary to what some might believe, a fairly rapid transition from the first-marriage family to the stepfamily is associated with fewer relationship problems in the new family (Montgomery, Anderson, Hetherington, & Clingempeel, 1992). Evidently, it is less disruptive to move from one two-parent household to another in rapid succession than it is to get settled into a single-parent household, only to then have to transition back into a two-parent household.

For the most part, research on child adjustment problems in stepfamilies supports the view that children in these contexts have slightly more behavior problems than do children in first-marriage families. Notwithstanding the environmental stress explanations for these effects, several theoretical explanations for these behavior problems focus on family relationship and communication problems in stepfamilies (Coleman et al., 2000). Most prominent among these are the family conflict explanation, which says that conflicts among divorced parents and within the stepfamily incite behavioral problems in children, and the deterioration of parental competencies theory, which explains child behavior problems in stepfamilies as a function of poor-quality parenting, including uninvolved parenting, minimal parental positivity, and more negatively toned communication behaviors from parents and stepparents.

CONCLUSION

When marriages end because of death or divorce, most people tend to remarry. However, remarriages have a divorce rate even higher than do first marriages. Many of the interpersonal behaviors that might have contributed to deterioration of the first marriage might work similarly in a remarriage. A natural consequent of abundant remarriage is a large number of stepfamilies. There are many negative images and views of stepfamilies in both the media and, more generally, the society. Where there are positive images of stepfamilies in the media, as in *The Brady Bunch*, they are often unrealistic and may engender expectations for relational harmony that simply cannot be met. People in stepfamilies often start out with great expectations, but the sometimes difficult realities of living in a stepfamily quickly become evident and create distance between stepparents and stepchildren. Family scholars have found that not all stepfamilies develop their relationships in the same way. Some develop rapidly, some slowly, and some never really develop a sense of "family." As stepfamilies develop, they often face disagreements about the role of stepparents in the family. Mothers in stepfather families often assume a variety of roles to regulate and referee the relationship between their children and their spouse. Research consistently shows that there are a wide variety of different stepfamily types and forms. However, most stepfamilies face communication challenges such as feeling caught, negotiating ambiguous parental roles, regulating boundaries, and vying for resources. Research findings also indicate that many stepfamilies have to contend with greater conflict, lower adaptability, lower cohesion, and more issues of boundary regulation than do nuclear families. Finally, children in stepfamilies exhibit more behavior problems than do children in nuclear families, and these are associated to some extent with the quality of the stepfamily relationships and communication.

Part V

EFFECTS OF INFIDELITY
AND ABUSE

13. Affairs and Children

By Jean Duncombe & Dennis Marsden

Concern over rising levels of marital breakdown has prompted a growth in research on divorce which has recently come to focus on the possibly damaging impact of divorce on children. Yet although affairs may also disrupt marriage and family life, the possible involvement of children in parental affairs is rarely discussed, still less researched. This gap in research reflects the wider neglect of affairs as a research topic, but also the general lack of research on children's own views about experiences that may deeply affect their lives. In this [article], although we introduce some evidence of the consequences of children's involvement in their parents' affairs, our main purpose is to draw attention to the need for further research in this area.

We begin by discussing why parents fail to consider children in relation to their affairs, and we present evidence that children may become involved in parental affairs to a greater extent than adults realize, We explore the extent to which research on the impact of divorce has tended to mask how the roots of continuing family disharmony may frequently lie in the influence of a parental affair. Finally, we describe from some of our own research how children's symptoms of distress from an affair may persist—or may only emerge—after they reach adulthood. Indeed children who are adults when one of their parents has an affair, or adults who learn of earlier parental affairs, may continue to suffer deeply.

The Need to "Hear the Voice of the Child"

We should stress that our purpose is not to focus narrowly on potential damage from affairs. Some have argued that not all affairs are necessarily damaging to children, and indeed others would claim that family disruption and transition may present children as well as adults with challenges and opportunities to grow and develop greater sensitivity and resilience (Duncombe & Marsden, 2003; Neale & Wade, 2000; Wallerstein & Blakeslee, 1989).1 Here we want to question the common assumption by many parents and researchers that what goes on between adults is not the business of children, who need to be protected from involvement because they are too immature or "innocent" to understand or too young to distinguish facts from lies and fantasy.[2] Instead of questioning children themselves about the impact of their parents' behavior, all too often researchers have explored children's feelings via their parents, prompting optimistic or pessimistic answers which reflect the parents' hopes and feelings about the outcomes of their actions rather than the reality of their children's experiences and lives (Brannen & O'Brien, 1996). This kind of research and writing about children has tended to render them socially invisible and to rob them of their agency in social interactions with adults.

It is only since the 1980s that sociologists have proposed the development of a new "Sociology of Childhood" (Jenks, 1982) that—with later backing from the United Nations Convention on the Rights of the Child, and in Britain the Children Act of 1989—has encouraged professionals and researchers to take into account how children describe their experiences (Alanen, 1988; Brannen & O'Brien, 1996; James & Prout, 1990). Subsequent research has revealed that children know much more about the "private sphere" of family life than adults appreciate and that they actively participate in ways that may shape their parents' behavior (Kitzinger, 1990).[3] This [article] is therefore an attempt to underline how—as in other areas of life involving children—in the area of parental affairs researchers should make the attempt to hear "the voice of the child."

The Failure to Consider the Impact of Affairs on Children

Recent much-cited theories concerning trends in adult and family relations fail to consider the possibility that children may become actively involved in affairs, still less that they may be adversely affected. For example, one theory argued that the growing insecurity of adult relationships will lead adults to invest more emotionally in their children (Beck & Beck-Gernsheim, 1995). Yet, as Smart and Neale (1999, pp. 17–18) pointed out: "the authors do not distinguish between the perception of a child as a provider of permanent unconditional love and the actuality of parent-child relationships." These authors also point out that Giddens's (1991, 1992) well-known discussion of:

> the pure relationship, where one can end a commitment once the relationship has ceased to be satisfactory, ignores the impact of having children. … Children, at least young children, are depicted somewhat as objects or burdens or a source of strain. Unlike the couple, they are not seen as having agency and thus are not seen as raising a voice at the point at which the adults decide to abandon their pure relationship. (Smart & Neale, 1999, pp. 12–13)

These major theorists of changing adult relationships show little understanding of how the disruption of parents' relationships—whether through divorce or an affair—may affect children's lives and relationships.

Most books or articles on affairs mention children only in passing or indirectly as a minor influence or constraint on parents' behavior. For example, Lawson (1988) introduced her large book on affairs by describing how she was worried not only by a female friend's affair but also by the risk it posed to the security of no fewer than nine children (equally divided between her friend, her friend's lover, and her friend's husband's lover). However, Lawson reveals nothing further about these children apart from the fact that one boy was missing his father because he was ostensibly "working away" too much. Elsewhere Lawson commented on how her interviewees rarely mentioned their children in connection with affairs, so that she had to introduce the topic. But even then, "There were rarely anxieties about the possible difficulties that children might experience simply because one of their parents was involved in a relationship with someone outside the family circle" (Lawson, 1988, p. 136). Men, in particular, tended to compartmentalize their views by saying, "It has nothing to do with my children, this is my private life outside, away from home" (Lawson, 1988, p. 138). Only about a quarter of the parents in Lawson's sample of parents said their decisions about starting the affair had been inhibited by the possibility of hurting their children should something "go wrong." Rather fewer (more women than men) said that such worries had influenced them in continuing with their affair once it had started, with 16% of mothers mentioning possible financial insecurity and emotional loss for their children and only 7% of fathers mentioning possible loss of their children.

In their discussion of a variety of case studies of affairs, Reibstein and Richards (1992) agreed that women are more likely than men to worry about the impact of affairs on children, but they suggest that the degree of concern that individuals show for their children is influenced by *family scripts* based on their own earlier experiences of their parents' behavior: "a powerful script around affairs or monogamy from one's past will influence one's sexual and marital boundaries" (Reibstein & Richards, 1992, p. 139). For example, remembering how she felt her mother's pain when her affair went wrong and her father's anguish at their subsequent marital breakdown and divorce, one woman said: "I would never do to my children what my mother did to my father" (Reibstein & Richards, 1992, p. 137). In contrast, another woman felt she could have affairs because the lives of her "bohemian" parents had demonstrated that affairs need do no damage. However adult behavior cannot be predicted entirely from childhood experience because some individuals resist family scripts and others may rewrite them to justify their own affairs.

The Impact of Affairs and Family Disruption on Children

The adverse reactions suffered by children as a result of parental affairs will, of course, depend partly on how badly family life is disrupted, but in general, children's reactions appear similar to those described in relation to disruptions from divorce (Duncombe & Marsden, 2003; Reibstein & Richards, 1992; Wallerstein & Kelly, 1990; although see also Neale & Wade, 2000). In particular, children's reactions vary with their age. For example, preschool children need more time and attention, so when they are neglected during parental crises they tend to feel bewildered and fear they are to blame and their parents no longer love them. Older and adolescent children are likely to learn more about the affair and to be drawn into parental arguments, perhaps as confidants. They tend to become angry and to suffer conflicts of loyalty, forming alliances with one parent against the other whom they blame for the conflict. Adolescents are probably more attuned to sexual undercurrents in adult relationships, and they are said to experience additional problems when faced with evidence of their parents' (previously invisible) sexuality and vulnerability just when they are having to cope with their own emergent sexuality. To adolescents, their parents' behavior seems to violate the generation gap, and to shake their belief in the possibility of stable partnerships so that they may respond with anger, depression, and withdrawal.

Reibstein and Richards (1992) provided one of the few empirically based discussions of the impact of affairs on children. They suggest that despite parents' attempts at secrecy, children may still learn about affairs indirectly, when their parents become preoccupied or depressed. Children may also pick up on—and react against—more subtle behavioral clues that there is a rival for a parent's affections "by witnessing some striking show of emotion or by the affair partner taking up too much of the parent's time, or performing the other parent's function" (Reibstein & Richards, 1992, p. 177). For example, a teenage boy had previously liked one of his mother's work colleagues, but when he detected from their expressions of intimacy that they had begun an affair, he showed his displeasure by behaving coolly toward them both (Reibstein & Richards, 1992, p. 178). A more striking instance was surprisingly mirrored in our own research. A woman had a daughter from an affair that ended when her husband agreed to adopt the child, but the daughter was never told the identity of her biological father. When the marriage broke down the mother resumed a more open relationship with her former lover, the daughter's biological father, but whenever he came near his daughter she moved away, sensing their relationship was a betrayal of the person whom she believed was her "real" father.

Sometimes children may discover an affair for themselves but in other instances a parent may reveal the existence of the affair to them. Where one parent confides the secret of an affair, the child (particularly an adolescent) may feel cross-pressured. For example, after Karen's father confided to her he was having an affair with his secretary, the parents' marriage deteriorated and Karen cut herself off from both parents and began to do badly in school. After her father told her his mistress had had a baby, "Karen left home, angry at her father, and also at her mother for not standing up to him" (Reibstein & Richards, 1992, p. 179). The impact of children's reaction on their parents was revealed in one of our own interviews, where a mother was afraid to tell her daughter about her husband's affair in case the daughter despised her for taking him back—as had happened to one of the mother's friends.

A final example from Reibstein and Richards's study reveals the power of the parent who remains resident, particularly the power of the mother who occupies a key role in interpreting the father's behavior to the children (Furstenberg & Cherlin, 1991). A father, who had previously been warm and affectionate with his teenage daughters, briefly left home for another woman. The mother, who had previously behaved coldly toward her daughters, now turned to them for comfort, presenting herself as blameless while denigrating their father. Although the father returned soon after he had left, even 30 years later the daughters still viewed him with contempt (Reibstein & Richards, 1992, p. 179).

This evidence describes how children may become aware of their parents affairs, and also how they may express disapproval in order to exert pressure on their parents. Yet it must be noted that evidence on the impact of affairs is limited, because research on family disruption has mostly concentrated on what have been seen as the outcomes of divorce. In the next section, we briefly "reread" the divorce literature to explore how far what have previously been regarded as the impacts of divorce may be traced back to the initial and ongoing impacts of affairs.

"Re-Reading" Divorce Research, Looking for the Influence of Affairs on Family Relationships and Children

Our proposal to "re-read" the research on the supposed impacts of divorce is in line with the ongoing reassessments of the divorce literature, which have already taken place over a number of years. Divorce is now viewed as only part of a potentially lengthy process of family disharmony, transition, and reordering, which may begin long before the actual divorce and continue well beyond it (Burghes, 1995). A major result of this reassessment has been to shift attention away from the "event" of divorce, and onto the question of what kind of family processes may have an adverse impact on children's lives, Unfortunately, however, the possible links between affairs, divorce and adverse impacts—or other effects—on children's lives have been little explored.

The relation between affairs and divorce is complex for a number of reasons. We have already noted the claims that not all affairs have damaging consequences for marital or family happiness, so affairs do not necessarily lead to divorce. Also, of course, there are other grounds for divorce apart from an affair, but in practice the legal grounds cited for divorce are unreliable indicators of the influence of affairs. For example, an affair may be a symptom or outcome of the marital unhappiness that leads to marital breakdown and divorce rather than the cause. In Britain, until recently the citing of an affair as legal grounds for divorce was often a convenient legal fiction to end a dead marriage or evidence that the innocent partner wished to publicly shame the adulterer. In the interests of reducing family conflict and promoting conciliation, Britain is now trying to move toward "no fault" divorce on general grounds of marital breakdown. However, a number of writers have commented that these legal moves run counter to common cultural understandings and emotions, where an affair still tends to be seen as betrayal and infidelity by a "guilty" spouse who consequently deserves to be blamed for the breakdown of the marriage (Simpson, 1998; Smart, 1999). We return to this point next, but it is clear that the divorce literature does not provide us with reliable evidence of how frequently affairs may be implicated in divorce—and hence, possibly in children's lives.

More indirect evidence comes from longitudinal and other types of studies, which have found relatively recently that a substantial proportion of children living in intact but conflictual families show adverse symptoms very similar to those formerly attributed to divorce (Amato & Booth, 1997; Burghes, 1995; Cherlin et al, 1991; Cockett & Tripp, 1994; Elliott & Richards, 1991). But if children are damaged primarily by parental conflict rather than divorce per se, we still need to ask what are the major sources of parental conflict. Specifically, how far is parental conflict before the divorce attributable to the discovery of an affair, sometimes leading to ongoing parental disharmony which may continue to be damaging for children after the divorce? Again, more research is needed to find out the extent of this phenomenon, but we do know that post-divorce relationships between ex-spouses are often still marred by recriminations over who is to blame, especially where one partner has had an affair (Arendell, 1994; Furstenberg & Cherlin, 1991; Simpson, 1998; Smart, 1999; Wallerstein & Kelly, 1990).

The divorce literature provides further, albeit indirect, evidence of the impact of affairs on children. Most divorced fathers quickly start "new" relationships (Smart, 1999; Wallerstein & Kelly, 1990) with a speed that suggests these may often be the continuation of affairs previously concealed from their wives, and fathers tend to develop quite different, more distant relationships with their children after divorce (Wallerstein & Kelly, 1990), with around half losing contact with their children within two years (Bradshaw et al., 1999). This may be because, after divorce, mothers are no longer prepared to perform their role of emotional mediation between their children and the children's fathers (Furstenberg & Cherlin, 1991; Smart, 1999). But we would also suggest that the deterioration in a father's relationship with his children may be exacerbated where his new partner is the person with whom he had the affair that the children perceive is responsible for the marital breakdown. Also, whereas the father's new partner may lack the inclination or skills to take over his ex-wife's role of mediation, any attempts she may make to substitute the mother's role are much more difficult where the children guess or feel they know that her affair with their father was instrumental in the breakdown of their parents' marriage. The problems of some children in stepfamilies may also be partly attributable to children's difficulties in relating to stepmothers who were formerly their fathers' mistresses.

It remains unclear how far the findings from the divorce literature may actually be attributable to the impact of affairs and, as we just suggested, the influence of affairs may also be hidden in some of the findings on conflict in stepfamilies (Cockett & Tripp, 1994; Kiernan, 1992). However we would tentatively suggest that even where affairs are not necessarily the primary cause of the marital disharmony that ends in divorce, they may often become the focus of conflict, and acrimonious arguments about affairs may color the breakdown of the marriage and sour subsequent relationships over lengthy periods of time or for life. Indeed, there is a trend for discussions of the research on divorce to extend the period over which the children of divorced parents are said to suffer the consequences of family disruption. For example, Wallerstein's 10-year follow-up study expresses concern at the failure of some individuals to "move on" psychologically, particularly some girls who seem to get angrier with the passage of time (Wallerstein et al., 1988, p. 198): "The danger in every crisis is that people will remain in the same place, continuing through the years to react to the initial impact as if it had just struck."

Clearly, there is a need for more research in this area. In the remainder of this [article] we will introduce some evidence from our own small study[4] of the way that some young adults were still struggling, years later to come to terms with their conflicting feelings about the affairs that lay at the heart of their parents' divorce (Duncombe & Marsden, 2003).

The Persistent Effects of Parental Affairs on Some Older Children

The common theme that emerged from our interviews was that these young adults tended to perceive themselves as searching for "the truth" about their parents' divorce which, however, they felt their parents were unwilling to give. To these "children" it was almost as though the parents were trying to keep their "secrets" through evasions, refusing to talk, or telling "lies."

In perhaps the most striking instance of how a long-standing affair had damaged the daughter's family relations, Gail, a friend of one of Holly's parents had taken it on herself to tell Holly what she thought she should know. Interestingly, even as Holly was recounting the story, she seemed to gain new insights:

> I was round at a friend's house, they're family friends, and suddenly they said, "Don't you mind about that woman?" I didn't know what they were on about. They said my Dad had been having an affair with her for years—since I was a baby, in fact! I can't believe it! I'd met her round his, but *he's* always told me he met her later. ... Looking back I can see all sorts of things. Stupid really. I wonder if Mum knew. ... Looking back she was always round our house, she was Mum's best friend, in fact. ... Now I come to think about it, it was only a couple of days after they'd split. ... I went round to see if Dad was all right ... and she was there then! Looking back, I suppose *that was* funny. Makes me question what it's all about ... makes me want to say to my Dad, "Is *this* why you split, was it really *your* fault?" Mum says I shouldn't blame Dad, but other times she says it *is* his fault. Tell you the truth, I'm a bit fed up with Mum for putting up with it, if she knew ... and not telling me. I don't see Dad anymore now. ... Mum thinks I'm wrong, I should still see him—she says I'll regret it—but I just don't wanna know. I'll always love him ... and actually I don't even mind the girlfriend. It's 'cos of all the lies ... yes, the lies. (Holly, 18)[5]

It is characteristic of these narratives that although these children had tried at various points to talk to one or both parents about the causes of divorce, including affairs, their questioning had not necessarily produced a more coherent story. Contrary to the recommendations in the literature on counseling and conciliation, parents tend to "behave badly" in justifying their own position and undermining their ex-partners by blaming them for having affairs.

> It's very hard. Some days my Mum says Dad's a bastard, and then she says everything—that's usually when she hasn't got the money [maintenance]—then she says, "He doesn't love us, he's had affairs, he drinks, he lies, he's a bully" and all that stuff. Some days I hate him. But then some days, she says to me? "He's a good man, a kind man. ... He really loves you." Sometimes she even says all the things in the *same* day, and I don't know what to think. (Rachel, 19)

Where parents had refused to give much information and seemed evasive, some young people had come across clues during casual explorations of their parents' homes. Others had developed such an intense desire to find out "the truth" of their parents' divorce that their search became deliberate, and any discoveries only seemed to heighten rather than satisfy their curiosity—particularly where they found something incriminating against the person they thought was to blame for the divorce. Among such clues, it seemed that the most damning proof of blame was evidence of an affair—evidence that could sometimes be all too graphic.

> When I was fourteen, I was searching around, you know how kids do, not bad or anything, and I found these photos—I can't hardly bear to speak about it even now—I found these photos of my Dad and "her" doing ... you know what ... and there was a date on the back and I couldn't *believe* it 'cos it's when I was only little! My Dad wouldn't usually talk, but once when he was angry he said they split 'cos Mum had an affair and he couldn't forgive her. But I looked at these ... I feel *sick to* think about it (Simon, 19)

> I was a really nosy teenager, I was always looking in drawers and things since I was small ... secret presents ... condoms ... but, well ... since they're not living together—I know it's awful ... I wouldn't tell anybody ... but I still look ... and only recently I found these letters—*old* letters—written when I was small ... written by my Dad to ... "the bitch" [laughs bitterly] that's what I call her, that's what I've always called her. He lives with her now, "the bitch." ... (Kerry, 23)

In instances like this, a daughter's hostility against the woman with whom her father had had an affair and who was now openly his girlfriend, was sometimes heightened by the father's behavior in always insisting on bringing his girlfriend when he met his daughter:

> He's always so preoccupied with his new life, he's got no time for me. He only sees me now when he wants a baby-sitter. I don't tell him but I can't bear it ... her, you know ... and him. ... (Claire, 19)

Unfortunately for young people's peace of mind, the different stories gained at various times from their parents and others—along with the information they discovered for themselves along the way—did not necessarily add up to what they felt was a complete explanation of their parents' divorce.

They might reach an explanation that seemed for a time to suffice. But then new knowledge reawakened old questions and provoked new ones, and the story might once again become contradictory and confusing, particularly when the parents exchanged accusations about which of them had had an affair, and when:

I always thought I knew the truth. Mum goes, Dad didn't talk to her, he drinks too much, and she was lonely … and 'cos Dad didn't talk to me much either, well, I could understand how she got fed up and they split up. So I've always been on her side. … I love my Dad. But just last year I found out *she* had an affair. … I just can't believe it … the lies. (Barbara, 21)

When I was sixteen I went to live with Dad … and I, sort of, thought … nice to hear his side, sort of thing. When I was little I tried to talk to my Dad … ask him why, sort of thing … he said, "It's none of your business. That's between me and your mother." … But when I was sixteen, I sort of needed to know … needed to know … *his* side, do you know what I mean … to know why …

I asked him again … he just shouted at me: "None of your business!" So I ask his girl-friend (she lives with him, you know) … I suppose she's a sort of a step-Mum—God, I hope not!—anyway I asked her why did Mum and Dad split up. She said, "I suppose you're old enough to know" and she told me it really was Dad that left, not Mum that left, 'cos Mum was having an affair. But when I went back to Mum, she said, "Dad's a liar, he *would* say that—that's because *he* was having an affair" and she told me that he was jealous. He thought she *was* having an affair but she wasn't. I don't know who to believe. I love my Mum *and* my Dad, and my Nan says to me, "It doesn't really matter now, it's all a long time ago "But I need to know. … (Simon, 19)

I find it's hard … I don't know the truth. … At the time, Mum left home she'd been having an affair—horrible bloke, *years* younger than her—but later Mum said that she couldn't stand Dad's drinking … he was always out the pub, that's why she left. He *did* drink a lot, when I think about it. … And now Dad says—when he's feeling "understanding"!—she probably married too young, they'd both grown apart. But the really peculiar thing … sometimes they seem to change and kind of regret getting divorced—well, Mum said to me once. … We'd sometimes be round Mum's for Christmas and Dad used to pop in, it was just like old times—well, I don't know if the boys liked it so much—and we thought—well, I hoped—perhaps they might … you know … be getting together again. But then later, they'd be quarrelling … things could get quite nasty. Then Dad says, "She always was a self-centred bitch. *She* had the affair, I didn't." … Then one day Mum even said he'd had affairs. It would go on like that, years and years. We *hated* it—I used to get really upset, I'd say, "For God's sake, act your age!" My brother says, it's *all* a pack of lies on both sides, and he shuts off from it, he doesn't wanna know. But I do How can I ever get married and make it work … or any sort of relationship really … if I can't understand what's happened. Sometimes I think their divorce has ruined my life. (Isobel, 21)

At times some siblings had fallen out quite badly over different versions of the divorce—which parent had had affairs and who was more to blame—and it may be a characteristically male response to try to cut off from any further discussion.

As some of the previous comments have indicated, a common outcome of parents' mutually contradictory stories could be a loss of trust in one or both of them, and often also a loss of respect:

> I want to love my Mum *and* my Dad, but I'm finding it really difficult. I just don't trust them any more. I can't trust them to tell the truth. (Simon, 19)

> I don't *trust my* Dad. He's a pathological liar, he just can't help it. As the years go by, I've come to think he doesn't know he's lying, he's come to believe his own lies. ... Like he says to me, "I didn't meet her until after me and your mother split," but I *know now* that's not true. But when I say to him, "I *know* Dad" he just won't have it, he goes mad! ... I used to respect him, but how can you respect someone who *lies* all the time I just want him to tell me the truth ... say he's sorry ... for how much he's hurt us. ... *Mum* tells me the truth, but he won't. He's a coward, and I don't respect him for that. He's too scared to tell me the truth. (Kerry, 23)

> How I see it now. ... I've got a mother, but I haven't got a father. There's a man involved in my birth, and he lives with that cow, but he's not my Dad. (Holly, 19)

Sadly, some young people's difficulties in "moving on" seemed integrally bound up with the concepts of "fault" and "blame" over affairs. As we just noted, in its attempt to alter cultural understanding and practice, the British law is in effect denying the continuing relevance of these concepts to many people's experience and perceptions of marital breakdown. Even if the parents had themselves "moved on" and come to some kind of truce or understanding that they would no longer argue over who had had affairs and who broke up the marriage, children sometimes still found this truce unsatisfactory. Before they could move on they wanted a clear and open acknowledgement of whose "fault" it was that they had been put through so much pain and insecurity.

> Mum's married now, and Dad's married, and Mum even seems like she's quite friends with Dad now, but I can't stand it! I can't bear it that they still do things together. After all it's *his* fault, and *her* fault, "the bitch "How can Mum forgive them, 'cos I can't forgive them 'cos those two have ruined my life. (Kerry, 23)

One son said he would no longer mind if his parents could arrive at a "true" story of which parent had an affair first, or whether they had both had an affair—in fact who was "to blame." What he wanted was to resolve the conflict between their stories about affairs, to provide one consistent story. But unfortunately (by his account) his parents—although prepared to behave amicably in public—would still not agree to share the blame equally:

> How I'd like it to be is *nobody's fault,* ideally that is, but my brother says, it's no good thinking that, because it is *somebody's* fault and we need to know whose fault it is, and I agree with that. But I can't stand all the rows, that's like it is now. Mum says it's Dad's fault. Dad says it's her fault, and don't care. I'd like them to be friends, and I really like it when they do things together, like they came to my school play, and my step-mum, she's all right. What I'd like is if they could both have ... a kind of shared story ... one that didn't blame anybody. but when I said that to my Mum ... what I'd like, she said, "That's not fair" 'cos she said, "He left us, I didn't ask him to go. Why should I take half the blame just to make *you* feel better" Mum said to me that Dad going off [leaving], *that's* the truth and I've got to learn to live with it (Simon, 19)

In this section, we presented evidence from our own research to show that the impacts of family disharmony may continue beyond formal "childhood" into the lives of young adults. Of course, we are not claiming that the distress and damage to relationships that may accompany divorce is entirely attributable to affairs. However, we draw attention to the role affairs may play in the family disruption and arguments that may lead to ongoing disturbance in children's lives.

Afterword: Living With Affairs

Our last quote posed the question of whether and how parents and children can learn to live with affairs in a more mature and potentially less damaging manner. Unsurprisingly, in view of what we have discussed about the failure to take account of children, there is a lack of literature dealing with how a parent who has had an affair may protect their children from any possible consequences. Significantly, Cole (a marriage counselor) recommends a number of steps very similar to those intended to minimize the impact of divorce (Duncombe & Marsden, 2003). For example, she suggests parents must talk honestly to one another and—both together—tell all their children at the same time about the affair, reassuring them that they are still loved. Parents should take care not to put down one another or "go into detail [that the children] don't need and won't understand." Cole acknowledges that owning up to your children that you have had an affair may be:

> One of the most difficult tasks you ever have to undertake … you will be admitting to something that most children find hard to accept about a parent. This is because children want to see their parents as caring people who would not willingly deceive another But … it is much better that they hear it from you than from a friend in the playground. (Cole, 1999, pp. 204–205)

The parents' aims should be to avoid burdening any child with secrecy, using a child as a go-between, or risking the possibility of a child forming an alliance with one parent against the other.

Unfortunately, however, in relation to these guidelines many parents appear to "behave badly." So the question arises whether they lack sensible advice or whether advice such as that provided by Cole is somewhat naïve, because there are deeper obstacles to parents meeting their children's demands to talk openly with them about "the truth" of their affairs. In fact, there are a number of reasons why parents would find it difficult to follow even the best advice from counseling (Duncombe & Marsden, 2003). Some parents may give distorted accounts because their children are still—in what may seem an unsophisticated way—searching for something *or* someone to blame. One or both of the parents may have undertaken considerable "repair work" on their relationship with their ex-spouse precisely with a view to covering over any elements of fault and blame, so they will not want their efforts to be undermined by their children's questioning. Also, even as their children grow older, there are some embarrassing "truths" or versions of events, particularly concerning sexual compatibility and affairs, that parents would rather conceal. Mothers may remain silent to avoid losing their "reputation" and "respectability"—indeed their aura of "maternal sanctity"—in the eyes of their children, who they know will not be immune from sexual double standards about affairs. As we saw earlier, fathers are prone to view their sexual behavior as "their own business"—although their relationship with a new partner (who may earlier have been their "mistress") may often drastically change their behavior toward their children in ways the children find puzzling and hurtful.

This [article] has primarily been a plea for research in a neglected area, but not only to hear "the voice of the child." The impacts of affairs on children extend so far that we also need to consider the voice of the "adult child" (as our colleague, Harrison, has described). There is a view that because they too are "grown ups," parental affairs do not matter. But the hurt of even these "adult children" reveals that the pain from a parental affair is not necessarily related to age. In looking at affairs, we are dealing with the disruption of the deep structures of family life, where the physical or psychic incursion into the family of an "alien lover" represents the "betrayal" of one parent by the other, and children of whatever age come up against some of the deeper family secrets that parents feel impelled to keep from them.

Endnotes

1. In many marriages there are affairs which appear to be condoned and even normalized so that they do not necessarily lead to marital disharmony and divorce This is evidenced in the marriages of some current politicians, and also in historical accounts of the Bloomsbury group and the early years of Soviet Russia, where private or state child care was thought to ensure that children did not suffer from the parental practice of free love. However, we may question the reliability of such accounts which mainly involve special pleading by adults!

2. Significantly, most respondents in our own research on affairs tended to deny their children might know about or be affected by their affairs, and among colleagues and friends the topic of this paper on "children and affairs" aroused surprise and even distaste.

3. For example, children involved in abuse and domestic violence have been grateful for the opportunity to talk about their experiences and to come to terms with their pain (Saunders, 1995). Recent research on divorce has also highlighted how children actively involved in marital breakdown may feel bitter about the way they tend to be marginalized (Duncombe & Marsden, 2003).

4. These case studies come from two focus groups and further follow-up discussions with groups of college students, plus follow up studies from a pilot project on divorce and step families.

5. Reibstein and Richards (1992, p. 180) described a similar situation but in relation to a much older "child." A man was upset when his mother left his father after 42 years of marriage, partly because she was "fed up with his other women." He suddenly felt deceived and angry when he recognized that the various women with whom his parents had made intensive friendships over a number of years were actually his father's girlfriends and that his mother had known. Subsequently, he fell out with his unmarried sister because she was sorry for his grief-stricken father and supported him. In a more dramatic case, Lake and Hills (1979, p. 16) cited a newspaper article in the *Guardian* newspaper about a 48-year-old man who murdered his mother after he heard that she had had an affair, because he had led a terrible childhood through his mother's constant criticisms of his father over a wartime affair. The persistence of the acrimony from affairs is illustrated by another instance from Lake and Hills (1979, p. 71). When his father left his mother to live with his mistress, the son decided to remain loyal to his mother and to disown his father. However, when the son grew up he married and had a child and his wife persuaded him to try to make it up with his father who was still with the mistress. When his mother discovered he had taken his wife and child to see his father, she saw this as a terrible breach of faith and cut him out of her life, refusing to ever see him or her grandson again.

14. Violence and Abuse in Families

By Kristin Anderson, Debra Umberson, & Simikka Elliott

For many women, men, and children around the world, the greatest risk of violent victimization occurs in the context of family relationships. A recent national survey conducted in the United States found that 25% of women and 8% of men reported that they were physically or sexually assaulted by a spouse, partner, or date in their lifetime (Tjaden & Thoennes, 1998). An estimated 9% to 30% of assaults between adult partners in the United States are witnessed by resident children (Edleson, 1999). Over 10% of U.S. children experience severe violence at the hands of their parents in a given year (Straus & Gelles, 1992). Available evidence suggests that an even larger number of children suffer from neglect than from physical abuse. Of the maltreated children who came to the attention of U.S. social service agencies in 1999, fifty-eight percent suffered neglect, 21% were physically abused, and 11% were sexually abused (U.S. Department of Health and Human Services, 2001). Family violence is a global problem; population-based surveys conducted in over 40 nations find that 10% to 50% of women report being the victim of an assault by an intimate male partner at some point in their lives (Heise, Ellsberg, & Gottemoeller, 1999).

The study of violence within families is a multidisciplinary enterprise. Sociologists study the ways in which the historical legitimacy of family violence, cultural notions of privacy, and inequalities of gender, age, race/ethnicity, and class facilitate high rates of violence within families (Straus & Gelles, 1992). Psychologists examine personality traits associated with violence perpetration and victimization (O'Leary, 1993). The central contribution of communication studies to this field is an emphasis on violence as a practice that is embedded within family interaction (Lloyd, 1999). Previous studies suggest that interpersonal communication processes are more powerful predictors of family violence than are individual or sociodemographic characteristics (Cahn, 1996).

Violence is a form of interactive communication. It is motivated by a desire to communicate a message—often a demand for compliance—to the victim. A large research literature describes how parents and intimate partners use violence to gain control over a family member (Dobash & Dobash, 1998; Kirkwood, 1993; Straus & Gelles, 1992). Although researchers have begun to make important distinctions among various patterns of spousal violence (Johnson, 1995, 2001), men's violence against their wives or partners is often linked to a general pattern of controlling behavior, including monitoring partners' activities and regulating their friendships (Dobash & Dobash, 1998; Kirkwood, 1993). Abusive parents often have rigid expectations for their children's behavior that they attempt to enforce through punishment (Anderson & Umberson, 1999). Violence can also be motivated by fear, shame, or a desire for revenge or recognition (Gilligan, 1996). As a communicative tool, violence serves both instrumental and expressive purposes. The perpetrator may desire to achieve control over the person or situation and/ or to express his or her anger or frustration (Umberson, Williams, & Anderson, 2002).

The use and legitimacy of family violence varies by status position within the family. In patriarchal societies, men's violence against wives and children is legitimized by custom and law (Dobash & Dobash, 1998; Heise et al., 1999; Pleck, 1987). Legal and political challenges to violence against wives and children began in the United States and Britain during the 19th century (Pleck, 1987). A global movement against family violence was in place by end of the 20th century (Heise et al., 1999). However, the hidden nature of family violence hinders intervention efforts. Most of the violence in families is unrecognized by those who come into contact with its victims.

Women and children suffer the most detrimental consequences of family violence. The physical punishment of children by their parents is considered a legitimate disciplinary tool within many nations, including the United States. Because children lack power within and outside of the family system, they are particularly vulnerable as targets of physical and sexual abuse (Gilgun, 1995). Girls are approximately three times more likely to be sexually abused than are boys (Sedlack, 1991). Although women and men report similar rates of violence against spouses or partners, women are much more likely to suffer injury and depression as a result of violence than are men (Tjaden & Thoennes, 1998). A context of gender inequality places women at a disadvantage within relationships marked by violence. When family interactions result in conflict and violence, men have an advantage due to their larger average physical size, their (increasingly contested) cultural authority as "head" of the family, and their control over economic resources (Anderson & Umberson, 2001).

This [article] considers how family interaction and communication patterns may be associated with family violence. Taken together, previous studies suggest that family interaction patterns are associated with violence in a bidirectional fashion. Particular interactive patterns may facilitate violence within families, but violence also *undermines* family communication and interaction. We first review the research on family interaction patterns that are associated with increased risk of family violence. Next, we examine the negative consequences of violence for family communication and interaction. Although family violence consists of spouse, partner, child, elder, parental, and sibling abuse, we emphasize the research on spousal/partner abuse and child maltreatment in this review, because the majority of published research studies focus on these forms of family violence.

COMMUNICATION PATTERNS AND THE RISK OF FAMILY VIOLENCE

Communication Skills

Violence within families has been associated with deficits in family members' communication skills. A number of studies find that partners in violent marriages or dating relationships lack problem-solving and positive negotiation skills (Bird, Stith, & Schladale, 1991; Sabourin, Infante, & Rudd, 1993). In a comparative study of conversations between 10 couples with a history of violence and 10 nonviolent couples, Sabourin and Stamp (1995) found several differences in communication styles. In contrast to nonviolent couples, the violent couples were more likely to use vague language, to be oppositional and interfering, and to express complaints and despair. Other studies find that spouses in abusive relationships are less argumentative, more verbally aggressive, and less likely to use mutual problem solving than are nonviolent couples (Feldman & Ridley, 2000; Infante, Chandler, & Rudd, 1989). Violence within relationships has also been associated with aversive–defensive communication patterns such as blaming, interrupting, invalidating, and withdrawing (Murphy & O'Farrell, 1997). Partners who use aversive or defensive forms of communication or who lack problem-solving skills may be at higher risk for violence because they lack the skills to communicate their needs clearly or to deescalate family conflict.

Less research has focused on positive communication patterns and family violence. Results from existing studies are mixed; some suggest that violent and nonviolent couples do not differ on positive forms of communication such as complimenting, apologizing, or displays of verbal or nonverbal affection (Lloyd, 1996; Murphy & O'Farrell, 1997). Other researchers find that violent couples report lower levels of caring behavior and positive interaction in everyday life than do nonviolent couples (Langhinrichsen-Rohling, Smultzer, & Vivian, 1994).

Abusive parents exhibit deficits in communication skills. Christopoulos, Bonvillian, and Crittenden (1988) compared the language inputs of mothers to their infants among a sample of abusive, neglectful, and adequate mothers. Adequate mothers spoke to their children more often and used more positive and accepting phrases than did the neglectful group, but the speech patterns of abusive mothers did not differ from those of adequate mothers. Neglectful parents are less verbally expressive and empathetic than parents who are not neglectful (Cowen, 1999). Prospective longitudinal studies find that physically abusive parents exhibit poor impulse control and antisocial behavior (Pianta, Egeland, & Erickson, 1989).

Lacking communication skills that would enable them to calm hurt feelings or create a compromise, spouses and parents may find that their conflicts with partners or children escalate in frequency and severity. However, because violence emerges in an interactive context, deficient communication skills are only part of the communication problem. Communication skills deficits may increase violence in those with a propensity, but deficits alone cannot account for differences between violent and nonviolent relationships (Babcock, Waltz, Jacobsen, & Gottman, 1993). Family members' interpretations of communication acts and their emotional responses to these interpretations are crucial components of the relationship between communication skills deficits and family violence.

Interpretive Processes

Communicative acts do not have a fixed meaning; they must be interpreted by others. For example, partners' critical words may be interpreted either as a signal of distress or as an attack. The interpretation determines the response; an interpretation of distress may lead to a comforting response, whereas an interpretation of attack may lead to a counterattack and an escalation of conflict (Blumer, 1969). The existing research evidence suggests that violent and nonviolent couples interpret their partners' words and actions differently. In a study of men's responses to written and videotaped scenarios of relationship conflict, domestically violent men responded with hostility and anger to scenarios in which wives displayed anger and emotional distress (Holtzworth-Munroe & Smultzer, 1996). In addition to displaying hostile reactions to hypothetical scenarios, violent men are more likely to attribute hostile intent to their female partner's actions (Dugan, Umberson, & Anderson, 2001; Holtzworth-Munroe & Hutchinson, 1993). Similar interpretative processes affect the relationships between parents and children in families harmed by spouse abuse. Holden and Ritchie (1991) examined mothers' reports of domestic violence and parenting practices. They found that men who perpetrated domestic assaults against their wives were more irritable and less physically affectionate in their interactions with their children than were nonviolent men.

The research on child maltreatment suggests that abusive parents also interpret their children's actions as hostile or threatening. In comparison to nonabusive parents, physically abusive parents express higher levels of annoyance and irritation in response to their children's behavior (Anderson & Umberson, 1999). Interpretive processes may also influence patterns of neglectful parenting. A child's cry is interpreted by some parents as a nuisance or deliberate misbehavior on the part of the child rather than as a signal of the child's needs (Ade-Ridder & Jones, 1996). These findings suggest that similar interpretive processes characterize different types of family violence. Individuals who engage in violence against family members, whether they are spouses, partners, or children, often attribute negative intentions to the victims' actions.

Interactive Patterns

Family violence is linked to particular styles of interaction, including insecure attachment, demand–withdrawal, and emotional reactivity. As these interactive patterns become galvanized in a relationship, "a pattern of coercive efforts can gradually develop, creating a rigid pattern of negative, polarized interaction" between family members (Holtzworth-Munroe, Smutzler, & Stuart, 1998; p. 732).

Insecure Attachment. Interactive patterns learned in childhood may set the stage for violence among family members in adulthood. Attachment theorists contend that children develop "working models" of relationships with others through their early interactions with their parents and that these models carry over into other intimate relationships (Bowlby, 1973). An insecure attachment style is characterized by the presence of anxiety, extreme dependency, and a fear of intimacy in relationships with others (Dutton, Saunders, Starzomski, & Bartholomew, 1994).

A few domestic violence researchers have examined the links between insecure adult attachment and male violence against intimate female partners. Dutton et al. (1994) found that men who exhibited insecure attachment patterns in their relationship with a female partner scored higher on measures of psychological abuse than securely attached men. Moreover, men referred for treatment for assault had significantly higher levels of insecure attachment than a matched control group. Insecure attachment may lead partners to interpret benign communication acts as dangerous or threatening: "The anxiously attached man, unaware that his dysphoria is intimacy produced, attributes it to real or perceived actions of his partner, and retaliates with abusiveness" (Dutton et al., 1994, p. 1379).

Abusive and neglectful parents also exhibit insecurity in their interpersonal relationships. In a prospective longitudinal study of mother–child interaction, Pianta et al. (1989) found that mothers' negative mood and lack of interpersonal trust were the most salient factors discriminating maltreating from nonabusive mothers. Additionally, they found that abusive mothers were unable to establish any type of intimate or supportive relationship characterized by mutual interdependence and trust.

Demand–Withdraw. Another interactive pattern that is associated with family violence is demand–withdrawal. In demand–withdraw interactions between adult partners, "one partner, the pursuer, tries to get the partner to change, while the other partner avoids change through withdrawal, passive inaction, or stonewalling" (Berns, Jacobson, & Gottman, 1999, p. 339). Partners who withdraw or stonewall are more often the dominant partners in the relationship (Jacobson & Gottman, 1998). Studies of demand–withdraw patterns suggest that wives often assume the "pursuer" role in seeking more intimacy and change, whereas husbands avoid change and are more likely to engage in withdrawal (Christensen & Shenk, 1991).

Only a few studies to date examine demand–withdraw interaction patterns in the context of violent relationships. The available evidence shows that demand–withdraw interaction is present in violent relationships, but in a guise different from how it appears in nonviolent couples (Babcock et al., 1993; Berns et al., 1999; Holtzworth-Munroe, Smutzler, & Stuart, 1998). Babcock et al. (1993) found greater levels of husband-demand and wife-withdraw interaction among couples experiencing husband violence than among nonviolent couples. Thus, the gendered pattern appears to be opposite to that observed in nonviolent couples. Husbands in abusive relationships may be more demanding than other husbands because they are often concerned with controlling and regulating the behavior of their wives or partners.

More recent studies suggest that violent relationships are characterized by interactive patterns in which both partners engage in demand and withdrawal. Berns et al. (1999) divided a sample of 47 batterers into separate categories according to unique characteristics. They identified two subtypes of batterers: Type I and Type II. Type I batterers, compared to Type II batterers, are quicker to anger, more likely to have used or threatened to use a knife or gun on their wives, and more likely to have histories of violence outside the marriage. Although both subtypes of batterers exhibited extreme demand *and* withdrawal patterns, the pattern of high husband-demand and wife-withdraw was stronger among Type I batterers. These men desired change from their partner but resisted their partner's demands that they change themselves.

Holtzworth-Munroe and colleagues (1998) compared demand–withdrawal patterns in interactions between four groups of couples: violent distressed, violent nondistressed, nonviolent distressed, and nonviolent nondistressed. Violent distressed couples reported the highest levels of conflict and negative behavior and they were the most demanding and withdrawing. Like previous researchers, Holtzworth-Munroe et al. observed that both wives and husbands in violent relationships engage in high levels of demand and withdraw.

In a recent study of 42 married couples, Sagrestano, Heavey, and Christensen (1999) examined relationships among power, violence, and the demand–withdraw interaction pattern. They found higher levels of verbal aggression and violence by both husbands and wives in couples in which the husbands perceive that they have less power than their wives have. Moreover, only wife-demand husband-withdraw interaction was associated with higher levels of violence. This finding suggests that violence is particularly likely to occur in a context in which husbands perceive their wives' demands as an indicator of power.

Emotional Reactivity. Research on domestic violence suggests that domestically violent men are more likely than nonviolent men to perceive their partner's words and actions as threatening, regardless of the objective content of those words and actions (Dugan et al., 2001; Holtzworth-Munroe & Hutchinson, 1993). Recent research further suggests that men with a propensity for violence often respond to perceptions of threat by avoiding further interaction and emotional engagement with their partner (Umberson, Williams, & Anderson, 2002). Although nonviolent men exhibit seemingly appropriate emotional reactions in response to interactions with their partners (e.g., negative emotion in response to partner disagreement), it is as if violent men experience a disconnection between ongoing interactions with their partners and their own emotional experiences. Umberson et al. argue that repressing and avoiding emotion only leads to a further buildup of anxiety that eventually surfaces in a violent act. They suggest that an increase in the expression of emotion in response to ongoing interactions with partners in the short run might serve to reduce the frequency of violence in the longer run.

Interrelationships Among Communicative Processes and Violence

There are theoretical reasons to expect that the communication skills deficits, interpretive processes, and interactive patterns identified in the literature on family violence are interconnected. For example, the pattern of higher rates of demand–withdrawal within violent relationships may be connected to specific interpretative processes. Abusers who attribute hostile or negative intent to their partners' actions may be more likely to perceive their partners' demands as an exertion of power that must be countered with violence. Abusers who feel fearful or anxious about intimacy within their relationships may be threatened by a partner's withdrawal. Communication skills deficits may be particularly likely to facilitate violence when they are combined with insecure attachment patterns or emotional repression. An individual who feels anxious or threatened but is unable to communicate these complex feelings verbally may lash out against a child or a partner.

THE IMPACT OF VIOLENCE ON FAMILY COMMUNICATION

The risk of violence within families may be increased by the communication skills deficits, interpretive processes, and interactive patterns described earlier. However, violence within families also has negative consequences for family communication and interaction. In a context of violence, family members may withdraw from social interaction or repress their concerns about the violence out of fear for themselves or for other family members. The pattern of controlling behavior enacted by perpetrators of family violence creates a family setting in which victims are unable to communicate their desires, needs, or emotions.

Communication Skills

Adults and children living in families marked by violence have limited opportunities to witness and practice positive communication skills. Violence decreases the communication skill level of victims because it creates a setting in which family members are not able to communicate freely. Family violence is associated with reports of fear and anxiety among children and women (Edleson, 1999; Jacobsen, Gottman, Waltz, Rushe, & Holtzworth-Munroe, 1994). Family members who live in a context of fear do not have opportunities to learn and develop effective communication skills.

Abused children exhibit deficient verbal language skills. Additionally, children who witness violence against a parent or sibling exhibit deficits in social competence and higher levels of fearfulness and anxiety than do nonexposed children. Children exposed to family violence inhibit their speech and interaction with others (Edleson, 1999). These communication skills deficits may help to explain the associations between child abuse and poor school performance and antisocial behavior (Anderson & Umberson, 1999).

Among adults, the experience of abuse at the hands of a loved one often leads to a loss of self-confidence and undermines the victim's ability to form and sustain healthy social relationships. Survivors of child sexual abuse report experiencing poor communication with their intimate partners as adults

(DiLillo & Long, 1999). Communication skills may be adversely affected by violence because victims lose self-confidence or learn to be fearful, secretive, and distrustful of others through the experience of abuse (DiLillo & Long, 1999). These characteristics may impede the victim's ability to engage in direct or open communication with others.

Interpretive Processes

Previous studies suggest that abusers' interpretations of specific communicative acts as dangerous or threatening may precede the perpetration of violence. However, interpretive processes are also important in the aftermath of a violent incident. Violence, in itself, is a communicative act that is given meaning through interpretative processes. The abuse that occurs within families must be assigned meaning by its perpetrators and victims. Available research evidence suggests that family members interpret abuse in a variety of ways.

Deviant patterns of social information processing are common in abused children, suggesting that children who learn to interpret communicative acts in a context of abuse will attribute hostile or aggressive intentions to others outside of their family context (Edleson, 1999). This pattern makes it difficult for abused children to form healthy relationships later in life. Additionally, children who are exposed to domestic violence may learn that violence is an effective means of conflict resolution. Child witnesses of adult domestic violence, particularly boys, report that violence is an effective strategy to address a problem or to enhance one's self-image (Edleson, 1999).

Adult female victims of partner violence struggle to define and interpret their experiences of victimization. Kelly (1990) argues that women have difficulty interpreting their experiences of domestic violence because violence within families is hidden and unnamed within U.S. culture. Wives or partners who experience infrequent assaults are hesitant to call it violence due to the stereotypical depictions of severe family violence that are presented in the media. Additionally, because cultural depictions of domestic assault attribute negative characteristics to the victim, women may be reluctant to interpret their experiences as domestic violence.

In a study of the ways in which women cope with physical and emotional abuse, Herbert, Silver, and Ellard (1991) examined characteristics that differentiated women who had left abusive partners from those who were still involved in the abusive relationship. They found that women who remained in the relationship framed their relationships in a positive light, emphasizing the loving and caring aspects of their partners' behavior. These women were also more likely to blame themselves for the abuse and to make downward comparisons, noting that their relationships were better than those of other people they knew.

Herbert and colleagues found that the frequency and severity of verbal abuse were more closely associated with women's decisions to leave than were the frequency and severity of physical abuse. Similarly, in her qualitative study of women's experiences of abuse, Kirkwood (1993) found that emotional abuse was constructed as more damaging and more difficult to overcome than was physical abuse. Many victims of violence report that the verbal abuse is characterized by constant degradation of their appearance, beliefs, and goals. Kirkwood found that abusive partners continually attack the victims' interpretations of violence. Over time, these attacks lead victims to question the validity of their own interpretations. Kirkwood's research suggests that perpetrators of abuse often manipulate the victims' interpretations of the abuse as a way to maintain power within the relationship.

Other strategies that wives and partners use to deal with violence include forgetting, minimizing, and self-medication with alcohol or drugs (Kelly, 1990). These coping strategies help victims to repress the physical and psychological pain caused by the abuse. However, they may reduce victims' chances of obtaining help from friends, family, or community members.

A different research literature focuses on the accounts that perpetrators of family violence offer in order to explain or rationalize their violent behavior. This research finds that violent male partners use several strategies to justify or rationalize past violence. These interpretative strategies include statements that they "lost control" due to intoxication or uncontrollable anger, that their female partners were responsible for their victimization because they failed to comply with demands or requests, and that their behavior was "minor" and thus not really violent (Anderson & Umberson, 2001; Ptacek, 1990).

Perpetrators of child sexual abuse also use interpretive processes to rationalize and justify their abusive behavior. In a study of incest perpetrators' accounts of sexual abuse, Gilgun (1995) found that perpetrators framed their abusive behavior as an act of love and caring for the victim. Perpetrators described the incest as a form of romantic love between equal partners and minimized the power and authority that they had over the victims. These strategies helped perpetrators to deny responsibility for behavior that they knew was illegal and immoral. Because family violence has been the focus of public education and reform efforts in recent decades, perpetrators feel that they must account for their abuse perpetration (Cavenaugh, Dobash, Dobash, & Lewis, 2001).

Few studies to date have examined children's interpretations of family violence. The scant evidence available suggests that the meanings that children attach to family violence between their parents vary; some children identify with the perpetrator of abuse and others identify with the victim (Anderson & Umberson, 1999). A small number of studies have examined children's attributions of their physical and sexual abuse victimization. Most children who suffer physical and sexual abuse define their experiences as abusive and do not self-blame (Kolko, Brown, & Berliner, 2002). However, attributions of abuse are linked to the severity of psychological consequences among children. Among physically and sexually abused children, higher levels of depression and posttraumatic stress disorder have been linked to self-blame and to labeling the behavior as abuse (Kolko et al., 2002).

In summary, the interpretations that abusers and victims use to make sense of the violence in their relationships influence the outcomes of the abuse. Interventions that focus on changing victims' and abusers' interpretations of violence may be necessary to challenge the legitimacy of family violence.

Interactive Patterns

Family violence has consequences for social interaction that occurs inside and outside of the family setting. The anxiety, fear, and isolation experienced by victims may make them less willing or less able to form positive relationships with others. Prospective longitudinal studies find that victims of child abuse are more likely to experience insecure attachment to others and to exhibit aggressive behavior (Corby, 1993; National Research Council, 1993). Additionally, child witnesses of domestic violence often exhibit aggressive and antisocial behaviors (Edleson, 1999). These interactive styles are not conducive to the creation of friendships or supportive relationships with other children or adults. In a study of the friendship patterns among severely abused and nonabused children, Howe and Parke (2001) found that abused children reported less caring and validation in their friendships and exhibited less proactive behavior in observed interactions with friends, than did nonabused children.

Childhood exposure to abuse and neglect has been linked to loneliness and isolation among young adults (Loos & Alexander, 1997). Henning, Leitenberg, Coffery, Turner, and Bennet (1996) found that young women who witnessed violence between their parents as children reported lower levels of social integration and attachment to others than did young women who did not witness parental violence.

Moreover, young adults' retrospective reports of child abuse have been associated with greater risk of aggression toward themselves and against others (Fergusson & Lynskey, 1997).

Previous studies find gender differences in the effects of child abuse or witnessing violence on aggressive behavior. Boys tend to respond to family violence by developing aggressive and antisocial behaviors, whereas girls tend to exhibit depression and other internalizing symptoms (Edleson, 1999). However, one recent study found that exposure to violence at home predicted higher levels of aggressive behavior among both adolescent boys and girls (Song, Singer, & Anglin, 1998). Girls' aggressive behavior was more closely associated with exposure to violence at home, whereas boys' aggressive behavior was more closely associated with exposure to violence at school or in the neighborhood. This gender difference may result from the fact that girls experience a high risk of violence victimization in the family setting, whereas boys experience violence in other social contexts in addition to the family.

Violence in partner relationships affects children directly because children observe, hear, or intervene in fights; but also indirectly, because violence increases negative communication between family members (Margolin, John, Ghosh, & Gordon, 1996). A number of studies find that abuse between spouses is linked to negative interaction patterns between parents and children. Domestic assaults between parents have been associated with fathers' use of power-assertive parenting techniques and physical punishment (Holden & Ritchie, 1991). Margolin and colleagues (1996), through analysis of videotaped family interactions in a laboratory setting, found that violence between parents was linked to a number of negative parenting practices. Parents who reported spousal violence showed higher levels of negative affect in interactions with their children. Fathers who were abusive toward their wives were controlling in interaction with their sons. Additionally, aggression between parents was linked to higher levels of withdrawal and distraction among boys. These findings suggest that exposure to parental violence leads children to feel fear and anxiety in social interactions with family members and others outside of the family.

Demand–withdraw interaction patterns have been conceptualized as a precursor to abuse in much of the literature. However, this interactive pattern could also reflect the consequences of abuse within a marital or cohabiting relationship. Withdrawal may be a way of showing contempt for a spouse or avoiding any external influence, but it might also be self-protective. Wives in violent relationships withdraw and demand to a greater extent than do wives in nonviolent relationships (Holtzworth-Munroe et al., 1998). This may be a learned response to the violence that characterizes an abusive relationship. A wife who has experienced violence in the past may demand change during times when she feels strong or safe in the relationship. At other times, she may withdraw in response to her partner's demands out of fear that the conflict will escalate into violence. Berns et al. (1999) found that severe levels of husband violence are associated with high levels of wife withdrawal. Because violence often escalates in frequency and severity over time, this finding suggests that withdrawal may be a response to abuse that is learned over time.

Isolation is another means by which abusive partners and parents attempt to gain control over their families. Women who report victimization at the hands of a male partner are often socially isolated and have less social support than do other women (Grisso et al., 1999; Kirkwood, 1993). Norms of family privacy and loyalty prevent victims from receiving help from friends, neighbors, or social service agencies. Abusive partners and parents often go to great lengths to prevent discovery of the violence that they perpetrate against family members. A recent newspaper story featured a photograph of a sign reading "We don't call 911" that police found hanging next to the telephone in the home of an abuser (Porter, 2001). The sign featured an image of a smoking gun. The victims of family violence were in this case directly warned that help seeking could result in further violence.

In summary, violence has detrimental consequences for family members' ability to learn positive forms of communication. Violence undermines the self-esteem and confidence of its victims, it teaches victims that aggressive and controlling styles of interaction are normative, and it isolates victims from other people. Children and adults who experience violence at the hands of a family member learn to be fearful, anxious, and insecure in their relationships with others.

BIDIRECTIONALITY

The links between negative communication patterns and family violence are well established. However, most studies have examined cross-sectional data and thus cannot address the issue of causal direction. There are strong theoretical reasons to believe that relationships between communication processes and family violence are bidirectional. On the one hand, communication skills deficits of one or both partners may lead to increasingly negative forms of interaction between partners and ultimately to the emergence of violence. On the other hand, past violence within the relationship may lead to a pattern in which one or both partners withdraw, become negative or critical, and report feelings of fear or anger when they attempt to communicate.

Two types of studies address the issue of causal direction. First, a few studies have examined the relationship between retrospective accounts of exposure to violence and communication patterns. Second, longitudinal studies address causal direction by documenting changes in attitudes or behaviors over time.

Retrospective Studies

To address the issue of causal order, researchers need information about the ways in which family members communicate prior to, and in the aftermath of, specific violent incidents. Although violence occurs in the context of social interaction, few studies have examined how communication processes influence actual incidents of domestic violence. It is difficult for researchers to access the daily interactions of family members as they naturally occur, and it is ethically and logistically problematic to study actual violent incidents that occur within families. Researchers must typically rely on retrospective narrative accounts of violent incidents supplied by victims or perpetrators. These accounts are influenced by individual interpretations of violence.

Despite these limitations, retrospective accounts of violence can provide information about the dynamics of violence in day-to-day life. Jacobsen and colleagues (1994) obtained descriptions of the events that preceded specific incidents of violence from a sample of 60 couples experiencing domestic violence and 32 maritally distressed couples who had never experienced violence. Results indicated that, according to wives, husbands continued their violence when wives were violent themselves, verbally defended themselves, or withdrew. Husband's descriptions suggested that they continued violence only when their wife was violent or emotionally abusive. Jacobsen et al. concluded that there were no wife behaviors that could stop the violence once it began; the violence escalated in response to nonviolent as well as to violent reactions by wives. This study suggests that, although communication patterns influence the violence that occurs within relationships, simply changing communication behaviors will not be enough to stop abusive behaviors that are already established. Because abusers often define the actions of victims as hostile or negative, victims' efforts to change their communication behaviors may have little impact.

Retrospective accounts can also provide information about the ways in which the experience of violence during childhood affects people later in life. Halford, Sanders, Matthew, and Behrens (2000) videotaped problem-focused discussions between 71 engaged couples to determine whether exposure to parental violence during childhood increased problematic communication patterns in adult relationships. They found significantly higher rates of invalidation, negative nonverbal behavior, conflict, and withdrawal among couples in which the male partner was exposed to parental violence. Female partners' exposure to parental violence was not associated with negative communication processes. Similarly, DiLillo and Long (1999) found that female victims of childhood sexual abuse reported significantly poorer communication with their spouses than did women who did not report childhood victimization. Thus, findings from retrospective accounts suggest that exposure to family violence leads to short-term and long-term problems with communication.

Longitudinal Studies

Because longitudinal studies are not subject to problems of memory errors or to other forms of retrospective bias, they are generally considered to be superior to retrospective studies for determining causal direction. Lloyd (1996) examined associations between violence and interaction patterns among 78 couples interviewed in two waves of data collection 18 months apart. Couples reporting aggression during both waves of data collection showed a pattern of increasingly negative interaction over time, suggesting that violence preceded the formation of negative communication. However, low levels of negative interaction at Time 1 were associated with a decrease in violence by Time 2. This study suggests that the relationship between violence and negative communication processes is bidirectional. Negative forms of communication increase the risk of violence, but violence also decreases opportunities for the development of positive styles of communicating and interacting.

Issues For Future Research

Communication patterns play a central role in the dynamics of family violence. The skills that parents and partners bring to family interactions, the interpretive processes that they use to attach meaning to communicative events, and the interactive styles that they develop are associated with the risk of violence within families. In turn, violence between family members undermines family communication and interaction. The effects of violence are not limited to the perpetrators and victims; relationships among all family members are impacted by violence. The dynamic and complex relationship between family violence and family communication should be the focus of future research.

Established research findings suggest that relationships between communication processes and family violence are bidirectional. Future research should examine changes in communication processes and family violence over time in order to clarify these reciprocal patterns. Research that examines how patterns in family interaction are linked to violence on a day-to-day basis is sorely needed. Additional longitudinal studies are needed to identify specific communication processes that precede family violence and the ways in which family communication changes in the aftermath of violence.

The majority of published studies on violence and family communication have focused on negative forms of communication. Findings from the few available studies that focus on positive forms of communication are mixed; some studies suggest that violence is associated with a decrease in positive communication, and others find that positive communication is not linked to violence within families. Future research should include measures of negative and positive communication in order to resolve this issue.

To date, most research on communication patterns and violence has examined samples consisting of married couples and two-parent families. Researchers should expand the definition of family to include single parents, stepfamilies, cohabiting couples and parents, and gay/lesbian/bisexual couples and parents in order to reflect the growing diversity in family structures. Previous research suggests that rates of family violence are higher among cohabiting couples and that child abuse and neglect rates may be higher within single-parent families and stepfamilies (Anderson & Umberson, 1999; Cowen, 1999; Stets, 1991). Additionally, communication patterns may differ within diverse family types. There is some evidence that parent–child conflict and communication problems increase following the formation of single-parent families and stepfamilies (Amato, 2000; Coleman, Ganong, & Fine, 2000).

Studies of family communication processes and violence have been limited by small samples consisting of middle-or high-socioeconomic-status families. There is some evidence that the income or educational levels of family members influence family communication patterns. Highly educated parents are more likely to using complex reasoning and less likely to use commands than are less educated parents when interacting with their children (Dekovic & Gerris, 1992). Heath (1983) found that middle-class and European American parents were more likely than working-class and African American parents to use discrete interrogative questions when they talked with their children. Because both family violence and language patterns have been linked to social class in past research, future research on the relationships between family communication and violence should include controls for socioeconomic status (Straus & Gelles, 1992).

The emphasis on violence as a form of communication that is embedded in family interaction has led family violence researchers to exciting new directions. Future research on the dynamic relationships between family violence and communication skills, interpretive processes, and interactive patterns will inform efforts to understand and prevent violence within families.

REFERENCES

Ade-Ridder, L., & Jones, A. R. (1996). Home is where the hell is: An introduction to violence against children from a communication perspective. In D. D. Cahn & S. A. Lloyd (Eds.), *Family violence from a communication perspective* (pp. 59–84). Thousand Oaks, CA: Sage.

Amato, K. (2000). The consequences of divorce for adults and children. *Journal of Marriage and the Family, 62,* 1269–1287.

Anderson, K. L., & Umberson, D. (1999). Child abuse. In L. Kurtz & J. Turpin (Eds.), *Encylopedia of violence, peace and conflict* (Vol. 1, pp. 223–238), San Diego: Academic Press.

Anderson, K. L., & Umberson, D. (2001). Gendering violence: Masculinity and power in men's accounts of domestic violence. *Gender & Society, 15,* 353–380

Babcock, J. C., Waltz, J., Jacobsen, N. S., & Gottman, J. M. (1993). Power and violence: The relation between communication patterns, power discrepancies, and domestic violence. *Journal of Consulting and Clinical Psychology, 61,* 40–50.

Berns, S. B., Jacobson, N. S., & Gottman, J. M. (1999). Demand-withdraw interaction patterns between different types of batterers and their spouses. *Journal of Marital and Family Therapy, 25*, 337–348.

Bird, G. W., Stith, S. M., & Schladale, J. (1991). Psychological resources, coping strategies, and negotiation styles as discriminators of violence in dating relationships. *Family Relations, 41*, 318–323.

Blumer, H. (1969). *Symbolic interactionism: Perspective and method.* Englewood Cliffs, NJ: Prentice Hall.

Bowlby, J. (1973). *Attachment and loss: Vol. 2. Separation, anxiety, and anger.* New York: Basic Books.

Cahn, D. D. (1996). Family violence from a communication perspective. In D. D. Cahn & S. A. Lloyd (Eds.), *Family violence from a communication perspective* (pp. 1–19). Thousand Oaks, CA: Sage.

Cavenaugh, K., Dobash, R. E., Dobash, R. P., & Lewis, R. (2001). Remedial work: Men's strategic responses to their violence against intimate female partners. *Sociology, 35*, 695–714.

Christensen, A., & Shenk, J. L. (1991). Communication, conflict, and psychological distance in nondistressed, clinic, and divorcing couples. *Journal of Consulting and Clinical Psychology, 59*, 458–463.

Christopoulos, C., Bonvillian, J. D., & Crittenden, P. (1988). Maternal language input and child maltreatment. *Infant Mental Health Journal, 9*, 272–286.

Coleman, M., Ganong, L., & Fine, M. (2000). Reinvestigating remarriage: Another decade of progress. *Journal of Marriage and the Family, 62*, 1288–1307.

Corby, B. (1993). *Child abuse: Toward a knowledge base.* Buckingham: Open University Press.

Cowen, P. S. (1999). Child neglect: Injuries of omission. *Pediatric Nursing, 25*, 401–418.

Dekovic, M., & Gerris, J. R. M. (1992). Parental reasoning complexity, social class, and child-rearing behaviors. *Journal of Marriage and the Family, 54*, 675–685.

DiLillo, D., & Long, P. J. (1999). Perceptions of couple functioning among female survivors of child sexual abuse. *The Journal of Child Sexual Abuse, 7*, 59–76.

Dobash, R. E., Dobash, R. P. (1998). Violent men and violent contexts. In R. E. Dobash & R. P. Dobash (Eds.), *Rethinking violence against women* (pp. 141–168). Thousand Oaks, CA: Sage.

Dugan, S., Umberson, D., & Anderson, K. L. (2001). The batterer's view of the self and others in domestic violence. *Sociological Inquiry, 71*, 221–240.

Dutton, D. G., Saunders, K., Starzomski, A., & Bartholomew, K. (1994). Intimacy-anger and insecure attachment as precursors of abuse in intimate relationships. *Journal of Applied Social Psychology, 24*, 1367–1386.

Edleson, J. L. (1999). Children's witnessing of adult domestic violence. *Journal of Interpersonal Violence, 14*, 839–870.

Feldman, C. M., & Ridley, C. A. (2000). The role of conflict-based communication responses and outcomes in male domestic violence towards female partners. *Journal of Social and Personal Relationships, 17*, 552–573.

Fergusson, D. M., & Lynskey, M. T. (1997). Physical punishment/maltreatment during childhood and adjustment in young adulthood. *Child Abuse and Neglect, 21*, 617–630.

Gilgun, J. F. (1995). We shared something special: The moral discourse of incest perpetrators. *Journal of Marriage and the Family, 57*, 265–281.

Gilligan, J. (1996). *Violence: Reflections on a national epidemic.* New York: Vintage Books.

Grisso, J. A., Schwartz, D. F., Hirschinger, N., Sammel, M., Brensinger, C., Santanna, J., Lowe, R. A., Anderson, E., Shaw, L. M., Bethel, C. A., & Teelpe, L. (1999). Violent injuries among women in an urban area. *New England Journal of Medicine, 341*, 1899–1905.

Halford, W., Sanders, K., R. Matthew, & Behrens, B. C. (2000). Repeating the errors of our parents? Family-of-origin spouse violence and observed conflict management in engaged couples. *Family Process, 39*, 219–235.

Heath, S. B. (1983). *Ways with words.* Cambridge: Cambridge University Press.

Heise, L., Ellsberg, M., & Gottemoeller, J. K. (1999). Ending violence against women. *Population Reports,* Series L, No. 11. Baltimore, MD: Johns Hopkins University School of Public Health, Population Information Program.

Henning, K., Leitenberg, H., Coffery, P., Turner, T., & Bennet, R. T. (1996). Long-term psychological and social impact of witnessing physical conflict between parents. *Journal of Interpersonal Violence, 11,* 35–51.

Herbert, T. B., Silver, R. C., & Ellard, J. H. (1991). Coping with an abusive relationship: How and why do women stay? *Journal of Marriage and the Family, 53,* 311–325.

Holden, G. W., & Ritchie, K. L. (1991). Linking extreme marital discord, child rearing, and child behavior problems. *Child Development, 62,* 311–377.

Holtzworth-Munroe, A., & Hutchinson, G. (1993). Attributing negative intent to wife behavior: The attributions of maritally violent vs. nonviolent men to problematic marital situations. *Journal of Abnormal Psychology, 102,* 206–211.

Holtzworth-Munroe, A., & Smultzer, N. (1996). Comparing the emotional reactions and behavioral intentions of violent and nonviolent husbands to aggressive, distressed, and other wife behaviors. *Violence and Victims, 11,* 319–340.

Holtzworth-Munroe, A., Smutzler, N., & Stuart, G. L. (1998). Demand and withdraw communication among couples experiencing husband violence. *Journal of Consulting and Clinical Psychology, 66,* 731–743.

Howe, T. R., & Parke, R. D. (2001). Friendship quality and sociometric status: Between-group differences and links to loneliness in severely abused and non-abused children. *Child Abuse and Neglect, 25,* 585–606.

Infante, D. A., Chandler, T. A., & Rudd, J. E. (1989). Tests of an argumentative skill deficiency model of interpersonal violence. *Communication Monographs, 56,* 163–175.

Jacobson, N. S., & Gottman, J. M. (1998). *When men batter women: New insights into ending abusive relationships.* New York: Simon & Schuster.

Jacobson, N. S., Gottman, J. M., Waltz, J., Rushe, R., & Holzworth-Munroe, A. (1994). Affect, verbal content, and psychophysiology in the arguments of couples with a violent husband. *Journal of Consulting and Clinical Psychology, 62,* 982–988.

Johnson, M. P. (1995). Patriarchal terrorism and common couple violence: Two forms of violence against women. *Journal of Marriage and the Family, 57,* 283–294.

Johnson, M. P. (2001). Conflict and control: Images of symmetry and asymmetry in domestic violence. In A. Booth, A. C. Crouter, & M. Clements (Eds.), *Couples in conflict* (pp. 95–104). Mahwah, NJ: Lawrence Erlbaum Associates.

Kelly, L. (1990). How women define their experiences of violence. In K. Yllo & M. Bograd (Eds.), *Feminist perspectives on wife abuse* (pp. 114–132). Newbury Park, CA: Sage.

Kirkwood, C. (1993). *Leaving abusive partners: From the scars of survival to the wisdom for change.* London: Sage.

Kolko, D. J., Brown, E. J., & Berliner, L. (2002). Children's perceptions of their abusive experience: Measurement and preliminary findings. *Child Maltreatment, 7,* 42–55.

Langhinrichsen-Rohling, J., Smultzer, N., & Vivian, D. (1994). Positivity in marriage: The role of discord and physical aggression against wives. *Journal of Marriage and the Family, 56,* 69–79.

Lawrence, E., & Bradbury, T. N. (2001). Physical aggression and marital dysfunction: A longitudinal analysis. *Journal of Family Psychology, 15,* 135–154.

Lloyd, S. A. (1996). Physical aggression, distress, and everyday marital interaction. In D. D. Cahn & S. A. Lloyd (Eds.), *Family violence from a communication perspective* (pp. 177–198). Thousand Oaks, CA: Sage.

Lloyd, S. A. (1999). The interpersonal and communication dynamics of wife battering. In X. B. Arriaga & S. Oskamp (Eds.), *Violence in intimate relationships.* Thousand Oaks, CA: Sage.

Loos, M. E., & Alexander, P. C. (1997). Differential effects associated with self-reported histories of abuse and neglect in a college sample. *Journal of Interpersonal Violence, 12,* 340–360.

Margolin, G., John, R. S., Ghosh, C. M., & Gordis, E. B. (1996). Family interaction process: An essential tool for exploring abusive relationships. In D. D. Cahn & S. A. Lloyd (Eds.), *Family violence from a communication perspective* (pp. 37–58). Thousand Oaks, CA: Sage.

Murphy, C. M., & O'Farrell, T. J. (1997). Couple communication patterns and aggressive and nonaggressive male alcoholics. *Journal of Studies on Alcohol, 58,* 83–90.

National Research Council. (1993). *Understanding child abuse and neglect.* Washington, DC: National Academy Press.

O'Leary, D. (1993). Through a psychological lens: Personality traits, personality disorders, and levels of violence. In R. J. Gelles & D. R. Loseke (Eds.), *Current controversies on family violence.* Newbury Park, CA: Sage.

Pianta, R., Egeland, B., & Erickson, M. F. (1989). The antecedents of maltreatment: Results of the mother-child interaction research project. In D. Cicchetti & V. Carlson (Eds.), *Child maltreatment: Theory and research on the causes and consequences of child abuse and neglect* (pp. 203–253). New York: Cambridge University Press.

Pleck, E. (1987). *Domestic tyranny: The making of American social policy against family violence from colonial times to the present.* New York: Oxford University Press.

Porter, M. (2001, October 5). Domestic violence kills, too. *Bellingham Herald,* pp. A1–A2.

Ptacek, J. (1990). Why do men batter their wives? In K. Yllo & M. Bograd (Eds.), *Feminist perspectives on wife abuse* (pp. 133–157). Newbury Park, CA: Sage.

Sabourin, T. C., Infante, D. C., & Rudd, E. J. (1993). Verbal aggression in marriages: A comparison of violent, distressed but nonviolent, and nondistressed couples. *Human Communication Research, 20,* 245–267.

Sabourin, T. C., & Stamp, G. H. (1995). Communication and the experience of dialetical tension in family life: An examination of abusive and non-abusive families. *Communication Monographs, 62,* 213–242.

Sagrestano, L. M., Heavey, C. L., & Christensen, A. (1999). Perceived power and physical violence in marital conflict. *Journal of Social Issues, 55,* 65–79.

Sedlack, A. (1991). *National incidence and prevalence of child abuse and neglect: 1988, revised report.* Rockville, MD: Westat.

Song, L., Singer, M., & Anglin, T. (1998). Violence exposure and emotional trauma as contributors to adolescents' violent behaviors. *Archives of Pediatric and Adolescent Medicine, 152,* 531–536.

Stets, J. E. (1991). Cohabiting and marital agression: The role of social isolation. *Journal of Marriage and the Family, 53,* 669–680.

Straus, M. A., & Gelles, R. J. (Eds). (1992). *Physical violence in American families: Risk factors and adaptations to violence in 8,145 families.* NJ: Transaction Publishers.

Tjaden, P., & Thoennes, N. (1998). Prevalence, incidence, and consequences from the National Violence Against Women Survey (Research in Brief), Washington, D.C.: U.S. Department of Justice, Bureau of Justice Statistics, November, NCJ 172837.

Umberson, D., Williams, K., & Anderson, K. L. (2002). Violent behavior: A measure of emotional upset? *Journal of Health and Social Behavior, 43,* 189–206.

U.S. Department of Health and Human Services, Administration on Children, Youth and Families. (2001). *Child maltreatment 1999.* Washington, D.C.: U.S. Government Printing Office.

Index